D1756752

Contents

Introduction

The whisky industry was definitely affected by the economic chaos that hit the world two years ago, no question about that. The record sales figures presented by Scotch Whisky Association may speak another language, but behind these figures lay hard work from producers who have been forced to re-visit their business activities and attune them to a new reality. The battle over market shares has become much tougher and it is not by coincidence that a majority of the mega brands have been re-vitalized through expensive marketing campaigns and new, lavish packaging. *Dominic Roskrow* touches on this very subject in **Malt Whisky Yearbook 2011** in his feature on re-launching and re-branding.

But not all markets have been so severely affected. While demand is increasing in India, the most dynamic whisky market in the world, *Charles MacLean* asks the question how the respective producers of Scotch and Indian whisky, shall cut the pie.

It is important to be in the right market position when times are harsh. Chivas Brothers did just that by starting a campaign to advocate the importance of age statements on the whisky label. In some quarters this was perceived as controversial and *Ian Buxton* reflects on the causes behind this strategy. And talking about labels - new regulations on what a producer may or may not print on the whisky label stimulates *Hans Offringa* to look back at how the whisky label has developed throughout time.

But despite new regulations, marketing spins and sales figures, there is always a concrete reality about whisky production. *Ian Wisniewski* looks deeply into one of the first steps in this process, the mashing, while *Gavin D. Smith* concentrates on the final part, the maturation. Find out how the flavour of the whisky is shaped during these two steps of the making.

In **Malt Whisky Yearbook 2011** you will also find the unique, detailed and much appreciated section on Scottish and Irish malt whisky distilleries. It has been thoroughly revised and updated, not just in text, but also including numerous, new pictures and tasting notes for all the core brands. The chapter on Japanese whisky is completely new and the presentation of distilleries from the rest of the world is larger than ever. You will also find a list of 130 of the best whisky shops in the world with their full details and a comprehensive list of 500 new bottlings. The summary of The Whisky Year That Was has been expanded again this year, in order to reflect on the exciting times. A special chapter describes the various steps in whisky production and you will also meet the people behind the whiskies - the distillery managers. Finally, the very latest statistics, gives you all the answers to your questions on production and consumption.

Thank you for buying **Malt Whisky Yearbook 2011**. We hope that you will have many enjoyable moments reading it and we can assure you that we will be back with a new edition in 2012.

Great care has been taken to ensure the accuracy of the information presented in this book. MagDig Media Ltd can, however, not be held liable for inaccuracies.

**Malt Whisky Yearbook 2012 will be published in October 2011.
To make sure you will be able to order it directly, please register at
www.maltwhiskyyearbook.com.**

**If you need any of the previous five volumes of Malt Whisky Yearbook,
they are available for purchase (in limited numbers) from the website
www.maltwhiskyyearbook.com**

Acknowledgments

First of all I wish to thank the writers who have shared their great specialist knowledge on the subject in a brilliant and entertaining way – Chris Bunting, Ian Buxton, Charles MacLean, Hans Offringa, Dominic Roskrow, Gavin D. Smith and Ian Wisniewski.

A special thanks goes to Gavin and Dominic who put in a lot of effort nosing, tasting and writing notes for more than 100 different whiskies. Thanks also to Ian W for the tasting notes for independent bottlings and to Chris for the Japanese notes.

The following persons have also made important photographic or editorial contributions:

Raymond Armstrong, Paul Aston, David Baker, Nick Ballard, Edward Bates, Keith Batt, Hans Baumberger, Jan Beckers, Kirsteen Beeston, Etienne Bouillon, Stephen Bremner, Graham Brown, Joanne Brownhill, Alex Bruce, Gordon Bruce, Stewart Buchanan, Alexander Buchholz, Sarah Burgess, Pär Caldenby, Douglas Campbell, John Campbell, Peter Campbell, Ian Chang, Ian Chapman, Ashok Chokalingam, Marco di Ciacca, Margaret Mary Clarke, Doug Clement, Willie Cochrane, Michael Cockram, Neal Corbett, Graham Coull, Jason Craig, Katherine Crisp, Jeremy Cunnington, Tim Danahy, Avishek Das, Susie Davidson, Stephen Davies, David Doig, Jean Donnay, Dennis Downing, Frances Dupuy, Gavin Durnin, Ben Ellefsen, Ralph Erenzo, Joanna Fearnside, Berle Figgins Jr, Hannah Fisher, Douglas Fitchett, Thomas Fleischmann, Robert Fleming, Gary Fleshman, Tim Forbes, Iain Gardiner, Gillian Gibson, Gregg Glass, John Glass, Jess Graber, Kenny Grant, Quyen Ha, Ueli Hagen, Monika Haider, Mike Haldane, Anna Hall, Andy Hannah, Jay Harman, Michael Heads, Robbie Hughes, Peter Hunt, Holger Höhler, Anne Jack, Pat Jones, Jens-Erik Jörgensen, Moritz Kallmeyer, Jenny Karlsson, Sanjeev Khanna, Shanth V Kumar, Ruedi Käser, Joe Lai, Cara Laing, Bill Lark, Gerhard Liebl, Karl Locher, Mark Lochhead, Jim Long, Alistair Longwell, Bill Lumsden, Horst Lüning, Urs Lüthy, Eddie McAffer, Iain MacAllister, Des McCagherty, Brendan McCarron, Alan McConnochie, John MacDonald, Polly MacDonald, Barbara McEwan, Frank McHardy, Ian MacMillan, Grant MacPherson, Patrick Maguire, Dennis Malcolm, Martin Markvardsen, Stephen Marshall, Tim Marwood, Lee Medoff, Jean Metzger, Marcin Miller, Euan Mitchell, Henric Molin, Nick Morgan, John Mullen, Robert Munro, Andrew Nelstrop, Stuart Nickerson, Jay Oddleifson, Linda Outterson, Richard A Pelletier, John Peterson, Stuart Pirie, Don Poffenroth, Michael Poulsen, Laci Poulter, Anssi Pyysing, Rachel Quinn, Robert Ransom, Donald Renwick, Carrie Revell, Patrick Roberts, David Robertson, Brian Robinson, Colin Ross, Niels Römer, Tyler Schramm, Bryan Schultz, Andrew Scott, Jacqui Seargeant, Sue Sellers, Abhishek Shahabadi, Andrew Shand, Rubyna Sheikh, Derek Sinclair, Sukhinder Singh, Alison Spowart, Jolanda Stadelmann, Jeremy Stephens, Billy Stitchell, Thomas Sundblom, Duncan Tait, Kazuyuki Takayama, Elizabeth Teape, Stephen Teeling, Marcel Telser, David Thomson, John Titto, Gerry Tosh, Zac Triemert, Erkin Tuzmuhamedov, Paul Verbruggen, Lasse Vesterby, Alistair Walker, Paul Wang, Claire Watson, Mark Watt, Andy Watts, Iain Weir, James Whelan, Kerry White, Nick White, Ronald Whiteford, Cristina Wilkie, Anthony Wills, Allan Winchester, Patrick van Zuidam

Thank you!

Ingvar Ronde
Editor
Malt Whisky Yearbook

What on earth were they thinking?

*Barely a week goes by
without one whisky company or another relaunching,
rebranding or reshaping one of its malt whiskies. Why do they do it,
and what are the consequences? Dominic Roskrow finds out.*

"Sometimes when I have been having a few whiskies I get some great ideas as to how we might reposition them, how to rebrand them or how to promote them and I scribble them down on pieces of paper."

"Then the next day when I have sobered up, I try and decipher what I wrote the night before. And most often I finally read what I've written down and wonder what on earth I was thinking of, and I throw the paper in the bin."

"It seems to me that the rebranding and re-positioning of some whisky brands is like that. Only the bits of paper don't get thrown away. The brand owners go ahead with their rebranding ideas and you end up thinking 'what on earth were they thinking of?'"

The speaker is a leading Scottish whisky maker but because his words are made off the cuff and in an unguarded moment, he shall remain nameless. Nevertheless, his words are pertinent and pointed.

Get the re-launch of a drinks brand right and you can turn its fortunes around and give it a new, extended and highly profitable lease of life. For aspiring and ambitious brand managers dreaming of future marketing directorships and a place on the company board, it's the Holy Grail.

Get it wrong though, and you can find yourself consigning your brand to history.
For proof, look no further than the world of beer. On the one hand take the success of Guinness, which was not so long ago an Irish stout consumed in pints by old men in parts of its homeland and in half-pints by old ladies just about anywhere else. Now it's a behemoth, in to its fourth decade at the top of the drinks chart and enjoyed as a cool drink – in all senses of the word – as much despite being a stout as because of it.

Then compare its fate with Stella Artois, reassuringly expensive and the sponsor of the prestigious Queens tennis tournament in London on the one hand, a cheap supermarket lager with an insulting nickname too libelous to reproduce here on the other.

Compare the cool image of Carlsberg, which is probably the best marketed lager in the world, with Hofmeister, whose strutting bear mascot marched it straight in to the 'where are they now?' file, along with Harp, which stayed sharp to the bottom of the glass – at least until nobody drank it any more.

So the risks are high, and never more so than in the world of malt whisky, where there has been a transformation in recent years and the temptation to change must have been hard to resist. Indeed, a huge number of malt whisky brands have undergone a facelift in recent years. What were their owners thinking of, and has it worked out for them?

When fresh air is not enough

One of the first companies to not only take the plunge with a rebranding of one of its malts but to give it a complete and utter overhaul, is Inver House. That brand is Balblair, a pleasant enough but largely ignored malt from the North East of Scotland. It comes from a region which can apparently boast the United Kingdom's cleanest air, so this was its marketing platform. One of its expressions was called Elements. It had, then, a marketing strategy which was quite literally a load of fresh air. Inver House's strategy was to reposition Balblair as a premium malt by effectively presenting it as a new brand.

"At the time we weren't under pressure from the market to make changes," recalls Iain Baxter, the company's senior brands manager.

"If I'm brutally honest we weren't doing the brand justice and it was being undersold by poor packaging. We felt we owed the brand more. We knew we had a fabulous liquid but we needed to show it off more."

Inver House had already re-launched its Knockdhu malt as AnCnoc, and given it a minimalist and smart new design. But that change had been semi-forced on the company in an agreement with Diageo to avoid confusion with Knockando. This was different.

"The AnCnoc redesign ended up being ahead of its time," says Baxter. "If you look at the simple stripped down design now it seems very modern and the brand has come of age. It's enjoying massive sales in Sweden and has gone completely wild, breaking all records. It's been hugely successful."

"But with Balblair we had to build a brand. We think integrity is very important and when people come to malt whisky they are looking for heritage and history. With a malt such as Pulteney that's easy – there are loads of angles to go for and it's a brand manager's dream. That wasn't the case with Balblair. So we looked at the region, looked at the Pictish connection, and brought that in. We focused on the Pictish stone because it just felt right."

The company didn't stop there. It moved away from age statements and introduced vintages, with a distillation date on the label instead. It came up with a stylish new bottle and a square box which didn't fit on the average whisky

The symbol for the new Balblair
– the Pictish Clach Biorach standing stone

shop shelf. It introduced bright and striking packaging. In essence it presented the consumer with not just a new Balblair, but a new direction for whisky. And it did it pretty much without a great deal of consumer research or focus groups.

"We knew we had a great spirit and we wanted to put across the idea that we would bottle it when it was ready like fine wine," says Baxter. "We also considered that it's very hard to wrap the sort of tube that most whisky was put in and the square box would be better. But we didn't have a lot more consumer insight than that."

Balblair has been a major success for Inver House but while the size of the rebranding exercise ensured that the company's strategy was a risky one, the relatively humble starting point for the distillery and its sales base meant that the potential rewards would always outweigh the risk.

"Yes the risk was always manageable," says Baxter. "The common perception of the brand was misaligned so we always felt we would succeed by changing it, and four years down the line we are ahead of where we thought we would be with Balblair and we are very pleased."

The danger of losing your soul

The situation for two other producers just along the road from Balblair was very different. Glenmorangie and Dalmore had far more at stake by seeking to reposition themselves in the luxury market, Glenmorangie because it already enjoyed large sales and had a lot to lose, The Dalmore because it enjoyed 'premier cru' status among serious whisky investors and was in danger of falling in to the Stella Artois trap if it changed its marketing tack and started sending out mixed messages,

Glenmorangie revamped its range extensively after it was bought by French luxury goods company Louis Vuitton Moët Hennessy. The purchase had already aroused the suspicions of some malt whisky purists. Now the company intended to scrap its core special finishes, whiskies which were widely seen as ground-breaking malts and leaders in their field, with three new whiskies in stylish bottles and with somewhat pretentious new names – Lasanta, Nectar D'Or and Quinta Ruban.

There was considerable disquiet about the changes and the company's head of distilling and whisky creation Bill Lumsden is diplomatic about the packaging and rebranding issues,

focusing instead on the quality of the whisky.

"The move away from the Madeira finish was inevitable anyway because we just couldn't continue to source the quality of casks we needed," he says. "But we also felt we had some outstanding whisky and the packaging should reflect that. Of course if you change a whisky there is a risk of upsetting some loyal drinkers and we do get letters from people complaining about the changes. But overall the response has been very good and we were very careful to make sure the qualities which are recognizably Glenmorangie have remained."

The changes also provided the platform for Lumsden and the company's blender Rachel Barrie to work on new expressions to excite and delight Glenmorangie drinkers – such as Sonnalta, the super premium and luxury Signet and the cask strength release Astar.

"Astar is almost my definitive Glenmorangie," says Lumsden. "It's got all the qualities that I would want from a Glenmorangie. The changes we made to our core range have allowed me to go in this direction."

Down the road the owner of neighbouring distillery Dalmore was having its own debate

Glenmorangie Original

David Robertson - Rare Whisky Director for Whyte & Mackay

The Dalmore Cigar Malt, for instance, was axed, seen in some quarters as past its sell-by date and linked with smoking.

That has caused a backlash among traditional drinkers and at the time of writing there were hints that opinion within Whyte & Mackay was divided over the Dalmore rebranding issue. Robertson wouldn't be drawn on whether the Cigar Malt would be reintroduced – "watch this space" was his only comment – nor on whether the rebranding exercise was to be reshaped.

"We sold 10,000 cases of Cigar Malt in the United States and we do not sell as much of Gran Reserva now," he says. "But that was because Cigar Malt was sold dirt cheap. We have moved away from that."

One company insider went one step further: "To go back to cheap and cheerful would, in my view, be a massive mistake," he said.

Fettercairn fights back

The jury is out on the long term future of Dalmore, but Whyte & Mackay is working its way through its malt range. It successfully repacka-

about rebranding. It, too, had changed ownership but it was faced with a dilemma: how do you square off a malt which sells for thousands of pounds a bottle at one end of the spectrum, and is sold off dirt cheap at the other? Whyte & Mackay chose to introduce a whole new range of malts, each one packaged in beautiful and simplistic designs based around the stag's head symbol.

"We wanted to stress the brand's fine quality, subtle craftsmanship and provenance," says the company's director for innovations David Robertson. "The stag's head links the brand to the Mackenzies, who owned Dalmore, and back to the incident in 1263 when a Mackenzie saved King Alexander III from being killed by a stag. We came up with a range of great tasting whisky each with a coherent and focused story."

But the changes meant a dramatic change in approach for Dalmore, highlighting the potential pitfalls of a rebranding exercise. There was some fall-out from the decision to move the malt to a higher price point and to scrap what some considered to be some iconic brands.

Fettercairn 40 year old - part of the brand's rebirth

ged Jura, introduced an excellent new peated expression of it in Prophecy, and has seemingly improved the spirit in the bottle across the range. Sales are up 30% in the last five years as a result. Now it's turning its attentions to Fettercairn, undoubtedly its biggest challenge so far. On the one hand the distillery has much going for it – it's a pretty Highland distillery close to a historic town with links to Queen Victoria. It was owned by one of Britain's most famous politicians and it has played a crucial role in the evolution of modern malt whisky as we know it.

But on the other, few malts have been so critically mauled as Fettercairn. It is despised by certain leading whisky writers. The Fettercairn fightback is in its infancy at the moment. Whyte & Mackay's approach is to change the malt offering entirely, scrapping the 12 year old and 1824 expressions and replacing them with Fior, a limited core brand with a premium price available only through select outlets. A new range of aged Fettercairns – a 24 year old, a 30 year old and a 40 year old have also been launched.

In a bid to ensure that the marketing was right 400 key industry people were sent potential designs, bottle shapes and logos. The resulting packaging combines the symbol of the gate in Fettercairn built to mark the visit of Queen Victoria and Prince Albert, and a unicorn symbol which relates to the family crest of Sir Alexander Ramsay, who founded the distillery.

"The process is similar to that for Dalmore," says Robertson. "We have got the stock, a strong back story and the brand DNA. That allows us to shape the whisky and being its story to life."

Only time will tell how successful the company has been, but it will no doubt be encouraged by the success of another brand which changed the liquid in the bottle, changed the whole image of the brand and increased sales despite a significant price hike.

Deanston was a not particularly exciting malt which sold well in America – it was the number three best selling malt there – and pretty much

Deanston Single Malt starting to rise from obscurity

nowhere else. Then owners Burn Stewart gave it a facelift. A better, fuller and fruitier malt was put in the bottle and it was repackaged in hip, environmentally friendly packaging, reflecting its green credentials – the distillery not only produces its own electricity but creates a surplus which powers the local village. The new premium proposition was also given a premium price. And to the delight of its owners, it's surging forward as a result.

"Prior to the change, Deanston's main market was the United States, with a few cases being sold in the United Kingdom," says brand manager Marco Di Ciacca.

"This however was purely based on price and the brand was treated as a commodity

by distributors and retailers...it was also not very well received by the maltheads due to sub-standard liquid which was distilled prior to the Burn Stewart takeover. We had to change people's attitudes and that's why there has been a huge amount of development work. It's now distributed to around 25 countries around the world with volumes increasing by around 19% even though the retail price has increased by over 30%."

And the rebranding exercise has provided a platform to launch a range of new Deanston expressions. Deanston Virgin Oak was launched in September, and an aged organic whisky and an older expression were also planned with the possibility of a small batch bottling in the future.

Unsurprisingly, whisky companies rebrand or reposition their malts to make more money. The ideal scenario is to both raise the price and to sell more, repositioning an expression in to a higher quality category. But the large number of malts being given a make-over is also born of necessity, reflecting the increasingly insatia-

ble demand among whisky lovers for new and better whisky. Stand still for too long, it seems, and you're toast.

Take the example of Bunnahabhain, another of Burn Stewart's malts and one with a strong unique selling point as 'Islay's gentle dram' or as many describe it, an unpeated Islay whisky. Can we say that about it any more?

In addition to some logical brand extension through expressions such as the 18 year old, the 25 year old and a sherried 16 year old, we have Toiteach, a peated version of the malt. A limited edition peated whisky under the name Moine was released as part of the Islay festival. And now the liquid in a bottle of the core 12 year old has changed – it's now non chill-filtered and has a strength of 46.3%, giving it a distinctly tangy, peaty taste. It's lovely but it's a definite step in a new taste direction.

When you put the new bottling alongside the peated Jura Prophecy and the Autumn 2010 release Machrie Moor, a peated malt from Arran, it would seem clear that whisky companies are responding to the demands of the malt drinker.

Scapa Single Malt is on the move

The whole range from Aberlour got a face lift in 2010

Low stock triggers a re-launch

One island malt which hasn't succumbed to the temptations of peat is Scapa. In fact since its new owner took it over it has benefited from a softly-softly approach. True, it's been re-launched as a 16 year old rather than a 14 year old – but according to brand director for malts at Chivas Brother, Neil Macdonald, the reason wasn't just one of moving the malt to a more premium category.

"We had to make the change because there were inventory issues," he says. "We had to take a long term view of the distillery and wait for everything to fall in to place. We had to get the liquid right and we knew that would take a considerable period of time.

"The spirit was just coming back on stream when we acquired it but it was all over the place. There was whisky in Canadian Club casks and all sort of things. We started filling all spirit into first fill American oak barrels and we revatted all existing stock as well. In terms of the change of packaging – well we went there and were amazed by this place, which was like a desert island, and we wanted to bring it to life in the packaging."

Macdonald says that other repackaging exercises by the company haven't always been just about cashing in on the brand. The 2010 repackaging of Aberlour, for instance, was about smartening up the overall image of the malt.

"Over the years different expressions have been introduced and each time there was a tweak in the design," he says. "This has meant that each bottle has been different and the differences between some had become quite large. There was an inconsistency so the new packaging has been introduced to remove that."

Consistency of packaging would be the thinking behind Diageo's The Singleton concept, though it's unique because it comes at the whole branding exercise from a different angle. Three different versions of The Singleton are on offer – Dufftown in Europe, Glen Ord in Asia, and Glendullan. The idea, according to Nick Morgan, Diageo's Scotch knowledge and heritage director, is to attract new drinkers to the malt whisky category.

單一麥芽威士忌

緩釀豐醇 完美平衡

後 不

Celebrity chef Curtis Stone from Australia
educating Taiwanese consumers how to pair
Singleton of Glen Ord with Asian cuisine

Nick Morgan, Diageo's Scotch Knowledge and Heritage Director

Photo: © Diageo

"I think there is a duty of all of us in the Scotch malt whisky category to satisfy the demands of experienced malt whisky drinkers which we do with our special releases, and to attract new people in to the category," he says.

"We can do that in a number of different ways but one of them is to offer consumers who might be intimidated by the category with something that is approachable and non threatening but delivers everything they would expect from a good single malt whisky."

"We did extensive research in different territories to find out what the consumer wanted and we provided a good quality single malt which delivers what they would expect. The Singleton has not only done this but it has surpassed all our expectations."

Walking a tightrope

But The Singleton is an exception. On the whole, rebranding is about growing and refreshing established brands or reinventing a little known one as a major force in the premium category.

For established malt brands it's a question of normally walking a tightrope – staying true to the brand's core values but finding space to dust themselves down to be more relevant for the future. But the stakes are high, and that's because as interest in the malt market continues to grow there are plenty of malts which are effectively unknown beyond a very small percentage of consumers and are therefore, to all intents and purposes, new brands for their owners. There are scores of them – Glen Garioch, GlenDronach, Ardmore, Benromach, even Glen Grant which has fallen from grace in recent years but is now set for a major push by owners Campari.

Bob Dalrymple, marketing manager for Maxxium, whose brands include Laphroaig, The Macallan, Highland Park and Ardmore, argues that of all the malts Scotland produces, only a handful are performing as brands in their own right.

"There are huge prices to be won with the right proposition," he says.

He points to Ardmore, which is a key ingredient in Teacher's but was virtually unknown as a single malt four years ago. It has a fascinating but challenging taste but it is growing as a single malt at a rapid pace. A 25 year old version released in to Travel Retail was being added to the core portfolio and to attract new drinkers a sample bottle of Ardmore Traditional was being given away with each bottle of Teacher's.

"Promoting what is effectively a new malt like this is a very different proposition to marketing an established malt," he says. "We were able to ditch the baggage which might come with malts which have been established for many years. The packaging is quite modern and distinctive. Ardmore stands apart from all the creams and beiges you find in the malt market place."

Undoubtedly, in the months ahead more malts will get a face lift and make-over. Some will work, some won't. What's clear, though, is that there's a dynamism at work in the industry, and no brand can afford to stand still, no matter how iconic it is.

If it does, it'll fall by the wayside, dated and unloved. And we'll look at what happened to it years later and ask: what on earth were its owners thinking of?

Dominic Roskrow is a freelance whisky writer and former editor of Whisky Magazine, which he edited for four years. He now edits Whiskeria, and writes regularly for Whisky Magazine, Malt Advocate, Harpers and Drinks International. He is the business development director for The Whisky Shop chain. He has been writing about drinks for nearly 20 years and is the author of Whiskies: From Confused to Connoisseur *and* Collins Gems Whisky. *In 2010 he provided new tasting notes and chapters for the sixth edition of* Michael Jackson's Malt Whisky Companion *and his coffee table book* The World's Best Whiskies - 750 Unmissable Drams from Tennessee to Tokyo *was published in autumn 2010. He lives in Norfolk, home of England's first malt whisky distillery, and is married with three children and is one of the few people in the world to be both a Keeper of the Quaich and a Kentucky Colonel.*

Mashing
-the basis
of a good distillation

*The lively, frothing wash in a washback
or the clear newmake flowing from the heated copper still.
To the distillery visitor, these are images that may leave stronger
impressions than the big mash tun silently doing its job.
But there lies the beginning of a successful distillation
and there is no one better than Ian Wisniewski
to explain the intricacies of mashing.*

Mashing may be considered a practicality that follows a specific formula, but that doesn't mean it's a straightforward process, as there are a number of variables to consider. Individual batches of the same delivery of malt can behave differently in the mash tun, let alone when changing to another barley variety, or to the next harvest, which can require adjustments to the milling specification, the water temperature and degree of stirring required in the mash tun. Consequently, it's a case of constant monitoring and not taking anything for granted.

The essential step prior to mashing is milling the malted barley into three separate grades. A typical milling specification is 20% husk, 70% grits (i.e. medium ground) and 10% flour (ie. finely ground), which is collectively termed grist. These percentages provide an ideal surface area for the hot water to work on, and enables the maximum amount of sugar to be extracted from the grist in the minimum amount of time (a crucial factor as every distillery has to maintain a strict timetable). But these percentages also reflect a balance between various considerations.

"I can't emphasise how important milling is, and the milling spec is crucial to mashing.

A higher percentage of flour (fine grind) can improve your yield of sugars, but too high a percentage of flour can potentially result in a sticky paste and problems with drainage. A higher percentage of husk improves drainage, but can also reduce extraction of sugars and therefore the yield, so it's a case of balancing all the options," says Russell Anderson, distillery manager, Highland Park.

Grist is conveyed from a container called a grist hopper to the steels mashing machine, where it meets the first batch of hot water (three batches of water are usually added at progressively higher temperatures and in specific amounts, although some distilleries use four waters). The combined water and grist, known as the mash, is fed into the mash tun through a spout.

Attaining the precise strike temperature requires some fine tuning, because the first batch of water is a case of recycling the final water of the previous mashing cycle. This water, known as the sparge, is always hotter than required, so it's mixed with cold water to reach the strike temperature.

Although 63.5° C is the usual strike temperature, variables such as moving onto another harvest means this may have to be revised.

"Sometimes it's a beautifully smooth transition from one harvest to the next, and other's it's not. In some years we'd have to raise the strike temperature to 64.5° C to gelatinise the starch and we might want to adjust the milling spec, and in other years we may lower the strike temperature to 60° C. It depends on the growing conditions of the harvest, with a lot of factors coming into play, such as the nitrogen level and soil conditions. We analyse early batches of malt which gives us an indication of what strike temperatures will be needed. We also measure the viscosity levels, which can vary from year to year, and a higher viscosity means the rate of drainage and extraction may not be as good," says Russell Anderson.

The first reactions

As soon as the water and grist meet various reactions begin, as groups of enzymes within the grist are activated when combined with hot water and hydrated. However, only a few of these enzymes are critical to mashing, with star performers including alpha amylase and beta amylase.

"Alpha amylase and beta amylase are the key enzymes as they generate the most alcohol potential by way of converting starch into sugar, so we check the level of these two enzymes when buying malted barley," says Douglas Murray, Process Technology Manager, Diageo.

Both enzymes are sensitive to different conditions, including levels of heat (ie. being damaged or destroyed at certain temperatures). This explains why the temperature of the first batch of water is 63.5° C when it meets or 'strikes' the grist (which gives rise to the term 'strike temperature').

"Alpha amylase is optimally active when the water temperature is at 70° C, but this is a bit too hot for beta amylase, for which 55° C is ideal. This means that a strike temperature of 63.5 is the ideal compromise for these two enzymes," says Dr Bill Lumsden, head of distilling and whisky creation, Glenmorangie.

Enzymes are already 'in position' to begin working as soon as they are hydrated, as the process of malting ensures the enzymes are distributed throughout the grain. Malting also breaks down the cell walls enclosing the starch, leaving only traces of cell walls for the enzymes to finish dismantling during mashing. However, the level of cell walls remaining after malting can be variable rather than uniform, and some grains may retain more cell wall than others.

Meanwhile, starch granules within the grist become gelatinised (i.e. change from a firmer to a softer texture). This is the first stage of the enzymes converting the starch into sugars, with the enzymes subsequently breaking down longer chain sugars into shorter units, with the range of sugars including glucose (comprising one glucose unit), maltose (comprising two glucose units linked together) and maltotriose (three glucose units).

"The fines and smaller particles convert first, with the middles and larger pieces taking longer. There is no sugar derived from the husk, as this doesn't contain starch. Alpha amylase attacks branches up to 25 glucose units long. Alpha amylase will attack the end of a long chain and lop off up to 4 maltose units. This enables beta amylase to follow up and work along the length taking off two units at at a time, so they make a good partnership," says Douglas Murray.

Meanwhile, an important preparatory stage when mashing is to cover the drainage plates at the bottom of the mash tun with a layer of sparge, pumped in from under the drainage plates. This ensures that when mash (ie. grist and water) falls to the base of the mash tun, it lands onto water rather than the drainage plates. Otherwise there could be serious consequences.

"At the start of the mashing process around eight inches of sparge water is added to the base of the mash tun before the grist is added to prevent the sparge/grist mix from striking the bottom plates and potentially choking the openings in the drainage plates," says James MacTaggart, distillery manager, Isle of Arran.

Furthermore, the initial water that drains through the plates is pumped to the top of the mash tun and re-introduced onto the bed, in a process known as vorlaufing. This water then continues it's journey through the bed, acquiring a higher level of sugars before draining from the mash tun.

"Another benefit of vorlaufing is the extra time this allows for the bed to settle, which optimises filtration of the wort and so promotes clear wort. Vorlaufing also allows extra contact between the liquid and the bed, which optimises the conversion of starches to sugars," says Dr Bill Lumsden.

The bed (i.e. mash that settles in the mash tun) acts as a filter, catching particles and solids while allowing liquid to drain through the base of the mash tun. This process would ideally be completed entirely of its own accord. However,

The newest mash tun in Scotland (Glenlivet) and the oldest from 1881 (Bruichladdich)

there can be problems such as the bed sticking together like a vast amount of porridge. One reason for this stickiness is a higher than usual level of protein in the malt (the protein level varies, being affected by annual harvest conditions, among other factors). Similarly, switching barley varieties can introduce surprises, as the grain size for example differs significantly among barley varieties, and may require adjustments to the milling spec.

If there are any problems, or if the rate of drainage simply needs to be enhanced, the bed can be stirred by rotating the arms fitted to a central column in the mash tun. Stirring opens up drainage channels, but needs to be as gentle as possible to avoid the risk of more particles and solids draining through in the wort.

The different types of mash tuns

The most traditional type of arms used in a mash tun are a rake, which are still in active service at a few distilleries such as Springbank.

"Our rakes are like the teeth of a comb, which go round doing a front crawl through the mash. When we mash in, we stir the bed a couple of times, then leave it sitting for 20 min-

utes before draining off the wort and adding a second water, which we also stir once, then drain off. A third and fourth water which are our sparge are then added to the mash tun," says Frank McHardy, director of production at Springbank distillery.

Developments in the brewing industry resulted in arms known as semi-lauters being introduced during the 1970s, and replacing rakes in various distilleries.

A semi-lauter comprises two horizontal arms each fitted with vertical attachments that carry smaller blades known as knives, which 'cut' through the bed as they rotate (either clockwise or anti-clockwise, with a choice of speeds available). The arms of a semi-lauter are fixed and extend through the depth of the bed to the drainage plates. This concept was taken a stage further during the 1970s-80s when the lauter (also referred to as a full lauter) was introduced. The arms of a lauter can be raised and lowered during mashing, enabling the arms to stir specific sections of the bed. The upper section of the bed, for example, can be stirred and gently broken up, while leaving the base of the bed unaffected. Consequently, the base of the bed is able to filter the wort to the

The inside of Bruichladdich's traditional rake and plough mash tun.

The mash tun at Linkwood distillery is cleaned. The removable plates and the sparge ring are clearly visible.

maximum degree, and limit the level of particles draining through.

Changing from a rake to a semi-lauter or lauter can improve the yield, and save a significant amount of time, which may mean only two-thirds of the mashing time compared to using a rake. Changing from a semi-lauter to a lauter also provides more options, though there are still plenty of semi-lauters in active service. But whatever the potential benefits of updating the arms, that doesn't mean every distillery seeks change.

"We consider that the extra yield and time saved by switching to a lauter tun is not enough of an advantage compared to main-taining our traditional production methods at Springbank Distillery," says Frank McHardy.

Mash tuns were traditionally made from cast iron, until stainless steel become a standard choice from the 1980's. This transition reflected ease of cleaning and manufacturing, with the dimensions of mash tuns increasing ever since.

Whether to have a lid on top of the mash tun is another part of the debate. A few distilleries, including Springbank, don't have lids. Most distilleries do, with some lids being

Frank McHardy, Springbank's Director of Production

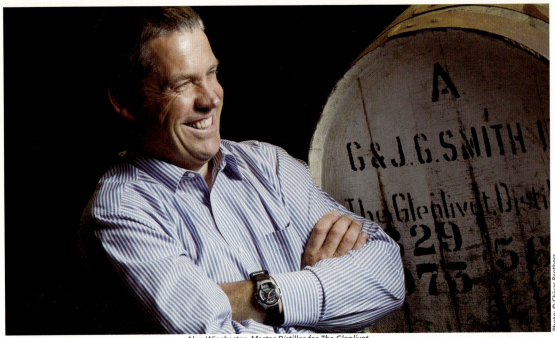
Alan Winchester, Master Distiller for The Glenlivet

copper and others stainless steel. One reason for having a lid is to help maintain the optimum water temperature within the mash tun. Another practical benefit is containing the steam (from batches of progressively hotter water) within the mash tun, and prevent it from dispersing and condensing in the mash house.

Another option is a canopy, which has become a rare feature in the industry.

"We decided to keep Strathisla's canopy, which dates from the 1950s. This is a domed copper lid that sits on legs slightly raised above the mash tun, with steam rising up the centre of the canopy to a chimney with vents," says Alan Winchester, master distiller, The Glenlivet.

The second water

Once all of the first water has been added, it's standard practise when using semi-lauters or lauters to add a second water at a higher temperature without any pause.

Rather than introducing the second water through the same spout as the first water, it's sprayed on from a sparge ring. This circular tube, running under the lid of the mash tun, is fitted with nozzles to ensure even distribution of water across the bed (where there is no lid the spout that introduces the first water can be used).

The second water is typically between 65-74° C, with this higher temperature required to flush out stickier sugars left behind by the first water. An additional effect is that the weight of the second water helps to 'drive' the remaining first water through the bed and drainage plates.

Good drainage is essential for an optimum rate of extraction, with individual drainage plates at the base of the mash tun fitting together like a jigsaw puzzle (and so easily removed for cleaning).

Drainage plates are generally stainless steel, though there's far more variety in the width of openings in the plates, narrower or broader, which helps to determine the rate of drainage. Larger openings naturally promote a greater rate of drainage, and allow a higher level of particles to drain through, which in turn determines whether the wort is clear or cloudy (and also the degree of cloudyness).

Whether clear or cloudy wort is preferable depends on each individual distillery, as this can have a significant influence on the character of the new make spirit. Cloudy wort can lead to a richer style of new make spirit, compared to clear wort. However, this also depends on the distillation regime, including key factors such as the spirit cut (ie. the strength of the spirit coming off the still), with a relatively higher strength such as 70% abv typically promoting a lighter, fruitier style than a lower strength.

In some mash tuns drainage plates sit above a 'valley' bottom, ie. a conical shape, as opposed to the other option which is a flat bottom, with this 'empty' space beneath the

plates promoting more uniform drainage to the underback.

Once the required volume of wort has been drained into the underback a third water is added at around 85-90° C, in order to rinse out any remaining sugars. However, the level of sugars in the third water, which is the sparge, is minimal. The sparge is conducted through a separate system from the wort, and used as the first water of the next mashing cycle. Some distilleries also use a fourth water, which can be stored as sparge and used as the second water of the next mashing cycle.

The result - fermentable sugars

Approximately 85-90% of the starches are broken down into fermentable sugars within the mash tun, with the first water achieving the greatest conversion rate. This provides a wort consisting mainly of maltose (comprising two glucose units linked together), with smaller amounts of glucose (comprising one glucose unit) and maltotriose (three glucose units). But the wort also includes longer chain sugars with the additional feature of a branch, and dealing with any branches requires a particular enzyme.

"Alpha amylase and beta amylase can only tackle long chain sugars (i.e. when the arrangement is like beads in a necklace), but neither can cope with any branches along a chain. Dealing with any branches is down to another enzyme called limit dextrinase," says Dr Bill Lumsden.

However, limit dextrinase requires specific conditions before it is 'activated' and able to debranch the longer chain sugars known as dextrins.

"Limit dextrinase can only operate in a more acidic environment than the mash tun provides. In the washback the pH falls and around pH 4.2 limit dextrinase is active and able to debranch dextrins. The alpha amylase and beta amylase are still able to convert the de-branched dextrins. This 'secondary conversion' is much slower and can potentially continue throughout fermentation," says Dr Bill Crilly, the Edrington Group's technical support manager.

While enzymes perform a vital role within the mash tun, a vital matching accessory outside the mash tun is a computer loaded with the appropriate program.

"You can control and monitor everything that happens in the mash tun on a computer screen, and it can be a fairly automated process, with a computer knowing what to do

next in certain situations, but even so an experienced mashman is needed to check on each stage of the process," says Alan Winchester.

Alasdair Anderson, distillery manager, Glenrothes, adds, "Our mash tun is computer controlled but not fully automated, we've reached a happy medium, and wouldn't like to loose the benefit of having a mashman monitoring the process. Each mash can have it's own peculiarities and drainage rates can vary hugely, so the input of the mashman is crucial."

Total mashing times vary widely among distilleries, though around 6-8 hours is a typical time frame. Once the mashing cycle is completed it's time to dispose of the draff (i.e. remnants of the mash). Needless to say, the design of the mash tun facilitates this process.

"Knives on the arms, which are straight during mashing, are angled to push the draff out, when we open up two draff doors among the drainage plates, then it's blown out with compressed air into holding tanks. The draff is then taken to a plant at the bottom of the village where it's converted into cattle feed," says Alasdair Anderson.

The process is slightly different at Springbank. "The fourth water and the draff are pumped to a drainer, water is drained from this vessel to the brewing tanks and local farmers take away the draff for feeding to cattle or sheep," says Frank McHardy.

With various ways of disposing of the draff, as well as different options for the type of arms fitted, the size of holes in the drainage plates, whether or not to have a lid on the mash tun, and so on, there are plenty of details to think about. But choice is a wonderful thing, and when purchasing new mash tuns a distillery manager can order 'a la carte,' and incorporate all the preferred features within an ultimate piece of kit.

*Ian Wisniewski is a food, drink and travel writer and broadcaster specialising in spirits.
He contributes to various publications, including Whisky Magazine, and has written 8 books on drinks, including* Classic Malt Whisky. *He is a regular visitor at malt whisky distilleries in Scotland, and also distilleries in various other countries, as he is fascinated by the production process. He is also chairman of the white spirits judges for the International Spirits Challenge, and frequently conducts tutored tastings.*

Age
and other matters

*A press release about the importance of age
sent out by Chivas Brothers this summer sparked a debate
within the whisky community. Why the controversy? Ian Buxton
asks the question whether it was a marketing spin
or a serious attempt to educate the customer.*

"…a message which is fraught with danger."
(Dave Broom)

"…a gargantuan load of fetid hooey."
(John Glaser)

"…a load of old bollocks." (caskstrength.net)

It's a wild guess of course, but I imagine that
that wasn't quite the reaction that Chivas
Brothers were hoping for when they launched
their Age Matters campaign. But, in case you
were on the dark side of the moon at the time,
let's begin at the beginning.

Back in June 2010, Chivas Brothers (that's the
Scotch whisky arm of Pernod Ricard) declared
that "age matters" and announced what they
described as "a global campaign to advocate
the importance and value of age statements to
consumers."

Just so as we're clear, the campaign applied
solely to Scotch whisky. "What about Irish
and American?" I asked them and the reply,
wrapped around with references to maturation
rates (Bourbon) and triple distillation (Irish
whiskey) was, in essence, "non".

The aim, apparently, was to "empower
consumers with knowledge, so that they fully

understand the value of what they are
buying." Which all sounds quite noble and
disinterested. The campaign had a very generic
feel and there were even faint suggestions that
the industry as a whole might like to pick up
the theme and adopt some kind of joint
marketing across the whole category.

But it stirred up quite some controversy,
especially amongst enthusiast blogs. While my
opening quotes are at the extreme end and
there was support from some commentators,
much of the reaction tended to the cynical and
dismissive. So what was going on?

The Chivas campaign appeared to be soundly
based. They had done extensive international
research amongst consumers to establish levels
of understanding of the age statements that
appear on bottles of Scotch and their attitude
to age in whisky. To summarise:

The sample consisted of more than 2,000
respondents in nine countries each evaluating
a set of statements. All respondents were male
and over 21 (or 25+ in India). All had purchased
whisky in the past month and the countries
where the research took place are all significant whisky markets: France, the UK, the US,
India, Korea, Russia, Mexico, China and Brazil.
All in all, it was a significant (and probably

LOOK FOR THE NUMBER

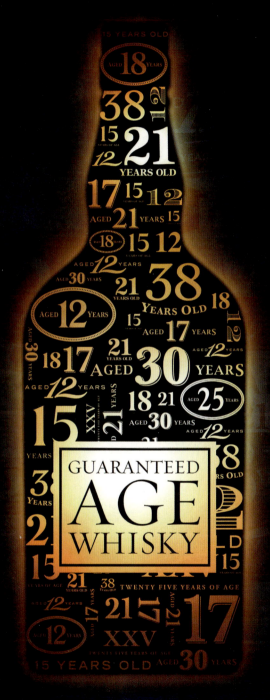

KNOW THE AGE, KNOW WHISKY

expensive) piece of work that wasn't undertaken lightly.

So what did they discover? The findings were as follows:

- Only 10% of consumers understand that an age statement on a bottle of Scotch refers to the youngest whisky in the bottle; nearly half (48%) believe it refers to the average age and 35% believe it signifies the oldest whisky present.

However,
- 94% of consumers believe that age is an important indicator of quality

- 93% believe that older whiskies are better quality

- 92% prefer to buy whisky with a clear age statement

- 97% agreed that whiskies that claim to be aged should clearly state the age on the bottle

- 89% look for an age statement when buying whisky, and

- 86% expect to pay a price premium for whiskies with an age statement

Ken Grier - Director of Malts at Edrington

That all seems straight-forward enough and actually quite helpful. After all, it's a legal requirement to age Scotch whisky and the regulations on how you describe that age are unambiguous. From one point of view, it's a straight-jacket but also a valuable piece of consumer protection that might just give Scotch an advantage, especially if age is so positively correlated with quality.

Age - just one of the factors

And here's where the problem starts, at least for the well-informed consumer. The well-informed consumer – such as readers of the Malt Whisky Yearbook – knows that age is only one factor in the quality of Scotch whisky.

It was a point that Chivas' competitors were keen to make when I discussed the campaign with them.

"The quality of a whisky is largely dependent on the quality of the oak casks it is matured in, the quality of the new make spirit and the time it is aged for," said Ken Grier, Edrington's Director of Malts (that puts him in charge of The Macallan and Highland Park).

"With around 60% of final whisky character determined by cask quality, the oak cask is the

Iain Kennedy - Global Brand Director at Bacardi (Dewar's)

John Glaser - owner of Compass Box Whisky

Serge Valentin - the man behind whiskyfun.com

most prominent factor in ensuring and delivering a quality spirit."

From Bacardi Global Brands, Iain Kennedy (he's in charge of Dewar's) went further.

"I do believe that 'age' does send a powerful quality message to consumers, and one that they understand with ease. It is however not the only one and in reality compared to a 12 year old whisky an 18 year old offers the drinker a different experience not a better one. Indeed some very old product that I have been privileged to sample has tasted more like chewing on a piece of wood rather than the pinnacle of the drinking experience that some may suggest. Age has importance but ultimately it is insufficient."

And John Glaser of Compass Box, who likened the campaign to "…a gargantuan load of fetid hooey" passionately stressed the complexity of the issue.

"The quality of a whisky is based on the quality and type of oak cask used, the quality and character of the spirit and the amount of time spent in the cask - in that order of importance," he blogged. "You can't skimp on any of those three variables, especially the quality of oak, if you want to make compelling whisky."

I'm sure you agree. As a reader of this publication you're likely keenly interested in such topics as cask type, wood finishing and so on. But let's be honest: fascinating as these are, they are pretty arcane topics and downright irrelevant to the vast majority of consumers and the vast majority of consumption occasions which, when we get right down to it, involve standard blends (and often copious amounts of ice. Sorry about that.)

And blends are, of course, what the industry has to sell in large quantities to survive (and, let it not be forgotten, by so doing maintain the survival, diversity and variety of the single malts that we all love so passionately). It's a point that Malt Maniac Serge Valentin made in a long and thoughtful piece (an e-pistle) on the 'age matters' campaign on the Maniacs' excellent website.

"Business is business. As for the distillers and retailers, they'll sell you what they have, and certainly not what they do not have (anymore). Why should we be surprised? They're doing their jobs," he wrote.

He's making a very important point about stocks that a number of commentators appear

The whisky loch of the 70s and 80s was created in dark warehouses like this, all over Scotland

to have forgotten; bear with me for a short history lesson. You don't have to look back very far in Scotch whisky marketing to see that older whiskies were not that highly regarded. The general view was that after 20 years or so whisky became unpleasantly woody – I recall the term "slimy" being used.

Then, due to the over-production of the late 1970s and early 1980s, the notorious "whisky loch" came into being. Industry stocks around 1980 were roughly equivalent to ten years of production. The short-term result was a painful round of distillery closures that are still remembered to this day but, less visibly, this meant warehouses filled with whisky that no-one wanted – a sinister, silent and faintly embarrassing reminder of the irrational optimism of the late 1970s. Unable to sell much of this whisky, the industry had no alternative but to keep it.. and keep it..and keep it until, eventually, it could be sold.

And, eventually, it was. Like a slow-moving glacier the whisky loch calved icebergs of older and older whisky that consumers came to love. And, in time, the whisky industry also came to love its old whisky because a new generation of marketing gurus were able to re-package it as luxury expressions and sell it at premium prices never previously achieved by whisky; prices that generated sexy profits and a glamorous brand image that those distillers are now reluctant to abandon.

But the loch has been largely drained and so now we're hearing a new mantra from the cohorts of youthfully enthusiastic and bright-eyed brand ambassadors that populate the whisky bars, fairs and festivals that have so proliferated in recent years.

"Age isn't every-thing," they cry. "It's really about the casks…or the skill of the blender" – curiously, the message will tend to vary depending on whether a luxury blend or single malt is being offered!

Serge Valentin certainly thinks the brand ambassadors are playing a role here and that age matters, though it's the age of the drinker as much as anything that counts for him.

"Younger guys, that is to say people who started in whisky very recently, also repeat what they are now told by a large part of the industry: that age does not really matter. They can't have any evidence, as their experience is short but let's face it; it's hard not to repeat what you're now told by a large proportion of the industry and their very engaging brand ambassadors."

Apparently out of the blue come the non-aged luxury expressions: we have Glenmorangie offering us Signet (at a thought-provoking £120 or so); Macallan releasing their 1824 Collection range for tax-free outlets (up to £1,200 for the 1824 Limited Release); Dewar's positioning Signature (around £160) as their ultimate blend, only to be trumped by Diageo's Johnnie Walker Blue Label King George V Edition (yours for £400 or so) and so on. Expect more of this sort of stuff.

A spin for those who have old whiskies to sell?

So you could be cynical about this and conclude that it's all about 'spin'. I'm reminded of Alice, lost in a kind of whisky wonderland and, in the words of Lewis Carroll, ask

"You are old, Father William," the young man said,
"And your hair has become very white;
And yet you incessantly stand on your head.
Do you think, at your age, it is right?"

But it probably would be cynical to suggest that the industry is simply standing years of received wisdom on its head. It's a lot more complex than that!

Undoubtedly, some of this is about stocks – or the lack of them. It's not a huge leap to conclude that while much of the Scotch industry has now exhausted much of its older inventory, Chivas Brothers have not and so, perfectly legitimately, they are seeking to maintain a commercial advantage and promote the idea that age matters.

And, conversely, many of their competitors are running out of older whisky but need to maintain the profitability and positive brand image that they were enjoying until recently. So they need a new message that transcends age. So wood is the new age.

Conveniently, though, that happens to be true. The science of whisky making has advanced significantly in the past decade (has anyone else noticed how the 'we make whisky the way we always have' message has been toned down recently?) and now we know a lot more about the relative contribution of cask type, finishing and aging than was the case in the 1970s and 80s. So Dewar's, Macallan and Compass Box have got a point but their point is as commercially driven as Chivas'.

So where can we find some disinterested information to try to resolve the question?

Once again Serge Valentin comes to the rescue. He analysed the Malt Maniacs' Malt Monitor to assess 865 bottlings, tasted 100% blind, each by a panel of more than 10 judges during the Malt Maniacs Awards – a staggering 10,303 tastings summarised in the graph below.

And what does it show? Well, his conclusion was that "unsurprisingly, aged whisky is indeed 'better' than young whisky. The widest gap, 5.32 points, lies between 11-13 years and 35-39 years. It's not totally huge, but it's very significant. 5.32 points within the usual '70-95' scale represents more or less 20% [variance]. It is also to be noted that peaty whiskies tend to get sold at younger age than unpeated ones, which may boost the lower ages a bit in the graph."

Now, to be fair to Chivas Brothers, we shouldn't misrepresent their message – as arguably some of the more excitable commen-tators have done. They only said 'age matters', not that age is the only thing, or the most important thing or that age was necessarily a guarantee of quality – though you might be excused for jumping to that conclusion or for thinking that they might want you to do that.

Of course, this isn't an altruistic exercise but let's consider a frightening statistic in the Chivas research: only around 10% of whisky consumers understand the age statement on the bottle they buy. That's scary and it's a useful reminder to the very well-informed (you, dear reader) that you are in a tiny minority.

Just to be clear: in a world where more than 90% of the Scotch whisky sold is a blend, 90% of consumers don't understand what they're buying. And, if they don't even understand the significance of the age statement what are the chances of them even being interested in, let alone understanding, messages about wood types; finishing; the relative merits of toasting vs. charring and the subtractive, additive and interactive contribution of the cask? That can only confuse.

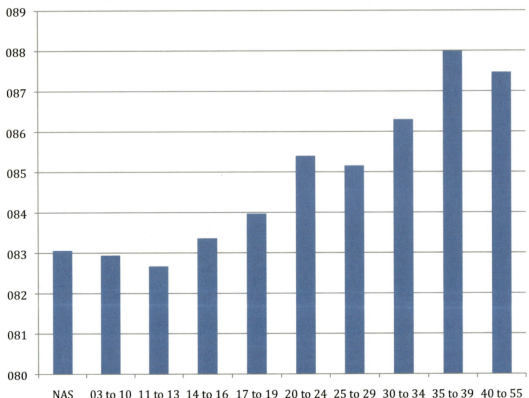

Malt Maniacs' Average Scores
(on 10,303 scorings - 100% blind only)

Photo: © Chivas Brothers

Christian Porta - Chairman and CEO of Chivas Brothers

Age must be put into a context

We need to take a step back. As Dr Bill Lumsden, Glenmorangie's Head of Distilling & Whisky Creation told me

"Age statements need to be understood in the context of the individual whisky – some is simply better younger, others need more age. There is no 'one size fits all' solution."

He's right, but I'd add that age statements also need to be understood in the context of the market and the drinker. We've got to get many more consumers to the point where they at least understand what the label is telling them. Only then can they move beyond whisky 1.01 (assuming they want to; they may, radical thought, prefer simply to enjoy their drams!)

As the old saw has it, in the kingdom of the blind the one-eyed man is king. But, to the extent that the 'age matters' campaign opens some eyes it will benefit the whole industry, not just Chivas Brothers and the fact that they evidently judge that they will benefit more than others need not concern us. After all, as Valentin remarks, "business is business".

For my part, I think Chivas have probably done us all a favour. An interesting debate has opened up and they claim to welcome the views and opinions surrounding the issue. It's certainly got them some attention amongst hard-core whisky fans; for the most part, though, all most Scotch drinkers will see of the campaign is a poster in the next airport shop they visit and perhaps a tiny logo on the bottle.

If it gives them pause for thought and distracts them from the blandishments of rum, vodka and cognac then Scotch as a whole will benefit. The campaign won't do much amongst enthusiasts but then it was probably never meant to – there is a whole world of blogs, websites, tutorials, tastings, whisky fairs and festivals, brand ambassadors (however partisan) and even books such as this to explore and, to be fair, the Chivas Brothers malt team are fully engaged in that more informed debate.

And, after all the study, research and debate are done the happy traveller in the world of whisky could do worse than remember Aeneas MacDonald's sage words. They may have been written in 1930 but remain as relevant today as ever – the enthusiastic student of whisky should fall back on "his mother-wit, his nose and his palate to guide him."

Age matters – but your taste matters more. Slainte!

Note: Thanks to Serge Valentin for permission to reproduce the chart from his Malt Maniacs E-pistle.

Keeper of the Quaich and Liveryman of the Worshipful Company of Distillers, Ian Buxton is well-placed to write or talk about whisky, not least because he lives on the site of a former distillery!
Ian began work in the Scotch Whisky industry in 1987 and, since 1991, has run his own strategic marketing consultancy business. In addition, he gives lectures, presentations and tastings; runs the annual World Whiskies Conference and writes regular columns for Whisky Magazine, WhiskyEtc, The Tasting Panel and various other titles. With Neil Wilson he established Classic Expressions to reprint facsimile editions of rare whisky classics.
During 2010 he has written four new books on whisky: The Enduring Legacy of Dewar's *(Angel's Share);* Highland Park: A Good Foundation *(for Highland Park Distillery);* Glenglassaugh – A Distillery Reborn *(Angel's Share) and his latest title* 101 Whiskies to Try Before You Die *(Hachette).*
During 2011 his ambition is to spend more time with his wife!

Focus on India
- the most dynamic whisky market in the world

When the Scots introduced whisky to India in the 1800s, they had no idea that 150 years later it would be the biggest market in the world! For the producers of Scotch, this would seem a goldmine to explore but the competition from Indian whisky is fierce. Charles MacLean explains the problems and opportunities.

D r. Vijay Mallya swept into the World Whiskies Conference 2008 – fresh from his private jet, fashionably late, diamond ear-stud glittering – and lambasted those who said that Indian whisky wasn't truly 'whisky' if it was made from molasses alcohol (as much of it is).

"It was you Scots who founded the first distilleries in India. It was you who first used molasses. And it was you who named the product 'whisky'".

He was able to stay for only a few questions, since he had to return immediately to Bangalore to watch his Premier League cricket team play an important match…

Vijay Mallya is ranked by Forbes Magazine as among the world's richest people. They describe him succinctly as an 'Indian liquor baron', but he is much more than this. He is immensely charismatic, venerated as a deity by the people who work for him, a leading philanthropist and a member of the Upper House of the Indian Parliament (the Rajya Sabha) since 2000.

He is also a keen sportsman – once a semi-professional racing driver, he is joint owner of India's first Formula One team, Force India, as well as a substantial collection of classic cars. He is an 'ardent aviator' and founded Kingfisher Airlines in 2005 (now India's leading airline, although it has had its difficulties recently); a 'yachtsman of distinction', owner of one of the largest private yachts in the world, Indian Empress [95 metres]. As well as the

aforementioned cricket team, Bangalore Royal Challengers – which he won in an auction - he also owns the Premier League football club, Kingfisher East Bengal, and a stud farm with 200 horses. In other words, he is a true 'whisky baron' in the style of Tommy Dewar, Peter Mackie and James Buchanan.

The Problem

Dr. Mallya is chairman of United Spirits Ltd (USL) –the largest distiller in India and the second largest distiller in the world, measured by volume. Understandably, he would like to be able to sell his products in Europe; unfortunately for him, Regulation EC No 110/2008 of the European Parliament is quite clear that:

"Whisky or whiskey is a spirit drink produced exclusively by distillation from a mash made from malted cereals with or without whole grains of other cereals…[and, inter alia] shall not contain any additives other than plain caramel used for colouring".

He is right to point out that the Indian spirits industry was founded by British expatriates in the 19th century to supply liquor to the colonial communities. Where religion permitted, it was enthusiastically adopted by the indigenous peoples. Western types of spirits such as brandy, gin, rum, vodka and whisky were collectively known throughout Asia as 'Locally Made Foreign Liquor' ('LMFL'). In India the British Raj named it 'Indian Made Foreign Liquor' ('IMFL').

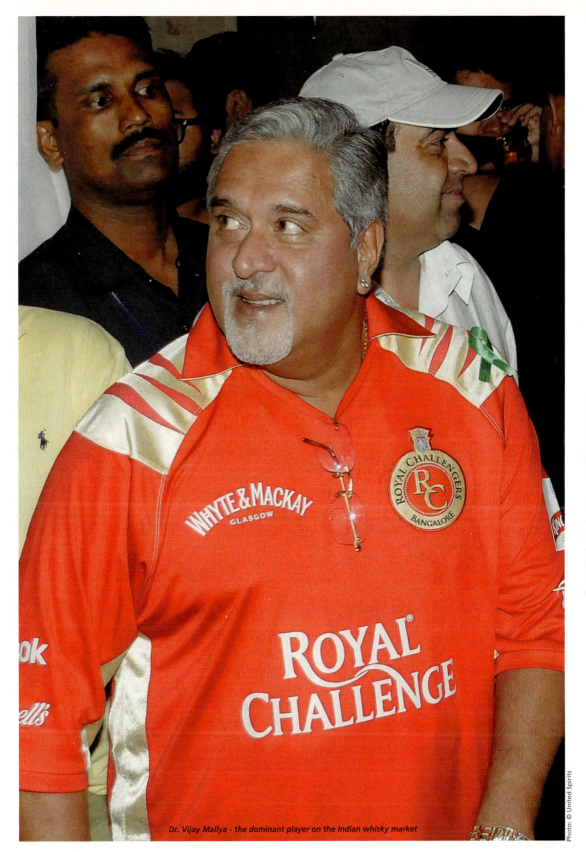

Dr. Vijay Mallya - the dominant player on the Indian whisky market

The raw materials, processes and maturation times for LMFL/IMFL are not defined by law, although if the product is to be sold in export markets it must meet the legal definition in these markets. Thus a brand of 'Indian Whisky' which is made from molasses alcohol and whisky essence cannot bear the name 'whisky' if it is offered for sale within the E.C., and many other export markets. Only a handful of Asian whiskies meet European legal requirements, although India is the largest consumer of whisky (or 'whisky') in the world, by a long way, consuming a staggering 200 million cases per annum in 2009 (IWSR estimate; around 60% of this is locally manufactured). Global sales of Scotch in the same period were 94.5 million cases.

Indian Whiskies and other IMFL spirits are often made in industrial ethanol plants, which make potable neutral alcohol as a side-line, although there are some dedicated grain distilleries, and a handful of pot still malt whisky distilleries on the sub-continent.

INDIAN WHISKY CATEGORIES

Extra Neutral Alcohol (ENA)
Made by fermentation and distillation in continuous stills - typically of molasses, rice, millet, buckwheat or any other fermentable agricultural product, including barley. The most basic Indian whiskies are made from ENA mixed with whisky essence and other artificial flavourings. They therefore do not meet the definition 'whisky' in most export markets.

Indian Blended Whisky
A mix of ENA and a varying amount of locally produced malt whisky and/or bulk imported malt whisky. Where an age statement is given, this is the age of the imported whisky. The product fails to pass the E.C. definition as whisky, unless the ENA is made from cereal grains.

Indian Blended Malt Whisky
Blends of 100% malt whiskies from two or more distilleries, domestic or foreign, qualify as 'whisky' in the E.C. so long as it is matured for at least three years.

Indian Single Malt Whisky
Made from malted barley in a single distillery. So long as this is matured for at least three years it meets E.C. regulations.

Notwithstanding this, many of the premium blended Indian whiskies I have tasted compare favourably with Scotch blends. My good friend Dr. Binod Maitin, Director of Production at USL, believes that the light style of ENA acts as a perfect background for the malts he uses in his blends. Indian blended and single malts are typically bottled a little over three years old

– the heat makes for a more rapid maturation, and with an angels' share (annual evaporation from the cask) at around 12%, they can't afford to leave it much longer!

Like everything else in India, penetrating the mysteries of style and operation is extremely difficult. Category definitions are loose (to say the least). Contacts and marketing people do not mean to be obscure, but, frankly, do not speak the same language as the rest of the whisky world. The web-sites are… well, look at them yourselves.

For decades India adopted a protectionist line for its home-made spirits, the IMFLs. Imported whisky is very highly taxed - until recently up to 550%. For years the Scotch Whisky Association and the World Trade Organisation pressed the Indian government to reduce duty, especially the discriminatory Additional Duty levy. In this they finally succeeded in July 2007, and Gavin Hewitt, SWA's Chief Executive reported that although tax would still be levied at 150% it "opens up new possibilities for Scottish distillers to compete with domestic producers on a level playing field for the first time. This is also good news for Indian consumers, who can look forward to a greater choice of internationally renowned Scotch whisky brands". Unfortunately, individual state governments control their own duties and excise, and many simply increased local taxes.

High tax is just one of the problems facing liquor companies in India. The overall regulatory framework for the alcoholic drinks market is highly complex. Licenses to produce alcohol are issued by both central and state governments, but state governments control duty and excise, and legislation relating to retailing. A raft of taxes, rules and regulations may apply in one state but be completely different in another. Some states, such as Gujarat, birthplace of Mahatma Ghandi, prohibit the production or sale of alcohol altogether. Such complexity and high costs inevitably lead to a thriving black market. Gujarat itself is among the top whisky consuming states, all of it supplied by the black market!

The complexity facing spirits companies seeking to trade in India is well exemplified by the variety of distribution methods. There are three types of markets in the states that permit the sale of liquor: open, auction and government-controlled. In open markets (eg Maharashtra) companies are permitted to appoint their own distributors. In auction markets (eg Punjab), governments auction off the wholesale and retail shops at the beginning of each

financial year. The state fixes the reserve price and the auction winners establish their own retail network and sourcing from manufacturers. In government-controlled distribution (southern Indian states), wholesale distribution is implemented by the particular state body, with consumer price decided upon by the state.

Sales in the off-trade, which accounts for around 80% of spirits volumes sold, are generally restricted to specialist retailers, although some states such as Delhi and Rajasthan allow sales in supermarkets. Across India, on-trade channels are crippled by the red tape that has to be endured before permission is obtained to open such establishments. The license fees that need to be paid by pubs and bars to operate are also considered to be very high.

The advertising of alcoholic products is banned, however companies get round this by sponsoring events or teams (such as Dr. Mallya's Bangalore Royal Challengers and Kingfisher East Bengal FC) and producing branded sales promotion materials. Celebrity endorsement is widely used, particularly from Bollywood stars. Soft drinks with the same packaging as the alcoholic drink has also provided a way to dodge the legislation – for a time a lavish TV commercial with all the trappings associated with the pleasures of alcohol was used to advertise 'Bagpiper' bottled water! (Bagpiper is the largest-selling brand of IMFL – see below)

If the myriad of restrictions and regulations were not difficult enough, any company doing business in India has to deal with the country's weak infrastructure. This can clearly be seen in its road transport. Between 1997 and 2004 the number of vehicles rose by 95% to 72.7 million. Although the National Highways network – the main arterial roads - has been, and continues to be, expanded, it cannot keep pace. Furthermore, many of the existing National Highways are in a poor state of repair and not wide enough, with the majority of the them no wider than two lanes.

The Opportunity

But never forget that India is the largest consumer of whisky (or 'whisky') in the world – 200 million cases in 2009. Indians have a well-established palate for whisky. While other 'key target markets' – China, Brazil, Russia and all other 'emergent' markets – are driven by fashion as well as flavour (and don't forget that in these markets imported whisky currently has huge cachet) – they are vulnerable: fashions change.

A senior manager at Pernod Ricard told me succinctly: "India represents potentially the most dynamic whisk(e)y market in the world. It consumes huge volumes of local Indian whiskies, some of which contain a percentage of Scotch, and many of the brands mirror Scotch in their style and apparance, preparing the Indian consumer with the product and image

Indian whisky brands often see the benefits of associating with Bollywood. The man holding the can is the famous actor Anil Kapoor.

cues of the Scotch whisky sector. However there are a number of issues which remain challenging for Western exporters, including high taxes and, for some, the availability of a distribution network".

Currently, the E.C. and the Indian government are negotiating a free trade agreement, and an important part of this is fair access for wines and spirits and a much more reasonable import duty, measured by international standards. For example, China's import tariff stands at 10%; Brazil's at 20%. In addition, the negotiators want imported and domestic products in each state to be treated in the same way, from a tax perspective.

Would Indian consumers immediately abandon Indian whisky if Scotch was more affordable? I don't think so. As I have mentioned, quality Indian whisky is very good; many of the leading premium and deluxe expressions cost as much as imported spirits. Scotch adds cachet - but it might also add significant state revenues if it were made more available. By and large the indigenous whisky companies are in favour, since duty parity across the subcontinent would make it simpler for them to operate. Some states have already adopted tax parity for imported and domestic spirits.

Recently there has been an increase in the production of 100% grain based Indian whisky, both malt and blended, which may well indicate preparations to enter the European market with these products. It may also presage preparations for increasing the supply of such whiskies to the ever-growing Indian market itself. In a recent article in Business India, Dr. Mallya was asked what his plans were for Whyte & Mackay, the established Scotch distiller he bought in 2007. He replied: "I did not buy W&M to buy into Scotch, but rather as a raw material for my brands... Though originally in the bulk business, the company has over 140 brands, of which Dalmore and Isle of Jura are very popular. Presently there is a management review to decide if we should be in the bulk business or do what we do best and build brands".

The year before he acquired W&M he had done just this with a blended Scotch named Black Dog, created in 1883 by Charles Mackinlay & Co for an ex-pat Scot in Calcutta, specifically for the Indian market. Co-incidentally, Mackinlay & Co. is now owned by W&M...

The Key Players

As I have stated, **United Spirits Limited** is the largest spirits producer in India, with 79 manu-

facturing and bottling plants, 64,000 retail outlets, 140 brands (23 of them selling over a million 9 litre cases per annum, with total spirits sales of 100 million cases [year to March 2010]) and commanding 60% of the Indian spirits market.

It is part of the United Breweries Group (UBG), the largest brewer in India, which was founded in 1915 by a Scotsman and bought in 1947 by Mr. Vittal Mallya, Vijay's father. Four years later he acquired the old established wine & spirits trading firm, McDowell & Co., built half a dozen distilleries and began to trade in IMFL – one of the first to do so – as well as imported spirits. Vijay Mallya succeeded his father as chairman of UBG in 1983, aged 28, and has expanded all areas of the business hugely. When UBG amalgamated with another well-established company, Shaw Wallace Distilleries Ltd in 2005, USL became the world's third (some say second) largest distiller. After more than a year of negotiation, the Glasgow-based Scotch whisky distillery, Whyte & Mackay, joined the fold in 2007.

USL's leading brands are:
Bagpiper, an IMFL launched in 1976 by Herbertsons Ltd, of Bombay, a subsidiary. Sales passed a million cases in 1987, five million in 1998, 10 million in 2006, and 17 million in 2009. The world's best-selling Scotch, Johnnie Walker, sells around 15 million cases globally. The brand has always been closely associated with 'Bollywood', and has won accreditation from many film stars.

Royal Challenge was introduced by Shaw Wallace in 1985, and was the best selling premium Indian whisky until 2008 but it is now challenged by Seagram's Blender's Pride (see below). It is associated by its owners with the up-market game of golf under the slogan "Game for Life".

McDowell's No.1 – a Blended Indian Whisky, was launched in 1968, and currently sells over 9 million cases per annum (the 4th largest selling whisky in the world), while McDowell's Single Malt is described as "the first ever indigenously developed single malt whisky in Asia".

Antiquity – a de luxe Indian blend from Shaw Wallace - still managed to win a Gold Award at the 2007 World Beverage Competition (USA) in the 'Scotch whisky' category! Also in the de luxe sector **Signature** is a blend of Indian and Scotch malts. A relative newcomer, it comes from the McDowell stable and has the tempting slogan "Success is Good Fun".

The second largest distiller in India is **Radico Khaitan**, owned and managed by Dr. Lalit Khaitan ("the country's second largest liquor baron") and his son Abhishek. Its HQ is at Rampur Distillery, Uttar Pradesh, a gigantic unit – the largest in Asia – with a capacity of over 90 million litres of alcohol per annum, producing ENA, rectified spirit (used in manufacturing IMFL brands - rum, brandy, gin and vodka as well as whisky), grain and malt whisky, as well as anhydrous alcohol, ethanol and gasohol (used as fuel, mixed with petrol).

Amongst Radico's leading brands of Indian whisky are **8PM**, launched in 1999. It had the singular distinction of selling a million cases in its first year (it now sells 3 million). It is made from "a mix of quality grains" and its core promise is 'thaath' [i.e. bold style, opulence] – "the reach of a man to the dream world" – while **Radico Supreme Gold** – Indian Blended Whisky, combines Indian spirits and Indian malt whisky "to impart a unique highland flavour".

Jagatjit Industries Limited (JIL) was founded in 1944 by the late L.P. Jaiswal, under the patronage of the Maharaja of Kapurthala, Jagatjit Singh, in the Punjab, with a large distillery, Jagatjit Nagar, at Hanira, the company's HQ.

It has 'manufacturing units' in eight other Indian states and the capacity to produce 14 million 9 litre cases per annum, so is ranked as the third largest producer of IMFL on the sub-continent.

JIL offers a range of spirits under the **Aristocrat** brand-name – brandy, gin and rum as well as whisky – and a couple of other Indian whiskies, including **Bonnie Scot**, which will enrage the Scotch Whisky Association!

Beyond India, perhaps the best-known Indian whisky is **Amrut Single Malt** from **Amrut Distilleries** in Bangalore. The 'Amrut' was a golden pot containing the Elixir of Life in Hindu mythology. This company was founded in 1948 by Shri J.N. Radhakrishna Jagdale, to supply bottled liquor to the Ministry of Defence. He was succeeded by his son and grandson. The latter, who is the company's Executive Director, trialed miniatures of Amrut Single Malt in 85 Indian restaurants in the U.K. It was particularly successful in Glasgow, and now the brand often features in whisky fairs around Europe and is also sold in the US.

Amrut Indian Single Malt Whisky is made from barley grown in the Punjabi foothills of the Himalayas, malted at Jaipur, Rajasthan, distilled in small batches at Bangalore (at 3,000 feet above sea level) where it is also matured in ex-bourbon and new oak casks and bottled without chill filtration. The range now consists of six different expressions.

United Spirits' leading brands

Amrut Distillery

Seagrams (now **Pernod Ricard India**) was the first international distiller to embrace the idea of producing IMFL whiskies for the Indian market and is still the only international company with a major presence in the country. It has fourteen manufacturing locations and ranks number three in volume production. Its main strength is in the north and west.

Pernod Ricard India's leading brand is *Royal Stag*, which broke the million cases a year barrier in 2000 and following further investment by Pernod Ricard since 2001, now sells in excess of five million cases per annum. *Imperial Blue* is a similar success story, jumping from under half a million cases to over a million by 2002 to become the company's second best selling brand, currently selling around 3.8 million cases per annum. *Blender's Pride* – has experienced a 30% rise in volume sales under Pernod Ricard, and is now neck and neck with Royal Challenge as the best seller in its sector, at around 1.10 million cases per annum.

In parallel with the company's local spirit production, Pernod Ricard India has been vigorous in promoting its leading Scotch brands on the sub-continent: *Chivas Regal* and *Royal Salute* in the premium and de luxe categories; *100 Pipers* and *Ballantines* as standard blends.
  "With Pernod Ricard's take-over of Seagrams and Allied, the business inherited a strong portfolio of local spirits, which is a big advantage for Chivas Brothers as a Scotch whisky

producer and also provides an excellent distribution network for our imported whiskies" a spokesman for the company told me.
  "Over the past couple of years, Chivas Regal has increased its share of the super premium sector significantly – it has long been a famous brand but recent investment in marketing has accelerated growth. India has the kind of growth among middle- and upper-class consumers which saw China become the biggest export market for Chivas. There is no doubt that image-led brands such as Chivas Regal are destined to do well if tax barriers are removed. Even the prestige sector is preparing for this and Chivas Brothers has begun promoting Royal Salute brand in India".

Royal Stag
- Pernod Ricard India's leading brand

Pernod Ricard's mighty competitor, **Diageo**, has until recently concentrated on selling Scotch (particularly Johnnie Walker, which is the most popular brand in India), but since 2007 has been engaged in a joint venture with Radico Khaitan (see above). The first fruit of the joint venture was *Masterstroke*, a de luxe whisky launched in February 2007. By May that year the brand was being endorsed by Bollywood super-star Shah Rukh Khan. The blend apparently uses a liberal amount of Blair Athol single malt, and the company's hope is that consumers will trade up to its international brands as well, as *Johnnie Walker Red* and *Black Label, VAT 69* and *Black & White* are all popular in India, and malts are establishing a high reputation, especially *The Singleton of Glen Ord*.

As I write this, (July 2010), the Indian press is reporting that Diageo is also considering launching its own IMFL brands, and/or buying existing Indian brands.

Like Pernod Ricard, **Bacardi** has a joint venture with a smaller company, Gemini Distilleries, in which it owns a 74% stake. Until 2004 Bacardi owned the popular *Whytehall* IMFL brand), but now seems to be focussing on selling its international brands in India, particularly the *Dewar's* brands. I caught Stephen Marshall, Dewar's Global Brand Ambassador, on his way from Moscow to Bombay. He said:

"We're working in India with new-found vigour now, and we're making decent progress. The honeyed character of Dewar's is ideally suited to the Indian palate and the feedback is enthusiastic. The new packaging will give us better presence, and Dewar's Discovery programme launches this month [September 2010]

Dewar's in new guise

and will be rolled out across the major India cities next year. India loves Scotch, and we love India; the people are delightful, and increasingly knowledgeable and discerning in regard to Scotch whisky".

Of the other international companies, only Fortune Brands has a production facility in India, following its acquisition of Allied Domecq's bottling operations in Rajasthan, but like Bacardi its presence is relatively weak. Other international spirits companies have a purely import operation in India and rely on third party distributors. These companies include Brown-Forman, William Grant & Sons and Edrington,

The latter has been concentrating on its leading single malts, The Macallan and Highland Park over the past three years. Ken Grier, Edrington's Marketing Director, is delighted by their reception.

" We are tremendously excited by the future opportunity for single malt whisky in India. We see a groundswell building among Indian connoisseurs to trade up and have already seen a tripling in demand for single malt in three years to just under the 100,000 cases. Consumers hone their knowledge through exposure to our products overseas, as well as through dining and enjoying with friends, and we are really benefiting from this with The Macallan alone showing growth rates of over 250% in the last year".

Fascinating, perplexing, frustrating, but totally committed to whisky, India is, as my friend at Chivas Brothers put it, "potentially the most dynamic whisky market in the world".

Charles MacLean has spent the past twenty-five years researching and writing about Scotch whisky and is one of the leading authorities. He spends his time sharing his knowledge around the world, in articles and publications, lectures and tastings, and on TV and radio. His first book (Scotch Whisky) was published in 1993 and since then he has published nine books on the subject, his most recent being Charles MacLean's Whiskypedia, published in 2009. He was elected a Keeper of the Quaich in 1992 and granted the rare honour of being elected Master of the Quaich, the industry's highest accolade, in October 2009. In 1997 Malt Whisky won the Glenfiddich Award and in 2003 A Liquid History won 'Best Drinks Book' in the James Beard Awards.

The Task of the Cask

*The importance of the casks
for defining the final flavour of the whisky
cannot be over-emphasised. But what makes the difference
between a good cask and a bad cask, and what influences
are there from the different types of oak?
Gavin D Smith helps us clear the matter.*

There is an old saying in the Scotch whisky industry that 'The cask is king.' It is generally accepted that between 60% and 80% of the character of whisky develops during maturation, so it follows that the casks in which spirit is matured are of paramount importance.

Nonetheless, although it has been known for several centuries that spirits improved while stored in wooden casks, most of the Scotch whisky industry has really only taken the business of 'wood management' seriously during the last three decades. Before that, the philosophy of 'If it doesn't leak, fill it,' all too often prevailed, with spirit sometimes being filled into exhausted, relatively inactive casks which served as little more than storage vessels. The regulations that legally define 'Scotch whisky' insist on a minimum maturation period of three years, and further specify that only oak casks may be used, and that these must not be of more than 700 litres in capacity. The stipulation about size is significant, since it highlights the importance of optimum contact between oak and spirit during the maturation process.

In general, the smaller the cask, the faster maturation occurs, as in a small cask there is greater liquid contact, and therefore inter-action, with the surface of the wood than there is in a larger cask. And 'interaction' is at the heart of maturation. Oak is specified as it is a hard wood with the porous quality necessary to allow the spirit to 'breathe,' and in the prevailing Scottish climate a reduction in both strength and volume occurs as time passes, with an average evaporation loss of around two per cent per annum. This is commonly referred to as the 'angels' share.'

Reactions occur during maturation between spirit, wood and external atmosphere, lending colour to the clear 'new-make' and helping to create a more rounded and less 'fierce' spirit. The ultimate colour of the whisky when bottled will depend on several factors, including the number of times the cask has been filled in the past, the length of time the spirit spends in it, and what the cask has been filled with prior to its adoption for Scotch whisky.

Analysts often refer to 'additive,' substitutive' and 'evaporative' elements in the complex chain of chemical activity taking place. Brian Kinsman, Glen Grant's Master Blender, defines 'additive' as "What the cask adds to the spirit as it matures. This has more to do with the variety of oak rather than the previous contents." Kinsman says of the 'substitutive' element

Charring of casks

that "With ex-Bourbon casks, for example, the active char layer will remove sulphur and some cereal notes," and referring to the 'evaporative' aspect, he confirms that "We lose around two per cent per year, and that is not wholly bad, as some volatile compounds get lost that way."

Two dominating types of oak

Quercus alba (American oak) and *Quercus robur* (European oak) are the two species of oak most commonly found in Scotch whisky warehouses, and American oak casks will usually have contained Bourbon prior to their acquisition by the Scotch whisky industry. By contrast, European oak casks, have generally been filled with sherry in a previous existence.

Britain was a major importer of Spanish sherry during the 19th century, and as that sherry was shipped into the country in casks, the Scotch whisky industry had a ready supply of relatively inexpensive containers available for maturation.

Ex-Bourbon barrels were first used for Scotch whisky maturation during the Spanish Civil War of 1936-39, but their widespread adoption came about from the 1950s onwards, as the Scotch whisky industry rapidly expanded and sherry casks became progressively scarcer. Scarcity inevitably equals expense, so it is not surprising that more and more distillers embraced Bourbon barrels rather than sherry butts, as ex-Bourbon wood was comparatively cheap and plentiful, due to the law which states that Bourbon must always be matured in new, charred oak barrels.

Casks which previously held Bourbon will have been 'charred' or fired internally for anything from 30 seconds to four minutes prior to being filled with Bourbon. This process creates a layer of carbon which aids the removal of undesirable sulphur compounds from the spirit and breaks up the surface of the oak, giving access to the 'toasted' layer which lies beneath the char. This toasted layer instigates various complex chemical reactions, including the creation of vanillin, which gives the maturing spirit its characteristic vanilla notes.

Former sherry casks undergo a similar firing process, known as 'toasting,' stimulating the

Sherry Bodega in Jerez

same sort of chemical reactions as in American oak, though toasting does not open up the surface of the oak to the same extent as charring. An ex-Bourbon barrel currently costs in the region of £50, while a sherry butt will sell for ten or twelve times that sum. Not surprisingly, some 90 per cent of all casks now used by the Scotch whisky industry formerly contained Bourbon! As a result, there has been a profound, yet rarely commented upon, character shift in many single malts.

The Macallan was one of the relatively few brands to persevere with the use of ex-sherry casks on a large scale, and Ken Grier, Malts Director for The Edrington Group, whose flagship is The Macallan, considers that "Many manufacturers made the conscious decision to use ex-Bourbon casks for maturation, purely due to lower costs and their availability. Also, as blended whiskies grew in importance in newer, emerging markets, there was a demand for lighter styles, and that demand made distillers want to fill their single malts into ex-Bourbon casks anyway. When single malts really began to sell in their own right that was the stock they had."

Along with The Macallan, Edrington's Orcadian 'stable mate' Highland Park continues to use ex-sherry casks for maturation, and Head of Brand Education Gerry Tosh explains some of the differences between European oak and American oak from a practical viewpoint.

"A Spanish oak tree is not poker straight, due to the climate," he explains, "and Scottish oak is an extreme example of the same effect. You certainly can't make big casks from it, because you can't get the straight lengths of wood you need. The grain of European oak is wider than that of American oak due to the way it grows, so as the spirit interacts with wood it can pull more colour and sweetness through, giving dark fruits, toffee, and chocolate notes to the spirit."

"American oak is almost exactly the opposite – it grows like a pencil! The grain is very tight. The spirit can't interact with the grain so much, so you don't get a lot of colour. But you do get citrus and coconut flavours."

A sherry cask is not about the sherry but about the wood

Gerry Tosh also contends that it is the type of oak which is truly influential in maturation rather than the casks' previous contents. "If you leave spirit in an-ex sherry cask for six

Gerry Tosh, Global Brand Manager for Highland Park

Photo: © Edrington

weeks you will get obvious sherry flavours," he says. "But if you leave it for 12 years you will go way past the sherry layer (4 - 5mm at maximum) in the wood. An ex-sherry cask is not about the sherry, it's about the wood. What brand of Oloroso sherry do you use, how does that flavour it? It doesn't. The sherry is a nuance, not the most profound influence in the whisky."

"Bourbon has been in wood for several years, so why does nobody talk about the Bourbon flavour? Nobody asks if it's a Jim Beam or a Heaven Hill flavour coming though. And it's not. It's from the type of wood. The tree is the most important thing, not the cask!"

Although most sherry casks are made of European oak, some are constructed from American oak, and Gerry Tosh says that "Highland Park 15 and 21-year-old expressions are matured in predominantly American oak sherry casks. These give very different flavours to European oak casks– more citrus, lemon and lime and coconut - yet they still contained sherry!

Diageo Malt Whisky Specialist Craig Wallace echoes Tosh's point about prior fillings, noting that "European oak is more porous than American oak – you get more of what we term

Craig Wallace, Diageo Malt Whisky Specialist

Japan's largest distiller, Suntory, uses some Japanese oak in its maturation 'mix' while the UK-based Number one Drinks Company has presented consumers with a number of whiskies from the Hanyu distillery, part-matured in Japanese oak.

Marcin Miller of the Number One Drinks Company says that "American oak grows quick and straight and is ready to fell for casks after 70 to 80 years, while European oak is less straight and takes probably more than 100 years to be ready to fell. Japanese oak is like Spanish oak only more so! It doesn't grow straight and is more prone to be difficult to work with, as it is hard due to the comparatively cold climate. There is also a tendency for leakage because of the coarseness of the grain, and it is difficult to cut and shape."

"It was in widespread use after the Second World War when, for political reasons, the Japanese couldn't source American or European oak. A new Japanese oak cask costs significantly more than a European oak cask: probably as much as £750, but when you fill whisky into Japanese oak for a final period of maturation, the underlying elegance of the spirit is overlaid with the benefits of Japanese oak. It's like the smell of the inside of a temple – incense, sandalwood and oriental spices."

an 'in-drink' from it. If you use a European oak cask, the sherry conditions the wood. The effects of the actual wood far outweigh any effect that you may pick up from the in-drink of previous contents. European oak will give rich fruits, intense notes, tannins and lots of mouth-feel."

"In American oak you get vanillin and lactose in greater concentration than in European oak, and consequently you get vanilla and coconut notes from the wood. Again, it's the actual wood rather than the previous fill that's really influential. How the wood-derived compounds then react with distillery character of the spirit, only time will tell."

Although American oak and European oak are the principal types used in Scotch whisky maturation, some distillers have experimented with Scottish oak, most notably Glengoyne, with its 15-year-old Scottish Oak Wood Finish and The Famous Grouse blend with its Scottish Oak Finish.

Japanese oak – *Quercus mongolica* - is also gaining wider currency as the Japanese whisky industry continues to grow and export its brands into a greater number of international markets.

Marcin Miller, owner of The Number One Drinks Company

Although conventional wisdom suggests that a previous filling of Bourbon or sherry aids maturation of whisky significantly, Benromach Organic employs virgin American oak casks in order to ensure its 'organic status.' According to Ewen Macintosh, Whisky Supply Manager for Benromach distillery owner Gordon & Macphail, "Obviously you get a lot more wood influence than if you used ex-Bourbon casks, because there hasn't been any Bourbon to soften off the oak. You still get sweetness, but not as much as with an ex-Bourbon cask, and a Bourbon barrel will give you fewer cedar-type aromas and flavours that you get from virgin American oak."

While Glenmorangie and Benromach have employed virgin American oak casks, William Grant & Sons has recently pioneered the use of new European oak casks for its Glenfiddich 14 year old Rich Oak expression.

"We were the first distillers to use virgin Spanish oak, as opposed to virgin American oak," says Grant's Master Blender Brian Kinsman. "It was a breakthrough flavour-wise. Essentially it was a case of what would happen if we just put whisky straight into a new Spanish oak cask, cutting out the sherry effect?"

"You're putting in whisky that's essentially good enough to bottle as it is, so you have to be careful not to overdo it, as it can easily become too woody. You don't need an active char layer, as you have in a former Bourbon cask, because you're not trying to mature whisky, not trying to get rid of immature notes. The tannins give the palate real texture; it is oaky and mouth-coating. In Rich Oak we use lots of American oak for sweetness and a percentage of virgin Spanish oak for mouth-feel and depth."

Size matters

It has already been noted that the size of the cask affects maturation, with Bourbon barrels, containing approximately 200 litres of liquid, being the smallest casks regularly employed by the Scotch whisky industry. A hogshead holds some 250 litres of spirit, and is constructed by adding extra staves to a barrel, with the barrel often being dismantled into 'shooks' for transportation from the USA to the UK and then rebuilt and expanded. The largest cask in regular use for Scotch whisky is the butt, which holds around 500 litres and is usually made of European oak.

"We still import shooks from the USA and build them into hogshead, says Willie Taylor of the Broxburn Cooperage Ltd, "but it would be fair to say that this type of business is now only a fraction of what it used to be. My understanding is that for most distillers this is due mainly to cost, as it is expensive to fit two new heads and six new hoops only to gain 60 extra litres' capacity! Mixed opinion prevails as to which cask size gives the best flavours and maturation."

"Butts are slowly disappearing, and their decline is partly due to price and quality, and I believe some of the older butts are also being culled, due to lack of warehouse space and the 'Health & Safety' legislation regarding manual handling of them."

If wood type, previous contents and size all matter in terms of how casks influence maturation, then so does the number of times the casks has previously been used. When a cask has held Bourbon or sherry prior to its acquisition by Scotch whisky distillers, it is referred to as a 'first-fill' cask. A 'second-fill' cask has been used once to mature Scotch whisky, while a 'refill' cask has had a minimum of two previous whisky fillings.

Not surprisingly, a first-fill cask has the most overt influence on the spirit within, and a cask may have a lifespan of half a century, depending on how many times it is filled and for how long the spirit remains in it on each occasion. In order to understand how distillers use a variety of cask permutations, Diageo's Craig Wallace outlines aspects of the company's 'wood policy.'

"We have 28 malt distilleries, so lots of unique flavours," he notes. "For us, it's not just about using first-fill American and European oak casks. Refill casks are very valuable to us as they allow the unique flavours of all our malts to shine through, both in single malt bottlings and in our range of blends. They take out immaturity but keep the flavours of the spirit intact. We also use rejuvenated – re-charred – casks, which tend to give spicy notes. They offer us another option, another permutation for our blends."

'Rejuvenated' casks 'will have been filled several times, to the point where they are not having sufficient effect on the maturing spirit to be viable. They are given a new lease of life by being reamed out and re-burnt in a process known as 'de-char/re-char.' In similar fashion, former sherry casks may be reamed and re-toasted.

Brian Kinsman, Master Blender for Grant's Blended Scotch Whisky

Good wood policy demands long-term planning... and money

Guaranteeing a supply of high-quality casks may mean going to the effort of sourcing the timber itself. "We don't buy anything at auction," says The Edrington Group's Gerry Tosh. "We have 10-year agreements with Spanish sawmills and cooperages. It's a very structured programme. The timber that we source in Spain is air-dried for four years, rather than kiln-dried, which cuts down on splits and breaks. Once the wood has been coopered into casks, they are handed over to sherry producers, who fill them with Oloroso sherry for about two years; then they empty them and ship them back whole."

If The Edrington Group takes its European oak seriously, then competitor Glenmorangie Company Ltd is equally fastidious about its American oak. Under the direction of Head of Distilling and Whisky Creation Dr Bill Lumsden, the company bought a tract of woodland in Missouri's Ozark mountain region, where slow-growing timber is carefully selected for future cask construction.

"It's very mature wood and breaks down the components that give bitterness and astringency," explains Lumsden.

Many consumers assume that once filled into a cask, most spirit destined for single malt bottling remains in that cask for its entire period of maturation, unless it is to undergo a period of 'finishing' in a secondary cask, which will give the whisky additional aroma and flavour facets.

However, it is not uncommon for distillers to re-cask spirit during maturation simply because the casks into which it has initially been filled are not doing their job effectively. This is sometimes because the casks in question are rather tired refills, though in other instances it is in order to alter the profile of the final product.

As Des McCagherty of Edradour distillery in Perthshire notes, "Edradour was traditionally presented as a single malt with a sherry wood profile, but lots of the stock we acquired from Campbell Distilleries when we bought the distillery in 2002 was in ex-Bourbon casks. This was because it had been destined for blending, so we have re-casked much of it into sherry casks so that we can offer the sherried style of Edradour we want to the public."

Edradour's parent company is the independent bottler Signatory Vintage Scotch Whisky Co Ltd, and McCagherty says that "In our ex-

perience there are no whiskies that don't work well with ex-sherry wood, if the sherry cask is a decent one. We've done sherried bottlings from distilleries like Rosebank, Cardhu, Tamdhu and Miltonduff, and they've all been excellent."

However, in many cases there is a clear correlation between new make spirit style and the type of casks into which it is filled, as Gerry Tosh explains.

"The flavour we get out of sherry butts is perfect both for The Macallan and Highland Park," he says. "The oily new-make of The Macallan can fight the Spanish oak and survive for 20 to 25 years and more. You can certainly put light spirit into a sherry cask, but if you do it for a length of time it usually overwhelms the distillery character."

Although certain malts are associated with specific wood styles, Craig Wallace of Diageo makes the point that "In terms of cask types, it's important to have a real range in the inventory, so we fill heavier new-make like Dailuaine and Mortlach into ex-sherry casks as a matter of course, but we also fill lighter spirit from other distilleries into ex-sherry wood to give us the diversity of components we require for the various permutation that go together to make up blends."

Some whiskies take longer time to mature than others

Each single malt differs in the optimum time it takes to reach its peak, with lighter-bodied whiskies generally maturing earlier than full-bodied ones, and The Macallan and Highland Park are good examples of whiskies that are generally able to withstand extended ageing.

Gerry Tosh notes that "With very old whiskies you have to have good new-make, good casks and the right warehouse location. As casks get older and there has been evaporation over the years there is more air and less liquid, and consequently more opportunities for the air to adversely affect the spirit. You can get mossy, musty flavours, which aren't desirable."

Brian Kinsman of William Grant & Sons declares that "To get a really good old whisky you need lots of luck! The maturation process slows as the spirit gets older and its strength drops. In every individual case there is a 'tipping point,' beyond which there is deterioration. It can't always be predicted, and it will even vary within a 'parcel' of whisky filled into the same type of casks at the same time."

When it comes to really old whiskies, Elgin-based distillers and bottlers Gordon & Mac-Phail are in a league of their own, offering 'the oldest whisky in the world', a 70-year-old Mortlach - in the spring of 2010. The firm's Ewen Mackintosh says that "One of the reason we are able to bottle some very old whiskies is that over the years Gordon & MacPhail has really understood the relationship between the style of whisky and the cask. It's been about choosing the optimum type of cask and size. A butt gives slow maturation due to the high surface to volume ratio, while you might use a second-fill cask for a lighter style of whisky, or one you want to keep for a long time, because you have already lost a lot of the heavy wood elements."

"Our warehouse in Elgin has quite a dry atmosphere, which means that strength and volume are retained. We are keeping surface to volume ratios quite high. If you have a small amount of whisky splashing around in the bottom of a cask it is likely to be very woody. It will oxidise, making the wood influence very noticeable."

Mackintosh's observation makes it clear that maturation variables do not begin and end in the cask, with climate, warehouse design and location, and even the location of individual casks within the warehouse, all being significant factors in the process.

While science has answered many of the outstanding questions about just what happens during maturation in the past couple of decades, there is still a pleasing element that remains stubbornly resistant to analysis. Ewen Mackintosh declares that "Maturation is a technically complex set of reactions.

Photo: © Gordon & MacPhail

Ewen Mackintosh, Whisky Supply Manager at Gordon & MacPhail

Getting it right is principally about experience, and there's no equation you can apply and say 'this is what we will get.'"

With that in mind it seems apposite to conclude with an observation by whisky consultant Dr Jim Swan, who likens maturation to the development of a butterfly.
A caterpillar (the new make spirit) enters a chrysalis (the cask), and ultimately what emerges is a beautiful butterfly!

Gavin D Smith is one of Scotland's leading whisky writers and Contributing Editor to www.whisky-pages.com He hosts whisky presentations and tastings and produces feature material for a wide range of publications, including Whisky Magazine, The Malt Advocate *and* Whisky Etc. *He is the author of more than 20 books, including* Whisky, Wit & Wisdom, The A-Z of Whisky, Worts, Worms & Washbacks, The Secret Still, The Whisky Men, Ardbeg: A Peaty Provenance *and* Goodness Nose *(with Richard Paterson). Most recently he has collaborated with Dominic Roscrow to produce a new edition of the iconic title* Michael Jackson's Malt Whisky Companion. *He is a Keeper of the Quaich and lives on the Fife coast in Scotland.*

Mortlach
70 year old from
Gordon & MacPhail

The Scotch Whisky Label

from simple decoration to true passport

The whisky label started as mere decoration and culminated in the ultimate passport of the drink. Hans Offringa travels through time, describing the development of the label and explaining the complicated rules and regulations on labelling today.

In the old days, some two centuries ago and longer, when distilling in Scotland was still an artisan craft, legal or illegal, the prospective buyer had to bring his own container to either tap the liquid straight from the still or the cask. Glassware, being rather expensive at the time, would have been rare. More likely earthenware jugs were used, similar to the ones sold today as a mere reminder of days gone by. Fortunate whisky drinkers could afford to buy whole casks and have those delivered to their cellars at home. The whisky inside would then be poured at measures in crystal decanters by a servant, taken upstairs to the library and poured into glasses for the distinguished guests. Not much attention was paid to specific brands or identifiers where the whisky came from, more to the whisky broker the cask was purchased from or the distillery where it was made.

Only when glass bottles became more affordable, around the 1850s, the need to distinguish one bottle from the other became more apparent. One of the first, if not the first to present his name on the bottle as a brand, was John Dewar, somewhere in the 1870s. He did not do this by pasting a label on the front, but by having his signature blown into the glass. He switched to paper a mere 15 years later - the oldest surviving bottle that carries his name on a paper label is from 1885.

Maybe it was another famous blended whisky that was the first to use labels. William Teacher and Sons owns two bottles with fragments of what might have been the first label ever. The remains cannot be accurately dated but the bottles on which they are glued were identified as the type used in the 1860s.

The first labels to appear on bottles were mostly printed in black on a white background. Sometimes with one or two colours, on a paper already coloured to add another tint. The back side of the label was covered with a type of glue which, when moistened, turned sticky and could then manually be applied to the bottle. Thanks to Alfred Barnard, who illustrated his tome *The Whisky Distilleries of the United Kingdom* with some examples of these labels, we know what they looked like in 1887, when the book was published.

At first the label was merely used as part of the packaging design and to create brand awareness. The majority didn't show any information regarding the alcoholic content or even the amount of whisky in the bottle. Designs were often taken from historical scenes or figures – Celebrated Mountain Dew showed two Highlanders enjoying a wee dram on the hillside and Roderick Dhu Old Highland Whisky portrayed the famous hero of the Scottish people in full regalia.

Teacher's were probably the first in
the industry to use labels

The first regulations came in 1905

As with all innovations there were no sound regulations for what should be mentioned on the label. The "What is Whisky" question started after a 1905 court case in Islington, London over blended whisky and led to a Royal Commission in 1909 clearly specifying which drink could be called whisky and which one not. As a logical consequence the brand owners would focus on giving more information on the label, like the number of years the whisky had matured and a statement about the percentage of alcohol by volume (ABV).

Blended whisky outnumbered single malt whisky by multitudes. The latter simply used its distillery name to distinguish itself from the next one, but the blenders had to fiercely compete for a place on the shelves and on the cornea of the prospective customer. The trusted old names like Teachers, Dewar's, Ballantines, Johnnie Walker, Bell's, Black & White and the like, were joined by fancy names - of which some would stay and others would utterly fail, regardless of the quality of the whisky in the bottle.

Once a brand was successfully launched onto the market, the brand owner protected the image and only slowly made small changes if needed. For instance the brand 100 Pipers did fairly well, but due to the dark design, it failed to be noticed in the dimly lit bars around the world. A decision was made to spice up the label, make it glossier. This was done in careful steps to avoid alienating the customer base. Certain changes not only applied to the label,

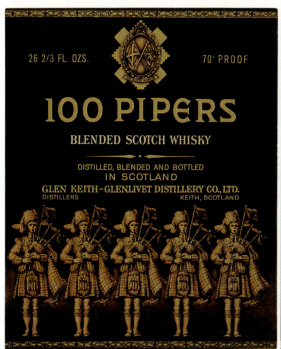

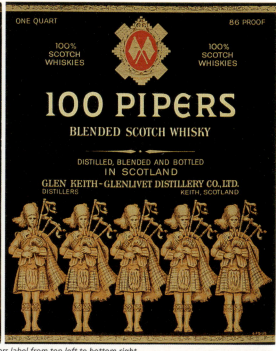

The gradual changes of the 100 Pipers label from top left to bottom right

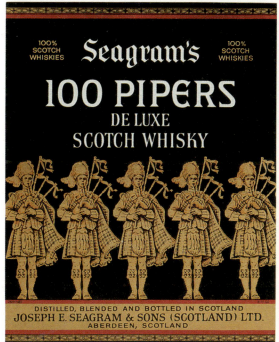

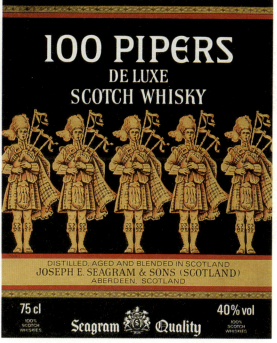

but stretched as far as replacing a metal screw cap for a plastic one or altering the shape of the bottle.

Changing the packaging and designing an new label means a lot of steps. It also means a great deal of money - another reason why owners are careful with changes.

Apart from that, each country to where the

brand is exported has its own set of rules and regulations. What can be done in one country is not allowed in another. In the USA for instance, after Repeal, all states drew up new laws regarding manufacture, sales and distribution. In one state the use of animals on a label was not allowed, in another state it was restricted to horses only. At the time it would

THE GLENFARCLAS "Scottish Classic"
Capturing the unique flavour of Scotland's rich, romantic past.
Sir Walter Scott -"Ivanhoe"

THE GLENFARCLAS "Scottish Classic"
Capturing the unique flavour of Scotland's rich, romantic past.
Robert Louis Stevenson -"Treasure Island"

The above label is available on the following Bottle Numbers:
9·39·69·99·129·159·189·219·249·279
309·339·369·399·429·459·489·519·549·579

The above label is available on the following Bottle Numbers:
15·45·75·105·135·165·195·225·255·285
315·345·375·405·435·465·495·525·555·585

Scottish Classics from Glenfarclas honouring Scottish literature and Diageo's Flora & Fauna labels

HIGHLAND
SINGLE MALT
SCOTCH WHISKY

BLAIR ATHOL

distillery, established in 1798, stands
on *peaty moorland* in the *foothills* of the
GRAMPIAN MOUNTAINS. An ancient
source of *water* for the *distillery*, ALLT
DOUR BURN ~'The Burn of the Otter',
flows close by. This *single MALT
SCOTCH WHISKY* has a *mellow deep
toned* aroma, a *strong fruity*
flavour and a *smooth* finish.

AGED **12** YEARS

43% vol   70cl
Distilled & Bottled in SCOTLAND.
BLAIR ATHOL DISTILLERY, Pitlochry, Perthshire, Scotland.

SPEYSIDE
SINGLE MALT
SCOTCH WHISKY

The Scots Pines beside *the ruins of*
ROTHES CASTLE, provide *an ideal habitat*
for the *GOLDCREST, Britain's smallest bird,*
and overlook the

GLEN SPEY

distillery. Founded in 1885, the distillery was
originally part of the *Mills of Rothes.* Water
from the DOONIE BURN is used to produce
this *smooth, warming single MALT SCOTCH
WHISKY.* A slight sense of *wood smoke* on
the nose is rewarded with a *spicy, dry* finish.

AGED **12** YEARS

43% vol   GLEN SPEY DISTILLERY Rothes Aberlour Banffshire, Scotland.   70cl

not have been possible to distribute Black &
White whisky USA-wide, although this brand
originally didn't carry the two little dogs on
the label. It was a nickname customers gave to
Buchanan's Blended Whisky, referring to the
simple design: black letters printed on a white
background. Sometimes a name would work
well in one country and be totally unaccepta-
ble in another. For instance the Japanese Black

Nikka Whisky is, phonetically speaking, a brand
name that will not go down well with a large
part of the American population.

Throughout the 20th century almost every
Scottish brand that managed to survive regularly changed the packaging design and with
it the label. At first many focused on the rich
traditions of Scotland, portraying on the label
things typically Scottish such as the ubiquitous

bagpipe and Highland dress, or wildlife in the form of salmons leaping over a river, stags roaming the hillsides, or Celtic designs. The series of beautiful labels dubbed Flora and Fauna by the late and great Michael Jackson show wildlife and describe various critters and flowers that can be encountered in the Scottish hills, rivers, lochs and mountains.

Others chose a purely graphical approach, like Laphroaig, Balvenie and Glenfarclas. The former two continue this tradition, while the latter made one exception for its millennium series Scottish Classics at the turn of the 20th century. Owner and Managing Director John Grant issued an assignment to a small group of Scottish designers to come up with a blend of Scottish literature and contemporary Scottish art. It became a highly sought after series of collectibles, with only 600 bottles featuring the artwork. Great stories, such as Ivanhoe (Sir Walter Scott), Treasure Island (Robert Louis Stevenson) and Tam O'Shanter (Robert Burns) inspired the artists.

The move from tweed to jeans

With Scotch whisky, blended as well as single malt, becoming increasingly popular outside the archetypical subculture (of gentlemen clad in tweed, relaxing in Chesterfields, smoking a cigar, whilst savouring their dram) the marketers realised they had to give their packaging a facelift to appeal to a newer, younger crowd.

Glenfiddich chose a careful path and stylised its famous stag, thus looking more modern. Others like Glenmorangie and Balblair were more daring and did extreme makeovers. The former went from a traditional whisky bottle with likewise label to a bottle resembling a luxury wine or cognac, undoubtedly influenced by French owner LVMH. The latter recreated the image of this lesser known, but very old distillery – it was founded in the 18th century – by reaching back in time to use a 4,000-year-old standing stone in a nearby field as the core image on the label and blowing an intricate Celtic design into the glass.

Johnnie Walker has been silently making small changes to its famous striding man and one who observes the bottles of this brand carefully might have noticed the character sometimes walks from left to right, then from right to left.

These were all changes in design, but with this came changes in the information to be conveyed on the label, which in some cases was now accompanied by a little booklet tied around the neck of the bottle. The booklet might contain a history-in-a-nutshell, tasting notes or praises from renowned whisky writers. Back labels would tell even more, and the packaging, tube or carton box became a large extension of the label.

Premium blends like The Century Malt, manufactured by Chivas Brothers, came with a small book, describing all 100 single malts that had gone into this rare and limited edition.

The Macallan did away with the oldfashioned embossed lettering, modernizing the type font, but kept Easter Elchies House as a clear symbol and statement of quality. The bottle was replaced by a more slender, somewhat longer and tapered one, now standing taller than its companions on bar shelving and thus immediately recognizable. But, the Rolls Royce among single malts went even further in the 21st century and took design to the extreme by cooperating with Lalique. The two companies so far have launched three very limited intricate crystal decanters, symbolising three of the six pillars The Macallan is built on, and containing very old versions of this single malt. The decanters come with a beautifully designed hard cover book with silver embossing, describing the philosophy behind the making and with elaborate tasting notes too. In years to come three more decanters will be launched.

This development was partly fuelled by marketers who now focus on heritage and want to convince consumers that pedigree is quality, partly fuelled by the increasing hunger for facts of that same crowd, which became more and more knowledgeable about whisky. At first this knowledge was acquired by visiting distilleries, where the manufacturers were willing to share what they knew, to be followed by brand ambassadors who travel the world and give tutored nosing and tastings to ever growing groups of whisky enthusiasts. And nowadays the many brand websites disperse a plethora of information about their product, their heritage and their idiosyncrasies. E-mail newsletters inform the whisky lover about new expressions and contain elaborate tasting notes and descriptions that previously went with the packaging. Social media and whisky blogs do the rest.

For history's sake it is important to manage archives, to keep the designs that were and the ones that are. In the digital age it is even easier to keep the images and descriptions from latter days. This has a downside too. It is relatively easy to make counterfeit labels, which unfortunately happens in certain countries.

The revered Malt Maniac and publisher of *whiskyfun.com* Serge Valentin was so annoyed

with this dubious practise that he started a War on Fakes on the Internet some time ago. However, one must bear in mind that fakes are of all times. A former employee of Laphroaig supposedly stole a stack of 30-year-old labels and glued them on 15-year-old bottles. He then sold them on an internet auction website, without the wooden box and with the wrong tag on the neck !

Passport to the whisky

But, there is something else at stake regarding the label. Where digital information can be modified, where tasting notes of dubious content might be taken for granted – everyone can present him or herself as a whisky expert on the web – the label is and will probably continue to be the only strictly legal document – the true passport to the whisky. Why?

With the coming and growing of stricter EU regulations describing what contents are in consumer goods, specifications on the bottle and packaging have to tell the "scientific truth" meaning what exactly is in the bottle, apart from a couple hundreds of years distilling history. Not every country displays the same information. For example whisky bottles in Germany have to be labelled mentioning if colour caramel is used - *Farbstoff* (the famous E-150a), whereas in The Netherlands such an obligation does not exist (yet). The size of the lettering differs from country to country as do the bottle sizes. All in all this means if a new or a restyled brand is launched, a whole new series of labels and packaging material has to be produced. This is one of the reasons why The Black Grouse is not available widely in the

USA. To distribute nationwide, an astonishing 27 different labels are needed to cover all wet states – skip that dry one Utah!

The US distillers suffer the same. Four Roses has one staff member who is employed full-time only to deal with regulations regarding the labelling of this iconic bourbon. The Department of the Treasury Alcohol and Tobacco Tax and Trade Bureau deals with bottle label approval and uses a complicated form for this, consisting of 23 different entries and a whole section where the actual label has to be attached, front side, back side, neck label and so forth. When the distiller changes so much as the alcohol percentage, which is common with the single barrel and small batch expressions, the procedure needs to be followed again in its entirety. The form is called a COLA – an acronym for Certificate of Label Approval. This application must be made for every brand of every distillery prior to production and shipment to the American distributor for sales to retailers, on premises accounts and the like. Once a brand is in a new market, some states may require semi-annual or annual renewals of registration. If a distillery wants to increase prices some states require a new registration, and some states require that price changes only occur at the time of registration renewal.

This can be a complete nightmare. The law also applies to imported whisky or whiskey. Whereas the 0.7 litre bottle is more or less standard in Europe, the Americans require 0.75 litre instead. Add to that the other sizes, from 5 cl miniatures up to 1.75 litre bottles and it becomes understandable that a full-time employee is needed to deal with all this red tape.

CATEGORIES OF SCOTCH WHISKY

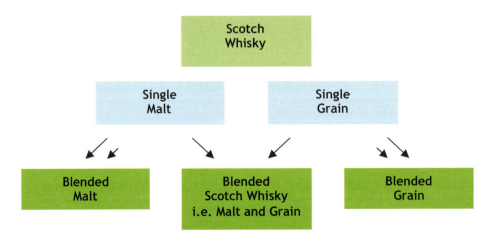

58

The do´s and dont´s of labelling

In Scotland the Scotch Whisky Association (SWA) has a 78-page guideline for producers and bottlers. Incorporated in that document is a section of an Official Journal of the European Union, entitled

REGULATION (EC) No 110/2008 OF THE EUROPEAN PARLIAMENT AND OF THE COUNCIL of 15 January 2008
on the definition, description, presentation, labelling and the protection of geographical indications of spirit drinks and repealing Council Regulation (EEC) No 1576/89

The SWA document ends with a four page basic checklist of do's and don'ts, for instance on Age Statement. One can assume it is common knowledge that the age of the youngest whisky is mentioned on the label, but it is much more complicated than that:

For instance, if an age statement is mentioned on the label it should only be referring to the youngest whisky.

Examples of acceptable age statements are:
"Aged 10 Years"
"12 Years Old"
"Over 10 Years Old"

Examples of statements that are prohibited are:
"aged five to ten years"
"minimum age 5 years: maximum age 10 years"
"The average age of the whiskies in the blend is ten years"
"Contains whiskies up to 60 years old"
"80% 10 year old; 20% 25 year old Scotch Whisky"

Also, the age should only consist of one number and be expressed in years.

Examples of statements that are prohibited are:
"Aged 36 months"
"Aged 3 Years – 36 Months"
"Aged for 12 maturation cycles"

If the distillation year is mentioned on the label, it should be referring to a single calender year.

Examples of statements which are prohibited are:
"This 21 year old whisky contains whiskies distilled in 1960 and 1970"
"Distilled 1991 or earlier"
"Contains whiskies dating back to the 1950s"

Source: SWA, The Scotch Whisky Regulations 2009 – Guidance for Producers and Bottlers.)

And this is only about something seemingly as simple as the age statement. Defining the category on the label shouldn't be that difficult, according to the drawing (shown on the opposite page) in the SWA document.

However, older bottlings still show "pure malt" or "vatted malt" on the label. Both terms are now prohibited by the SWA, a regulation that fuelled many debates in the past years.

Neither John Dewar nor William Teacher could foresee, back in the mid to late 19th century, what complicated matters their innovative approach would cause over time. Luckily the stuff in the bottle still tastes good. Let's hope the EU doesn't make it obligatory to specify which single malts and grain whiskies go into which blends, in what proportions. It would take the myth out of the craft and turn a centuries old art into a scientific exercise.

And … it would take up too much space on the label!

* Due to space restrictions Mr. Offringa focused on Scotch Whisky, but emphasises that similar stories apply to whiskies and whiskeys from other countries, as the paragraph on Four Roses Bourbon illustrates.

The label images in this article come from Hans Offringa's 1998 publication *The Craigellachie Collection of Scotch Whisky Labels*, now a well-sought after collector's item.

Hans Offringa is an internationally published author, media expert and whisky connoisseur. His written works include more than 20 books on whisky, among which The Road to Craigellachie, The Legend of Laphroaig, A Taste of Whisky *and* Whisky & Jazz. *He regularly contributes to various newspapers, magazines and websites around the globe, has been producing mini documentaries for singlemalt.tv and translated Michael Jackson's Malt Whisky Companion and* WHISKY – the Definitive Guide *into Dutch.*

In 1998 he won a prestigious prize from the Dutch Ministry of Economic Affairs, for developing a new business model in the publishing world.

from Barley to Bottle

the different stages of Malt Whisky production

Barley

Barley (*Hordeum vulgare*) is the fourth most important cereal crop in the world after wheat, maize and rice and it is one of three raw materials needed to produce malt whisky. The other two are water and yeast. Barley is grown all over the world and is mainly used for feeding animals or for producing beer and spirits. The total barley production in Scotland in 2009 was 1.9 million tonnes (of which more than 80% was spring barley and the rest winter barley). The Scottish whisky industry uses about 500,000 tonnes of barley per year and the major part comes from Scottish farms. In 2005, the share grown in Scotland was 90% but it has decreased since then and an increasing share is imported from, e. g. Denmark, Germany, France and Australia not to mention England.

There are two forms of barley that are of interest to producers of beer and whisky: *two-row* and *six-row barley*, with the names alluding to how the kernels are arranged on the plant.

Furthermore, barley can be divided into *spring barley* (planted in spring and harvested in late summer or early autumn) and *winter barley* (planted in autumn and harvested the following autumn).

Finally, through continuous improvement, there are probably over 100,000 different varieties of barley today.

The most common barley for distilling malt whisky is two-row spring barley. This form can be divided into many different varieties, each more or less suitable for whisky production. Until the early 1800s, the traditional *Bere barley*, a six-row variety, was used for making whisky in Scotland but through plant refinement new kinds with better

characteristics were developed. Despite that, both Bruichladdich and Springbank have tried Bere barley for whisky production recently, albeit with mixed results.

In modern times, new varieties were introduced such as Golden Promise in 1966. It was replaced by Prisma and Chariot in the early nineties. The dominating barley strain today is Optic which was introduced in 1995. At its peak it was responsible for two thirds of all distilling barley used in Scotland but is now down to 40%. Recent new varieties include Oxbridge, Belgravia and Publican.

Research is ongoing to find new and better varieties by hybridising and refining existent varieties. The key factors to take into consideration when searching for new varieties are:

• Low percentage of protein content, which is inversely related to the percentage of starch which will be transformed into sugar and finally alcohol. This is measured as *spirit yield* (litres of alcohol/tonne of barley). A good yield, by today's standards, will be considered to be around 405-420 litres per tonne compared to older varieties with a spirit yield of 380 litres. It depends, however, whether peated or unpeated whisky is produced. Figures will be slightly lower with peated whiskies, as they will when using floor malted barley rather than malt from commercial maltsters.

• Resistance to diseases like mildew, brown rust and leaf spotting.

• A good capability to germinate, which is a prerequisite for malting.

• A high yield (from the farmer's point of view) from the fields. The yield of the old variety, Golden Promise, was about two tonnes per acre, whereas Optic produces a yield of three tonnes.

Quite recently experiments have been made using *hull-less barley*, a genetically improved type. Normally the grain is surrounded by a husk, which makes up about 10% of the whole grain, and contains mostly cellulose and lignin. The husk is glumellae which disappear after threshing of hull-less varieties. By modifying the malting regime for hull-less barley, one does not only shorten the steeping time during the malting, but also reduces

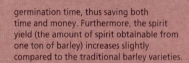

germination time, thus saving both time and money. Furthermore, the spirit yield (the amount of spirit obtainable from one ton of barley) increases slightly compared to the traditional barley varieties.

The harvested grain is laboratory-tested when it arrives at the maltings and before the consignment is accepted and brought to the barley store. Thereafter, it is dried by warm air and screened which also functions as purification. It is then cooled to ca 150°C and can subsequently be stored for months before use. The barley is now dormant and it will take several weeks before it wakes up and can germinate.

Malting

Malting is the process during which the barleycorn is modified so that it is possible to extract the sugar in the next step - the *mashing*. This process is used for producing both beer and whisky but when making malt for whisky, low protein barley with a high, starch content is chosen which can be turned into sugar and then alcohol. The largest part of the malt produced in the world is used to make beer while only 3% is used for whisky production.

The barleycorn consists of three parts - the *husk* which is wrapped around a piece of *starch* to which the *embryo* (or germ) is attached. By consuming the starch the embryo will, if not controlled, develop into the roots and shoots of a new barley plant. So what malting is all about is controlling the germination process.

The harvested barley is dormant between

six to sixteen weeks before germination can begin. To determine if the barley is ready a viability test is performed. When the barley has rejuvenated, it is sent to the *steepings* where the barley is immersed in water in order to raise moisture content, so that the germination can begin. Dry barley has a water content of less than 12%. The first steeping water has a temperature of 14-17 degrees and after eight hours the barley has absorbed and contains 32-35% water. At that time the water is drained off and the barley rests in air for 12 hours. Water is, once again, added and finally after another 16 hours the water content has reached the optimal 46% threshold.

During the steeping, a variety of enzymes have become active. *Cytase* starts breaking down the cell walls exposing the starch and *amylase* invades the starch itself, breaking it down into smaller parts. The moist malt is left to germinate either on traditional malting floors or in modern vessels (but more about that later).

The germination process will take about 7-10 days on a malting floor and 2-4 days at modern, commercial maltings. Germination produces heat so at this stage it is vital to turn the barley, so that air is allowed to pass through the grains in order to control temperature. Also, if it is left unturned, the roots tend to grow into each other leaving a rug of entangled grain that can weigh up to 500 tonnes.

During the germination process the enzymes that have been awoken by the steeping continue to do their job, but the germ also starts

feeding on the modified starch. In order not to "lose" too much starch, which will then be converted into sugar and in the end alcohol, the maltster needs to terminate the germination at the correct time. This process, known as *kilning*, entails drying the *green malt* (as it is now called) with the help of heat.

At this stage, we can take a look at the different types of maltings. The traditional way is *floor malting* where, after steeping, the grain is spread out on a floor made of stone or concrete in a layer 30 cm thick. Two to three times a day for about a week, the green malt has to be turned with shiels (wooden shovels). Thereafter the malt is brought to the kiln where it is spread out on a perforated metal floor. Here it is dried, either directly fired when the smoke from the furnace below passes through the malt bed, or indirectly when heated air passes from a radiator through the malt. The whole process takes between 24 and 48 hours, depending on the size of the kiln and the amount of malt. There are only a handful of distilleries that use this traditional method and when they do, it is generally only for a small part of their requirements.

A peated malt obtains its peaty character during the kilning. *Peat* consists of acidic and decayed vegetation and the place where it has been sourced is important for the character it adds to the finished whisky. Some peat bogs can be up to 10,000 years old and up to 10 metres deep. In the old days, peat was the predominant fuel source of the Highlands. Today it is used to complement other fuels and only to impart flavour to certain whiskies. The smoke from the peat contains *phenols*, of which there are many different kinds; some of the most important are isomeric cresols, xylenols and guaiacol. The peat is used during the first part of kilning when the green malt has a moisture content of 40-45% and usually stops when the content has reached 18-20%. The kilning then continues until reaching 4% moisture. The content of phenols in malt (or the finished whisky for that matter) is measured in *ppm* (parts per million) of phenols. Commercial maltsters divide their different kinds of peated malt into lightly peated (1-5ppm), medium peated (5-15ppm) and heavily peated (15-50+ppm). The big malting companies actually

do not use solid peat at all for their peated malt. Instead, a solution of water and phenols is sprayed on to the barley.

Commercial maltsters use any of three techniques - *Saladin box, Drums* or *SGKV* (Steeping, Germination and Kilning Vessel).

The SGKV, which was developed in the seventies, is the most recent and can process up to 500 tonnes in one batch, performing all the steps in one process.

Saladin boxes can be found at Tamdhu distillery, at Baird's in Inverness, as well as at Crisp in Alloa. They were invented by the Frenchman Charles Saladin in the late 19th century and can handle up to 200 tonnes.

The third method is drum maltings which came into use in the late 1960s. The drums are reliable and easy to use, but have a disadvantage in that only 30 to 50 tonnes of barley can be loaded at a time.

Apart from different varieties of peated and unpeated malt, some distilleries have recently started experimenting with malt types usually developed for the brewing industry - *chocolate malt, roasted malt* and *crystal malt* - adding new flavours to the whisky. From 100 kilos of barley, 80 kilos of malt is produced, and when the malting process is finished, the malt is taken to the mill and then to the mash tun.

Mashing

Before it is possible to start extracting soluble sugars from the malted barley during the mashing, it has to be crushed in a *mill*. The passage from the malt bin leads through a dressing machine where unwanted parts (rootlets etc.) are removed and put into the mill. There are different types of mills but the basic concept is that rollers crack the husks of the barleycorn and grind them to grist.

The most common type is the Porteus two or four roll mill, but some distilleries use a more modern version called Bühler-Miag with up to seven rolls. A few distilleries still use an old but reliable mill called Boby mill. During the milling it is vital that the size of the particles is perfect in order to have an as efficient as possible mashing process.

The requirement depends on the type of mash tun in use and varies between different distilleries. The optimum distribution if one is using a traditional mash tun is 10% *flour*, 70% *grits* and 20% *husk*. With too much flour, the filter in the mash tun can become clogged and with too much husk the water will flow through too quickly. If a lauter mash tun is used, the mash is more shallow (perhaps 0.5-1 metres deep) which gives a quicker drainage and therefore makes it possible to use a finer grind.

The *grist* (as the milled barley malt is called) flows from the mill to the grist hopper where it is stored before taken to the *mash tun*. The latter is a large circular vessel made either of stainless steel or (more uncommon) cast iron. Just one distillery (Glenturret) still uses a wooden mash tun. Most mash tuns are covered with a dome but some that are open are still operated. The sizes vary a great deal,

from Glenturret where the mash tun holds 1 tonne of grist, to the giants at Glenfarclas; 10 metres in diameter and loaded with 15 tonnes of grist per mash.

The grist is then mashed with hot water in order to extract sugars from the barley. The enzymes, amylase, that were awoken during the malting process, but deactivated during the kilning, now start to transform starch to sugars. Two to five (but usually three) waters are used in the mashing.

The *first water* (which is actually the third water from the previous mashing) is heated to about 65 degrees. The temperature is crucial – if the water is too warm then the enzymes are killed. During the process it is important to keep in mind that certain enzymes are most active at 50 degrees while others are active at higher temperatures.

After the water has been mixed with the grist it is stirred to increase the extraction of sugars. In the olden days this was done manually with large wooden spades. The only distillery which practices that method today is Glenturret.

Today, when talking about *traditional mash tuns*, it refers to the ones where revolving mechanical rakes stir the mash. Many distilleries have switched to the more modern lauter mash tuns commonly used in breweries.

In this newer version, a rotating arm is equipped with blades that cut through the mash. Two varieties exist: *semi-lauter* and *full lauter*. In the latter, the knives can be moved not only horizontally, but also vertically. After about 30 minutes the first batch of *wort*, as the mash is now called, is drained off through the perforated floor into the underback or wort receiver.

The *second water* is now filled into the mash tun, this time heated to anywhere between 70 and 85 degrees, depending on the distillery´s different preferences. The same procedure follows and the wort is drained off after 30 minutes. By this time, 90% of the starches have been converted into fermentable sugars, but there is still some soluble starch left in the mash and, in order to make use of it, a *third water* is added. The temperature of this water will typically vary between 80 and 95 degrees and after 15 minutes it is drained off. Since this water only contains about 1% sugar, it should not be mixed with the wort already collected, so it is pumped to the hot water tank to be used as part of the first water in the next mashing.

The resulting residue in the mash tun is now called *draff*, consisting of husks and spent grains, which is collected, processed and used for cattle feed. Sometimes it is mixed with the *pot ale* from the distillation and transformed into pellets, so called *dark grains*. Before the collected wort in the wort receiver goes into the washbacks for fermentation, the temperature has to be reduced to 18-20 degrees, otherwise the yeast would be destroyed.

The whole mashing procedure will take about three hours in a modern lauter mash tun and, in the case of Glenfarclas, a batch of 15 tonnes of grist will produce around 75,000 litres of wort. One thing which is important to measure before the fermentation starts is the *Original Gravity (OG)* of the wort, i. e. how rich the wort is in sugars. This will determine the amount of yeast that can be used during the next phase – namely *fermentation*. The density of water at 20 degrees is 1000 and when whisky is produced the OG of the wort will be around 1050.

Fermentation

The part of the whisky production when sugar is transformed into alcohol is called the *fermentation*. From the mash tun, where the enzyme amylase breaks down the starch into maltose sugar (almost 50% of the wort), the wort is pumped through a heat exchanger to the *washbacks*. Reducing the heat of the wort to around 20 degrees is essential. If the wort is too hot, the yeast will be destroyed in the next step.

The washbacks, where the fermentation takes place, are large vats, traditionally made of wood but nowadays often made of stainless steel. Wooden washbacks, usually made of larch or Oregon pine, are more difficult to clean, but supporters claim that the wood has a positive effect on the wash. Others say that the material of the washbacks is irrelevant and prefer the efficiency of the stainless steel washbacks. One thing is true though: few distilleries today dare

change the material of their washbacks for fear of changing the established character of their whisky. The size of the washbacks can vary between 1,000 and 70,000 litres and they are usually filled two-thirds full.

Now the yeast goes into the wort to start transforming the sugar into alcohol. The process is often described as yeast cells feeding frantically on sugar, which is not entirely correct. During the first (aerobic) phase, the yeast cells reproduce and, in order to do so, they assimilate free, dissolved oxygen from the wort. As the oxygen is reduced and the carbon dioxide increased, the environment becomes anaerobic and hostile to the yeast cells. They need more oxygen and now get this from the sugar molecules. The resultant by-products contain even more carbon dioxide, alcohol and various congeners.

Unlike beer production, the making of malt whisky is not a sterile process. In the mash there will be a variety of wild yeast and bacteria, which will influence the flavour of the spirit. The magnitude of this influence depends on the fermentation time, what kind of distiller´s yeast is used and if

the washbacks are made of wood or stainless steel. The wooden washbacks are virtually impossible to rid 100% of the bacteria.

All sugar has been utilised after roughly 48 hours and the yeast cells sink to the bottom. The third fermentation then takes place caused by the different bacteria, mainly lactic acid ones, in the wort which no longer face competition from the yeast. The pH decreases and many new congeners are created and the ones present are enhanced. This is called a *malolactic fermentation*. If allowed to ferment for too long, the pH can become too low and the wash destroyed.

So the final result after 48 to 120 hours of fermentation is actually an ale without hops and with an alcohol content between 5 and 8%. Approximately 85% of the solids in the wash have been converted into alcohol and the remaining 15% goes with the wash to the wash still for the first distillation.

Until the early seventies, there was only one type of yeast available, namely *Brewer´s Yeast*. Not only did this yeast transform sugar into alcohol, but by being less efficient than modern yeast strains, it also left some sugar and esters in the wash, thus contributing to the flavour of the whisky.

In search of a more efficient yeast strain which could give a higher alcohol content, some producers came up with the cultivated *Distiller´s Yeast*. It gave a better financial yield, but there were worries that it would affect the taste of the whisky too much. Since 2005, Brewer´s Yeast has not been available outside the brewing industry, so even if the distilling industry would have wanted to, there was no turning back. This is the reason why a lot of research has gone into finding a substitute for Brewer´s Yeast that can be used, if not by itself, then in combination with Distiller´s Yeast. Yeast is used either in a dried or compressed state or as a liquid (slurry) and the major part of yeast for distilling today comes from two large food companies, Kerry Group and AB Mauri (an affiliate of Associated British Foods).

A great deal of the final character of the new make spirit is determined during fermentation. Some say that 55% is due to fermentation and 45% to distillation. Please note that this is the character of the new make spirit and not the matured whisky. For the latter, the wood and the casks are of the utmost importance.

Factors to take into consideration are fermentation time, temperature and alcohol strength of the finished wash. Some distilleries have practised short fermentation times for years, but to suddenly cut down on the fermentation time in order to produce more spirit could easily backfire. The malolactic fermentation, important to create certain congeners, will be shorter and this could also have an impact on the character of the spirit. Some advocates are of the opinion that a fermentation time of at least 60 hours is necessary in order to achieve complexity.

Wash Still

With the exception of Auchentoshan and Hazelburn which both are *triple distilled* and Springbank, Benrinnes and Mortlach, all of which are partially triple distilled, Scottish malt distilleries all practise *double distillation*. This means there are two stills usually working in pairs: a *wash still* and a *spirit still*.

The stills are made of copper which is of the utmost importance. The reaction between the copper and the spirit will reduce any unwanted impurities in the spirit and the more copper contact there is the cleaner the spirit will be. Therefore one could argue that distillers always aim for as much copper contact as possible in order to get as pure spirit as possible. This, however, is not true. In these impurities are also congeners that give each whisky its distinctive taste, so if you are known to produce a full-bodied, powerful spirit you will want to keep more congeners, as opposed to a distillery known for its light and clean whisky.

From the washbacks, where the fermentation has taken place, the (often pre-heated) wash is pumped into the wash still. Thereafter the wash starts to warm up and the first of two distillations commences.

There are different ways of heating the still. The commonest method today is through indirect heating by steam. The steam, which has been heated by either oil or gas, is transported into the bottom of the still by steam coils. The steam coils are, in their turn, connected to round steam kettles, rectangular steam pans or steam plates which heat the wash.

A few distilleries still use the old way of heating the stills by burning an open flame under the still. Glenfiddich has 28 stills, all direct-fired by a gas flame, at Glenfarclas all six stills are directly fired by gas and, finally, at Springbank, the wash still is directly fired using oil but also has steam coils installed.

One disadvantage with direct firing is that solids will have a tendency to stick to the bottom and burn, thus affecting the taste of the spirit. To deal with that, a *rummager* is installed at the inside bottom of the kettle. Basically it is a copper chain that revolves, scraping off solids before they burn.

When the temperature in the still has reached 95 degrees, the alcohol will rise as vapours to the top of the still, but before we go into what happens next, let´s have a look at the different shapes of the pot stills.

There are three main types:

Onion still (traditional still) - as the name indicates, shaped like an onion

Boiling ball still (reflux bulge still) - with a bulb fitted between the pot and the neck

Lantern still - with a narrow "waist" between pot and neck

Within these three groups there is a plethora of variations with wide or narrow necks, long or short necks and with the lyne arm (the copper pipe leading from the top of the neck to the condenser) inclined at various angles.

The reason for having different shapes as well as sizes, is that the shape decides how much copper contact the spirit will have and also how much reflux is obtained when distilling. *Reflux* is the term used for re-distillation of the spirit vapours. If there are tall or narrow necks or a lyne arm that is angled upwards, the result will be that a large portion of the heavier spirit vapours will not make it to the condenser in the first try, but will instead go down to the bottom of the still to be distilled once more. This process will give a lighter spirit.

The boiling ball still will add more copper contact to the spirit and often results in a less heavy spirit than the onion still. The lantern still also adds more copper contact due to its often wide neck and the narrow waist also reduces the risk of the wash frothing and rising up the neck. If the wash cannot be stopped from frothing (or "boiling over") and reaches the condenser, the distillation will be wasted. To avoid frothing (which only

appears in the wash still during the first distillation) anywhere between 60 and 80% of the full capacity of the still should be charged. There is a sight glass on the side of the neck to monitor if the level is rising and then the temperature has to be lowered.

Once the spirit vapours have made their way through the neck and down the lyne arm, they are condensed into liquid and gathered in the low wines and feints receiver. Low wines collected correspond to one third of the wash still charge and the strength is slightly over 20%. When it is pumped to the low wines & feints receiver it is mixed with the foreshots and feints (read more about that under spirit still, below) from the previous distillation in the spirits still. This will raise the alcohol strength to 28% which is extremely important for the next distillation. If the spirit still would have been charged with just the low wines at 20%, the alcohol strength would never reach more than 60% from the spirit still which is too low for the spirit to fractionate, i. e. it would not be possible to collect all the congeners needed to create whisky. When the strength is raised to 28%, it means the distillate from the spirit still will reach the desired 70% in its turn.

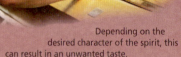

Spirit Still

After the spirit from the wash still has been collected in the *low wines & feints receiver*, it is pumped through the low wines charger into the *spirit still*.

At the beginning of the second distillation, the strength of the spirit is around 28%. After a while, when the temperature of the still has increased, the strength will have reached 82%. The risk of frothing that prevails during the first distillation is minimal during the second distillation due to the fact that no carbon dioxide is left in the low wines. On the other hand, it is more important during the second distillation to keep a close watch on the temperature. A high temperature will lessen the reflux and bring heavy congeners through the neck and the lyne arm to the condenser.

Depending on the desired character of the spirit, this can result in an unwanted taste.

Traditionally the spirit vapours were condensed using a *worm tub*. This is a large tub, 3 to 5 metres deep, made of wood or cast iron and placed outside the still house. Inside the tub, which is filled with water, is a copper spiral which sometimes measures up to 120 metres long. The spirit flows through it and is cooled by the surrounding water. Worm tubs are still in use at 13 distilleries.

A more modern cooling device, placed at the end of the lyne arm, is called a *shell and tube condenser*. This is a wide copper tube with a number of smaller copper pipes on the inside, through which cold water flows condensing the surrounding vapours.

The *spirit safe* is divided into two parts - the wash safe and the spirit safe. All of the low wines, distilled in the wash still, are collected into one glass bowl with a hole in the bottom. The spirit from the spirit still, on the other hand, is divided into three fractions - *foreshot, middle cut* and *feints*. The stream of these three parts of the spirit run is directed by a pipe that can be moved to any of two glass containers with openings at the bottom. Traditionally it was the stillman's job to switch the handle but, nowadays, it is often done by computers.

The first part of the run, called the foreshots and which takes 15-30 minutes, has a high percentage of impurities and unwanted congeners and would have damaged the final spirit if collected. So this part, with an alcoholic strength of 75-80%, goes back to the low wines & feints receiver to be re-distilled.

The next fraction, the middle cut, is the part which will be saved for maturation. This part of the run, which goes into the intermediate spirit receiver, contains up to 100 different aromatic esters that will give the spirit its fruity and fragrant character. After a while, the esters start to decrease and the feints increase.

The feints (the third part) are pleasant to start with and necessary in the spirit. After a while, though, the feints change into a variety of unpleasant aromas and this is where the stillman (or the computer) stops the middle cut and turns the pipe to the first glass container in the spirit safe. Just like the foreshots, the feints are directed to the low

wines & feints receiver to become a part of the next distillation.

So, it is obvious that determining the start and end of the middle cut is crucial. To ascertain this, hydrometers are used to measure alcohol strength. Depending on what character one is aiming for in the final whisky, the length of the middle cut differs from distillery to distillery. If a fruity and flowery whisky is desired, the stillman will start collecting the middle cut at around 75% and stop at perhaps 68%. Others, looking for a heavier, more pungent spirit, will start at 70% and will not stop until 60% or even lower. During the middle cut, it is important to run the still as slowly as possible in order to increase the reflux and this will typically take somewhere between two and three hours.

The middle cut is often called the *new make* (the proper term is BPS British Plain Spirit) and has an alcohol strength of around 70%. The new make is finally pumped from the intermediate spirit receiver to the spirit vat, where the spirit from several distillations is mixed to even out the differences. The spirit vat is placed in the filling store which is the last step before the spirit goes into casks.

Before we go on to Maturation, just a few words on another type of still frequently mentioned in the "*Distilleries around the globe*" section of this book. It is often called *Holstein still*, after one of the biggest manufacturers, but there are other companies producing the same type of still; Christian Carl and Vendome for example. Basically it is a copper pot with a *rectification column* attached to the top. The column is equipped with a number of different plates which, by creating reflux, force parts of the spirit vapours to be re-distilled before entering up the column again and finally cooled into liquid. Normally this type of still is used for distilling eaux de vie and similar spirits but it is, in central Europe and in the US in particular, also used for whisky production. This type of still comes in many shapes and sizes and with a number of plates ranging from two up to over 40.

Maturation

Prior to being filled into the casks for maturation, the new make spirit is diluted and, until recently, the majority of the industry followed the rule that 63.5% was the optimal strength. One argument was that at a higher alcohol strength, maturation would take longer and the formation of certain congeners which would give the final whisky its character, was made difficult. However, this routine has started to change and several producers now fill at a higher strength or even without diluting. The main reason for this is a saving in the number of casks and, thus, warehouse space.

Also, many producers have not followed this routine for all of their production during the years. That is why one can sometimes find cask strength bottlings that are more than 20 years old, but still have an alcohol strength of more than 60%. If it had been filled at 63.5%, two decades of evaporation

would have brought the strength down to somewhere below 50% at the least.

The evaporation we are talking about here is what is generally called the *Angel's Share*. The yearly evaporation in Scotland is around 1.5-2%. Oak is a semi-porous material and alcohol, as well as water, will evaporate during maturation. The rate depends very much on the temperature of the warehouse. Higher temperature means a higher degree of evaporation. The air humidity also plays an important role. High humidity surrounding the cask means that water evaporation is less, which in its turn means that the alcohol is reduced in relation to the amount of water, thus creating a lower alcohol content from year to year. This is the case in Scotland with its high humidity, especially in the winter.

In other places, for example southern USA, temperature is high and humidity low, so more water than alcohol will be lost from evaporation and this may result in the alcohol strength growing higher during maturation.

Oak & Casks

The importance of the wood for the final character of the whisky cannot be underestimated! It is often claimed that up to 80% of the whisky's flavour depends on the cask. After diluting, the spirit is filled into wooden casks and, according to the Scotch Whisky Act of 1988, it has to be oak to be allowed to be called Scotch whisky. Sometimes different types of wood are used in other parts of the world and there have been occasional experiments in Scotland in the old days with casks made of for example chestnut.

There are more than 400 different kinds of oak in the genus *Quercus* (200 in the USA alone) but only three that are of major interest to the distilleries, all of them belonging to the category white oak:

Pedunculate Oak or English Oak (*Quercus robur*)

Sessile Oak or Durmast Oak (*Quercus petraea*)

American White Oak (*Quercus alba*)

The first two grow in Europe and the last, obviously, in North America, particularly in Arkansas, Kentucky, Missouri and Tennessee. American White Oak is often preferred because it brings in better revenue. The trees grow faster and it is tighter grained which means it can be sawn rather than split by an axe. This also results in less wasted wood.

The European Oak on the other hand, is more porous which means that whisky is lost at a higher speed, but the increased oxidization can often be of benefit during the maturation. European Oak also contains more tannin whereas American Oak has a higher content of vanillin, both contributing to the flavour of the whisky.

A fourth variety of oak which has become increasingly interesting is Japanese Oak (*Quercus mongolica*) or Mizunara Oak as it is also known as. Sherry casks were difficult to get hold of just after the second World War and several Japanese distilleries filled whisky into casks of this indigenous oak. They were not fully satisfied with the wood's ability to hold the spirit, so when sherry casks once again became available, these were preferred. Decades later, however, it was discovered that the whisky that had matured in Japanese Oak had a unique sandal or cedar flavour and now most of the distilleries

in Japan have started using Japanese Oak again, at least to some extent.

The oak's importance for the maturation of whisky can be divided into three parts: subtractive, additive and interactive.

The *subtractive* part is about breaking down and removing especially sulphury compounds in the spirit. Actually, it is not the oak itself doing this job but rather carbon derived from the toasting or charring of the inside of the cask. In order to put the cask together, the oak staves are heated to the point where they obtain a toasted character. For a bourbon cask, however, that is not enough. After the cask has been put together, the inside is exposed to an open flame and the walls are charred to a depth of about one to three millimetres. An American bourbon cask will therefore be more efficient in reducing the sulphur in the spirit.

The *additive* mechanism is about lending both flavour and colour to the spirit. From the wood oils, acids, sugar and esters are extracted which all, to a varying degree, affect the flavour. Another addition to the flavour, at least for shorter maturations or finishes, comes not from the oak itself, but from whichever wine or spirit was in the cask previously (sherry, bourbon, Port etc). Depending on how many times a cask has been used, the effect on the colour will differ. The tannin in the wood also influences the colour and European Oak, being more tannic than American Oak, results in a darker colour.

The *interactive* process is yet the least understood of the three maturation elements. Evaporation and oxidation (when oxygen replaces the evaporated water and alcohol) is one part and this eliminates harshness and adds complexity to the spirit. But interaction also means oak and spirit together creating compounds that were not present from the beginning. While the first of the two maturation processes are active during the first couple of years, the interactive part will continue during the entire time of maturation and is also very dependent on how the cask is stored (temperature, humidity, atmospheric pressure).

In the olden days, the distilleries would fill their spirit into any wooden cask that they could find because the cask was merely seen as a transport vessel. In the late 1800s, a new regime came into being when distillers started using empty sherry

casks from Spain. Huge amounts of sherry were imported to England and casks were cheap. In the mid 1900s, though, the demand for sherry, at least in the UK, had diminished substantially and the producers had to look for other solutions. One was to make their own casks in Spain and lend them to the sherry bodegas for a few years and then bring them to Scotland. The other alternative was to import empty bourbon barrels from the USA. By law, bourbon has to be matured in new, charred oak casks so there was always a good supply to be had from across the Atlantic.

There are about 18 million casks of whisky maturing in Scotland and 95% of these are made of American Oak with 300,000 new casks being shipped every year from the USA to Scotland.

It is important to understand that it really is not the sherry or bourbon itself that affects the oak when speaking of sherry versus bourbon casks and the impact the various types have on the flavour of the whisky. With just a few exceptions, the spirit destined to become whisky is always filled into a cask that has once held spirit or wine. If it was to be filled into new or virgin oak casks, one needs to be very careful that the wood does not overpower the whisky.

Bourbon, sherry or any other previous filling will soften the oak and help degrade the polymers in the wood into flavour compounds. Basically, it can be said that it conditions the wood. Obviously, a bourbon with its high alcohol content will affect the oak differently than a lower-alcohol sherry or wine. The different levels of alcohol will simply extract or transform different kinds of compounds. If comparing an American Oak cask and a European Oak cask, both having been previously filled with sherry, it will be noticed that the two casks contribute very different flavours to the whisky.

American Oak will, for example, provide a vanilla and coconut flavour while European oak contributes with rich fruits and tannins. This being said, with very

less and are therefore easier to use in a blend or to sell as a single cask whisky (with no blending). After each filling, most bourbon casks are rejuvenated, which means that a thin layer is shaved off on the inside and then the wood is re-charred, i. e. burnt with a flame to create a carbon surface. Sherry casks are often toasted and sometimes seasoned with new sherry.

Blending & Bottling

If we disregard single cask bottlings, which is what the name indicates; one single cask of whisky bottled and almost always at cask strength, all Scotch whisky can be considered blended - also single malts. Blended in this case means two or more casks vatted together before bottling. The process varies considerably among producers and whether it is blended Scotch or single malt, but the basics remain as follows;

Different casks are blended together in big vats where filtered air passes through the whisky to make the blending proper. This is called *rousing*. The whisky is then diluted using de-mineralised water to the appropriate bottling strength, but never below the legal minimum of 40%. Before the next step, which is colouring, the vatted whisky is sometimes left to "marry". The time varies but can sometimes take up to 12 weeks. Colouring of the whisky is obtained by using caramel (E150). At least among whisky aficionados this step is controversial. Some producers

will perform it while others don't, and sometimes the one and the same producer chooses to colour parts of the range and not interfere with others. The reason for colouring is to obtain a consistency between batches and, as opponents to the procedure emphasize, to make the whisky look older. Those against this process state that the caramel will affect the taste.

After the caramel has been added, the whisky is again roused for 10-15 minutes. The next step is *filtering*. Any solids derived from the cask are filtered away using mechanical filters. *Chill filtration* is an extended type of filtering, which is as debated as colouring. This means that the whisky is chilled to anywhere between -4C and 2C which will make it turbid. The cloudiness consists of, among other things, various fatty acids, which get caught in the different filters that the whisky will pass through afterwards.

The reason for chill filtering whisky is to avoid the liquid (when the strength is brought down below 46%) becoming less clear if the consumer adds water to it or drinks it with ice, i. e. purely out of a cosmetical regard.

The controversy over chill filtration is due to the fact that during the process, various congeners and esters that might add to the flavour of the whisky, will get caught in the filters as well. To what degree this happens, depends on the temperature of the chilling and also of the filters' sizes and the speed with which the whisky flows through the filters. Independent bottlers rarely chill filter their whisky and several producers have also decided to go for unchill filtered whisky for all, or parts of their production.

After chill filtration the whisky is finally bottled. As previously mentioned, this is the standard procedure when blending and bottling, but the details will vary hugely from producer to producer and from product to product. In recent years, the lack of colouring and chill filtration, have become strong marketing arguments, at least for those producers aiming for the dedicated whisky drinkers.

short maturations or so called finishes (see more about that below), the character of sherry, bourbon or any other previous wine and spirit will influence the flavour of the final product

During the last two decades, new types of casks have entered the scene, besides bourbon and sherry. Today, it is quite common to find whisky that has matured in Port pipes, Madeira casks, rum casks or casks that have held different kinds of wine. In some cases the spirit has been in the same cask for the whole period of maturation, but more frequent is that the whisky is re-racked from a bourbon or sherry cask to obtain a final maturation of a few months or a couple of years in a second cask. There are different terms for this procedure - finishing, enhancing, acing - which aims to give the whisky an added flavour profile.

Casks are also categorised depending on how many times they have been used. The first time a cask is used for maturing whisky, it is called *first-fill*, then comes *second-fill* and from the third filling it is often simply called *re-fill*. A first-fill cask has to be handled with great care when blending the whisky, as the oak and/or previous spirit or wine will sometimes dominate the whisky character. Second-fill and third-fill contribute

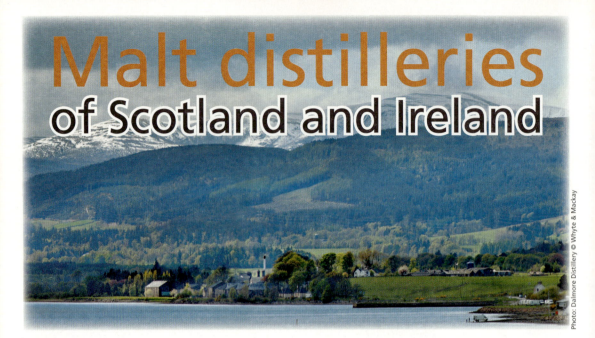

Malt distilleries
of Scotland and Ireland

Photo: Dalmore Distillery © Whyte & Mackay

On the following pages, 128 Scottish and Irish distilleries are described in detail. Most are active, while some are mothballed, decommissioned or demolished.

Long since closed distilleries from which whisky is very rare or practically unobtainable are described at the end together with four new and upcoming distilleries.

Japanese malt whisky distilleries and distilleries in other countries are covered on pp. 200-235.

Just a brief explanation with regards to where in the book the different distilleries are placed.

I have decided that the owners must have released at least one bottling of single malt whisky (not just new make spirit) to warrant a place of its own in the alphabetical part of the distillery directory of Scottish and Irish distilleries. That is, for example, why Kilbeggan, thanks to their newly released single malt, has a page of their own this year in the directory instead of being mentioned under the owner, Cooley distillery.

Distilleries that are about to be built or have not left the planning phase yet are treated in the part The Whisky Year That Was (pp. 236-249).

Explanations

Owner:
Name of the owning company, sometimes with the parent company within brackets.

Region/district:
There are four formal malt whisky regions in Scotland today; the Highlands, the Lowlands, Islay and Campbeltown. Where useful we mention a location within a region e.g. Speyside, Orkney, Northern Highlands etc.

Founded:
The year in which the distillery was founded is usually con-sidered as when construction began. The year is rarely the same year in which the distillery was licensed.

Status:
The status of the distillery's production. Active, mothballed (temporarily closed), closed (but most of the equipment still present), dismantled (the equipment is gone but part of or all of the buildings remain even if they are used for other purposes) and demolished.

Visitor centre:
The letters (vc) after status indicate that the distillery has a visitor centre. Many distilleries accept visitors despite not having a visitor centre. It can be worthwhile making an enquiry.

Address:
The distillery´s address.

Tel:
This is generally to the visitor centre, but can also be to the main office.

website:
The distillery's (or in some cases the owner's) website.

Capacity:
The current production capacity expressed in litres of pure alcohol (LPA).

History:
The chronology focuses on the official history of the distillery and independent bottlings are only listed in exceptional cases. They can be found in the text bodies instead.

Tasting notes:
For all the Scottish and Irish distilleries that are not perma-nently closed we present tasting notes of what, in most cases, can be called the core expression (mainly their best selling 10 or 12 year old).

We have tried to provide notes for official bottlings but in those cases where we have not been able to obtain them, we have turned to independent bottlers.

The whiskies have been tasted by *Gavin D Smith* (GS) and *Dominic Roskrow* (DR), well-known and eperienced whisky profiles who, i.a., where assigned to write the 6th edition of Michael Jackson´s Malt Whisky Companion.

New for this year is that we also have tasting notes, prepared by Chris Bunting, for some of the Japanese malts. All notes have been prepared especially for Malt Whisky Yearbook 2011.

Brief distillery glossary

A number of terms occur throughout the distillery directory and are briefly explained here. We can recommend for example *A to Z of Whisky* by Gavin D Smith for more detailed explanations.

Blended malt
A type of whisky where two or more single malts are blended together. The term was introduced a few years ago by SWA to replace the previous term vatted malt. The term is controversial as those who oppose the use of it are of the opinion that it can be confused with 'blended whisky' where malt and grain is blended.

Cask strength
It has become increasingly common in recent times to bottle malt whisky straight from the cask without reducing the alcohol contents to 40, 43 or 46%. A cask strength can be anything between 40 to 65% depending on how long the cask has been matured.

Chill-filtering
A method used for removing unwanted particles and, especially used to prevent the whisky from appearing turbid when water is added. Some producers believe that flavour is affected and therefore avoid chill-filtering.

Continuous still
A type of still used when making grain whisky. The still allows for continuous distillation and re-distillation. Can also be called column still, patent still or Coffey still.

Cooling
The spirit vapours from the stills are cooled into liquids usually by a shell and tube condenser, but an older method (worm tubs) is still in use at some distilleries.

Dark grains
The draff and pot ale from the distillation process is used for making fodder pellets, so-called dark grains.

Drum maltings
The malting method used on all major malting sites today.

Dunnage warehouse
Also called traditional warehouse. The walls are made of stone and the floors of earth. The casks (up to three) are piled on top of each other.

Floor maltings
The traditional method of malting the barley on large wooden floors. This method is only used by a handful of distilleries today.

Lyne arm
The lyne arm leads the spirit vapours from the wash or spirit still to the condenser. The angle of the lyne arm has great significance for reflux and the final character of the whisky.

Mash tun
The procedure after the malt has been milled into grist is called the mashing. The mash tun is usually made of cast iron or stainless steel, but can sometimes be made of wood. The grist is mixed with hot water in order to release the sugars in the barley. The result is the wort which is drawn off through a perforated floor into the underback. The mashed grains in the mash tun are called draff and are then used for making animal feed.

Pagoda roof
A roof shaped as a pagoda which was built over the kiln to lead the smoke away from the drying peat. The pagoda roof was invented by the famous architect Charles Doig. These days pagoda roofs provide mainly aesthetical value as the majority of distilleries usually buy their malt elsewhere.

Peat
A soil layer consisting of plants which have mouldered. Used as fuel in drying the green malts when a more or less peaty whisky is to be produced. In other cases the kiln is usually heated by oil or gas.

PPM
Abbreviation for Parts Per Million. This is used to show the amount of phenols in the peated malt. Peated Islay whisky usually uses malt with 40-60 ppm, which is reduced to 10-20 ppm in the new make spirit.

Purifier
A device used in conjunction with the lyne arm which cools heavier alcohols and lead them back to the still. A handful of distilleries use this technique to make a lighter and cleaner spirit.

Racked warehouse
A modern warehouse with temperature control and built-in shelves. Casks can be stored up to a height of 12.

Reflux
When the heavier vapours in the still are cooled and fall back into the still as liquids. The amount of reflux obtained depends on the shape of the still and the angle of the lyne arm. A distillation process with high reflux gives a lighter, more delicate spirit while a small amount of reflux gives a more robust and flavour-rich whisky.

Saladin box
A method of malting barley which replaced floor maltings. It was invented by the Frenchman Charles Saladin in the late 19th century and was introduced in Scottish distilleries in the 1950s. The only distillery using the method today is Tamdhu.

Shell and tube condenser
The most common method for cooling the spirit vapours. It is a wide copper tube attached to the lyne arm of the still. Cold water is led through a number of smaller copper pipes and cools the surrounding vapours.

Spirit still
The second still, usually a little smaller that the wash still. The low wines are collected in the spirit still for redistilling. Alcohol increases to 64-68% and unwanted impurities disappear. It is only the middle fraction of the distillate (the cut) which is utilized.

Vatted malt
See blended malt.

Washback
Large tubs of stainless steel or wood in which fermentation takes place. Yeast is added to the worts and the sugars change into alcohol. The result is a wash with an alcoholic content of 6-8% which is then used for distillation.

Wash still
The first and usually largest of the stills. The wash is heated to the boiling point and the alcohol is vaporized. The spirit vapours are cooled in a condenser and the result is low wines with an alcohol content of c 21%.

Worm tub
An older method for cooling the spirit vapours in connection with distilling. This method is still used in approximately ten distilleries. The worm tub consists of a long, spiral-shaped copper pipe which is submerged in water in a large wooden tub, usually outdoors. The spirit vapours are led through the copper spiral so they can condense.

Aberfeldy

Owner:
John Dewar & Sons
(Bacardi)

Region/district:
Eastern Highlands

Founded: 1896

Status:
Active (vc)

Capacity:
3 500 000 litres

Address: Aberfeldy, Perthshire PH15 2EB

Tel:
01887 822010 (vc)

website:
www.dewarswow.com

History:

1896 – John and Tommy Dewar embark on the construction of the distillery, a stone's throw from the old Pitilie distillery which was active from 1825 to 1867. Their objective is to produce a single malt for their blended whisky - White Label.

1898 – Production starts in November.

1917-19 – The distillery closes.

1925 – Distillers Company Limited (DCL) takes over.

1972 – Reconstruction takes place, the floor maltings is closed and the two stills are increased to four.

1991 – The first official bottling is a 15 year old in the Flora & Fauna series.

1998 – Bacardi buys John Dewar & Sons from Diageo at a price of £1,150 million.

2000 – A visitor centre opens and a 25 year old is released.

2005 – A 21 year old is launched in October, replacing the 25 year old.

2009 – Two 18 year old single casks are released.

2010 – A 19 year old single cask, exclusive to France, is released.

Aberfeldy 12 year old

GS – Sweet, with honeycombs, breakfast cereal and stewed fruits on the nose. Inviting and warming. Mouth-coating and full-bodied on the palate. Sweet, malty, balanced and elegant. The finish is long and complex, becoming progressively more spicy and drying.

DR – The nose is a mix of fresh and clean barley, honey and a hint of smoke. The honey carries through to the palate and the pleasant finish is shaped by a touch of smoke and peppery spice.

Dewar's, the whisky part of the Bacardi conglomerate, is concentrated to two brands; Dewar's and William Lawson's. Both are blended Scotch while the single malt side of the business only accounts for 1% in terms of volume. Despite this, Aberfeldy is an essential part of the business: it illustrates the heritage back to the Dewar brothers who built the distillery. This heritage is also emphasized by Dewar's World of Whiskies, a visitor centre which opened at the distillery in 2000. Furthermore, Aberfeldy is an important part of the Dewar's blend. The big blended Scotch brands took a beating in 2009 as volumes declined and Dewar's was no exception. Being the category leader in USA (with 15% of the market), it was, of course, affected when the overall market for Scotch whisky there fell by 6% and Dewar's even more (-15%). However, while Johnnie Walker, Ballantine's, J&B and Chivas Regal decreased with two-digit percentages, Dewar's managed to restrict the decrease to a minimum and sold 3.2 million cases worldwide, making it the sixth most sold brand.

The equipment at Aberfeldy consists of a stainless steel mash tun, eight washbacks made of Siberian Larch, two stainless steel washbacks placed outdoors and two pairs of stills. There are six warehouses on site, though they are no longer used for storage. A seven-day working week was introduced a year ago, but Aberfeldy is now back at five-day weeks producing 2.85 million litres of alcohol.

The core range consists of *12* and *21 year old*. For the first time ever, the owners released *two single casks* in 2009. Both were *18 year olds* distilled in 1991 and, while one was aimed at Duty Free, the other was released to commemorate Chris Anderson, the Distilleries Manager's retirement. The next single cask was a *19 year old* exclusive for La Maison du Whisky in September 2010 and yet another bottling was announced for release later in the year.

12 years old

Aberlour

Owner:
Chivas Brothers Ltd
(Pernod Ricard)

Region/district:
Speyside

Founded: 1826   **Status:** Active (vc)   **Capacity:** 3 700 000 litres

Address: Aberlour, Banffshire AB38 9PJ

Tel: 01340 881249   **website:** www.aberlour.com

History:

1826 – James Gordon and Peter Weir found the first Aberlour Distillery.

1827 – Peter Weir withdraws and James Gordon continues alone.

1879 – A fire devastates most of the distillery. The local banker James Fleming constructs a new distillery a few kilometres upstream the Spey river.

1892 – The distillery is sold to Robert Thorne & Sons Ltd who expands it.

1898 – Another fire rages and almost totally destroys the distillery. The architect Charles Doig is called in to design the new facilities.

1921 – Robert Thorne & Sons Ltd sells Aberlour to W. H. Holt & Sons, a brewery near Manchester.

1945 – S. Campbell & Sons Ltd buys the distillery.

1962 – Aberlour terminates floor malting.

1973 – Number of stills are increased from two to four.

1975 – Pernod Ricard buys Campbell Distilleries.

2000 – Aberlour a´bunadh is launched. A limited 30 year old cask strength is released.

2001 – Pernod Ricard buys Chivas Brothers from Seagrams and merges Chivas Brothers and Campbell Distilleries under the brand Chivas Brothers.

2002 – A new, modernized visitor centre is inaugurated in August.

2008 – The 18 year old is also introduced outside France.

Aberlour 12 year old

GS – The nose offers brown sugar, honey and sherry, with a hint of grapefruit citrus. The palate is sweet, with buttery caramel, maple syrup and eating apples. Liquorice, peppery oak and mild smoke in the finish.

DR – The nose combines horse chestnut casing then sweet melon and fresh spearmint, the taste is beautifully fresh and clean, with mint and gentle fruit.

In 2008 Aberlour surpassed Glenfiddich on the French market and thus became the single malt leader there. To make it big in France is an important step in developing a brand. France is, since 1998 when the US was left behind, without comparison the biggest market for Scotch whisky in the world in terms of volume. The equivalent of 179 million bottles (including bulk imports) of Scotch whisky were imported last year, which corresponds to 15% of the total volume sold in the world. This can be compared to 89 million bottles 20 years ago. If one looks at the other big markets in the Mediterranean area, France fared well in 2009 with a 12% increase, despite a declining single malt segment.

The distillery is equipped with one semi-lauter mash tun, six stainless steel washbacks and two pairs of stills. There are five warehouses on site (three racked and two dunnage) but only two racked, holding a total of 27,000 casks, are used for maturation. About half of the production is used for single malts.

The packaging of the whole range was upgraded in 2010 to achieve a more consistent look and also to include more information on production and maturation of the different expressions.

The core range of Aberlour includes a *10 year old* (sherry/bourbon), a *12 year old Double Cask* matured, a *16 year old Double Cask* matured and *a'bunadh*, of which there are 30 batches launched up to and including summer of 2010. A new expression in spring 2008 was the *18 year old*, previously sold exclusively in France. In France, a *10 year old Sherry Cask Finish* and the *15 year Cuvée Marie d'Ecosse* are available. Two 'exclusives' are available for the duty free market – *12 year old sherry matured* and *15 year old Double Cask* matured. Recent independent bottlings include two from Duncan Taylor (1993 and 1995) and a 16 year old from Speciality Drinks.

a'bunadh batch 30

Allt-a-Bhainne

Owner: **Region/district:**
Chivas Brothers Ltd   Speyside
(Pernod Ricard)

Founded: **Status:**   **Capacity:**
1975   Active   4 000 000 litres

Address: Glenrinnes, Dufftown,
Banffshire AB55 4DB

Tel: **website:**
01542 783200   -

History:
1975 – The distillery is founded by Chivas
Brothers, a subsidiary of Seagrams, in order to
secure malt whisky for its blended whiskies. The
total cost amounts to £2.7 million.

1989 – Production has doubled.

2001 – Pernod Ricard takes over Chivas Brothers
from Seagrams.

2002 – Mothballed in October.

2005 – Production restarts in May.

Deerstalker 12 year old

GS – Cereal and toffee on the sherbety nose,
with mildly metallic notes. The palate is
light, with fresh fruits. Medium length and
warming in the finish.

DR – Autumn fields and damp hay on the
nose, a richer, sweeter earth and heathery
taste on the palate and a gentle rounded
finish.

Allt-a-Bhainne is definitely one of the most unknown distilleries in Scotland. There are two reasons for this; one is that the whisky has never been bottled by the owner and the second is that its location is in a remote part of the Highlands, halfway between Dufftown and Glenlivet. There is no visitor centre. Allt-a-Bhainne, like its sister distillery Braeval a few kilometres away, were both established by Seagrams in the mid seventies, in order to produce malt whisky for blended Scotch and that is exactly what they have been doing ever since. In the case of Allt-a-Bhainnes it is to become a part of, especially, Chivas Regal and 100 Pipers. The latter brand, introduced in 1966, peaked in 2005 with a 340% increase in six years to 3.5 million cases. It has been going downhill since and in 2009, 100 Pipers 'only' sold 2 million cases. The main market is Thailand and the general decrease in whisky sales there has affected the brand.

The modern distillery is, surprisingly, equipped with a traditional mash tun with rake and ploughs, despite the modern production novelty called the lauter mash tun being introduced for whisky production already a decade prior to Allt-a-Bhainne's commissioning. The reason was that the Distilleries Director of Chivas Brothers at the time, Stuart McBain, was not in favour of this innovation and decided that traditional mash tuns should be installed at both Allt-a-Bhainne and its sister distillery Braeval. The rest of the equipment consists of eight stainless steel washbacks and two pairs of stills. There is capacity for 25 mashes per week. The whisky is not filled in casks on site but transported by lorry to a facility in Keith.

There are no official bottlings of Allt-a-Bhainne and according to Chivas Brothers there are no plans for any either. Independent bottlings can be found, though, in the form of Deerstalker 12 year old from Aberko.

Deerstalker 12 year old

Whisky Chronology

continued on page 143

1644 The Scottish parliament instates a new law on Excise Duty to be paid for each pint of aqua vitae that is produced.

1698 Berry Bros. is founded.

1756 Arthur Guinness Son & Co. is established.

1774 A law prohibiting wash stills less than 400 gallons and spirit stills less than 100 gallons is passed.

1784 The Wash Act is introduced to encourage legal distilling in the Highlands.

1805 Seager Evans (producer of gin) is formed.

1814 Matthew Gloag embarks on a career as a whisky merchant in Perth.

1814 The Excise Act states that the smallest size of a Highland still is to be 500 gallons.

1816 The Small Stills Act states that the smallest allowed size of a still is 40 gallons in all of Scotland.

1820 John Walker establishes himself as a grocer and wine and spirits merchant in Kilmarnock.

1823 An Excise Act states that a licence is required to suppress illicit distilling.

1826 Robert Stein invents a patent still for continuous distilling.

1827 George Ballantine becomes established as a grocer and wine merchant in Edinburgh.

1828 J. & A. Mitchell & Co. (Springbank) is founded.

1830 Aenas Coffey patents an improved version of Robert Steins patent still which is named Coffey still.

1830 William Teacher obtains a liquor licence for a shop in Glasgow.

1831 Justerini & Brooks is formed.

1841 James Chivas forms a company in Aberdeen.

1842 William Cadenhead Ltd is formed.

1846 John Dewar is established as a wholesale wine and spirit merchant in Perth.

1853 Andrew Usher & Co. starts to produce blended whisky.

1857 Walter and Alfred Gilbey start their career as wine merchants in London.

1857 Joseph Seagram & Sons is founded.

1857 William and Robert Hill join forces with William Thomson and found Hill Thomson & Co.

1858 James and John Chivas found Chivas Brothers.

1860 Roberston & Baxter is established.

1865 Eight Lowland grain distilleries form Scotch Distillers Association.

1865 The passing of The Blending Act allows for malt and grain whisky being blended.

1869 W. P. Lowrie & Co. is founded.

1870 Greenlees Brothers is established.

1874 The North of Scotland Malt Distillers Association is founded.

1875 William Teacher founds William Teacher & Sons.

1877 Distillers Company Limited (DCL) is founded by six grain distilleries.

1882 James Whyte and Charles Mackay found Whyte & Mackay.

1885 The North British Distillery Co. is formed.

1886 Alexander Walker brings in his sons to the company and founds John Walker & Sons Ltd.

1886 William Grant and Sons is founded.

1887 Highland Distillers is founded.

1888 John Alicius Haig founds Haig & Haig Ltd.

1890 Mackie & Co. is established.

1893 McDonald & Muir is founded.

1895 Gordon & MacPhail is founded.

1895 Arthur Bell & Sons is founded.

1896 Matthew Gloag & Son establish The Grouse.

1898 The Pattison crash.

1906 Buchanan takes over W. P. Lowrie.

1907 Robertson & Baxter buys Haig & Haig.

1914 Scottish Malt Distillers is founded.

1915 Buchanan and Dewars merge into Scotch Whisky Brands.

1915 Immature spirits act requires that whisky must be bonded for two years prior to bottling.

1916 The bonding time is increased to three years.

1917 The Whisky Association, a predecessor to SWA, is formed.

1919 James Barclay and R. A. McKinlay acquire Ballantines.

1919 Scotch Whisky Brands becomes Buchanan & Dewar.

1919 John Haig & Co. and Andrew

Usher & Co. join DCL.

1920 Prohibition is introduced in the United States.

1922 Roberston & Baxter is acquired by DCL, Walker and Buchanan-Dewar.

1924 Sir Peter Mackie dies and the company changes name to White Horse Distillers.

1925 The Big Amalgamation – DCL merges with Buchanan-Dewar and Walker.

1925 DCL acquires W. P. Lowrie & Co.

1925 DCL buys Scottish Malt Distillers.

1926 Pot-Still Malt Distillers replaces North of Scotland Malt Distillers Association.

1927 DCL acquires White Horse Distillers.

1928 Distillers Corporation of Canada buys Joseph E. Seagram & Sons.

1933 The Prohibition ends in the USA.

1934 Arthur Bell & Sons buys P. Mackenzie & Co.

1935 William Sanderson & Son merges with Booth's Distillers.

1935 Hiram Walker acquires George Ballantine & Son.

1936 Seager Evans buys W. H. Chaplin and the brand Long John.

1936 Lundy & Morrison buys Chivas Bros.

1937 Hiram Walker (Scotland) is formed.

1942 Scotch Whisky Association (SWA) is formed.

1949 Lundie & Morrison sells Chivas Bros to Robert Brown & Co. (subsidiary of Seagrams).

1950 Seagrams buys Strathisla and transfers administration to Chivas Brothers.

1950 Douglas Laing & Co. is founded.

1951 Morrison Bowmore Distillers Ltd is founded.

1952 George & G. J. Smith Ltd and J. & J. Grant form The Glenlivet & Glen Grant Distillers Ltd.

1952 Justerini & Brooks merges with Twiss, Browning & Hallowes and form United Wine Traders.

1956 Inver House is founded.

1956 Seager Evans is acquired by Schenley Industries Inc.

1958 Watney Mann is formed through merger between Watney, Coombe Reid & Co. and Mann, Crossman & Paulin Ltd.

Ardbeg

Owner:
Glenmorangie Co
(Moët Hennessy)

Region/district: The
Islay

Founded: 1815

Status: Active (vc)

Capacity: 1 150 000 litres

Address: Port Ellen, Islay, Argyll PA42 7EA

Tel: 01496 302244 (vc)

website: www.ardbeg.com

History:

1794 – First record of a distillery at Ardbeg. It was founded by Alexander Stewart.

1798 – The MacDougalls, later to become licensees of Ardbeg, are active on the site through Duncan MacDougall.

1815 – The current distillery is founded by John MacDougall, son of Duncan MacDougall.

1853 – Alexander MacDougall, John's son, dies and sisters Margaret and Flora MacDougall, assisted by Colin Hay, continue the running of the distillery. Colin Hay takes over the licence when the sisters die.

1888 – Colin Elliot Hay and Alexander Wilson Gray Buchanan renew their license.

1900 – Colin Hay's son takes over the license.

1959 – Ardbeg Distillery Ltd is founded.

1973 – Hiram Walker and Distillers Company Ltd jointly purchase the distillery for £300,000 through Ardbeg Distillery Trust.

1974 – Widely considered as the last vintage of 'old, peaty' Ardbeg. Malt which has not been produced in the distillery's own maltings is used in increasingly larger shares after this year.

1977 – Hiram Walker assumes single control of the distillery. Ardbeg closes its maltings.

1979 – Kildalton, a less peated malt, is produced over a number of years.

1981 – The distillery closes in March.

1987 – Allied Lyons takes over Hiram Walker and thereby Ardbeg.

1989 – Production is restored. All malt is taken from Port Ellen.

1996 – The distillery closes in July and Allied Distillers decides to put it up for sale.

Lord Robertson inspecting his cask

Ardbeg retains its position as a cult whisky with thousands of dedicated followers around the world. This was clearly shown when its website crashed on two occasions during 2010 - when Rollercoaster and Supernova 2010 were put up for sale. It comes as no surprise that Distillery Manager, Mickey Heads made every effort to increase production capacity by 15% to 1.15 million litres of alcohol with the whisky in such high demand. The whole output is used for their own needs and the owners have not furnished independent bottlers with Ardbeg spirit since 1997.

The distillery is equipped with a stainless steel mash tun, six washbacks made of Oregon pine and one pair of stills. In the spirit still, installed as recently as 2001, lies a large part of the secret of Ardbeg's taste; compared to its neighbours Laphroaig and Lagavulin the peatiness is supplemented by a fruitiness which gives Ardbeg its own very special style and sometimes the nickname "the peaty paradox". The character is achieved by a purifier attached to the spirit still and increasing the reflux. An unpeated Ardbeg known as Kildalton is produced for a few weeks a year since 1999 and was released in 2004. The peated malt is bought from Port Ellen and the unpeated from the mainland. The specification of Ardbeg's malt is 55 ppm which gives c 23 ppm in the finished spirit.

The core range consists of the *10 year old, Uiegedail* and *Corryvreckan*. In 2008 the lightly peated (8 ppm) *Blasda* was released. The peatiest ever release from Ardbeg, at the opposite end of the scale from Blasda, is called *Supernova* and was released in early 2009. Its phenol level was well in excess of 100ppm. This whisky is from 2001 and has been matured in first fill bourbon casks (70%) and sherry butts (30%). The second edition of this heavily peated expression, *Supernova 2010*, was released in May 2010 with the same phenols level but slightly higher alcohol strength. A couple of months earlier, *Rollercoaster* was released to celebrate the 10th anniversary of the Ardbeg Committee to which 50,000 Ardbeg fans can count themselves as members. The Rollercoaster was a vatting of one cask from each year between 1997 and 2006 and, although most casks were ex bourbon, there were also a couple of ex sherry butts included. A special single cask was also launched in summer of 2010 when former Secretary General of NATO, Lord Robertson, donated a cask that was laid down 10 years ago when he visited his native Islay and Ardbeg distillery. All 220 bottles were sold for charity.

History (continued):

1997 – Glenmorangie plc buys the distillery for £7 million (whereof £5.5 million is for whisky in storage). On stream from 25th June. Ardbeg 17 years old and Provenance are launched

1998 – A new visitor centre opens.

2000 – Ardbeg 10 years is introduced. The Ardbeg Committee is launched and has 30 000 members after a few years.

2001 – Lord of the Isles 25 years and Ardbeg 1977 are launched.

2002 – Ardbeg Committee Reserve and Ardbeg 1974 are launched.

2003 – Uigeadail is launched.

2004 – Very Young Ardbeg (6 years) and a limited edition of Ardbeg Kildalton (1300 bottles) are launched. The latter is an un-peated cask strength from 1980.

2005 – Serendipity is launched.

2006 – Ardbeg 1965 and Still Young are launched. Distillery Manager Stuart Thomson leaves Ardbeg after nine years. Almost There (9 years old) and Airigh Nam Beist are released.

2007 – Ardbeg Mor, a 10 year old in 4.5 litre bottles is released.

2008 – The new 10 year old, Corryvreckan, Rennaissance, Blasda and Mor II are released.

2009 – Supernova is released, the peatiest expression from Ardbeg ever.

2010 – Rollercoaster and Supernova 2010 are released.

Ardbeg 10 year old

GS – Quite sweet on the nose, with soft peat, carbolic soap and Arbroath smokies. Burning peats and dried fruit, followed by sweeter notes of malt and a touch of liquorice in the mouth. Extremely long and smoky in the finish, with a fine balance of cereal sweetness and dry peat notes.

DR – Intense smoke and tar on the nose but with some distinctive sweet lemon notes, a mouth-coating palate with honeyed but firey peat, completely balanced and impressive, and a long smoke tail at the finish.

Uigeadail   *Supernova 2010*   *Rollercoaster*

10 years old   *Corryvreckan*

Ardmore

Owner:
Beam Global
Spirits & Wine

Region/district:
Highland

Founded: 1898

Status: Active

Capacity: 5 200 000 litres

Address: Kennethmont,
Aberdeenshire AB54 4NH

Tel: 01464 831213

website: www.ardmorewhisky.com

History:

1898 – Adam Teacher, son of William Teacher, starts the construction of Ardmore Distillery which eventually becomes William Teacher & Sons' first distillery. Adam Teacher passes away before it is completed.

1955 – Stills are increased from two to four.

1973 – A visitor centre is constructed.

1974 – Another four stills are added, increasing the total to eight.

1976 – Allied Breweries takes over William Teacher & Sons and thereby also Ardmore. The own maltings (Saladin box) is terminated.

1999 – A 12 year old is released to commemorate the distillery's 100th anniversary. A 21 year old is launched in a limited edition.

2002 – Ardmore is one of the last distilleries to abandon direct heating (by coal) of the stills in favour of indirect heating through steam.

2005 – Jim Beam Brands becomes new owner when it takes over some 20 spirits and wine brands from Allied Domecq for five billion dollars.

2007 – Ardmore Traditional Cask is launched.

2008 – A 25 and a 30 year old are launched.

Ardmore Traditional

GS – A nose of smoked haddock and butter, plus sweet, fruity malt and spices. Sweet and initially creamy on the palate, spices, peat smoke, tobacco and vanilla emerge and blend together. The finish is long and mellow.

DR – Unique and remarkable mix of burnt meat savouriness on the nose, and a delicatessen of flavours on the palate, smoked vanilla, burnt fruit and a distinctive and highly addictive sweet and savoury mix towards the peated finish.

Ardmore single malt gained wider recognition in 2007 when Ardmore Traditional Cask was launched. The current owner, Beam Global, certainly shows a greater interest for the distillery's opportunities on the single malt market than the previous owner, Allied Domecq, did.

Twelve bins, holding more than 1,000 tonnes of malted barley, gives Ardmore unusually good possibilities to store its malt. The distillery is also equipped with a large (12.5 tonnes charge) cast iron mash tun, 14 Douglas fir washbacks and four pairs of stills equipped with sub-coolers to give more copper contact. The process of adding water to the mash to extract sugar, is often done in three rounds with a temperature that is successively increased. Most distilleries add the second water at circa 80-85 degrees, but Ardmore does it at a staggering 95 degrees! This regime can be traced back many years when temperature was raised following a bad harvest and as malt quality improved, the temperature was never brought down to typical levels again.

Ardmore has always been known to use peated malt (12-14 ppm), but for 18 of the 47 production weeks, an unpeated version called Ardlair is produced, which is used by other companies as a blending malt. At the moment, Ardmore is doing 24 mashes per week resulting in 4.9 million litres. Mostly ex bourbon barrels are filled, but also a few Pedro Ximenez sherry, port and cognac can be found in the warehouses, where the oldest cask is from 1978. Plenty of smaller quarter casks are also in use as a result from the trials that former owner, Allied Domecq, started years ago.

Ardmore is an important part of the Teacher's blend and 35% of the 36 different malts (corresponds to 15% of the total quantity) which are included in this blend is Ardmore.

The core expression is the *Traditional* with no age statement and with a 10 months finish in quarter casks. In 2008 a *25 year old* was launched for UK and duty free while a *30 year old* was released for the American market.

Ardmore Traditional Cask

Arran

Owner: Isle of Arran Distillers   **Region/district:** Islands (Arran)

Founded: 1993   **Status:** Active (vc)   **Capacity:** 750 000 litres

Address: Lochranza, Isle of Arran KA27 8HJ

Tel: 01770 830264   **website:** www.arranwhisky.com

History:

1993 – Harold Currie founds the distillery.

1995 – Production starts in full on 17th August.

1996 – A one year old spirit is released.

1997 – A visitor centre is opened by the Queen.

1998 – The first release is a 3 year old.

1999 – The Arran 4 years old is released.

2002 – Single Cask 1995 is launched.

2003 – Single Cask 1997, non-chill filtered and Calvados finish is launched.

2004 – Cognac finish, Marsala finish, Port finish and Arran First Distillation 1995 are launched.

2005 – Arran 1996 is launched (6,000 bottles). Two more finishes are launched - Chateau Margaux and Grand Cru Champagne.

2006 – After an unofficial launch in 2005, Arran 10 years old is released as well as a couple of new wood finishes.

2007 – Arran is named Scottish Distiller of the Year by Whisky Magazine. Four new wood finishes and Gordon's Dram are released.

2008 – The first 12 year old is released as well as four new wood finishes.

2009 – Peated single casks, two wood finishes and 1996 Vintage are released.

2010 – A 14 year old, Rowan Tree, three cask finishes and Machrie Moor (peated) are released.

Arran 14 year old

GS – Very fragrant and perfumed on the nose, with peaches, brandy and ginger snaps. Smooth and creamy on the palate, with spicy summer fruits, apricots and nuts. The lingering finish is nutty and slowly drying.

DR – The precocious ten year old becomes a testy teenager. If the 12 year old was a diversion this is right on track - with sweet, fresh and zesty nose, and rich creamy and rounded palate defined by vanilla, lemon and cream soda. The finish is long and full.

The sales of Arran single malt has certainly gathered momentum since the official release of their 10 year old in 2006. More than 150,000 bottles are sold annually while the first batch to China is now ready for dispatch. In 2009, Arran was listed by the Norwegian monopoly and had, after five months, become the second best selling malt in Norway after Glenfiddich. The North American market is also in focus and a new sales manager was hired in 2010 with the specific task of increasing sales across the Atlantic.

The semi-lauter mash tun, the four Oregon Pine washbacks and the two stills all stand in one room, which allows the production to be easily overviewed by the 60,000 annual visitors to the distillery. One dunnage warehouse holds 3,000 casks and a racked warehouse is of a similar capacity. Total capacity is 750,000 litres and the planned production for 2010 is 250,000 litres. Of that, 8,000-10,000 litres has since 2004 been a peated version with a phenol content of 12ppm.

When the distillery launched the new 14 year old, in August 2010, with a combination of 2/3 ex bourbon and 1/3 ex sherry, it was a desired replacement of the 12 year old. Thus, phase two of its plan for three core expressions - 10, 14 and 18 year old – was completed. The final step will be the 18 year old due for release in 2014. In addition to the *10* and *14 year olds*, the current core range consists of *100 Proof* and *Robert Burns*. The latter is a single malt usually bottled as a 5 year old. Apart from the yearly single casks from ex sherry and ex bourbon casks, limited releases in 2010 include the second edition of *Icons of Arran* called *Rowan Tree*, a 1999 Vintage released to celebrate the 15th anniversary of the distillery, three *cask finishes* (*port, sauternes* and *amarone*) and, finally, a peated expression which was released in September. This received a new brand name, *Machrie Moor*, after a peat bog on Arran and is made up from stock from 2004 and 2005.

14 years old

Auchentoshan

Owner:
Morrison Bowmore (Suntory)

Region/district:
Lowlands

Founded: 1823
Status: Active (vc)
Capacity: 1 750 000 litres

Address: Dalmuir, Clydebank, Glasgow G81 4SJ

Tel: 01389 878561
website: www.auchentoshan.com

History:

1800 – First mention of the distillery Duntocher, which may be identical to Auchentoshan.

1823 – An official license is obtained by the owner, Mr. Thorne.

1903 – The distillery is purchased by John Maclachlan.

1923 – G. & J. Maclachlan goes bankrupt and a new company, Maclachlans Ltd, is formed.

1941 – The distillery is severely damaged by a German bomb raid and reconstruction does not commence until 1948.

1960 – Maclachlans Ltd is purchased by the brewery J. & R. Tennant Brewers.

1969 – Auchentoshan is bought by Eadie Cairns Ltd who starts major modernizations.

1984 – Stanley P. Morrison, eventually becoming Morrison Bowmore, becomes new owner.

1994 – Suntory buys Morrison Bowmore.

2002 – Auchentoshan Three Wood is launched.

2004 – More than a £1 million is spent on a new, refurbished visitor centre. The oldest Auchentoshan ever, 42 years, is released.

2006 – Auchentoshan 18 year old is released.

2007 – A 40 year old and a 1976 30 year old are released.

2008 – New packaging as well as new expressions - Classic, 18 year old and 1988.

2010 – Two vintages, 1977 and 1998, are released.

Auchentoshan 12 year old

GS – The nose features fruit & nut chocolate, cinnamon and oak. Smooth and sweet in the mouth, with citrus fruits and cloves. Drying gently in a gingery finish.

DR – Toffee, rose water and Milk Chocolate Crisp on the nose, grape and crisp apple on the palate before a spicy fruity interplay in a lengthy finish.

Most Scottish distilleries lost sales volumes during 2008 and 2009 due to the recession, but Auchentoshan was an exception. The total increase between 2007 and 2009, when 41,000 cases were sold, was almost 30%. Taiwan, the UK, Scandinavia and USA are the biggest markets.

The distillery lies embedded in a valley near the busy A82. This has created problems with floods, most recently in 2008, but ramps that lead the water away are now in place.

The distillery is equipped with a semi-lauter mash tun, four Oregon Pine washbacks and three stills. Auchentoshan is the only distillery in Scotland, except for Springbank with its Hazelburn expression (and recently BenRiach), that practises triple distillation. There are another three washbacks which are not in use at the moment. The spirit matures in three dunnage and two racked warehouses. For several years now, Auchentoshan has produced at levels far below its capacity. 500,000 litres are, for example, planned for 2010. The reason is not that there is a low demand for its produce, but a decision that dates to 2005, when it was decided that sales to blenders would cease.

Comparatively few visitors reach Auchentoshan, despite its proximity to Glasgow, but they are on the increase, thanks to an exquisite visitor centre which was inaugurated in 2005. The style is very contemporary which includes a wooden bar, shaped as a circle, where the distillery tour ends.

The Auchentoshan Ale - an idea originating from Jeremy Stephens, the Distillery Manager and former brewer, was launched for the first time in connection with the Auchentoshan Whisky Festival in 2009. Wort, from the mash tun, is used and the "brewery" is fitted into a small, converted yeast store next to the washbacks.

The core range consists of *Classic, 12 years, Three Wood, 18 years* and *21 years. Select* (no age statement) has been moved to the duty free range. A *1978* bourbon matured was released in 2009 and limited bottlings from 2010 include a *Vintage 1977* and a *Vintage 1998* matured in a fino sherry cask.

12 years old

Meet the Manager

JEREMY STEPHENS
DISTILLERY MANAGER, AUCHENTOSHAN DISTILLERY

When did you start working in the whisky business and when did you start at Auchentoshan?

I started at Auchentoshan in March 2006, my first whisky distillery.

Had you been working in other lines of business before whisky?

I began my career as a Lab Technician at The Badger Brewery in 1997 before moving to Fullers a year later, where I learned production brewing. After 5 years in brewing, I moved to Bairds Malt and managed their Grantham Maltings for 4 years.

What kind of education or training do you have?

I hold an honours degree in Chemistry and Maths, the Diploma in Brewing, the General Certificate in Distilling, and am currently reading for the Diploma in Distilling.

Describe your career in the whisky business.

Auchentoshan is my first and only distillery.

What are your main tasks as a manager?

To ensure the production of a high quality new make spirit in accordance with Health and Safety, Environmental and Quality systems, while maximising profitability and minimising liability. I also enjoy promoting our brand internationally and giving our visitors a memorable experience at Auchentoshan.

What are the biggest challenges of being a distillery manager?

We have a great team at Auchentoshan, so the day-to-day running of the plant usually presents few problems, bar the occasional technical breakdown. The main challenges are satisfying legislative demands, so I need to keep abreast of industry affairs and understand where we fit into the bigger picture. However, the biggest challenge is a personal one, and that is to dispel untruths about whisky and promote a more embracing and inclusive image, in which everyone can find their place, and enjoy!

What would be the worst that could go wrong in the production process?

In order of importance:
Loss of life
Loss of brand image
Loss of product
Loss of sanity!

How would you describe the character of Auchentoshan single malt?

Exceptionally smooth and delicate. For me, there is real elegance and balance to our expressions, which makes them accessible, yet distinct.

What are the main features in the process at Auchentoshan, contributing to this character?

Our traditional practice of triple distillation gives the new make spirit its unique and gentle qualities into which wood characters can easily infuse. This gives a fresh, clean whisky, which carries the distinct flavour of the new make while openly expressing the nature of the casks.

What is your favourite expression of Auchentoshan and why?

I would have to say Three Wood. The intense, sweet and complex nature of the whisky has instant appeal, and often takes people by surprise. Many have been persuaded into the world of whisky by this unusual expression as it challenges the perception of malt whisky as something difficult by offering something accessible, yet still full of character. It also has no age statement on the bottle, which I like, as it transcends the pretensions of age. An older whisky is not necessarily a better whisky, it's a matter of personal choice. The character of a whisky changes over time, but quality is timeless.

If it were your decision alone – what new expression of Auchentoshan would you like to see released?

I'd like to see more wine matured whisky coming out of Auchentoshan as the 1999 Bordeaux sold out too quickly. I believe the purer nature of the new make spirit can mature relatively more quickly, and is well placed to hold its own character while bringing out the elements of different wood.

If you had to choose a favourite dram other than Auchentoshan, what would that be?

Although loyal to my brand, I am mostly governed by fickleness as to what I drink from day to day, so I try to keep a fairly eclectic mix of whiskies. I'm also discovering the wonderful world of rum…

What are the biggest changes you have seen the past 10-15 years in your profession?

A move from the old dogma that a Distillery Manager should be able to fit a round of golf comfortably into his day while closely guarding his distilling secrets to the new and more benevolent philosophies of knowledge-sharing and securing the integrity of the brand by careful and informed management. Of course, this needs to be balanced by making time to relax and enjoy the finished product!

Do you see any major changes in the next 10 years to come?

While already a relatively green industry, we have targets to meet to further help the environment. This is an enjoyable part of my job as it's beneficial to both the planet and our industry's image. I'm also pleased to see new micro-distilleries coming through, and I'm looking forward to sampling some potentially unusual products in the coming years.

Do you have any special interests/hobbies that you pursue?

I have played keyboards with bands most of my adult life and I try to attend music concerts as often as I can.

You have a background as a beer brewer. How does that help you in your job as distillery manager?

Brewing taught me to be disciplined and hygienic. In distilling, I learned to enjoy a more natural process. The management side of the job is essentially the same, except whereas brewing is immediate, distilling takes its time!

Auchentoshan distillery is surprisingly unknown to the local community despite being situated a few miles from Glasgow. How can you change that?

That's a good question and is most certainly something we're hoping to change – and not just amongst the local community. We really believe the style of Auchentoshan, created by our triple distillation process offers something completely unique and distinct from other single malts, and is something people need to know about! We'll be holding our third annual Auchentoshan Whisky Festival in August and are looking forward to welcoming the people of Glasgow to the Distillery once again!

Auchroisk

Owner:
Diageo

Region/district:
Speyside

Founded: **Status:**   **Capacity:**
1974   Active   3 800 000 litres

Address: Mulben, Banffshire AB55 6XS

Tel: **website:**
01542 885000   www.malts.com

History:

1972 – Building of the distillery commences by Justerini & Brooks (which, together with W. A. Gilbey, make up the group IDV) in order to produce blending whisky. In February the same year IDV is purchased by the brewery Watney Mann which, in July, merges into Grand Metropolitan.

1974 – The distillery is completed and, despite the intention of producing malt for blending, the first year's production is sold 12 years later as single malt thanks to the high quality.

1986 – The first whisky is marketed under the name Singleton.

1997 – Grand Metropolitan and Guinness merge into the conglomerate Diageo. Simultaneously, the subsidiaries United Distillers (to Guinness) and International Distillers & Vintners (to Grand Metropolitan) form the new company United Distillers & Vintners (UDV).

2001 – The name Singleton is abandoned and the whisky is now marketed under the name of Auchroisk in the Flora & Fauna series.

2003 – Apart from the 10 year old in the Flora & Fauna series, a 28 year old from 1974, the distillery's first year, is launched in the Rare Malt series.

2010 – A Manager's Choice single cask and a limited 20 year old are released.

Auchroisk 10 year old

GS – Malt and spice on the light nose, with developing nuts and floral notes. Quite voluptuous on the palate, with fresh fruit and milk chocolate. Raisins in the finish.

DR – Young and zesty and citrusy on the nose, warming tangerine and citrus fruits and a touch of salt on the palate, medium long malty finish.

Auchroisk distillery was built at the same time as Braeval and Allt-a-Bhainne, around 1973, and (with the exception of Kininvie in 1990) they were to be the last big distilleries to be developed for more than 30 years until 2007, when Ailsa Bay and later Roseisle were founded.

Auchroisk is equipped with one stainless steel mash tun, eight stainless steel washbacks and four pairs of stills which are situated in a modern and very spacious still room. The washbacks are large (holding 50,000 litres each) and one washback can serve all four wash stills (which can hold 12,700 litres each). Fermentation in the washbacks can often be quite vigorous and to prevent overflow most distilleries have rotating blades to keep the froth away. At Auchroisk, however, each washback is equipped with four stainless steel bars containing a fibre-based solution to prevent frothing.

The huge warehouses at Auchroisk which can store 250,000 casks have a special role in Diageo's production of blended whiskies. New make comes by tanker from many other distilleries, especially Knockando, Glen Spey and Strathmill. They are all, in common with Auchroisk, vital parts of J&B and filled into casks for maturation. The matured malt whisky is then blended at Auchroisk and shipped to any of the bottling plants where the final blending with grain spirit as well as bottling takes place. This blend of malt whiskies is called part blend.

The core range from Auchroisk is simply the *10 year old Flora & Fauna* bottling. In 2010, the distillery became better known when two new, limited, releases appeared. The first was a *single sherry cask* distilled in 1999 and released as part of the *Manager's Choice* series. Six months later a *20 year old* from 1990 was launched in connection with the traditional *Special Release*. It was, again, a cask strength but was a mix of American and European oak. The very first time that the whisky was bottled, it was under the name Singleton, as Auchroisk was considered too difficult to pronounce. The name Singleton is now used for single malts from Dufftown, Glendullan and Glen Ord.

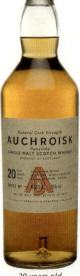

20 years old

Aultmore

Owner:
John Dewar & Sons
(Bacardi)

Region/district:
Speyside

Founded:
1896

Status:
Active

Capacity:
3 030 000 litres

Address: Keith, Banffshire AB55 6QY

Tel:
01542 881800

website:
-

History:
1896 – Alexander Edward, owner of Benrinnes and co-founder of Craigellachie Distillery, builds Aultmore.

1897 – Production starts.

1898 – Production is doubled; the company Oban & Aultmore Glenlivet Distilleries Ltd manages Aultmore.

1923 – Alexander Edward sells Aultmore for £20,000 to John Dewar & Sons.

1925 – Dewar's becomes part of Distillers Company Limited (DCL).

1930 – The administration is transferred to Scottish Malt Distillers (SMD).

1971 – The stills are increased from two to four.

1991 – UDV launches a 12-year old Aultmore in the Flora & Fauna series.

1996 – A 21 year old cask strength is marketed as a Rare Malt.

1998 – Diageo sells Dewar's and Bombay Gin to Bacardi for £1,150 million.

2004 – A new official bottling is launched (12 years old).

Aultmore 12 year old

GS – Gentle spice and fudge notes on the fragrant nose. Fresh fruits and restrained vanilla in the mouth. Nutty and drying in a medium-length finish.

DR – Orange blossom and flowers on the nose, lemon and lime Starburst on the palate, with late sherbet spicy and drying and more-ish finish. Altogether, zesty and very pleasant.

Aultmore distillery was built towards the end of perhaps the greatest whisky boom we have ever witnessed - the last two decades of the 19th century. Many more distilleries were founded at that time and the future looked bright. Just two years after Aultmore was completed, the market plummeted through the Pattison crash. One would have thought that with Aultmore being one of the major suppliers of whisky to the Pattison brothers blending operations, it would be forced into liquidation, like so many other distilleries at that time, but somehow it survived. It was first when the repercussions of WWI and the ensuing Prohibition in the US affected the owners, that they were forced to sell to the larger company, Dewar & Sons, in 1923, to which Aultmore still belongs. Today, virtually nothing of the old Aultmore Distillery is left and the visitor encounters rather traditional industrial buildings which were erected in the early seventies.

Since 2008 production has been running seven days a week which, for 2010, means full capacity of 3 million litres. A Steinecker full lauter mash tun, six washbacks and two pairs of stills are operated. The stillhouse control system was modernised in 2008. All the warehouses were demolished in 1996; in fact, Dewar's no longer has any maturation capacity at any of its distilleries. Instead, the company has redeveloped its headquarters at Westthorn in Glasgow, where another five warehouses have been constructed. A new site at Poniel has been bought where the first two, of 18 planned, warehouses with a total capacity of 140,000 casks were opened in 2009 followed by another four in 2010. Most of the output is, above all, used in Dewar's blended whiskies, but a *12 year old* official bottling appeared on the market in 2004. Recent independent bottlings include a 1997 from Ian MacLeod and a 35 year old distilled in 1974, released by Adelphi Distillery.

12 years old

Balblair

Owner:
Inver House Distillers
(Thai Beverages plc)

Region/district:
Northern Highlands

Founded: 1790   **Status:** Active   **Capacity:** 1 330 000 litres

Address: Edderton, Tain, Ross-shire IV19 1LB

Tel: 01862 821273

website: www.balblair.com

History:

1790 – The distillery is founded by John Ross.

1836 – John Ross dies and his son Andrew Ross takes over with the help of his sons.

1872 – New buildings replace the old.

1873 – Andrew Ross dies and his son James takes over.

1894 – Balnagowan Estate signs a new lease for 60 years with Alexander Cowan. He builds a new distillery, a few kilometres from the old.

1911 – Cowan is forced to cease payments and the distillery closes.

1941 – Balnagowan Estate goes bankrupt and the distillery is put up for sale.

1948 – The lawyer Robert Cumming from Keith buys Balblair for £48,000.

1949 – Production restarts.

1970 – Cumming sells Balblair to Hiram Walker. A third still is installed.

1988 – Allied Distillers becomes the new owner through the merger between Hiram Walker and Allied Vintners.

1996 – Allied Domecq sells the distillery to Inver House Distillers.

2000 – Balblair Elements and the first version of Balblair 33 years are launched.

2001 – Thai company Pacific Spirits (part of the Great Oriole Group) takes over Inver House.

2004 – Balblair 38 years is launched.

2005 – 12 year old Peaty Cask, 1979 (26 years) and 1970 (35 years) are launched.

2006 – International Beverage Holdings acquires Pacific Spirits UK.

2007 – Three new vintages replace the entire former range.

2008 – Vintage 1975 and 1965 are released.

2009 – Vintage 1991 and 1990 are released.

2010 – Vintage 1978 and 2000 are released.

Balblair 2000

GS – Peach and pineapple on the nose, with coconut and honeyed vanilla. Toasted marshmallows with time. Relatively light-bodied, sweet, with lively spice, ginger and youthful oak on the palate. Fudge in the finish, and a contrasting hint of dark chocolate at the last.

DR – Exotic sweet tinned fruits on the nose, syrupy sweet pear, apple and peach on the palate and a dollop of sweet spice towards the end. The finish is sweet, spicy and fruity.

The relaunch of Balblair back in 2007, when the entire range of bottlings with age statements was replaced by vintages, did not have an immediate impact on sales' figures, at least not in terms of volume. Momentum was picked up in 2009, however, when 8,000 cases were sold – double that of the previous year. The main markets are France, Spain, Germany and the UK with plans to develop USA and Taiwan.

Balblair can trace its distilling origins back to the 18th century, but the buildings we see today were initially constructed around the mid 1890s. The equipment consists of a stainless steel mash tun, six Oregon Pine washbacks and one pair of stills. There is actually a third still but it has not been used since 1969. The spirit is matured in eight dunnage warehouses with a capacity of 26,000 casks. Some 12-15% of the production is bottled as single malt, which is filled and stored on site. Currently, a six-day week is in place with 17 mashes per week, and the target for 2010 is to produce 1.4 million litres of alcohol. The water is drawn from Ault Dreag more than 4 miles from the distillery and is pumped to a tank, equipped with a copper filter, on the other side of the road.

In 2007, the first range of vintages appeared - *1979, 1989* and *1997*. All three had been matured in first or second fill bourbon casks. The 1979 was replaced by the *1975*, this time from second filled sherry butts. In autumn 2010, the 1975 was repla-ced by a *1978* and the 1997 by a *2000 vintage*. In 2009, Balblair *1990* was released as a duty free exclusive and in October a limited edition of Balblair *1988* was launched in France, Switzerland and the UK. Early 2010 saw the launch of the bourbon-matured Balblair *1991* for the American market. At least three independent bottlings appeared in 2010; a 19 year old from Dewar Rattray and two 20 year olds released by Cadenheads and Adelphi Distillery.

Balblair 2000

Balmenach

Owner:
Inver House Distillers
(Thai Beverages plc)

Region/district:
Speyside

Founded: **Status:** **Capacity:**
1824   Active   2 000 000 litres

Address: Cromdale, Moray PH26 3PF

Tel:
01479 872569

website:
www.inverhouse.com

History:
1824 – The distillery is licensed to James MacGregor who operated a small farm distillery by the name of Balminoch for decades.

1897 – Balmenach Glenlivet Distillery Company is founded.

1922 – The MacGregor family sells to a consortium consisting of MacDonald Green, Peter Dawson and James Watson.

1925 – The consortium becomes part of Distillers Company Limited (DCL).

1930 – Production is transferred to Scottish Malt Distillers (SMD).

1962 – The number of stills is increased to six.

1964 – Floor maltings replaced with a Saladin box

1992 – The first official bottling is a 12 year old.

1993 – The distillery is mothballed in May.

1997 – Inver House Distillers buys Balmenach from United Distillers.

1998 – Production recommences.

2001 – Thai company Pacific Spirits takes over Inver House at the price of £56 million. The new owner launches a 27 and a 28 year old.

2002 – To commemorate the Queen's Golden Jubilee a limited edition of 800 bottles of 25-year old Balmenach is launched.

2006 – International Beverage Holdings acquires Pacific Spirits UK.

Deerstalker 18 year old

GS – An intriguing and inviting nose, with herbal notes, eucalyptus, heather and hints of sherry. Rich and warming on the palate, big-bodied, with well harmonised malt and sherry flavours prevailing. The finish is long and sophisticated.

DR – Pine needles, lemon and grapefruit and flu powder on the nose, rich sherry and a trace of sulphur on the palate, with savoury lemon and a traces of peat. A medium and citrusy finish.

Balmenach distillery lies along the A95, on the periphery of the Speyside area with Grantown-on-Spey as its closest larger community. It was one of the first distilleries in the area to obtain a distillery licence and soon established a reputation for being a whisky perfectly suitable for blending.

Among InverHouse's five distilleries, Balmenach has the largest production capacity. Their traditional mash tun can hold 8 tonnes which is double that of the other distilleries. While all other distilleries in the group have just the one pair of stills, Balmenach has three pairs. In terms of litres produced in a year, it has been able to increase even further in 2010 to 2.3 million litres. The six washbacks are made of wood and the distillery also practises the traditional way of cooling the spirit vapours, namely by a worm tub with a 94 metre long worm. The three dunnage warehouses have space for 14,000 casks.

However, in spite of its size, Balmenach is the only distillery in the group that does not have an official bottling. One reason for that is that when Inver House Distillers took over from United Distillers in 1997, there was no maturing whisky included in the deal so they had to start from scratch. The entire output, at least for the moment, goes to the company's range of blended whiskies and to the own label blends sold to other companies. This part of the business is 90% in terms of volume and single malts only make up 10%. InverHouse's most famous blended Scotch are MacArthur's, Catto's and Hankey Bannister. Blairmhor blended malt, as well as vodka and gin are also included in the portfolio.

The only "official" bottling so far is the *12 year old Flora & Fauna* from the previous owner and this is now becoming increasingly difficult to find. There are, however, other Balmenach on the market. One is produced by an independent company called Aberko in Glasgow under the name Deerstalker 18 years.

Deerstalker 18 years

Balvenie

Owner:		Region/district:
William Grant & Sons		Speyside

Founded:	Status:	Capacity:
1892	Active (vc)	5 600 000 litres

Address: Dufftown, Keith,
Banffshire AB55 4DH

Tel:	website:
01340 820373	www.thebalvenie.com

History:

1892 – William Grant rebuilds Balvenie New House to Balvenie Distillery (Glen Gordon was the name originally intended). Part of the equipment is brought in from Lagavulin and Glen Albyn.

1893 – The first distillation takes place in May.

1957 – The two stills are increased by another two.

1965 – Two new stills are installed.

1971 – Another two stills are installed and eight stills are now running.

1973 – The first official bottling appears.

1982 – Founder's Reserve, in an eye-catching Cognac-reminiscent bottle, is launched.

1990 – A new distillery, Kininvie, is opened on the premises.

1996 – Two vintage bottlings and a Port wood finish are launched.

2001 – The Balvenie Islay Cask, with 17 years in bourbon casks and six months in Islay casks, is released.

2002 – Balvenie releases 83 bottles of a 50 year old that has been in sherry casks since January 1952. Recommended price £6,000 a bottle.

2004 – The Balvenie Thirty is released to commemorate Malt Master David Stewart's 30th anniversary at Balvenie.

2005 – The Balvenie Rum Wood Finish 14 years old is released.

2006 – The Balvenie New Wood 17 years old, Roasted Malt 14 years old and Portwood 1993 are released.

2007 – Vintage Cask 1974 and Sherry Oak 17 years old are released.

2008 – Signature, Vintage 1976, Balvenie Rose and Rum Cask 17 year old are released.

2009 – Vintage 1978, 17 year old Madeira finish, 14 year old rum finish and Golden Cask 14 years old are released.

2010 – A 40 year old, Peated Cask and Carriban Cask are released.

The Balvenie Doublewood 12 year old

GS – Nuts and spicy malt on the nose, full-bodied, with soft fruit, vanilla, sherry and a hint of peat. Dry and spicy in a luxurious, lengthy finish.

DR – Red fruits and berries, a hint of smoke on the nose, on the palate mouth filling, rich and fruity and, surprisingly, with a peat presence. Lots of sherry and some toffee in the finish.

Balvenie is one of few distilleries still doing some of their own maltings. Thirty tonnes of malt, corresponding to 10% of requirements, are produced every week. For the first six hours the malt is dried using peat and for the remaining 42 hours it is dried with coal. The malted barley is used exclusively for Balvenie single malt and not for the other two malt distilleries in the group - Glenfiddich and Kininvie. The distillery has a full lauter mash tun, nine wooden and five stainless steel washbacks.

The number of wash stills was increased to five and spirit stills to six, divided into two still rooms, in 2008 when the facilities were expanded. This means that 28 mashes per week with an annual capacity of 5.6 million litres of alcohol is now possible. Both bourbon and sherry casks are used, stored in a total of 44 dunnage, racked or palletised warehouses shared with Kininvie and Glenfiddich.

A new Master Blender started his work at William Grant towards the end of 2009, when Brian Kinsman succeeded David Stewart. David had been Master Blender since 1974 and will now continue his work as The Balvenie Malt Master.

The core range consists of *Doublewood 12 years old, Signature 12 years, Single Barrel 15 years, Portwood 21 years* and the *30 year old*. The Signature 12 years (now in its third edition) is a marriage between first fill bourbon barrels, refill bourbon and Oloroso sherry butts and replaced the 10 year old Founder's Reserve a couple of years ago. The most exciting amongst new limited expressions was, of course, *The Balvenie 40 year old* released for travel retail in July 2010. Only 150 bottles were released. Another limited bottling was *The Balvenie Peated cask 17 year old* and the US exclusive rum finish, *Carribean Cask*, launched in autumn 2010. Limited releases during 2009 included *1978 Vintage*, a *17 year old* finished in *Madeira* casks and a new duty free exclusive, *Golden Cask 14 years old* with a finish in Carribean rum.

17 year old Peated cask

Ben Nevis

Owner:
Ben Nevis Distillery Ltd
(Nikka, Asahi Breweries)

Region/district:
Western Highlands

Founded: 1825

Status: Active (vc)

Capacity: 1 800 000 litres

Address: Lochy Bridge, Fort William PH33 6TJ

Tel: 01397 702476

website: www.bennevisdistillery.com

History:

1825 – The distillery is founded by 'Long' John McDonald.

1856 – Long John dies and his son Donald P. McDonald takes over.

1878 – Demand is so great that another distillery, Nevis Distillery, is built nearby.

1908 – Both distilleries merge into one.

1941 – D. P. McDonald & Sons sells the distillery to Ben Nevis Distillery Ltd headed by the Canadian millionaire Joseph W. Hobbs.

1955 – Hobbs installs a Coffey still which makes it possible to produce both grain and malt whisky.

1964 – Joseph Hobbs dies.

1978 – Production is stopped.

1981 – Joseph Hobbs Jr sells the distillery back to Long John Distillers and Whitbread.

1984 – After restoration and reconstruction totalling £2 million, Ben Nevis opens up again.

1986 – The distillery closes again.

1989 – Whitbread sells the distillery to Nikka Whisky Distilling Company Ltd.

1990 – The distillery opens up again.

1991 – A visitor centre is inaugurated.

1996 – Ben Nevis 10 years old is launched.

2006 – A 13 year old port finish is released.

2007 – 1992 single cask is released.

2010 – A 25 year old is released.

Ben Nevis 10 year old

GS – The nose is initially quite green, with developing nutty, orange notes. Coffee, brittle toffee and peat are present on the slightly oily palate, along with chewy oak, which persists to the finish, together with more coffee and a hint of dark chocolate.

DR – Grape skins, over-ripe pear on the nose, baked apple and liquorice roots on the palate, pleasant malty finish.

On the northern outskirts of Fort William and at the foot of the highest mountain in Britain, Ben Nevis, lies the distillery with the same name, the last surviving whisky producer in town. Ben Nevis is currently equipped with one lauter mash tun, six stainless steel washbacks and two made of Oregon pine and two pairs of stills. Two distinctive spirits are distilled at Ben Nevis. Fermentation is 48 hours in the steel washbacks and the spirit is destined to become either single malt or part of the Dew of Ben Nevis blend. In the wooden washbacks, on the other hand, fermentation time is 96 hours and this version, called Coire Leis, is sent as newmake directly to the owners, Nikka, in Japan. It is used there at a very young age in the popular blend Nikka Black (or just Black as it was renamed in 2009). At the moment, the distillery is doing nine mashes per week, which equals 800,000 litres per year.

Ben Nevis had produced peated whisky for some time, filling it into sherry casks, but stopped four years ago. No peated bottlings have yet been released though. The vatting of Dew of Ben Nevis blend, takes place at the distillery and it is bottled at Glen Turner in the Highlands. The single malts and Glencoe vatted malt are both bottled by Duncan Taylor. A combination of bourbon and sherry casks is used for maturation.

Since 1996 the core of the range has been a *10 year old*. Some one-off bottlings have appeared at regular intervals, such as the *13 year old Port finish* released in 2006 and the *1992 single cask* released in 2007. In early 2010, a limited release was made of a *25 year old* which sold out quickly. Another batch was released again in June 2010. It has spent the first 12 years in a fresh bourbon cask that was then re-racked to a fresh sherry cask.

The blended whisky, Dew of Ben Nevis, which occurs in several varieties, is the main seller (40,000 cases per year compared to the single malts 1,000 cases). Glencoe, a vatted malt, is also produced.

10 years old

Meet the Manager

COLIN ROSS
DISTILLERY MANAGER, BEN NEVIS DISTILLERY

When did you start working in the whisky business and when did you start at Ben Nevis?

I started working in the Scotch whisky industry on leaving school in June 1965 and became distillery manager at Ben Nevis the first time in 1983.

Had you been working in other lines of business before whisky?

I have worked in this industry since June 1965 until the present day, all my working life, a total of 45 years.

What kind of education or training do you have?

I was educated to Higher Leaving Certificate level at Milne's High School in Fochabers from 1953 – 1965

Describe your career in the whisky business.

In 1965 I started work as a trainee manager with Chivas Brothers. In 1971, I was appointed Head Brewer at Tormore Distillery where I was to remain for 12/13 years progressing to Assistant Manager. During 1982 I also worked at Ben Nevis distillery when the company were conducting some trial production runs. The next year I was appointed to my first real distillery manager's position at the Ben Nevis distillery. In 1987 I took up the post of manager at Laphroaig Distillery, where I remained for two years until Nikka had purchased Ben Nevis distillery, and I was transferred back to Ben Nevis to be employed as Managing Director for the Ben Nevis Distillery (Fort William) Limited company.

What are your main tasks as a manager?

My main tasks as a manager are to ensure that we operate the distillery to the level of production demanded and within budget and ensuring the safety of staff whilst at work. Then I try to ensure that all our customers and stakeholders receive their orders on time with payments being made on time to maintain cashflow in order that we can keep the business running smoothly.

What are the biggest challenges of being a distillery manager?

The main challenges are satisfying legislative demands, so I need to keep abreast of industry affairs and understand where we fit into the bigger picture. However, the biggest challenge is a personal one, and that is to dispel untruths about whisky and promote a more embracing and inclusive image, in which everyone can find their place, and enjoy!

What would be the worst that could go wrong in the production process?

By far the worst nightmare at a distillery would be to have the warehouses go up in fire. In the production process itself it would be having a still collapse.

How would you describe the character of Ben Nevis single malt?

I feel that the character of Ben Nevis malt is quite unique, not as soft as a typical Speyside although we use the same specification of malted barley, yet not as full-bodied and characterful as the Islays. I suppose we lie somewhere in between, just as we do geographically. It is a sweet whisky with flavours of chocolate and dried fruit, well worth trying!

What are the main features in the process at Ben Nevis, contributing to this character?

The unique selling point with Ben Nevis is the water, running off Britain's highest mountain - possibly the purest water being used in whisky production and we are the only distillery tapping into this source. I also think that the size of the pots of the stills play a significant part in producing such a big whisky.

What is your favourite expression of Ben Nevis and why?

My personal preference is for the younger expressions of Ben Nevis up to and including 21 years old, although our recent 40 years old single blend "Blended at Birth" whisky was just fantastic.

If it were your decision alone – what new expression of Ben Nevis would you like to see released?

Several years ago we produced a port wood finish. I felt that the combination between the Ben Nevis malt and the port cask worked very well and I would like to see this as an on going release.

If you had to choose a favourite dram other than Ben Nevis, what would that be?

I really enjoyed a 15 years old Laphroaig when I worked there but was also fond of the odd Tormore but Glenfarclas has to rank among the finest there is available.

What are the biggest changes you have seen the past 10-15 years in your profession?

When I started in distilling the managers were all totally committed to their post, responsible for all that went on throughout 24 hours a day, 7 days a week. It was not so much a job, more a way of life! This seems to have changed, not only in distilling but in all spheres these days with people enjoying a better work/life balance.

Do you see any major changes in the next 10 years to come?

In recent years we have seen Japanese whiskies being awarded accolades for their quality and being voted the best whisky in the world. We have seen more Irish and American whiskies winning awards and I personally believe that this is something we shall see more and more of in the years to come with quality whiskies being produced all around the world eg. Taiwan, Sweden, India.

Do you have any special interests/hobbies that you pursue?

I enjoy spending time with my family, particularly my two grandsons who are 2 and 3 years old, and when they are not around I do enjoy a good book.

How does it affect your work having the owners and managers sitting in Japan?

It can be quite difficult working with the owners and managers being based in Japan. When I first joined the company in 1989 there was a representative from Nikka based in London. It was great having him in the same time zone and any questions could be raised through him. Not only was he a colleague, but a dear friend.

You used to produce some peated spirit. Any chance we will see that released as a Ben Nevis single malt?

Yes, we experimented with heavily peated malt some years ago, but it is only about 5 years old and some of it has already been sold as bulk malt to a dear customer of ours. I do not know what the longer term plans are for this whisky.

BenRiach

Owner:
Benriach Distillery Co

Region/district:
Speyside

Founded: **Status:** **Capacity:**
1897 Active 2 800 000 litres

Address: Longmorn, Elgin, Morayshire IV30 8SJ

Tel:
01343 862888

website:
www.benriachdistillery.co.uk

History:
1897 – John Duff & Co founds the distillery.

1899 – Longmorn Distilleries Co. buys the distillery.

1903 – The distillery is mothballed.

1965 – The distillery is reopened by the new owner, The Glenlivet Distillers Ltd.

1978 – Seagram Distillers takes over ownership.

1983 – Seagrams starts producing a peated Benriach.

1985 – The number of stills is increased to four.

1994 – The first official bottling is a 10 year old.

1999 – The maltings is decommissioned.

2002 – The distillery is mothballed in October.

2004 – Intra Trading, buys Benriach together with the former Director at Burn Stewart, Billy Walker. The price is £5.4 million including stock.

2004 – Standard, Curiositas and 12, 16 and 20 year olds are released.

2005 – Four different vintages are released in limited editions - 1966, 1970, 1978 och 1984.

2006 – Sixteen new releases, among them a 25 year old, a 30 year old and 8 different vintages.

2007 – A 40 year old and three new heavily peated expressions are released.

2008 – New expressions include a peated Madeira finish, a 15 year old Sauternes finish and nine single casks.

2009 – Two new wood finishes (Moscatel and Gaja Barolo) and nine different single casks are released.

2010 – Triple distilled Solstice, heavily peated Horizons and The Firkin Cask are released.

BenRiach Curiositas

GS – The nose is medicinal, with tarmac and a balancing heathery fragrance. Sweet fruits and beeswax in the mouth merge with major peat smoke flavours. Iodine and black pepper. Spicy, phenolic and tar-like in the finish.

DR – Complex nose with sooty smoke, cocoa powder and lemon. Lots of charcoal smoke and heavy peat on the palate, but melon and peach too. A long finish mixing sweet fruit with an acerbic wood fire smokiness.

BenRiach 12 year old

GS – Malt, orange and pineapple on the nose, floral with vanilla notes. Soft fruits, brittle toffee and honey on the smooth palate, with a finish of spicy milk chocolate.

DR – Classic Speyside nose, with a rich blend of fruits, vanilla and honey. On the palate ripe fruits are balanced by crisp barley and sweet honey, and the finish is balanced, rounded and pleasant.

The least that can be said about the people behind BenRiach distillery is that they have a vision to expand the business. Two years ago, they bought Glendronach distillery and in July 2010 they took over Chivas Brothers' Newbridge bottling plant as part of a £6m investment to increase the sales volumes from the two distilleries. One side of the business that will become increasingly important in the future, is the blended whiskies, for example Clan Murray - a big hit in Africa.

The distillery is equipped with a traditional cast iron mash tun, eight washbacks made of stainless steel and two pairs of stills. One of the old stills was replaced by a new in January 2010. The annual production of this independent distillery has increased from year to year and has now reached 1.6 million litres. It is worth to note that a small amount of triple distilled spirit has been produced every year since 2005, just like previous owners Chivas Bros did in 1998. This makes up for 25,000 litres, while the peated whisky amounts to 175,000 litres.

The core range of BenRiach is *Heart of Speyside* (no age), *12, 16* and *20 years old* in what the distillery itself calls Classic Speyside style and *Birnie Moss, Curiositas 10 year old, Authenticus 21 year old* and the *four 12 year olds* named *Fumosus* - heavily peated whiskies with different finishes as the peated varieties. *Four different 15 year olds* with different finishes were supplemented in 2008 with a *16 year old Sauternes finish* and in August 2009 with *Moscatel* and *Gaja Barolo*, both *18 year olds*. Some old BenRiachs of between *25-40 years* of age complete the range.

New for 2010 are three *16/17 year old wood finishes* (Claret, Burgundy, Rioja) released in June and then, in July, no less than *10 vintages* from 1976 to 1993 were also released. And as if that was not enough; later in autumn, three specials - *Solstice, a 12 year old triple distilled, Horizons - 15 year old, heavily peated* and with a *Tawny port finish* and, finally, *The Firkin Cask* which has matured for 32 years in a 45 litre firkin cask, appeared.

Curiositas 10 year old

Benrinnes

Owner:
Diageo

Region/district:
Speyside

Founded: **Status:** **Capacity:**
1826 Active 2 500 000 litres

Address: Aberlour, Banffshire AB38 9NN

Tel: **website:**
01340 872600 www.malts.com

History:
1826 – The first Benrinnes distillery is built at Whitehouse Farm by Peter McKenzie.

1829 – A flood destroys the distillery.

1834 – A new distillery, Lyne of Ruthrie, is constructed a few kilometres from the first one. The owner, John Innes files for bankruptcy and William Smith & Company takes over.

1864 – William Smith & Company goes bankrupt and David Edward becomes the new owner.

1896 – Benrinnes is ravaged by fire which prompts major refurbishment. David Edward dies and his son Alexander Edward takes over.

1922 – John Dewar & Sons takes over ownership.

1925 – John Dewar & Sons becomes part of Distillers Company Limited (DCL).

1955/56 – The distillery is completely rebuilt.

1964 – Floor maltings is replaced by a Saladin box.

1966 – The number of stills doubles to six.

1984 – The Saladin box is taken out of service and the malt is purchased centrally.

1991 – The first official bottling from Benrinnes is a 15 year old in the Flora & Fauna series.

1996 – United Distillers releases a 21 year old cask strength in their Rare Malts series.

2009 – A 23 year old (6,000 bottles) is launched as a part of this year's Special Releases.

2010 – A Manager's Choice 1996 is released.

Benrinnes 15 year old

GS – A brief flash of caramel shortcake on the initial nose, soon becoming more peppery and leathery, with some sherry. Ultimately savoury and burnt rubber notes. Big-bodied, viscous, with gravy, dark chocolate and more pepper. A medium-length finish features mild smoke and lively spices.

DR – Cucumber, water melon and some caramel on the nose, sherried and full palate with some figs and harsher notes. The finish is medium long and complex.

Benrinnes Distillery has been subjected to at least three major refurbishings since its inception in 1826. The first entailed rebuilding a completely new distillery after a serious flooding and the most recent, in the fifties, gave it the current, rather charmless, appearance. The surroundings at the foot of the mountain, Ben Rinnes, are however unrivalled.

The distillery is equipped with a stainless steel lauter mash tun, eight washbacks made of Oregon pine and six stills. For a long time the stills have been run three and three instead of in pairs. This technique is reminiscent of Springbank's partial triple distillation and was probably adopted in connection with rebuilding the distillery in 1955. For the last two years, though, this has changed and two wash stills are now feeding four spirit stills; two of which were originally the intermediate stills. The change was made for inventory requirements and it remains to be seen if this is a permanent change. Worm tubs are used for condensation. During 2010, Benrinnes is producing at full capacity, which means 16 mashes at 8.5 tonnes, amounting to 2.5 million litres of alcohol.

The lion's share of Benrinnes' production is used in blended whiskies - J&B, Johnnie Walker and especially the standard blend Crawford's 3 Star. The latter brand was established in the early 19th century by the Leith blender and bottler A & A Crawford, and was followed up by a 5 Star in 1920, which now has been discontinued.

The only core expression is the Flora & Fauna 15 years old. In autumn 2009, a surprise appeared in Diageo's annual Special Releases when a new bottling of Benrinnes was launched - a 23 year old from 1985. In May 2010 came another new release, a Manager's Choice from 1996, drawn from a refill bourbon cask. Independent bottlings are quite rare but it was recently revealed that the well-known single malt Stronachie (12 and 18 year olds) from Dewar Rattray is in fact distilled at Benrinnes.

Flora & Fauna 15 years old

Benromach

Owner:	**Region/district:**
Gordon & MacPhail	Speyside
Founded: **Status:**	**Capacity:**
1898 Active (vc)	500 000 litres

Address: Invererne Road, Forres,
Morayshire IV36 3EB

Tel: **website:**
01309 675968 www.benromach.com

History:
1898 – Benromach Distillery Company starts the distillery.

1911 – Harvey McNair & Co buys the distillery.

1919 – John Joseph Calder buys Benromach and sells it to recently founded Benromach Distillery Ltd owned by several breweries.

1931 – Benromach is mothballed.

1937 – The distillery reopens.

1938 – Joseph Hobbs buys Benromach through Associated Scottish Distillers and sells it on to National Distillers of America (NDA).

1953 – NDA sells Benromach to Distillers Company Limited (DCL).

1966 – The distillery is refurbished.

1968 – Floor maltings is abolished.

1983 – Benromach is mothballed in March.

1993 – Gordon & McPhail buys Benromach from United Distillers.

1998 – The distillery is once again in operation. A 17 year old is released to commemorate this and the distillery's 100th anniversary.

1999 – A visitor centre is opened.

2004 – The first bottle distilled by the new owner is released under the name 'Benromach Traditional' in May. Other novelties (although distilled in UD times) include a 21 year Tokaji finish and a Vintage 1969.

2005 – A Port Wood finish (22 years old) and a Vintage 1968 are released together with the Benromach Classic 55 years.

2006 – Benromach Organic is released.

2007 – Peat Smoke, the first heavily peated whisky from the distillery, is released.

2008 – Benromach Origins Golden Promise is released.

2009 – Benromach 10 years old is released.

2010 – New batches of Peatsmoke and Origins are released.

The world of Scotch whisky has become more diversified and, in a positive sense, more unpredictable this last decade, as several distilleries have been bought by smaller, independent companies with plenty of exciting ideas. Bruichladdich, BenRiach, Bladnoch and Edradour are a few of them. Another is Benromach - the smallest distillery in Speyside. The owner, Gordon & MacPhail, has worked calmly and systematically over the years, retaining the traditional ways but, at the same time, excelling in innovative production angles, especially when it comes to maturation. They were also the first to release a single malt that was fully certified organic by the Soil Association (Benromach Organic).

Benromach is equipped with a semi-lauter mash tun, four washbacks made of larch and one pair of stills. Only two people are employed in the production and, although it has the capacity to produce 500,000 litres per annum, the output for 2010 is approximately 130,000 litres of alcohol. There is a filling store on site and some of the production is stored in the three warehouses, while the rest is taken to the owner's facilities in Elgin.

The core range consists of *Traditional* (around 6 years old), *10 year old* (released last year and the first Benromach distilled by Gordon & MacPhail to carry an age statement), *21 years old, 25 years old, Cask Strength 1981* (to be replaced by a younger vintage this year) and *Vintage 1968*. There is also *Organic, Peatsmoke*, produced using peated barley and *Origins*, which was made using Golden Promise barley and matured in first and second fill sherry casks. In August 2010 the third batch of *Peatsmoke* was released, this time less peated (35ppm) that than the first batch (55ppm). At the same time batch 2 and 3 of *Origins* were launched - the first fully matured in Port pipes since 1999 and the other distilled in 2000 from Optic barley having matured in an ex-sherry cask. Previous limited editions include *Benromach Classic 55 years* and *Madeira Wood Finish*.

10 year old

Benromach 10 year old

GS – A nose that is initially quite smoky, with wet grass, butter, ginger and brittle toffee. Mouth-coating, spicy, malty and nutty on the palate, with developing citrus fruits, raisins and soft wood smoke. The finish is warming, with lingering barbecue notes.

DR – Lemon custard creams, apricots and then pine table polish on the nose, spicy virgin oak, refreshing sharp barley and pine needles on the palate, and a complex and intriguing spicy and wood shaving finish

Bladnoch

Owner: **Region/district:**
Co-ordinated   Lowlands
Development Services

Founded: **Status:**   **Capacity:**
1817   Active (vc)   250 000 litres

Address: Bladnoch, Wigtown,
Wigtonshire DG8 9AB

Tel: **website:**
01988 402605   www.bladnoch.co.uk

History:

1817 – Brothers Thomas and John McClelland found the distillery.

1825 – The McClelland brothers obtain a licence.

1878 – John McClelland's son Charlie reconstructs and refurbishes the distillery.

1905 – Production stops.

1911 – Dunville & Co. from Ireland buys T. & A. McClelland Ltd for £10,775. Production is intermittent until 1936.

1937 – Dunville & Co. is liquidated and Bladnoch is wound up. Ross & Coulter from Glasgow buys the distillery after the war. The equipment is dismantled and shipped to Sweden.

1956 – A. B. Grant (Bladnoch Distillery Ltd.) takes over and restarts production with four new stills.

1964 – McGown and Cameron becomes new owners.

1966 – The number of stills is increased from two to four.

1973 – Inver House Distillers buys Bladnoch.

1983 – Arthur Bell and Sons take over.

1985 – Guiness Group buys Arthur Bell & Sons which, from 1989, are included in United Distillers.

1988 – A visitor centre is built.

1993 – United Distillers mothballs Bladnoch in June.

1994 – Raymond Armstrong from Northern Ireland buys Bladnoch in October.

2000 – Production commences in December.

2003 – The first bottles from Raymond Armstrong are launched, a 15 year old cask strength from UD casks.

2004 – New varieties follow suit: e. g. 13 year olds 40% and 55%.

2008 – First release of whisky produced after the take-over in 2000 - three 6 year olds.

2009 – An 8 year old of own production and a 19 year old are released.

Bladnoch 8 year old

GS – Bright, fresh and citric, with lemon, cereal, soft toffee and nuts on the nose. Medium in body, the palate is gingery and very lively, with vanilla, hot spices and hazelnuts. The finish offers persistently fruity spice.

Bladnoch, the southernmost of the Scottish distilleries, was owned by United Distillers (later Diageo) when it was moth-balled in 1993. One year later, Raymond Armstrong, a builder from Northern Ireland bought it with the reservation from Diageo that it should not be used for whisky production. In 2000, after lobbying from the local community and Armstrong, Diageo gave permission for Bladnoch to start producing again. The distillery is equipped with a stainless steel semi-lauter mash tun, six washbacks made of Oregon Pine (of which only three are in use) and one pair of stills. There are only two people employed in the whisky production. Normally they do four mashes per working week and the highest annual volume produced was 250,000 litres in 2007. When owned by United Distillers the distillery used to produce over 1 million litres per year. When Armstrong bought the distillery, Diageo dictated that a maximum of 100,000 litres were to be produced annually, but this restriction is no longer applied.

The distillery has an excellent visitor centre which attracts 25,000 visitors per year. To make a profit the company relies on three corner stones; sales of whisky, the visitor centre and, most significantly, warehouse rents. Of the 11 warehouses on site, Bladnoch uses only one for their own purposes (3,000 casks) while the others, holding 40,000 casks are rented to other distilleries.

Until recently, all official bottlings have come from the previous owner's production from casks that Armstrong has bought. These included *13* to *19 year olds* but in spring of 2010 a couple of *20 year olds* were also released. In 2008 the first release from stock distilled under the current ownership appeared. Three *6 year old cask strengths* were released - a bourbon matured, a sherry matured and one lightly peated from a bourbon barrel. During 2009/2010 a range of *8 year olds* were released with similar maturation. A *Distiller's Choice* with no age statement has also been released.

8 year old

Blair Athol

Owner:
Diageo

Region/district:
Eastern Highlands

Founded: **Status:**   **Capacity:**
1798   Active (vc)   2 500 000 litres

Address: Perth Road, Pitlochry,
Perthshire PH16 5LY

Tel:
01796 482003

website:
www.malts.com

History:
1798 – John Stewart and Robert Robertson found Aldour Distillery, the predecessor to Blair Athol. The name is taken from the adjacent river Allt Dour.

1825 – The distillery is expanded by Robert Robertson and takes the name Blair Athol Distillery.

1826 – The Duke of Atholl leases the distillery to Alexander Connacher & Co.

1832 – The distillery closes.

1860 – Elizabeth Connacher runs the distillery.

1882 – Peter Mackenzie & Company Distillers Ltd of Edinburgh (future founder of Dufftown Distillery) buys Blair Athol and expands it.

1932 – The distillery is mothballed.

1933 – Arthur Bell & Sons takes over by acquiring Peter Mackenzie & Company.

1949 – Production restarts.

1973 – Stills are expanded from two to four.

1985 – Guinness Group buys Arthur Bell & Sons.

1987 – A visitor centre is built.

2003 – A 27 year old cask strength from 1975 is launched in Diageo's Rare Malts series.

2010 – A distillery exclusive with no age statement and a single cask from 1995 are released.

Blair Athol 12 year old

GS – The nose is mellow and sherried, with brittle toffee. Sweet and fragrant. Relatively rich on the palate, with malt, raisins, sultanas and sherry. The finish is lengthy, elegant and slowly drying.

DR – The nose is rich and full, with orange and citrus fruit. The palate, too, is big and chunky, with some tannin and spice in the mix, and with water, parma violet notes.

Blair Athol's fame is, to a certain extent, tied to its single malt as an integral part of Bell's blended whisky, but the distillery has earned a reputation by its own force as well. The 12 year old single malt is selling rather well and in May 2010 the range was extended with a new distillery-exclusive bottling, while the excellent visitor centre attracts almost 40,000 visitors per year. Still, with the relationship between the distillery and Bell's dating back to the mid 1800s, it is perhaps not so surprising that Bell's comes to mind as soon as Blair Athol is mentioned. Of the top ten blended Scotch in 2008, six increased their volumes since the year 2000, one decreased, while three (Bell's included) remained at about the same volumes. But from the same list, Bell's was the only brand that managed to increase volumes from 2008 to 2009, with 5% to 2.3 million cases sold.

Part of the success was caused by Russia where consumer interest diminished as the financial crisis set in. To keep customers from choosing other spirits than whisky, Diageo introduced Bell's as an alternative to the more expensive Johnnie Walker and, thereby, managed to sell 100,000 cases in less than a year.

Blair Athol is one of the oldest distilleries in Scotland and is equipped with a semi-lauter mash tun, six washbacks of stainless steel and two pairs of stills. The washbacks replaced eight old ones (four wooden and four steel) in 2010. The wooden ones were 75 years old and were brought in from Mortlach. In 2008, the distillery was running seven days a week giving a production of 2.5 million litres of spirit. The malt is acquired from Diageo's own Roseisle maltings.

Until 2010, the only official bottling was the *12 year old Flora & Fauna*. In May, a *first fill sherry* bottled at cask strength and without age statement was released as a *distillery exclusive*. A couple of months earlier, a *single cask* distilled in *1995* was released as part of the Manager's Choice series.
Independent bottlings are rare.

Distillery Exclusive no age

Bowmore

Owner:
Morrison Bowmore
Distillers (Suntory)

Region/district:
Islay

Founded: **Status:**   **Capacity:**
1779   Active (vc)   2 000 000 litres

Address: School Street, Bowmore, Islay,
Argyll PA43 7GS

Tel:
01496 810441

website:
www.bowmore.com

History:
1779 – Bowmore Distillery is founded by John Simpson and becomes the oldest Islay distillery.

1837 – The distillery is sold to James and William Mutter of Glasgow.

1892 – After additional construction, the distillery is sold to Bowmore Distillery Company Ltd, a consortium of English businessmen.

1925 – J. B. Sheriff and Company takes over.

1929 – Distillers Company Limited (DCL) takes over.

1950 – William Grigor & Son takes over.

1963 – Stanley P. Morrison buys the distillery for £117,000 and forms Morrison Bowmore Distillers Ltd.

1989 – Japanese Suntory buys a 35% stake in Morrison Bowmore.

1993 – The legendary Black Bowmore is launched. The recommended price is £100 (today it is at least ten times that if it can be found). Another two versions are released 1994 and 1995.

1994 – Suntory now controls all of Morrison Bowmore.

1995 – Bowmore is nominated 'Distiller of the Year' in the International Wine and Spirits competition.

Volumes of global single malt whisky sales dropped by 5% in 2009. This did not seem to bother Morrison Bowmore, owner of Bowmore distillery. Its top brand increased its sales by an impressive 12% and reached 164,000 cases. Laphroaig has, since overtaking Lagavulin in 2001, been the number one selling Islay single malt but the strong performance from Bowmore is bringing it close behind. The complete overhaul of the range in 2007 and focus on the Duty Free market in favour of selling through supermarkets are behind recent years' successes. Bowmore is one of few Scottish distilleries with its own malting floor (three in fact), with as much as 40% of the malt requirement produced in-house. Whereas most cost-conscious distilleries shop around for malt from different maltsters and often change the type of barley when it is convenient, Bowmore buys all their externally malted barley from Simpsons and have exclusively been using Optic for many years now. The spirit yield from their own malt is 408 litres of spirit per tonne barley and for the malt from Simpsons 416 litres. The distillery has a stainless steel semi-lauter mash tun, six washbacks of Oregon Pine and two pairs of stills. 27,000 casks are stored in two dunnage and one racked warehouse. The building closest to the sea and dating back to the 1700s, is probably the oldest whisky warehouse still in use in Scotland. Bowmore has a capacity of 2 million litres, but during 2010, there will be nine mashes per week, i. e. 1.2 million litres.

The core range for domestic markets includes *Legend* (no age), *12 years*, *Darkest 15 years*, *18 years* and *25 years*. The duty free line-up contains *Surf*, *Enigma*, *Mariner* (15 years old), *17 year old* and *Cask Strength*. Two limited bottlings were released in September 2010. One was a *40 year old* in a spectacular bottle surrounded by molten glass. The whisky has matured in an American bourbon cask and only 53 bottles were released. The second bottling was a *Vintage 1981* (402 bottles). Other recent limited bottlings are Craftman´s Collection, a new range introduced at the beginning of 2009. The first version was the *Maltmen´s Selection*, a sherry-matured 13 year old. May 2009 also saw the release of *Laimrig*, an exclusive for the Swedish market, and in autumn of 2009 finally, *Bowmore Tempest*, a 10 year old cask strength matured in first fill Bourbon casks. For Feis Isle 2010, another 500 bottles of Tempest were released as well as 100 bottles of a *25 year old*. A handful of extremely rare bottlings distilled in 1964 were released during 2007-2009; *Black Bowmore*, *White Bowmore* and *Gold Bowmore*.

History (continued):

1996 – A Bowmore 1957 (38 years) is bottled at 40.1% but is not released until 2000.

1999 – Bowmore Darkest with three years finish on Oloroso barrels is launched. A Claret cask strength is also released in 12,000 bottles.

2000 – Bowmore Dusk with two years finish in Bordeaux barrels is launched.

2001 – Bowmore Dawn with two years finish on Port pipes is launched. A bottle from 1890 is sold at an auction in Glasgow and brings in £14,300 which is a new world record.

2002 – A 37 year old Bowmore from 1964 and matured in fino casks is launched in a limited edition of 300 bottles (recommended price £1,500).

2003 – Another two expressions complete the wood trilogy which started with 1964 Fino - 1964 Bourbon and 1964 Oloroso.

2004 – Morrison Bowmore buys one of the most outstanding collections of Bowmore Single Malt from the private collector Hans Sommer. It totals more than 200 bottles and includes a number of Black Bowmore.

2005 – Bowmore 1989 Bourbon (16 years) and 1971 (34 years) are launched.

2006 – Bowmore 1990 Oloroso (16 years) and 1968 (37 years) are launched. A new and up-graded visitor centre is opened.

2007 – Dusk and Dawn disappear from the range and an 18 year old is introduced. New packaging for the whole range. 1991 (16yo) Port and Black Bottle are released.

2008 – White Bowmore and a 1992 Vintage with Bourdeaux finish are launched.

2009 – Gold Bowmore, Maltmen´s Selection, Laimrig and Bowmore Tempest are released.

2010 – A 40 year old and Vintage 1981 are released.

Bowmore 12 year old

GS – An enticing nose of lemon and gentle brine leads into a smoky, citric palate, with notes of cocoa and boiled sweets appearing in the lengthy, complex finish.

DR – Rich peat and seaweed and the merest hint of characteristic palma violets on the nose, smoked fish in butter, menthol cough sweets and lemon on the palate, sweet peat in the finish.

Vintage 1981   40 years old   Bowmore Tempest

12 years old   15 years old Darkest   18 years old

93

Braeval

Owner: **Region/district:**
Chivas Brothers Ltd   Speyside
(Pernod Ricard)

Founded: **Status:**   **Capacity:**
1973   Active   4 000 000 litres

Address: Chapeltown of Glenlivet,
Ballindalloch, Banffshire AB37 9JS

Tel: **website:**
01542 783042   -

History:
1973 – The Chivas and Glenlivet Group founds Braes of Glenlivet, the name which will be used for the first 20 years. The Glenlivet, Tomintoul and Tamnavulin are the only other distilleries situated in the Livet Glen valley. Production starts in October.

1975 – Three stills are increased to five.

1978 – Five stills are further expanded to six.

1994 – The distillery changes name to Braeval.

2001 – Pernod Ricard takes over Chivas Brothers.

2002 – Braeval is mothballed in October.

2008 – The distillery starts producing again in July.

Deerstalker 10 year old

DR – Grass and violin bow on the nose, zippy sherbet and citrus fruit on the palate, with a clean and refreshing finish.

Braeval Distillery opened in 1978 and its owner, famous blending company Chivas Brothers (founded in 1858), was then owned by Canadian company Seagrams (founded in 1857). Seagrams already entered the Scottish market in 1936 when legendary owner, Sam Bronfman, initiated the acquisition of the Glasgow whisky house, Robert Brown Ltd in 1936. The crusade then continued with the acquisition of Chivas Brothers (1949), Strathisla (1950) and Glenlivet, Glen Grant and Longmorn (1977). The fall of the succesful Seagram Co. came when Sam Bronfman's grandson, Edgar Bronfman Jr., diversified the company into film and record companies. Debts built up and the Vivendi Group then took over the company. It sold the wine part of the operation to Diageo and the spirits part to Pernod Ricard in 2001. This move, together with the acquisition of Allied Domecq four years later, awarded Pernod Ricard the position of the second largest alcohol producer in the world (in terms of volume), a position that Indian company United Spirits recently took over.

Braeval is situated in a very remote part of the Highlands with Tamnavulin as its closest distillery neighbour and it is both impressive and surprisingly handsome, despite that it was built to function as a typical working distillery.

Braeval was reopened in 2008 after having been mothballed for six years. The distillery is equipped with a stainless steel traditional mash tun, fifteen washbacks made of stainless steel and six stills. There used to be four pairs but now each of the two wash stills serve two spirit stills. The capacity is 25 mashes per week. The whole production is used for blended Scotch and there are no official bottlings. Independent bottler, Aberko Ltd., have two versions from the distillery in their range of Deerstalker single malts - a 10 year old and a 15 year old. Recently, there has also been a release of a 20 year old from 1989 by Speciality Drinks.

Deerstalker 10 year old

New Websites To Watch

www.whiskynotes.be

This blog, started by Ruben end of December 2008, is almost entirely about tasting notes plus some news. Ruben is hard-working and has published 400 tasting notes since the start. He concentrates on newly released bottlings and this is a great site especially to get acquainted to releases from the independent companies.

www.dramming.com

This website, emminently hosted by Oliver Klimek, takes a wide-angle view of the whisky world. Included are such diverse subject as whisky knowledge, trip teports, whisky ratings, whisky business and articles on various topics. You may know this site from before under the name Whisky Ratings.

www.whiskyintelligence.com

Lawrence Graham has made this into the best site on all kinds of whisky news. He does not miss out on a single press release, newsletter or comment concerning all kinds whisky. The first website you should log into every morning!

www.ardbegproject.com

We all know how devoted the followers of Ardbeg can be. Well, this is clearly evidenced by Californian Tim Puett who has made this extraordinary site a temple for those of you who want to know everything about the Islay distillery and, especially, all the bottlings. Do not miss this site if you are an Ardnut too!

www.guidscotchdrink.com

Jason (and sometimes guest contributors) reflects on what goes on in the world of whisky. Tasting notes is one part of the site but the highlights are the many comments on current events and trends.

www.whiskywhiskywhisky.com

Mark Connelly started this forum for whisky friends a couple of years ago and it is now one of the more active forums on the internet with lots of daily comments on new whiskies, industry news, whisky events or if you just want to chew the fat with fellow whisky lovers.

Some of Our Old Favourites

www.maltmadness.com
Our all-time favourite with something for everyone. Managed by malt maniac Johannes van den Heuvel.

www.maltmaniacs.org
A bunch of knowledgeable whisky lovers dissect, debate, attack and praise the varying phenomena of the whisky world.

blog.maltadvocate.com
John Hansell is well situated with his unique contacts in the business to write a first class blog on every aspect of whisky.

www.whiskyfun.com
Serge Valentin, one of the Malt Maniacs, is almost always first with well written tasting notes on new releases.

www.nonjatta.blogspot.com
A blog by Chris Bunting with a wealth of interesting information on Japanese whisky as well as Japanese culture.

drwhisky.blogspot.com
Sam Simmons delivers tasting notes that include exciting stories and reflections about distilleries, people and events.

www.whiskyreviews.blogspot.com
Ralfy does this video blog with tastings and field reports in an educational yet easy-going and entertaining way.

www.caskstrength.net
Joel and Neil won a Drammie Award for this blog and deservedly so. Initiated, entertaining and well written reports.

www.edinburghwhiskyblog.com
Lucas and Chris review new releases, interview people from the industry and cover various news from the whisky world.

www.whiskycast.com
The best whisky-related podcast on the internet and one that sets the standard for podcasts in other genres as well.

www.whisky-news.com
Apart from daily news, this site contains tasting notes, distillery portraits, lists of retailers, whisky clubs, events etc.

www.spiritofislay.net
This site is of course about the famous Islay whiskies but Gordon Homer also covers many other aspects of the island.

www.whiskyforum.se
Swedish whisky forum with more than 1,800 enthusiasts. Excellent debate as well as more than 2,000 tasting notes.

www.whisky-pages.com
Top class whisky site with features, directories, tasting notes, book reviews, whisky news, glossary and a forum.

www.whiskyforeveryone.com
Educational site, perfect for beginners, with a blog where both new releases and affordable standards are reviewed.

blog.thewhiskyexchange.com
Tim Forbes from The Whisky Exchange writes about new bottlings as well as the whisky industry in general.

www.whiskynyt.dk
A Danish whisky site with emphasis on an active members' forum. Updated news on whisky is also presented.

www.whiskymag.com
The official website of the printed 'Whisky Magazine'. A very active whisky forum with over 3000 registered members.

www.whisky.de
German whisky dealer with more than 7 500 photos of 168 distilleries on the site.

www.scotch-whisky.org.uk
The official site of SWA (Scotch Whisky Association) with i.a. press releases and publications about the industry.

www.whisky-distilleries.info
A great site that is absolutely packed with information about distilleries as well as history and recent bottlings.

www.whiskyguiden.se
An excellent Swedish site with thorough descriptions of most distilleries as well as continuously updated whisky news.

Bruichladdich

Owner: **Region/district:**
Bruichladdich Distillery Co   Islay

Founded: **Status:**   **Capacity:**
1881   Active (vc)   1 500 000 litres

Address: Bruichladdich, Islay, Argyll PA49 7UN

Tel: **website:**
01496 850221   www.bruichladdich.com

History:

1881 – Barnett Harvey builds the distillery with money left by his brother William III to his three sons William IV, Robert and John Gourlay. The Harvey family already owns the distilleries Yoker and Dundashill.

1886 – Bruichladdich Distillery Company Ltd is founded and reconstruction commences.

1889 – William Harvey becomes Manager and remains on that post until his death in 1937.

1929 – Temporary closure.

1936 – The distillery reopens.

1938 – Joseph Hobbs, Hatim Attari and Alexander Tolmie purchase the distillery for £23 000 through the company Train & McIntyre.

1938 – Operations are moved to Associated Scottish Distillers.

1952 – The distillery is sold to Ross & Coulter from Glasgow.

1960 – A. B. Grant buys Ross & Coulter.

1961 – Own maltings ceases and malt is brought in from Port Ellen.

1968 – Invergordon Distillers take over.

1975 – The number of stills increases to four.

1983 – Temporary closure.

1993 – Whyte & Mackay buys Invergordon Distillers.

1995 – The distillery is mothballed in January.

The people at Bruichladdich are rarely idle when it comes to producing new expressions and 2010 was no exception to this rule, as can be seen below. But this year the staff have also been occupied by an extensive refurbishing of the still room and construction of a new warehouse (at a cost of £600,000). In January, the oldest wash still, dating back to 1881, was sent to Forsyth´s in Rothes for refurbishing at the same time as the pot ale vat, intermediate spirits receiver and feints charger were removed. The space that was freed up was filled with such a unique item as the only functioning Lomond still in the industry. Originally built in 1955, but not in use since 1985, it was brought to Bruichladdich in 2004 just before Inverleven distillery (where it had been working) was to be demolished. Contrary to ordinary pot stills, Lomond stills have a rectifying column attached with plates that can be adjusted to achieve the desired amount of reflux. The first distillation in the new still took place at the beginning of August 2010 but, surprisingly, not of whisky but gin! During a 13 hour-long distillation, 2,500 cases were produced and the Islay gin was made available to the public in September.

Apart from the new Lomond still (named Ugly Betty), Bruichladdich distillery is equipped with a cast iron, open mash tun from 1881, six washbacks of Oregon pine and two pairs of stills. All casks are stored either at Bruichladdich or at the old Port Charlotte site. The yearly production at Bruichladdich has now increased to 800,000 litres of alcohol and all whisky produced is based on Scottish barley. Twenty-three farmers are contracted and eight of these grow the barley organically. The latter are responsible for 50% of the annual requirements. There are three main lines in Bruichladdich's production; lightly peated Bruichladdich, moderately peated Port Charlotte and the heavily peated Octomore. A traditional core range has become increasingly difficult to identify as many of the first bottlings with an age statement are sold out. *Rocks, Waves, Peat, Laddie Classic* and *Infinity* are all part of the current range as are *18, 20* and *21 year old*. Three new bottlings were released in early autumn - *Octomore/3_152*, a 5 year old version with 152 ppm in the malted barley, *PC Multi Vintage*, the fifth version of Port Charlotte and *Organic MV* which is a multi vintage based on organic Chalice barley grown on Islay. Another three bottlings were announced for a later release, namely *Bruichladdich 1977, Bruichladdich 40 year old* and *Black Art 2 1989*. From the last years, limited releases such as *Octomore Orpheus* with a second maturation in Chateau Petrus casks deserve mention.

History (continued):

1998 – In production again for a few months, and then mothballed.

2000 – Murray McDavid buys the distillery from JBB Greater Europe for £6.5 million.

2001 – Jim McEwan from Bowmore becomes Production Director. The first distillation (Port Charlotte) is on 29th May and the first distillation of Bruichladdich starts in July. In September the owners' first bottlings from the old casks are released, 10, 15 and 20 years old.

2002 – The world's most heavily peated whisky is produced on 23rd October when Octomore (80ppm) is distilled.

2003 – Bruichladdich becomes the only distillery on Islay bottling on-site. It is awarded Distillery of the Year for the second time and launches the golf series, Links, 14 years old.

2004 – Second edition of the 20 year old (nick-named Flirtation) and 3D, also called The Peat Proposal, are launched.

2005 – Several new expressions are launched - the second edition of 3D, Infinity (a mix of 1989, 1990, 1991 and Port Charlotte), Rocks, Legacy Series IV, The Yellow Submarine and The Twenty 'Islands'.

2006 – Included in a number of new releases in autumn is the first official bottling of Port Charlotte; PC5.

2007 – New releases include Redder Still, Legacy 6, two new Links, PC6 and an 18 year old.

2008 – More than 20 new expressions including the first Octomore, Bruichladdich 2001, PC7, Golder Still and two sherry matured from 1998.

2009 – New releases include Classic, Organic, Black Art, Infinity 3, PC8, Octomore 2 and X4+3 - the first quadruple distilled single malt.

2010 – PC Multi Vintage, Organic MV, Octomore/3_152, Bruichladdich 40 year old are released.

PC Multi Vintage *Octomore/3_152* *Organic Multi Vintage*

Bruichladdich 12 year old

GS – A light, elegant nose of fresh fruit and vanilla fudge. Medium-bodied, smooth, and malty. Becoming nuttier. Spicy oak in the finish.

DR – Very welcoming mix of melon, grape and pear on the nose, and over-ripe peach, soft melon and other sweet fruits on the palate, with a delightful clean and fresh finish.

Port Charlotte PC8

GS – A big hit of sweet peat and malt on the nose. Liquorice and a hint of rubber when water is added. Quite dry on the slightly peppery palate; sweeter and fruitier when diluted. Lingering ash notes in the lengthy, plain chocolate finish.

DR – Classic Port Charlotte peaty smoky nose, but a maturer note on the palate. It's big and bold with citrus fruits, but with sweet honeycomb and Horlicks malt drink in the mix. The peat coats the mouth and lingers on.

Rocks

Laddie Classic

18 year old 2nd edition

Bunnahabhain

Owner:
Burn Stewart Distillers
(CL Financial)

Region/district:
Islay

Founded: 1881

Status: Active (vc)

Capacity: 2 500 000 litres

Address: Port Askaig, Islay, Argyll PA46 7RP

Tel: 01496 840646

website: www.bunnahabhain.com

History:

1881 – William Robertson of Robertson & Baxter, founds the distillery together with the brothers William and James Greenless, owners of Islay Distillers Company Ltd.

1883 – Production starts in earnest in January.

1887 – Islay Distillers Company Ltd merges with William Grant & Co. in order to form Highland Distilleries Company Limited.

1963 – The two stills are augmented by two more.

1982 –The distillery closes.

1984 – The distillery reopens. A 21 year old is released to commemorate the 100th anniversary of Bunnahabhain.

1999 – Edrington takes over Highland Distillers and mothballs Bunnahabhain but allows for a few weeks of production a year.

2001 – A 35 year old from 1965 is released in a limited edition of 594 bottles during Islay Whisky Festival.

2002 – As in the previous year, Islay Whisky Festival features another Bunnahabhain – 1966, a 35 year old in sherry casks. Auld Acquaintance 1968 is launched at the Islay Jazz Festival.

2003 – In April Edrington sells Bunnahabhain and Black Bottle to Burn Stewart Distilleries (C. L. World Brands) at the princely sum of £10 million. A 40 year old from 1963 is launched.

2004 – The first limited edition of the peated version is a 6 year old called Moine.

2005 – Three limited editions are released - 34 years old, 18 years old and 25 years old.

2006 – 14 year old Pedro Ximenez and 35 years old are launched.

2008 – Darach Ur is released for the travel retail market and Toiteach (a peated 10 year old) is launched on a few selected markets.

2009 – Moine Cask Strength is released during Feis Isle.

2010 – The peated Cruach-Mhòna and a limited 30 year old are released.

Bunnahabhain 12 year old

GS – The nose is fresh, with light peat and discreet smoke. More overt peat on the nutty and fruity palate, but still restrained for an Islay. The finish is full-bodied and lingering, with a hint of vanilla and some smoke.

DR – Ginger and barley candy on the nose, then sweet and sour mix on the palate, lots of sweetness but with a distinctive savoury and earthy undertow.

Burn Stewart´s big seller is without doubt Scottish Leader, a blended whisky selling almost six million bottles in, mainly, Asia and South Africa. Among the single malts, however, Bunnahabhain is the star with 220,000 bottles sold yearly.

The distillery is equipped with a stainless steel mash tun, six washbacks made of Oregon Pine and two pairs of stills. The spirit destined for single malt bottling and for the Black Bottle blend is stored on site in six dunnage and one racked warehouse, (totalling 21,000 casks) while the rest is shipped to other sites for maturation. Last year production equalled 1.2 million litres (using five mashes per week) and it will remain the same for 2010. The lion's share of this is, of course, the traditional unpeated version but 250,000 litres will be peated (38 ppm). This version is called Moine and is primarily used as a part of the blend Black Bottle, but has also been released as a single malt a couple of times.

In spring of 2010 the distillery manager, John MacLellan, who had been with the distillery since 1989, resigned in order to commence as General Manager at Kilchoman distillery. Andrew Brown, with 20 years working experience at Bunnahabhain, has taken over as Team Leader since April while waiting for a new Distillery Manager to be appointed.

The core range consists of *12, 18* and *25 years old* as well as a 10 year old version of the peated Bunnahabhain called *Toiteach* (smoky in Gaelic). There are also two travel retail exclusives. The first, released in 2008, is *Darach Ur* ("New Oak") with no age statement and in autumn of 2010, *Cruach-Mhòna* ("Peat Stack") was released. The latter is a peatier version of Toiteach and bottled at 50% as it is made up from young (5-7 years old), heavily peated Bunnahabhain matured in ex bourbon and refill casks along with 20-21 years old matured in ex sherry butts. For Islay Festival 2010, an *18 year old* matured for the last four years in a PX sherry butt, was launched and in September came a rare treat - a *30 year old* (357 bottles).

Cruach-Mhòna

Bushmills

Owner: **Region/district:**
Diageo   N Ireland (Co. Antrim)

Founded: **Status:**   **Capacity:**
1784   Active (vc)   4 500 000 litres

Address: 2 Distillery Road, Bushmills,
Co. Antrim BT57 8XH

Tel: **website:**
028 20731521   www.bushmills.com

History:
1608 – James I issues Sir Thomas Philips a licence for whiskey distilling.

1784 – The distillery is formally registered.

1885 – Fire destroys part of the distillery.

1890 – S.S. Bushmills, the distillery's own steamship, makes its maiden voyage across the Atlantic to deliver whiskey to America and then heads on to Singapore, China and Japan.

1923 – The distillery is acquired by Belfast wine and spirit merchant Samuel Wilson Boyd. Anticipating the end of US prohibition, he gears Bushmills up for expansion and increases production.

1939-1945 – No distilling during the war. The distillery is partly converted to accommodate American servicemen.

1972 – Bushmills joins Irish Distillers Group which was formed in 1966. Floor maltings ceases.

1987 – Pernod Ricard acquires Irish Distillers.

1996 – Bushmills 16 years old is launched.

2005 – Bushmills is sold to Diageo at a price tag of €295.5 million as a result of Pernod Ricard's acquisition of Allied Domecq.

2007 – The 40 year old cast iron mash tun is replaced by a new one of stainless steel at a cost of £1.4m.

2008 – Celebrations commemorate the 400th anniversary of the original license to distil, granted to the area in 1608.

Bushmills 10 year old

DR – Autumn orchard of over-ripe apples on the nose, soft red apples and pear on the palate, soft sweetie finish.

Irish whiskey has been one of the most successful segments in the whisky industry for the past five years. Today it sells 4.5 million cases worldwide with USA as the biggest market.
In 2009, 1.2 million cases were sold there compared to 615,000 in 2005. This success has inspired the two biggest rivals to set optimistic goals. Jameson (Pernod-Ricard) aimed for 3.5 million cases in 2009, but managed only 2.75 while Bushmills (Diageo) have their eyes set on selling 1 million cases in 2012. In 2009 they sold half of that.

Diageo have clearly shown that Bushmills is a brand to invest in, even if the plans may seem somewhat unrealistic. Since take-over in 2005, no less than £10 million has flowed into the distillery, resulting in a new mash tun, new stills, more warehouses and a new bottle design. Bushmill's now has ten stills and since 2008 the production runs seven days a week. This means 4.5 million litres a year, a tripling in only three years.

Two kinds of malt are used, one unpeated and one slightly peated. The distillery uses triple distillation, which is the traditional Irish method, contrary to Cooley which uses double distillation.

Bushmills' core range of single malts consists of a *10 year old*, a *16 year old Triple Wood* with a finish in Port pipes for 6-9 months and a *21 year old* finished in *Madeira* casks for two years. There is also a *12 year old Distillery Reserve* which is sold exclusively at the distillery and the *1608 Anniversary Edition*, launched in 2008 to celebrate the 400th anniversary. The malt whiskey part for that expression was distilled using a proportion of crystal malt which gave the blend distinct toffee/chocolatey notes.

Black Bush (with a high proportion of grain whiskey distilled in a pot still) and Bushmills Original (the big seller in the US) are the two main blended whiskeys in the range. Bushmills is open to the public and the visitor centre receives more than 100,000 visitors per year.

21 years old

Caol Ila

Owner:
Diageo

Region/district:
Islay

Founded: **Status:** **Capacity:**
1846   Active (vc)   5 800 000 litres

Address: Port Askaig, Islay, Argyll PA46 7RL

Tel:
01496 302760

website:
www.malts.com

History:

1846 – Hector Henderson founds Caol Ila.

1852 – Henderson, Lamont & Co. is subjected to financial difficulties and Henderson is forced to sell Caol Ila to Norman Buchanan.

1863 – Norman Buchanan encounters financial troubles and sells to the blending company Bulloch, Lade & Co. from Glasgow.

1879 – The distillery is rebuilt and expanded.

1920 – Bulloch, Lade & Co. is liquidated and the distillery is taken over by Caol Ila Distillery.

1927 – DCL becomes sole owners.

1972 – All the buildings, except for the warehouses, are demolished and rebuilt.

1974 – The renovation, which totals £1 million, is complete and six new stills are installed.

1999 – Experiments with a completely unpeated malt are performed.

2002 – The first official bottlings since Flora & Fauna/Rare Malt appear; 12 years, 18 years and Cask Strength (c. 10 years).

2003 – A 25 year old cask strength is released.

2005 – A 25 year old Special Release is launched.

2006 – Unpeated 8 year old and 1993 Moscatel finish are released.

2007 – The second edition of the unpeated 8 year old is released.

2008 – The third edition of unpeated 8 year old is released.

2009 – The fourth edition of the unpeated version (10 year old) is released.

2010 – A 25 year old, a 1999 Feis Isle bottling and a 1997 Manager's Choice are released.

Caol Ila 12 year old

GS – Iodine, fresh fish and smoked bacon feature on the nose, along with more delicate, floral notes. Smoke, malt, lemon and peat on the slightly oily palate. Peppery peat in the drying finish.

DR – Barbecued fish and seaweed on the nose, oily bacon-fat, squeezed lemon and sweet smoke on the palate, immensely satisfying citrusy seaside barbecue of a finish.

Talisker is, no doubt, one of Diageo's success stories in recent years. The brand increased by 145% to 110,000 cases from 2000 to 2009. Perhaps Diageo's next fastest growing single malt brand will also be a peated malt, namely Caol Ila. Last year, its sales were at Talisker's year 2000 levels, at around 45,000 cases. The range has expanded in recent years and production increased for the first time in many years from October 2010, when the five-day week was replaced by a seven-day week. This will entail impressive 24 mashes per week and 5.8 million litres of alcohol in a year.

Caol Ila is, already by far, the biggest distillery on Islay with a cast iron mash tun that can take 13 tonnes of grist per mash, eight washbacks made of Oregon Pine and three pairs of stills in a still room with a stunning view of Jura across the Sound of Islay. There is a three-storey warehouse on site, but today's production is sent by lorry to the mainland for filling and maturation.

The whisky from Caol Ila is peated but trials with low phenol started already in the 1980's. The result, destined for blended whisky, was that unpeated Caol Ila was produced annually until 2005. In recent years, the increasing demand for peated whisky has put an end to the production of the unpeated, so called Highland, Caol Ila. This variety was bottled for the first time in 2006.

The core range consists of *12* and *18 years old, Distiller's Edition Moscatel finish* and *Cask Strength*, but was extended with a *25 year old* in summer 2010. The fourth edition of the unpeated, a *10 year old*, was released in autumn of 2009. In connection with the 2010 Islay Festival, a *1999 sherry-matured* from European oak was released. One month earlier, another ex-sherry distilled in *1997* was released in the *Manager's Choice* series.

The number of independent bottlings is huge. Recent releases include two 30 year olds from Dewar Rattray and Berry Brothers, three 25 yeard olds from Cadenheads, Signatory and Duncan Taylor and a 13 year old Sauternes finish from Ian MacLeod.

10 year old unpeated

Cardhu

Owner:		Region/district:
Diageo		Speyside

Founded:	Status:	Capacity:
1824	Active (vc)	3 200 000 litres

Address: Knockando, Aberlour, Moray AB38 7RY

Tel:	website:
01340 872555 (vc)	www.malts.com

History:

1824 – John Cumming applies for and obtains a licence for Cardhu Distillery.

1846 – John Cumming dies and his son Lewis takes over.

1872 – Lewis dies and his wife Elizabeth takes over.

1884 – A new distillery is built to replace the old.

1893 – John Walker & Sons purchases Cardhu for £20,500 but the Cumming family continues operations. The whisky changes name from Cardow to Cardhu.

1908 – The name reverts to Cardow.

1960-61 – Reconstruction and expansion of stills from four to six.

1981 – The name changes to Cardhu once again.

1998 – A visitor centre is constructed.

2002 – Diageo changes Cardhu single malt to a vatted malt with contributions from other distilleries in it.

2003 – The whisky industry protests sharply against Diageo's plans.

2004 – Diageo withdraws Cardhu Pure Malt.

2005 – The 12 year old Cardhu Single Malt is relaunched and a 22 year old is released.

2009 – Cardhu 1997, a single cask in the new Manager´s Choice range is released.

Cardhu 12 year old

GS – The nose is relatively light and floral, quite sweet, with pears, nuts and a whiff of distant peat. Medium-bodied, malty and sweet in the mouth. Medium-length in the finish, with sweet smoke, malt and a hint of peat.

DR – Honeycomb and chocolate Crunchie bar on the nose, fluffy over-ripe apples, toffee, boiled sweets on the palate, delightful clean and crisp finish.

Cardhu was the fastest growing single malt in the 1990s, increasing by 100,000 cases in just three years. This lasted until 2003 when Cardhu sold 295,000 cases and, at that time, was bigger than both Macallan and Glenmorangie. Since then until 2009, it has been the fastest declining brand and seen a 40% decrease. The reason for this fluctuation is the heavy exposure to just a few countries - Spain, Greece, Portugal and, to some extent, France. In these countries, even in the tiniest shop on the remotest island, one could find Cardhu which sometimes was the only Scotch single malt available. All these markets have been badly hit by the latest recession and Cardhu is now back to the same figures it showed in the mid-nineties. Cardhu is still by far the biggest selling of the Diageo single malts, with Talisker coming in as number two. But Cardhu is not just single malt. It is also one of the most important ingredients of Johnnie Walker and c. 70% of production goes to the various versions of that blend. Cardhu and Johnnie Walker have been intimately close since the 19th century and the distillery was actually bought by Johnnie Walker in 1893. Cardhu distillery's location is unrivalled; situated on a small hill, it overlooks Ben Rinnes, with Knockando and Tamdhu as its closest neighbours. The distillery is equipped with one stainless steel full lauter mash tun, ten washbacks (eight made of Scottish larch and two of stainless steel) and three pairs of stills. At least until 2008, Cardhu was working a seven-day week with a production of almost three million litres of alcohol. The core range consists of the *12 year old* only. In October 2006, a *Special Cask Reserve* with no age statement was released in Spain. A *single cask from 1997* was released in autumn 2009 as part of the new series Manager´s Choice.

12 years old

Clynelish

Owner: Diageo

Region/district: Northern Highlands

Founded: 1967 | **Status:** Active (vc) | **Capacity:** 4 200 000 litres

Address: Brora, Sutherland KW9 6LR

Tel: 01408 623003 (vc) | **website:** www.malts.com

History:

1819 – The 1st Duke of Sutherland founds a distillery called Clynelish Distillery.

1827 – The first licensed distiller, James Harper, files for bankruptcy and John Matheson takes over.

1846 – George Lawson & Sons become new licensees.

1896 – James Ainslie & Heilbron takes over.

1912 – James Ainslie & Co. narrowly escapes bankruptcy and Distillers Company Limited (DCL) takes over together with James Risk.

1916 – John Walker & Sons buys a stake of James Risk's stocks.

1931 – The distillery is mothballed.

1939 – Production restarts.

1960 – The distillery becomes electrified.

1967 – A new distillery, also named Clynelish, is built adjacent to the first one.

1968 – 'Old' Clynelish is mothballed in August.

1969 – 'Old' Clynelish is reopened as Brora and starts using a very peaty malt.

1983 – Brora is closed in March.

2002 – A 14 year old is released.

2006 – A Distiller's Edition 1991 finished in Oloroso casks is released.

2009 – A 12 year old is released for Friends of the Classic Malts.

2010 – A 1997 Manager's Choice single cask is released.

Clynelish 14 year old

GS – A nose that is fragrant, spicy and complex, with candle wax, malt and a whiff of smoke. Notably smooth in the mouth, with honey and contrasting citric notes, plus spicy peat, before a brine and tropical fruit finish.

DR – Fresh green fruit and unripe melon on the nose, sweet almost fizzy lemon sherbet on the palate, a wispy hint of peat and pepper, and satisfying and balanced finish.

Heading north on the A9 towards Thurso, just north of the village Brora, one finds Clynelish distillery on the left side of the road. This is the second most northerly distillery on mainland Scotland (with Pulteney being the northernmost).

Clynelish is actually the site of two distilleries - the closed Brora which was originally founded as Clynelish in 1819 and the operating distillery which was built in 1967. The two distilleries ran in parallel for one year in 1967/1968 after which the older closed. The demand for peated malt to be used for blends was, however, great and it was reopened in 1969 under the name Brora and with a completely new recipe for the whisky – strongly peated at 40ppm. Finally, in 1983 it was closed which probably is for good. The old buildings are still there but only the warehouses are used for maturation of Clynelish. The mash tun, washback and the two old stills are intact in the old still house.

The distillery we today call Clynelish lies on the other side of the small road and is a modern creation made of glass, steel and concrete. It is equipped with a cast iron full lauter mash tun, eight wooden washbacks, two stainless steel washbacks installed in 2008 and three pairs of stills (with the spirit stills being larger than the wash stills). Since 2008, the distillery has been running at full capacity doing 18 mashes per week, producing 4.2 million litres of alcohol. The whisky is much less peated than Brora. The Clynelish single malt sells around 8,000 cases per year. Official bottlings include a *14 year old* and a *Distiller's Edition* with an Oloroso Seco finish. The first distillery shop exclusive, a *cask strength*, was released in 2008. In 2009 another addition was made to the range, a *12 year old* for Friends of the Classic Malts and in May 2010 a *single cask* (first fill bourbon) distilled in *1997* was released as part of the Manager's Choice series.

Recent independent bottlings include a 28 year old from 1982 by Berry Brothers, a 16 year old from Cadenhead, a 12 year old from Dewar Rattray and a 1995 Chateau Lafite finish released by Murray McDavid.

14 years old

Meet the Manager

SARAH BURGESS
SENIOR SITE MANAGER, CLYNELISH DISTILLERY

When did you start working in the whisky business and when did you start at Clynelish?

I started as a tour guide at Cardhu distillery on my 21st birthday. (If I told you the year, I would have to kill you!) It was in August 2008 that I took up my role as Site Operations Manager here at Clynelish.

Have you been working in other lines of business before whisky?

I was brought up on Speyside so whisky was in my blood, as it were. But before working at Cardhu, I had just been doing the usual fairly temporary jobs that people do before finding their true career.

What kind of education or training do you have?

I went to High School at Aberlour. I didn't have any formal training in brewing or distilling. But the technical training I have received throughout my Diageo career has been excellent.

Describe your career in the whisky business.

All my career has been in Diageo. After working as a tour guide at Cardhu, I filled in as Brand Home Manager at Oban for a year to cover someone on maternity leave. Then I went back to Speyside. In October 2004, I started my Site Operations Manager training, working at Dailuaine and Glenspey. In October 2005 I was appointed to the post of Site Operations Manager for Northern Warehousing, based at Auchroisk. Then in August 2008, I moved up to Brora to my present position.

What are your main tasks as a manager?

Above all, to make sure that everyone goes home safely at the end of their shift each day.

What are the biggest challenges of being a distillery manager?

Making sure that we produce precisely the right spirit, at the right time, cost-effectively, safely and consistently.

What would be the worst that could go wrong in the production process?

Someone getting injured on the site is every distillery manager's nightmare. That apart, anything happening that could jeopardise the quality of our spirit.

How would you describe the character of Clynelish single malt?

A light suggestion of scented candle wax, with some sugar and a faint floral fragrance: dried flowers on a beach and a touch of saltiness.

What are the main features in the process at Clynelish, contributing to this character?

We run a lengthy (80) hour fermentation: and, as some commentators have observed, the deposits on the low wines and feints receivers play a part too.

What is your favourite expression of Clynelish and why?

The 14 year old is quite a star! But apart from that, perhaps my favourite is the Distillery Only bottling, which, as the Michelin guides say, is worth the journey! If you can't get that, the Distillers Edition, which miraculously manages to be both rich and unctuous while also being balanced and dry.

If it were your decision alone – what new expression of Clynelish would you like to see released?

We've done a special limited-edition bottling, for the Friends of the Classic Malts, of a 12 year old Clynelish which was terrific.

If you had to choose a favourite dram other than Clynelish, what would that be?

Cardhu, for old times' sake...

What are the biggest changes you have seen the past 10-15 years in your profession?

It's been all change for me over the last 15 years -- I'm afraid I've been too busy learning to notice whether the demands of our job have changed.

Do you see any major changes in the next 10 years to come?

I'm pretty sure the major changes will involve working towards a lighter environmental footprint, through the more efficient use of energy resources, water and by-products.

Do you have any special interests/hobbies that you pursue?

By the time this guide appears, I will hopefully have had my first baby. So for the next few years at least, any other special interests and hobbies will just be a dream!

After you had started as distillery manager at Clynelish you were still a student of Robert Gordon University in Aberdeen. It's a 3,5 hour drive one way! How was it possible combining these two activities?

Yes, it was not an easy time. I had already embarked on a course studying for a BA in Management which involved classes every Monday and Tuesday evening. When I was on Speyside, this was not too difficult. When I moved up to Brora, this as you say involved two 7-hour round trips each week. I persevered because I really did want to graduate.

Usually the distillery manager is not involved in selecting what is bottled. What was it like to be a part of choosing the Managers' Choice of Clynelish?

You're right, it is very rare for a distillery manager to get the chance to sample carefully selected single casks of their whisky with a view to choosing something to be released. I wouldn't be surprised if this opportunity never occurred again for the rest of my career. It was a revelation and a fantastic privilege, to be tasting from a cask that had been filled years before I personally arrived at the distillery.

Cooley

Owner:
Cooley Distillery plc

Region/district:
Ireland (County Louth)

Founded: 1987 **Status:** Active **Capacity:** 3 250 000 litres

Address: Riverstown, Cooley, Co. Louth

Tel: +353 (0)42 9376102 **website:** www.cooleywhiskey.com

History:

1987 – John Teeling purchases Ceimici Teo Distillery in Dundalk. Previously it has produced spirits in column stills (e. g. vodka) and is now renamed Cooley Distillery.

1988 – Willie McCarter acquires part of A. A. Watt Distillery and the brand Tyrconnell and merges with Teeling. Teeling simultaneously buys decommissioned Locke's Kilbeggan Distillery.

1989 – A pair of pot stills is installed for production of both malt and grain whiskey.

1992 – Locke's Single Malt, without age statement, is launched as the first single malt from the distillery. Cooley encounters financial troubles and and stops production.

1995 – Finances improve and production resumes.

1996 – Connemara is launched.

2000 – Locke's 8 year old single malt is launched.

2003 – The Connemara 12 year old is launched.

2006 – Five Connemara Single Casks from 1992 are released.

2007 – Kilbeggan distillery is reopened.

2009 – New packaging for the Connemara range and release of the first in The Small Batch Collection.

2010 – The heavily peated Connemara Turf Mor is released.

Connemara 12 year old

DR – Soft fruit and tarry peat on the nose, then fluffy red apples, toffee and smoke intriguingly mixed into an unusual and very enticing whole. Smoke in the finish.

In the late 1980s the Irish whiskey business was nothing less than a monopoly. From a country where, in the mid 18th century, there were more than 1,000 legal and illegal whiskey distilleries, the numbers had been reduced to two, both of which were owned by the mighty Irish Distillers Group. None other than John Teeling could be better suited to challenge a huge dominant player like that. He is a man of action who, aside from the whisky business, is also involved in a diamond mine in Botswana, oil fields in Iraq and gold deposits in Iran, for example. In addition to that he also holds a doctorate from Harvard Business School. He bought a disused distillery, restarted it under the name Cooley and has managed to create a strong brand that can ride on the success of Irish Whiskey world wide.

The owner has recently invested in new bottling equipment at Cooley, a new warehouse (with another one potentially being added) and embarked upon maintenance work on both the grain and malt distilleries. Today, the equipment consists of a mash tun and washbacks made of stainless steel, two copper pot stills and two column stills. There is a production capacity of 250,000 cases of malt whiskey and 800,000 cases of grain whiskey.

The Cooley range of whiskies consists of several brands. *Connemara* single malts, which are all more or less peated, consist of a no age, a *12 year old*, a *cask strength* and a *sherry finish*. The latter is part of a series of limited expressions called The Small Batch Collection. A new member of this range will be launched in November 2010 - the heavily peated *Turf Mor*. The rest of Cooley's single malt range includes *Tyrconnel no age*, *Tyrconnel 15 year old single cask* and *Tyrconnel wood finishes* as well as *Locke's 8 years old*.

A number of blended whiskeys are also produced as is a single grain, *Greenore 8 years old*. An *18 year old* version of the latter is due for release towards the end of 2010.

Connemara 12 years old

Cragganmore

Owner: Diageo

Region/district: Speyside

Founded: 1869

Status: Active (vc)

Capacity: 2 000 000 litres

Address: Ballindalloch, Moray AB37 9AB

Tel: 01479 874700

website: www.malts.com

History:

1869 – John Smith, who already runs Ballindalloch and Glenfarclas Distilleries, founds Cragganmore.

1886 – John Smith dies and his brother George takes over operations.

1893 – John's son Gordon, at 21, is old enough to assume responsibility for operations.

1901 – The distillery is refurbished and modernized with help of the famous architect Charles Doig.

1912 – Gordon Smith dies and his widow Mary Jane supervises operations.

1917 – The distillery closes.

1918 – The distillery reopens and Mary Jane installs electric lighting.

1923 – The distillery is sold to the newly formed Cragganmore Distillery Co. where Mackie & Co. and Sir George Macpherson-Grant of Ballindalloch Estate share ownership.

1927 – White Horse Distillers is bought by DCL which thus obtains 50% of Cragganmore.

1964 – The number of stills is increased from two to four.

1965 – DCL buys the remainder of Cragganmore.

1988 – Cragganmore 12 years becomes one of six selected for United Distillers' Classic Malts.

1998 – Cragganmore Distillers Edition Double Matured (port) is launched for the first time.

2002 – A visitor centre opens in May.

2006 – A 17 year old from 1988 is released.

2010 – Manager's Choice single cask 1997 and a limited 21 year old are released.

Cragganmore 12 year old

GS – A nose of sherry, brittle toffee, nuts, mild wood smoke, angelica and mixed peel. Elegant on the malty palate, with herbal and fruit notes, notably orange. Medium in length, with a drying, slightly smoky finish.

DR – The nose has honey, soft fruits and sweet spring meadow notes and is very inviting, and on the palate soft barley, summer fruits and a sweetness lead up to an almost tangy finish.

Cragganmore distillery is one of the original six Classic Malts but in spite of their provenance and nice visitor centre, only a couple of hundred people used to find their way here every year. The problem was that visitors focus their attention on the imposing Tormore distillery just along the A95 and consequently miss the small side road leading down to Spey and Cragganmore. A couple of years ago, more visible road signs were erected and suddenly the number of visitors tripled and still continues to increase.

The distillery is equipped with a stainless steel full lauter mash tun which was installed in 1997. There are also six washbacks made of Oregon Pine and two pairs of stills. The two spirit stills are peculiar with flat tops, which had already been introduced in the times of the founder, John Smith. As if that was not enough, the unusually T-shaped lyne arms increase the reflux which, together with the long fermentation time, sets the character of the spirit. The stills are attached to cast iron worm tubs on the outside for cooling the spirit vapours. Part of the production matures in three dunnage warehouses on site.

Cragganmore sells around 350,000 bottles per year and also plays an important part in two blended whiskies; Old Parr and White Horse.

The core range is made up of a *12 year old* and a *Distiller's Edition* with a finish in Port pipes. Two new limited bottlings appeared in 2010. First, in January, came a *single sherry cask* distilled in *1997* and released as part of the Manager's Choice series. In autumn, Cragganmore was part of the yearly Special Releases with a *21 year old*. Older limited bottlings include a *14 year old* destined for 'Friends of Classic Malts', a *1973 29 year old*, a *10 year old cask strength* released in 2004, a *1993 Bodega Cask* from the same year and, finally, a *17 year old* released in 2006. Recent independent bottlings include a Dewar Rattray from 1997, 12 years old.

21 years old

Craigellachie

Owner:
John Dewar & Sons
(Bacardi)

Region/district:
Speyside

Founded: 1891

Status: Active

Capacity: 4 000 000 litres

Address: Aberlour, Banffshire AB38 9ST

Tel: 01340 872971

website: -

History:
1891 – The distillery is built by Craigellachie–Glenlivet Distillery Company which has Alexander Edward and Peter Mackie as part-owners. The famous Charles Doig is the architect.

1898 – Production does not start until this year.

1916 – Mackie & Company Distillers Ltd takes over.

1924 – Peter Mackie dies and Mackie & Company changes name to White Horse Distillers.

1927 – White Horse Distillers are bought by Distillers Company Limited (DCL).

1930 – Administration is transferred to Scottish Malt Distillers (SMD), a subsidiary of DCL.

1964 – Refurbishing takes place and two new stills are bought, increasing the number to four.

1998 – United Distillers & Vintners (UDV) sells Craigellachie together with Aberfeldy, Brackla and Aultmore and the blending company John Dewar & Sons to Bacardi Martini.

2004 – The first bottlings from the new owners are a new 14 year old which replaces UDV's Flora & Fauna and a 21 year old cask strength from 1982 produced for Craigellachie Hotel.

Craigellachie 14 year old

GS – Citrus fruits, cereal and even a whiff of smoke on the nose. Comparatively full-bodied, with sweet fruits, malt and spice on the palate, plus earthy notes and a touch of liquorice in the slightly smoky and quite lengthy finish.

DR – Intriguing and deep mix of light fruits on the nose, a spicy bite then clean and smooth mouth feel, and a soft finish.

The Craigellachie distillery and the surrounding village takes its name from the huge cliff which dominates the landscape and the name actually means "rocky hill". The village dates back to the mid 18th century with the distillery being built around a century and a half later. This is right in the heart of the whisky country and while Craigellachie itself is a rather anonymous distillery, it is surrounded by famous neighbours - Macallan to the west, Glenfiddich to the south and Glen Grant to the north. Malted barley is bought from Glenesk Maltings and the distillery has a modern Steinecker full lauter mash tun, installed in 2001, which replaced the old open cast iron mash tun. There are also eight washbacks made of larch wood and two pairs of stills. A new cooling tower and heat recovery system has been installed recently. Craigellachie runs 24/7 and has managed to squeeze out even a little more than last year and are now producing 3.98 million litres of alcohol.

The distillation at Craigelllachie gives an interesting insight into how the shape, size and running of the stills will influence the final spirit. The stills are some of the biggest in the industry with a capacity of 56,370 litres each. Wide, big stills offer less contact with the copper, resulting in a heavy spirit. But the result will also depend on how much is charged into the stills. At Craigellachie the stills are only charged at 40%, creating a lot of space where spirit vapours can react with the copper to become less powerful. But it does not stop there. When the spirit vapours run down the lye pipe and condensate, it takes place in worm tubs which gives less copper contact than the more modern tube condensers. Therefore, the end product is an unusually robust whisky compared to other Speyside whiskies.

Most of the production goes into Dewar's blends but a *14 year old* was launched in 2004 and this is, so far, the only official bottling. Recent independent bottlings include a 10 year old from distilled in 1999 from Duncan Taylor.

14 years old

Dailuaine

Owner:
Diageo

Region/district:
Speyside

Founded: 1852
Status: Active
Capacity: 3 300 000 litres

Address: Carron, Banffshire AB38 7RE

Tel: 01340 872500
website: www.malts.com

History:
1852 – The distillery is founded by William Mackenzie.

1865 – William Mackenzie dies and his widow leases the distillery to James Fleming, a banker from Aberlour.

1879 – William Mackenzie's son forms Mackenzie and Company with Fleming.

1891 – Dailuaine-Glenlivet Distillery Ltd is founded.

1898 – Dailuaine-Glenlivet Distillery Ltd merges with Talisker Distillery Ltd and forms Dailuaine-Talisker Distilleries Ltd.

1915 – Thomas Mackenzie dies without heirs.

1916 – Dailuaine-Talisker Company Ltd is bought by the previous customers John Dewar & Sons, John Walker & Sons and James Buchanan & Co.

1917 – A fire rages and the pagoda roof collapses. The distillery is forced to close.

1920 – The distillery reopens.

1925 – Distillers Company Limited (DCL) takes over.

1960 – Refurbishing. The stills increase from four to six and a Saladin box replaces the floor maltings.

1965 – Indirect still heating through steam is installed.

1983 – On site maltings is closed down and malt is purchased centrally.

1991 – The first official bottling, a 16 year old, is launched in the Flora & Fauna series.

1996 – A 22 year old cask strength from 1973 is launched as a Rare Malt.

1997 – A cask strength version of the 16 year old is launched.

2000 – A 17 year old Manager's Dram matured in sherry casks is launched.

2010 – A single cask from 1997 is released.

Dailuaine 16 year old

GS – Barley, sherry and nuts on the substantial nose, developing into maple syrup. Medium-bodied, rich and malty in the mouth, with more sherry and nuts, plus ripe oranges, fruitcake, spice and a little smoke. The finish is lengthy and slightly oily, with almonds, cedar and slightly smoky oak.

DR – Rich and full nose, with plum, apricot jam and some treacle toffee. The palate is very full, rich, rounded and sweet with apricot and red berries. The finish is medium, fruity and sweet.

One of the most familiar sights when travelling around in, especially, the Speyside area are the pagoda roofs. One can sometimes spot a distillery miles away just with the help of the typical roof that covers the kiln where the malt was dried, at least in the olden days. But this oriental-looking roof is fairly new. No distilleries had this efficient construction for drawing off smoke from the kiln fire in old times. The first roof was designed by the famous architect and civil engineer, Charles Cree Doig, (1855-1918) at Dailuaine distillery in 1889 and was soon followed by all the other distilleries. In fact, even today when a distillery is built, it is sometimes fitted with a pagoda roof even if it does not have a kiln, just for ornamental reasons.

The distillery is equipped with a stainless steel full lauter mash tun installed in 1993, eight washbacks made of larch and three pairs of stills. There are also eight magnificent granite warehouses but they are no longer used for storing whisky. Instead, the spirit is tankered away to Cambus for filling and then to the Diageo warehouses in Blackrange.

Apart from distilling whisky which becomes a part of Johnnie Walker, Dailuaine has also turned into an "environmental hub" to seven distilleries nearby. On the site lies one of two dark grains plants in the Diageo group. It was built in 1960 to process draff and pot ale into cattle feed. The capacity of the plant is 900 tonnes per week. There is also an effluent treatment plant just below the other buildings, which treats spent lees and wastewater using various filters. The effluent is discharged into the river when the BOD level (biological oxygen demand) is less than 20 ppm.

The core range is only the *16 year old* in the *Flora & Fauna* series. In April 2010 a limited ex-sherry *single cask* from *1997* was released as part of the Manager's Choice series.

Flora & Fauna 16 years old

Dalmore

Owner:
Whyte & Mackay Ltd
(United Spirits)

Region/district:
Northern Highlands

Founded: 1839

Status: Active (vc)

Capacity: 3 700 000 litres

Address: Alness, Ross-shire IV17 0UT

Tel: 01349 882362

website: www.thedalmore.com

History:

1839 – Alexander Matheson founds the distillery.

1867 – Three Mackenzie brothers run the distillery.

1874 – The number of stills is increased to four.

1886 – Alexander Matheson dies.

1891 – Sir Kenneth Matheson sells the distillery for £14,500 to the Mackenzie brothers.

1917 – The Royal Navy moves in to start manufacturing American mines.

1920 – The Royal Navy moves out and leaves behind a distillery damaged by an explosion.

1922 – The distillery is in production again.

1956 – Floor malting replaced by a Saladin box.

1960 – Mackenzie Brothers (Dalmore) Ltd merges with Whyte & Mackay and forms the company Dalmore-Whyte & Mackay Ltd.

1966 – The number of stills is increased to eight.

1982 – The Saladin box is abandoned.

1990 – American Brands buys Whyte & Mackay.

1996 – Whyte & Mackay changes name to JBB (Greater Europe).

2001 – Through management buy-out, JBB (Greater Europe) is bought from Fortune Brands and changes name to Kyndal Spirits.

2002 – Kyndal Spirits changes name to Whyte & Mackay.

2004 – A new visitor centre opens.

2007 – United Spirits buys Whyte & Mackay. 15 year old, 1973 Cabernet Sauvignon and a 40 year old are released.

2008 – 1263 King Alexander III and Vintage 1974 are released.

2009 – New releases include an 18 year old, a 58 year old and a Vintage 1951.

2010 – The Dalmore Mackenzie 1992 Vintage is released.

Dalmore 12 year old

GS – The attractively perfumed nose offers sweet malt, thick cut orange marmalade, sherry and a hint of leather. Full-bodied, with an initially quite dry sherry taste, though sweeter sherry develops in the mouth, along with spice and balancing, delicate, citrus notes. The finish is lengthy, with more spices, ginger, lingering Seville oranges and a suggestion of vanilla.

DR – Orange jelly and squidgy fruit on the nose, an impressive full confectionery and fruit salad taste to the softest of peat beds, and a wonderful and warming finish.

If one would choose a distillery that epitomizes the trend of premiumisation, it should probably be Dalmore. Lately, this distillery has excelled in releasing more premium expressions at higher age and demanding higher prices. This could raise some concern if one looks at sales' figures; Dalmore is down in volume by 36% and the other single malt brand in the group, Jura is up 100%. But this, of course, is a deliberate strategy by the owner who wishes to position Dalmore as a rare and prestigious brand. The distillery is working at full steam, despite diminishing volumes of Dalmore single malt. The spirit is needed for the blends Whyte & Mackay, Claymore, John Barr and Cluny and not least for producing own label brands for supermarkets. For Whyte & Mackay Ltd this latter part of the business amounted to 25 million bottles in 2008.

The distillery is equipped with a semi-lauter mash tun, eight washbacks made of Oregon Pine and four pairs of stills. The spirit stills have water jackets, a peculiar device that cannot be seen anywhere else. This allows cold water to circulate between the reflux bowl and the neck of the stills, thus increasing the reflux. Two weeks per year a heavily peated spirit is produced using 400 tonnes of malt peated at 50 ppm. Following a longer quiet season in 2009 due to refurbishment of the millroom, the distillery is back to the full production of 3.7 million litres of alcohol in 2010.

The core range consists of a *12 year old* (since 2008 a 50/50 combination of sherry and bourbon), *15 year old*, *18 year old* (launched in autumn 2009), *Gran Reserva* and *1263 King Alexander III*. Limited releases have been plentiful lately, especially in late 2009/early 2010, when the extremely rare *Candela, Selene* and *Sirius* were launched. The total retail value of these 120 bottles was a staggering £1 million! In spring 2010, *Dalmore Mackenzie*, a 1992 Vintage was released. It has matured in ex-bourbon casks for 11 years with an additional 6 years in Port pipes.

15 years old

Dalwhinnie

Owner:
Diageo

Region/district:
Northern Highlands

Founded: 1897

Status: Active (vc)

Capacity: 2 000 000 litres

Address: Dalwhinnie, Inverness-shire PH19 1AB

Tel: 01540 672219 (vc)

website: www.malts.com

History:

1897 – John Grant, George Sellar and Alexander Mackenzie from Kingussie commence building the facilities. The first name is Strathspey and the construction work amounts to £10,000.

1898 – Production starts in February. The owner encounters financial troubles after a few months and John Somerville & Co and A P Blyth & Sons take over in November and change the name to Dalwhinnie.

1905 – America's largest distillers, Cook & Bernheimer in New York, buys Dalwhinnie for £1,250 at an auction. The administration of Dalwhinnie is placed in the newly formed company James Munro & Sons.

1919 – Macdonald Greenlees & Willliams Ltd headed by Sir James Calder buys Dalwhinnie.

1926 – Macdonald Greenlees & Williams Ltd is bought by Distillers Company Ltd (DCL) which licences Dalwhinnie to James Buchanan & Co.

1930 – Operations are transferred to Scottish Malt Distilleries (SMD).

1934 – The distillery is closed after a fire in February.

1938 – The distillery opens again.

1968 – The maltings is decommissioned.

1986 – A complete refurbishing takes place.

1987 – Dalwhinnie 15 years becomes one of the selected six in United Distillers' Classic Malts.

1991 – A visitor centre is constructed.

1992 – The distillery closes and goes through a major refurbishment costing £3.2 million.

1995 – The distillery opens in March.

1998 – Dalwhinnie Distillers Edition 1980 (oloroso) is introduced for the first time. The other five in The Classic Malts, each with a different finish, are also introduced as Distillers Editions for the first time.

2002 – A 36 year old is released.

2003 – A 29 year old is released.

2006 – A 20 year old is released.

2010 – A Manager's Choice 1992 is released.

Dalwhinnie 15 year old

GS – The nose is fresh, with pine needles, heather and vanilla. Sweet and balanced on the fruity palate, with honey, malt and a very subtle note of peat. The medium length finish dries elegantly.

DR – Full honey and sweet peat on the nose, a rich creamy mouthfeel and a delicious honey and exotic fruits mix all layered on soft peat foundations.

Being one of the original six Classic Malts, Dalwhinnie single malt has received special attention already since the mid 80s. Sales figures have also increased steadily, even if the last two years of harsher financial climate has decreased sales by 15% to circa 65,000 cases. But another brand associated with Dalwhinnie has made an even more impressive journey; Buchanan blended Scotch. Dalwhinnie single malt is, since the twenties, an important ingredient in this brand. Although established as long ago as in the late 19th century, it fell into oblivion during the 1980s and 1990s. Sales have increased by 100% in recent years though, due to its enormous popularity in South America, particularly in Venezuela and Mexico where Buchanan, together with Johnnie Walker, is the dominating blend. The Buchanan range of three varieties recently increased to four when Buchanan´s Master was introduced.

Dalwhinnie, beautifully set in the Grampians and visible from the A9 between Perth and Inverness, is equipped with a full lauter mash tun, six wooden washbacks and just the one pair of stills. From the stills, the lyne arms lead out through the roofs to the wooden wormtubs outside. In the eighties, the owners replaced the existing worm tubs with tube condensers but, after a while, discovered that the spirit's character changed and the worms were reinstalled. The distillery is doing 15 mashes per week, resulting in 2.2 million litres per year. Two racked warehouses are able to store approximately 5,000 casks.

The core range is made up of a *15 year old* and a *Distiller's Edition*. Some older versions have also been released in recent years. In January 2010, a *1992 Dalwhinnie single cask* from refill American Oak was released as part of the Manager´s Choice series.

It is very difficult to find an independently bottled Dalwhinnie.

15 years old

Deanston

Owner: **Region/district:**
Burn Stewart Distillers   Eastern Highlands
(C L Financial)

Founded: **Status:**   **Capacity:**
1965   Active   3 000 000 litres

Address: Deanston, Perthshire FK16 6AG

Tel: **website:**
01786 841422   www.burnstewartdistillers.com

History:
1965 – A weavery from 1785 is transformed into Deanston Distillery by James Finlay & Co. and Brodie Hepburn Ltd (Deanston Distillery Co.). Brodie Hepburn also runs Tullibardine Distillery.

1966 – Production commences in October.

1971 – The first single malt is named Old Bannockburn.

1972 – Invergordon Distillers takes over.

1974 – The first single malt bearing the name Deanston is produced.

1982 – The distillery closes.

1990 – Burn Stewart Distillers from Glasgow buys the distillery for £2.1 million.

1991 – The distillery resumes production.

1999 – C L Financial buys an 18% stake of Burn Stewart.

2002 – C L Financial acquires the remaining stake.

2006 – Deanston 30 years old is released.

2009 – A new version of the 12 year old is released.

2010 – Virgin Oak is released.

Deanston 12 year old (new bottling)

GS – A fresh, fruity nose with malt and honey. The palate displays cloves, ginger, honey and malt, while the finish is long, quite dry and pleasantly herbal.

DR – Fresh and young crystallized barley on the nose with some cut hay and grass. On the palate it's a fruit sandwich, with orange and yellow fruits at first, then a cough candy honey and aniseed centre, and orange marmalade late on. The finish is intensely fruity with some spice.

The owner of Deanston, Burn Stewart Distillers, was founded as a company in 1948. By the late eighties, the company was in a financial crisis and a management buy-out took place. Bill Thornton, later accompanied by his son, the current CEO Fraser Thornton, started thinking about how the trend could be reversed. The company lacked a big brand of its own, and so entered the blend, Scottish Leader. Today it is selling 500,000 cases and is one of the biggest brands in, for example, Taiwan.

One of the most important parts of Scottish Leader is Deanston single malt, a whisky that has just recently started selling on its own merits as well. Much money has been invested in refurbishing the distillery these past two years and, today, the equipment consists of an open top cast iron mash tun, eight stainless steel washbacks and two pairs of stills. During 2010, the distillery will be running at two thirds of its capacity, producing 2 million litres of alcohol, which is up by 35% compared to 2009. There are two warehouses, one modern racked and one listed building from the old mill, which altogether can contain 45,000 casks with the oldest dating back to 1971.

The rebranding of Deanston which started in 2009 with the new version of the *12 year old* - non-chill filtered and at a higher strength (46,3%) - continues in 2010/2011 with a couple of exciting bottlings. First out was a non-age statement malt with a finish in *Virgin Oak* casks. Beginning of 2011 *Organic Deanston* (10 years old) will follow. The distillery has been performing one week of organic production every year in August since 2000. They use Optic barley sourced from a farm in Perthshire. Later in 2011 an *older (16-19 years)* expression will be released. Deanston also produces a special 12 year old bottling for *Marks & Spencer*.

Virgin Oak

Dufftown

Owner: **Region/district:**
Diageo   Speyside

Founded: **Status:**   **Capacity:**
1896   Active   5 800 000 litres

Address: Dufftown, Keith, Banffshire AB55 4BR

Tel: **website:**
01340 822100   www.malts.com

History:
1895 – Peter Mackenzie, Richard Stackpole, John Symon and Charles MacPherson build the distillery Dufftown-Glenlivet in an old mill.

1896 – Production starts in November.

1897 – The distillery is owned by P. Mackenzie & Co., who also owns Blair Athol in Pitlochry.

1933 – P. Mackenzie & Co. is bought by Arthur Bell & Sons for £56,000.

1968 – The floor maltings is discontinued and malt is bought from outside suppliers. The number of stills is increased from two to four.

1974 – The number of stills is increased from four to six.

1979 – The stills are increased by a further two to eight.

1985 – Guinness buys Arthur Bell & Sons.

1997 – Guinness and Grand Metropolitan merge to form Diageo.

2006 – The Singleton of Dufftown 12 year old is launched as a special duty free bottling.

2008 – The Singleton of Dufftown is made available also in the UK.

2010 – A Manager's Choice 1997 is released.

Singleton of Dufftown 12 year old

GS – The nose is sweet, almost violet-like, with underlying malt. Big and bold on the palate, this is an upfront yet very drinkable whisky. The finish is medium to long, warming, spicy, with slowly fading notes of sherry and fudge.

DR – Honeycomb and tinned peach and apricot in syrup on the nose, sharp and spicy clean barley on the palate, with some bitter orange notes towards the finish.

Using long fermentation and slow distillation combined with much reflux due to the shape of the stills, Dufftown distillery produces a smooth, easy-drinking whisky. This was also what Diageo was seeking when it launched the new series of Singleton single malts for different markets a couple of years ago. The 12 year old Dufftown was earmarked for the Duty Free market but was released in Europe in autumn of 2008.

The 12 year old was supplemented with a 15 year old, a mix of European and American Oak, in 2010.

Dufftown is a giant among distilleries when it comes to capacity. It is Diageo's second largest after Roseisle and the eighth largest malt distillery in Scotland. Dufftown also has one of the biggest mash tuns in the industry, with a capacity of no less than 13 tonnes. It is a full lauter model and was installed in 1979. There are twelve stainless steel washbacks which replaced old wooden ones in 1998 when the distillery closed for four months for refurbishing. No less than £3m were invested in the distillery during 1998-2000. Throughout the years, stills have been added and it is a bit of a mystery how all of them have managed to fit into such small premises. The still house, with its three pairs of stills, must certainly be one of Scotland's most cramped.

Dufftown was the sixth distillery to be built in the whisky capital bearing the same name as the distillery. There has been a total of nine distilleries in the town, but Convalmore and Parkmore have closed, even though the buildings remain, and Pittyvaich was demolished a few years ago.

About 97% of the production goes into blended whiskies, especially Bell's. The core range consists of *Singleton of Dufftown 12 year old* and *15 year old*. In January 2010, a *1997 Dufftown* with a maturation in rejuvenated American Oak was released as a part of the *Manager's Choice* range.

The Singleton of Dufftown

Edradour

Owner:
Signatory Vintage
Scotch Whisky Co. Ltd

Region/district:
Eastern Highlands

Founded: 1825   **Status:** Active (vc)   **Visitor centre:** 90 000 litres

Address: Pitlochry, Perthshire PH16 5JP

Tel: 01796 472095   **website:** www.edradour.com

History:

1825 – Probably the year when a distillery called Glenforres is founded by farmers in Perthshire.

1837 – The first year Edradour is mentioned.

1841 – The farmers form a proprietary company, John MacGlashan & Co.

1886 – J. G. Turney & Sons acquires Edradour through its subsidiary William Whitely & Co.

1922 – William Whiteley buys the distillery. The distillery is renamed Glenforres-Glenlivet.

1975 – Pernod Ricard buys Campbell Distilleries.

1982 – Campbell Distilleries (Pernod Ricard) buys Edradour and builds a visitor centre.

1986 – The first single malt (10 years) is released.

2002 – Edradour is bought by Andrew Symington from Signatory Vintage Scotch Whisky for £5.4 million. The product range is expanded with a 10 year old and a 13 year old cask strength.

2003 – A 30 year old and a 10 year old are released. A heavily peated variety is also distilled.

2004 – A number of wood finishes are launched as cask strength.

2006 – James McGowan becomes the new distillery manager. The first bottling of peated Ballechin is released.

2007 – A Madeira matured Ballechin is released.

2008 – A Ballechin matured in Port pipes and a 10 year old Edradour with a Sauternes finish are released.

2009 – Fourth edition of Ballechin (Oloroso) is released.

2010 – Ballechin #5 Marsala is released.

Edradour 10 year old

GS – Cider apples, malt, almonds, vanilla and honey ar present on the nose, along with a hint of smoke and sherry. The palate is rich, creamy and malty, with a persistent nuttiness and quite a pronounced kick of slightly leathery sherry. Spices and sherry dominate the medium to long finish.

DR – Lemon and lime, rich fruits and some mint on the nose, sharp grape, berries and honey on the palate, and a lingering and pleasant fruity finish with hints of smoke.

Ballechin No 4 Oloroso Sherry

GS – A nose of profound, yet polished, notes of peat and sherry, which merge nicely. The palate is luxurious and smooth, with warm leather and stewed fruit notes to the fore, while insistent, spicy peat develops and lasts through a long, warming finish.

After 15 years as an independent bottler, Andrew Symington finally got what he was looking for: a distillery of his own that could supplement his other business. He had made several attempts at buying distilleries such as Scapa, Glenturret and Ardbeg, but did not score until Pernod Ricard sold Edradour to him in 2002. Immediately after the take-over a flood almost drowned the distillery, but since then the curve has pointed mainly upward and, today, Edradour is a busy place in many ways. Not so much because of a huge production (they only do 90,000 litres per year) but because of almost 100,000 visitors who are attracted to one of the most picturesque distilleries in Scotland. Since 2007 it has become even busier when the owner, independent bottler Signatory, moved from Edinburgh to a purpose-built bottling hall and warehouse next to the distillery.

The equipment at Edradour consists of an open, cast iron mash tun, two Oregon pine washbacks and one pair of stills with a purifier connected to the spirit still. The vapours are cooled in a wormtub from 1910. Edradour is the only distillery still using a Morton refrigerator to cool the worts.

The original one, dating back to 1934, was replaced by a replica in 2009. The existing warehouse with room for only 700 casks, will be demolished and a new one will be built to store 6,000 casks.

The core expression is the *10 year old*. A large number of single casks, vintages and wood finishes have been released in addition to this. A series of *wood finishes* was commenced in 2004. The most recent ones have been *Sauternes, Moscatel, Sassicaia, Port, Madeira* and *Rum*. In June 2010, a *single sherry cask* from 2000 was released as a *10 year old*.

An exciting experiment got under way in 2003, initiated by then Distillery Manager, Iain Henderson, with the first distilling of a heavily peated (no less than 50 ppm) malt. The first bottling of *Ballechin*, as it is called, appeared on the market in 2006. In August 2010 came the fifth edition, with a *Marsala finish*.

Ballechin #5 Marsala

Meet the Owner

ANDREW SYMINGTON
OWNER OF EDRADOUR DISTILLERY AND
SIGNATORY VINTAGE SCOTCH WHISKY COMPANY

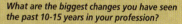

When did you start working in the whisky business?

In the mid 1980's when I was working at The Prestonfield House Hotel, overseeing events organised by the large whisky companies.

Had you been working in other lines of business before whisky?

After leaving school I pursued a career in hotel and hospitality management.

Describe your career in the whisky business.

I was 25 when I bought my first cask of whisky in 1988, which I sold by the case to a number of European customers. I then bought and sold 2 casks, and built up from there. I formed Signatory in 1988, and had casks bottled for me by various distillers. Single malts had not really caught on yet so there were many interesting bottlings that I could bring to the market. Independent bottlers provided an awareness of the variety and quality of single malts, which was not an area of focus for the majors, who were primarily focused on their big selling blends. This proved to be a great time to start out, since the whisky industry had massive surplus stocks referred to at the time as "The Whisky Loch". Several distilleries had been closed between 1983 and 1985. At this time Port Ellen, Ardbeg and Brora in particular, had still to be appreciated as producers of outstanding single malts.

What were the reasons for also adding a distillery to the company?

Building up Signatory involved considerable travel to establish a network of international distributors and to create an awareness of single malts. Whilst very rewarding and enjoyable, I was acutely aware that I was dependent upon market surpluses, and owning my own distillery was a logical way to secure my future in the industry. I had made unsuccessful bids on a number of distilleries over the years, including Ardbeg. But in 2002, I was fortunate and bought Edradour from Pernod Ricard. It was a very special day for me when George Nectoux, handed over the keys. Edradour was a perfect fit with Signatory. Its output at only 90,000 litres of alcohol per year, meant I did not have to worry about selling new make spirit to survive. Edradour sales in 2001 only accounted for about 20% of its output. Due to use in blends, there were only small stocks of casks over 12 years old and the first full year of inventory intact was 1998. So stocks were very tight until quite recently.

What are the biggest challenges of owning and managing a distillery?

Owning a distillery, brings large responsibilities. We have been true to the character of the site in our major build program. I have tried to move it on to the next level. Much is still to come in terms of product development and in the experiences that will be available to visitors to the distillery. Charging for visits to the distillery was introduced in 2010 so we could offer a more intimate experience. Our new facilities, in 2011, will allow us to also offer more in depth tours.

How would you describe the character of Edradour single malt?

The small dumpy stills at Edradour produce a heavy, oily style of spirit with a nutty sweet character. These characteristics are also very evident in our heavily peated new spirit, which we call Ballechin and which we have made each year since 2003 (min 50ppm).

What are the main features in the production process at Edradour, contributing to this character?

The quality and tradition of what we produce is of paramount importance. That is why I had a replica wort cooler made and installed in 2009. It is why we will only use casks for 2 cycles of maturation, and why we probably spend more per litre produced than any other distiller on new wood. Fresh sherry casks are used extensively in the maturation of Edradour and fresh Bourbon barrels in the maturation of Ballechin. I enjoy fine wines, so experimenting with finishing Edradour in wine casks has been something I have enjoyed doing. We contuinue to experiment with wine casks with both new spirit and in "finishes" of mature whisky. From 2011 all Edradour stocks will be matured on site.

What is your favourite expression of Edradour and why?

My favourite Edradour is the 13 year old Sherry Matured cask strength, which compares very favourably with older malts from other distilleries. I guess over time, as we release older sherry casks, I will be drinking those.

What are the biggest changes you have seen the past 10-15 years in your profession?

This would have to be the substantial consolidation in the industry amongst the big players, their much greater focus on premium blends and the single malt sector in particular. It is evident that with the higher cost of ingredients and casks, that there has been a much greater focus on quality within the industry and that has been a good thing. However, the scale and level of automation in some of the modern developments, is at the expense of tradition and skill of the individual distiller.

The emergence of China and Russia in particular as major markets for premium and Rare whiskies has also been an interesting development.

Do you see any major changes in the next 10 years to come?

The untapped growth potential, particularly in the Far East is likely to see more and more of the better quality whiskies gravitating towards those markets at the expense of the more established European markets. Many of the stocks from closed distilleries from the mid 1980's will have been consumed and scarcity value will therefore increase further. In the same vein, stocks of malts generally available to Independent bottlers, will be reduced dramatically, as economic recovery returns around the world. Independent bottlers who have not built up stocks will struggle to survive, or be competitive. Hence a number of us having diversified already into owning our own distillery.

I am looking forward to the next 10 years with great relish, to see our efforts at Edradour since 2002, translating into a mainstream Ballechin offering and the introduction of a more traditional age line up for Edradour products.

Fettercairn

Owner:
Whyte & Mackay Ltd
(United Spirits)

Region/district:
Eastern Highlands

Founded: 1824
Status: Active (vc)
Capacity: 2 300 000 litres

Address: Fettercairn, Laurencekirk,
Kincardineshire AB30 1YB

Tel: 01561 340205
website: www.whyteandmackay.co.uk

History:
1824 – Sir Alexander Ramsay, owner of Fasque Estate, founds the distillery.

1830 – Sir Alexander Ramsay sells Fasque Estate and the distillery to Sir John Gladstone.

1887 – A fire erupts and the distillery is forced to close for repairs.

1890 – Thomas Gladstone dies and his son John Robert takes over. The distillery reopens.

1912 – The company is close to liquidation and John Gladstone buys out the other investors.

1926 –The distillery is mothballed.

1939 – The distillery is bought by Associated Scottish Distillers Ltd. Production restarts.

1960 – The maltings discontinues.

1966 – The stills are increased from two to four.

1971 – The distillery is bought by Tomintoul-Glenlivet Distillery Co. Ltd.

1973 – Tomintoul-Glenlivet Distillery Co. Ltd is bought by Whyte & Mackay Distillers Ltd.

1974 – The mega group of companies Lonrho buys Whyte & Mackay.

1988 – Lonrho sells to Brent Walker Group plc.

1989 – A visitor centre opens.

1990 – American Brands Inc. buys Whyte & Mackay for £160 million.

1996 – Whyte & Mackay and Jim Beam Brands merge to become JBB Worldwide.

2001 – Kyndal Spirits, a company formed by managers at Whyte & Mackay, buys Whyte & Mackay from JBB Worldwide.

2002 – The whisky undergoes a major makeover including new bottle and packaging and the name is changed to Fettercairn 1824.

2003 – Kyndal Spirits changes name to Whyte & Mackay.

2007 – United Spirits buys Whyte & Mackay. A 23 year old single cask is released.

2009 – 24, 30 and 40 year olds are released.

2010 – Fettercairn Fior is launched.

Fettercairn Fior

DR – A big whisky from the off, earthy and rustic on the nose, with bitter orange, cocoa, nuts and burnt toffee on the nose, full mouth feel with toasty orange marmalade, chocolate and peat. The finish includes wood, burnt toffee and spice.

Fettercairn distillery is set in tranquil surroundings in the fertile part of eastern Highlands, that sometimes goes under the name Howe of Mearns. But the best way to reach the distillery is not from the south through the farmland, but from the north on the B974 road. It runs from Banchory, 20 kilometres to the north and down to Fettercairn village and is, indeed, a scenic route to travel. The Scottish Tourist Board describes it as an "adventurous" road and it is often impassable due to snow or flooding in the winter.

The distillery is equipped with a traditional mash tun made of cast iron, eight washbacks made of Douglas fir and two pairs of stills. One feature makes it unique among Scottish distilleries: cooling water is allowed to trickle along the spirit still necks and is collected at the base for circulation towards the top again, in order to increase reflux and thereby produce a lighter and cleaner spirit. The stills are connected to copper condensers where the spirit vapours turn to liquid. This is the common way of doing it, but until 1995, these condensers were made of stainless steel which probably will result in a heavier, more sulphury spirit. There are 14 dunnage warehouses on site holding 32,000 casks with the oldest from 1962.

In 2010 the distillery is doing 17 mashes per week which equals 1.5 million litres of alcohol.

Since 2002 when the bottle, name and packaging of the whisky was changed, nothing much has happened to the range of Fettercairn. The core simply consisted of a *12 year old* and a few single casks saw the light of day over the years. Now, all of a sudden, there is an *18 year old single cask* at 50% for sale at the distillery, a range of very old and limited bottlings launched in autumn 2009 (*24, 30* and *40 year olds*) and last, but not least, in May 2010 the 12 year old was discontinued and replaced by an expression without age statement. The new core bottling is called *Fettercairn Fior* which is bottled at 42% and it also contains a portion of peated Fettercairn. Independent bottlings are very rare but turn up occasionally.

Fettercairn Fior

Glenallachie

Owner: **Region/district:**
Chivas Brothers   Speyside
(Pernod Ricard)

Founded: **Status:** **Capacity:**
1967   Active   3 000 000 litres

Address: Aberlour, Banffshire AB38 9LR

Tel: **website:**
01542 783042   -

History:
1967 – The distillery is founded by Mackinlay, McPherson & Co., a subsidiary of Scottish & Newcastle Breweries Ltd. William Delmé Evans is architect.

1985 – Scottish & Newcastle Breweries Ltd sells Charles Mackinlay Ltd to Invergordon Distillers which acquires both Glenallachie and Isle of Jura.

1987 – The distillery is decommissioned.

1989 – Campbell Distillers (Pernod Ricard) buys the distillery, increases the number of stills from two to four and takes up production again.

2005 – The first official bottling for many years becomes a Cask Strength Edition from 1989.

The fame of the whisky architect, William Delmé-Evans, rests on the construction of three distilleries. The first was Tullibardine when he bought and reconstructed a brewery in the late forties. He also became the owner for a short period of time. The second was Isle of Jura where he helped local landowners in resurrecting the long closed distillery and eventually also became the Distillery Manager. The last distillery that he was involved in was Glenallachie and it was here that his long-time dream came true - a gravity-fed distillery with liquids flowing through without the aid of pumps. Delmé-Evans retired in the 70s and died at the age of 83 in 2003.

Glenallachie distillery, just outside Aberlour and in the shadow on Ben Rinnes, is equipped with a semi-lauter mash tun, six stainless steel lined washbacks and two pairs of stills. The wash stills are lantern-shaped while the spirit stills are of the onion model. All four stills are unusually connected to horizontal tube condensers, rather than vertical ones and the capacity is 18 mashes per week. The spirit is filled into bourbon casks and matured in 12 racked and two palletised warehouses. The distillery is currently running at full capacity, which entails 3 million litres of alcohol.

Glenallachie 16 year old 56,7%
GS – Major Sherry influence right through this expression, starting with warm leather and a hint of cloves on the fragrant nose, progressing through a Christmas pudding palate, featuring sultanas, dates and lots of spice, to a lengthy, sherried, leathery finish.

The trickle of Glenallachie reaching the market as single malt is feeble. It is used instead in, among others, Pernod Ricard's fourth largest (after Ballantine's, Chivas Regal and 100 Pipers) blended Scotch - Clan Campbell. Clan Campbell, a medium priced whisky, was one of few Scotch blends which managed to survive 2009 with an increase in sales' volumes - up 2% to 1.8 million cases.

Currently the only official bottling is a *16 year old cask strength* matured in first fill Oloroso casks and released in 2005. Independent bottlings have also been scarce, but in 2010 an old expression (36 years) from 1973 was released by Adelphi Distillery.

1989 16 years old

Glenburgie

Owner:
Chivas Brothers
(Pernod Ricard)

Region/district:
Speyside

Founded: 1810

Status: Active

Capacity: 4 200 000 litres

Address: Glenburgie, Forres,
Morayshire IV36 2QY

Tel: 01343 850258

website: -

History:
1810 – William Paul founds Kilnflat Distillery. Official production starts in 1829.

1870 – Kilnflat distillery closes.

1878 – The distillery reopens under the name Glenburgie-Glenlivet, Charles Hay is licensee.

1884 – Alexander Fraser & Co. takes over.

1925 – Alexander Fraser & Co. files for bankruptcy and the receiver Donald Mustad assumes control of operations.

1927 – James & George Stodart Ltd buys the distillery which by this time is inactive.

1930 – Hiram Walker buys 60% of James & George Stodart Ltd.

1936 – Hiram Walker buys Glenburgie Distillery in October. Production restarts.

1958 – Lomond stills are installed producing a single malt, Glencraig. Floor malting ceases.

1981 – The Lomond stills are replaced by conventional stills.

1987 – Allied Lyons buys Hiram Walker.

2002 – A 15 year old is released.

2004 – A £4.3 million refurbishment and reconstruction takes place.

2005 – Chivas Brothers (Pernod Ricard) becomes the new owner through the acquisition of Allied Domecq.

2006 – The number of stills are increased from four to six in May.

Glenburgie 10 year old G&M

GS – Fresh and fruity on the nose, with toasted malt and a mildly herbal note. Soft fruits and mild oak on the palate, while the finish is subtly drying, with a touch of ginger.

DR – Classic sherry, barley and prickly wood on the nose, sweet and gentle red berry on the palate, and a warming mouth-filling soft and pleasant finish.

Glenburgie, together with Miltonduff, is one of the cornerstones in the Ballantine blend. The brand became the second most sold Scotch whisky in the world in 2007 when it surpassed J&B. It still holds that position even if sales decreased by 11% in 2009 to 5.8 million cases. On the other hand, a similar decrease was experienced by most of the bigger blends. The weak economy made consumers trade down to less premium brands and it becomes very obvious when one analyses which brands actually increased their numbers - the less expensive William Peel, Label 5 and Sir Edward's among others.

When the old Glenburgie distillery was knocked down in 2003, a new purpose-built and highly efficient distillery was built just behind it. All the equipment fits on one level in one gigantic room. Most of the equipment is new but four stills, the mill and the boiler were brought in from the old distillery. The only remaining building of the old distillery is the customs house which is now used as a tasting room. A huge lawn fills up the rest of the view. The distillery is equipped with a full lauter mash tun, 12 stainless steel washbacks and three pairs of stills.

The majority of production is filled into bourbon casks and part thereof are matured in four dunnage, two racked and two palletised warehouses.

The distillery changed to a five-day week in April 2009 and during that year "only" 2.6 million litres of alcohol were produced. As from 2010 it is on full production again, distilling 4.2 million litres.

A single malt from Glenburgie named Glencraig can still be found on the market. It came into being by Hiram Walker's experimenting with Lomond stills in the fifties. Glenburgie's first Lomond still was a small model, originating in Dumbarton. It was replaced in 1958 by a pair of full-size Lomond stills and it is the make from these stills that received the name Glencraig.

An official *15 year old cask strength* Glenburgie appeared in 2008. Apart from Gordon & MacPhail 10 year old, independent bottlings are rare. A recent one is an 18 year old from Speciality Drinks.

*Gordon & MacPhail
Glenburgie 10 years old*

Glencadam

Owner:
Angus Dundee Distillers

Region/district:
Eastern Highlands

Founded: 1825

Status: Active

Capacity: 1 300 000 litres

Address: Brechin, Angus DD9 7PA

Tel: 01356 622217

website: www.glencadamdistillery.co.uk

History:

1825 – George Cooper founds the distillery.

1827 – David Scott takes over.

1837 – The distillery is sold by David Scott.

1852 – Alexander Miln Thompson becomes the owner.

1857 – Glencadam Distillery Company is formed.

1891 – Gilmour, Thompson & Co Ltd takes over.

1954 – Hiram Walker takes over.

1959 – Refurbishing and modernization of the distillery.

1987 – Allied Lyons buys Hiram Walker Gooderham & Worts.

1994 – Allied Lyons changes name to Allied Domecq.

2000 – The distillery is mothballed.

2003 – Allied Domecq sells the distillery to Angus Dundee Distillers.

2005 – The new owner releases a 15 year old.

2008 – A re-designed 15 year old and a new 10 year old are introduced.

2009 – A 25 and a 30 year old are released in limited numbers.

2010 – A 12 year old port finish, a 14 year old sherry finish and a 21 year old are released.

Glencadam 10 year old

GS – A light and delicate, floral nose, with tinned pears and fondant cream. Medium-bodied, smooth, with citrus fruits and gently-spiced oak on the palate. The finish is quite long and fruity, with a hint of barley.

DR – Fruity and treacle toffee nose, sweet, fruity and with uncluttered malt on the palate, and a clean medium long fruity finish.

GRIST MILL

This part of Scotland, Tayside, was never as strewn with distilleries as Speyside currently is, but until the mid 1980s there were at least five distilleries, with just one remaining today - Glencadam. The other four (Glenesk, Glenury Royal, Lochside and North Port) have all been demolished or are used for other purposes. The same destiny probably awaited Glencadam, had Angus Dundee Distillers not bought it in 2003.

Today it is not only a busy distillery, but also hosts a huge filling and bottling plant with 16 large tanks for blending malt and grain whisky. Owner, Angus Dundee, is responsible for 4-5% of the total export of Scotch and 3.8 million litres per year can be blended at Glencadam.

There is a traditional cast iron mash tun from the eighties and the mashing time is quite long - nine hours. There are six stainless steel washbacks (four with wooden tops and two with stainless steel ones) and one pair of stills. The external heat exchanger on the wash still is from the fifties and perhaps the first in the business. The distillery is currently working seven days a week, which enables 16 mashes per week and 1.3 million litres of alcohol per year. It was closed temporarily in October 2009 due to flooding.

On site are two dunnage warehouses from 1825, three from the 1950s and one racked. There are 23,000 casks maturing, the oldest from 1978.

Not much happened in terms of bottlings the first two years after Angus Dundee's take-over, but the owners have not been idle since. The first official bottling appeared in 2005, a *15 year old*, which was later redesigned and bottled at 46% and without chill filtration. This also goes for the *10 year old*, introduced in autumn of 2008. Two very limited releases appeared at the beginning of 2009 - a *25 year old* from 1983 and a *30 year old* from 1978, both bottled in elegant glass decanters. In 2010, three new expressions were released - a *12 year old* with 20 months of *port wood finish*, a *14 year old* with a 16 months *Oloroso sherry finish* and a *21 year old*.

10 years old

Glendronach

Owner:
Benriach Distillery Co

Region/district:
Speyside

Founded: Status:
1826   Active (vc)

Capacity:
1 400 000 litres

Address: Forgue, Aberdeenshire AB54 6DB

Tel: website:
01466 730202   www.glendronachdistillery.com

History:
1826 – The distillery is founded by a consortium. James Allardes is one of the owners.

1837 – The major part of the distillery is destroyed in a fire.

1852 – Walter Scott (from Teaninich) takes over.

1887 – Walter Scott dies and Glendronach is taken over by a consortium from Leith.

1920 – Charles Grant buys Glendronach for £9,000 and starts production three months later.

1960 – William Teacher & Sons buys the distillery.

1966-67 – The number of stills is increased to four.

1976 – A visitor centre is opened.

1976 – Allied Breweries takes over William Teacher & Sons.

1996 – The distillery is mothballed.

2002 – Production is resumed on 14th May.

2005 – Glendronach 33 years old is launched. The distillery closes to rebuild from coal to in-direct firing by steam. Reopens in September. Chivas Brothers (Pernod Ricard) becomes new owner through the acquisition of Allied Domecq.

2008 – Pernod Ricard sells the distillery to the owners of BenRiach distillery.

2009 – Relaunch of the whole range - 12, 15 and 18 year old including limited editions of a 33 year old and five single casks.

2010 – A 31 year old, a 1996 single cask and a total of 11 vintages and four wood finishes are released. A visitor centre is opened.

Glendronach Original 12 year old

GS – A sweet nose of Christmas cake fresh from the oven. Smooth on the palate, with sherry, soft oak, fruit, almonds and spices. The finish is comparatively dry and nutty, ending with bitter chocolate.

DR – Sherry, red berries, vanilla and traces of mint-flavoured toffee on the nose, an intriguing palate of cranberry and blueberry, a peaty carpet and some pepper, and a medium savoury and peaty finish.

When BenRiach bought Glendronach distillery in 2008, the goal was to sell 150,000 bottles during 2009. Instead, they sold 300,000 bottles, establishing strongholds in markets like USA, France, Taiwan and Scandinavia. In spring of 2010, they also opened a new visitor centre in spite of suffering two floods. 5,000 visitors are expected this first season.

The sherried whisky from Glendronach has always had a faithful following around the world and forty years ago, Glendronach was amongst the top five most popular malts in the world. The new owner has ambitious plans to restore the brand's former status. A £5m investment in sherry casks over the next four years and another £2m on brand promotion and extra staff was announced in September 2009.

The distillery equipment consists of a cast iron mash tun with rakes, eight Oregon Pine washbacks, two wash stills with heat exchangers and two spirit stills. Glendronach was the last Scottish distillery to fire the stills with coal. This old, traditional process continued until September 2005 when indirect heating using steam coils replaced it.

The new owners took over 9,000 casks of maturing whisky when they bought the distillery and the oldest expression in the three dunnage and three racked warehouses is from 1968.

This year there will be an average of 18 mashes a week resulting in 1.1 million litres of alcohol. Some 50% are aimed for own releases and the rest will be sold to Pernod Ricard for its blended whiskies. The core range is the 12 year old, the biggest seller 15 year old Revival and 18 year old Allardice, the last two matured in Oloroso casks. March 2010 saw the release of the 31 year old Grandeur and, to celebrate the opening of the visitor centre, a single cask from 1996 was launched. After that no less than 16 new bottlings were released - in June seven vintages (1971, 1972, 1978, 1989, 1990, 1991 and 1993), in July four wood finishes (Virgin Oak, Sauternes, Moscatel, and Port) and in September another four vintages (1989, 1990, 1991 and 1996).

20 year old Tawny Port finish

Meet the Manager

ALAN MCCONNOCHIE
DISTILLERY MANAGER, BENRIACH AND GLENDRONACH DISTILLERIES

When did you start working in the whisky business and when did you start at BenRiach?

I started working in the business in 1973 and I joined the BenRiach Distillery in 2004.

Had you been working in other lines of business before whisky?

No. I went into the business straight from school.

What kind of education or training do you have?

I achieved my Highers (Scottish Certificates of Education) at school, before commencing my career in whisky, where all of my skills were learnt in house.

Describe your career in the whisky business.

I have worked for a number of companies over the past 37 years, including:
White Horse (1973 – 1977)
Long John (1977 – 1984)
Plymouth Gin (1984 – 1988)
Laphroaig (1988 -1990)
Ben Nevis (1990 – 1991)
Bunnahabhain (1991 – 1994)
Tobermory (1994 – 2004)
BenRiach (2004 – present)

What are your main tasks as a manager?

My role as a distillery manager is challenging, but very rewarding. It is my responsibility to oversee the running of all aspects of the distillery and it is paramount that the site runs in a precise manner at all times. The main responsibilities of my role include overseeing production, warehousing and the tourism division (distillery's visitor centre and gift shop).

What are the biggest challenges of being a distillery manager?

I have to be accountable at all times and responsible for everything and everyone on site. This requires a lot of time and attention to ensure that all runs smoothly. There is never a dull moment and there are always new challenges that need addressing, however we have a great team at BenRiach/GlenDronach, who are very passionate and dedicated, so I can always be sure that work will be carried out to the highest standard.

What would be the worst that could go wrong in the production process?

The teams' safety is always of the highest importance; therefore one of my biggest concerns is injury to staff. Aside from this, we've faced serious problems with flooding at both BenRiach and GlenDronach. Last year the burn burst at GlenDronach and the site was submerged in 4ft of water. This was very problematic as it caused considerable

damage and slowed down production for a short time. Luckily though, the warehouses were not affected, so all of the casks were safe.

How would you describe the character of GlenDronach single malt?

The GlenDronach Distillery is renowned for producing richly sherried single malts. GlenDronach is rich, creamy, silky-smooth and full of character.

What are the main features in the process at GlenDronach, contributing to this character?

Firstly the water source is key. The water at GlenDronach is sourced from the Balnoon Dam, which contains a high mineral content. Secondly, our traditional practises, without a doubt, make a significant contribution to the character of GlenDronach malts. We have a rare and very traditional copper mash tun, which is scarcely found in other distilleries. Our washbacks are made from Oregon pine, rather than stainless steel, and we are proud to have traditional dunnage warehouses on site, which provide the perfect environment for maturing our whisky, as they remain cool in the summer and keep out the harsh Scottish winters. Finally, our cask selection is one of the most important factors in the process. We use the finest Pedro Ximinez and Oloroso sherry casks, sourced from bodegas in the south of Spain.

What is your favourite expression of GlenDronach and why?

The GlenDronach 12 year old is my favourite expression, as the PX and Oloroso sherry casks compliment the whisky perfectly.

If it were your decision alone – what new expression of GlenDronach would you like to see released?

It is very important to us that we don't expand the GlenDronach range too much, as we want to protect its heritage – it's richly sherried style. However, this summer we released 4 new wood finishes (Sauternes, Moscatel, Virgin Wood and Port), which I think will be a nice addition to the range and something which I personally would have hoped for. These expressions have some interesting characteristics and will help to build our product portfolio. They offer GlenDronach fans something a little different to what has been released from the distillery before.

If you had to choose a favourite dram other than GlenDronach, what would that be?

The BenRiach 16 year old is a favourite of mine. It's a really well balanced Speyside whisky, full of character.

What are the biggest changes you have seen the past 10-15 years in your profession?

The introduction of technology has made a big difference to the way distilleries operate. In addition to this, a lot of smaller companies are now coming into the business. This is great as it allows for flexibility and creativity.

Do you see any major changes in the next 10 years to come?

Yes, I'm sure technology will remain influential in the industry. There are always new advancements, which endeavour to improve the way in which distilleries operate.

Do you have any special interests/hobbies that you pursue?

I have a number of hobbies outside of work. These include reading, listening to music and following sports (especially football).

When you bought GlenDronach, could you start distilling right away or did you have to make any adjustments first?

We started distilling straight away. Production started pretty much as soon as we got the keys. There were very few adjustments that we had to make.

Any chance we will see floor maltings in operation at either BenRiach or GlenDronach in the future?

There is a high possibility that we may re-introduce the floor maltings at BenRiach. However there are a number of factors that we need to consider first – such as the impact of shift programming as well as costs. Of course it would really be worth it though as it would be great to see this aspect of the distillery reinstated.
At GlenDronach, unfortunately this isn't something that will be possible. However, the old malting floor still remains for our visitors to see.

Glendullan

Owner: | **Region/district:**
Diageo | Speyside

Founded: | **Status:** | **Capacity:**
1897 | Active | 3 400 000 litres

Address: Dufftown, Keith, Banffshire AB55 4DJ

Tel: | **website:**
01340 822100 | www.malts.com

History:

1896-97 – William Williams & Sons, a blending company with Three Stars and Strahdon among its brands, founds the distillery.

1902 – Glendullan is delivered to the Royal Court and becomes the favourite whisky of Edward VII.

1919 – Macdonald Greenlees buys a share of the company and Macdonald Greenlees & Williams Distillers is formed.

1926 – Distillers Company Limited (DCL) buys Glendullan.

1930 – Glendullan is transferred to Scottish Malt Distillers (SMD).

1962 – Major refurbishing and reconstruction.

1972 – A brand new distillery, accommodating six stills, is constructed next to the old one and both operate simultaneously during a few years.

1985 – The oldest of the two distilleries is mothballed.

1995 – The first launch of Glendullan in the Rare Malts series becomes a 22 year old from 1972.

2005 – A 26 year old from 1978 is launched in the Rare Malts series.

2007 – Singleton of Glendullan is launched in the USA.

Singleton of Glendullan 12 year old

GS – The nose is spicy, with brittle toffee, vanilla, new leather and hazelnuts. Spicy and sweet on the smooth palate, with citrus fruits, more vanilla and fresh oak. Drying and pleasingly peppery in the finish.

DR – The nose has a mix of fruits including grapefruit melon and even banana, the taste is moreish, with the citrus and melon notes coming through. Warm and pleasant finish.

The old distillery

In the quest to find new customers to sell their produce to, the whisky producers have to be rather innovative. They can, e. g., create ready-to-drink mixes with whisky and soft drinks, launch whisky specifically produced to be served with ice and make the whisky as colourless as possible to resemble vodka - the favorite tipple of many young people. But sometimes a brand becomes successful without these, sometimes perceived as drastic, approaches. The Singleton of Glendullan was marketed specifically towards first-time Scotch consumers when it was introduced in 2008 as an exclusive for the American market. The style was kept smooth as market research had shown this was favoured by newcomers to the drink. The brand has since become a success (just like its sister malts Singleton of Glen Ord in Asia and Singleton of Dufftown in Duty Free and Europe) and Diageo puts much effort into strengthening it further.

Glendullan is one of the largest distilleries in the Diageo group with a brand new full lauter stainless steel mash tun fitted in spring 2010, eight washbacks made of larch and three pairs of stills. It is one of the original seven distilleries of Dufftown and the last of them to open. However, the distillery that opened in 1896 is not the one distilling today; a new Glendullan was built in 1972 next to the old one. The two were operated in parallel for a few years until 1985 when the old distillery closed. It is now used as a workshop for Diageo´s distillery engineering team. The old distillery was equipped with one pair of stills with a capacity of 1 million litres a year. Apart from being bottled as a single malt, Glendullan is an important part of the blend Old Parr, already launched in 1909, and a big seller in Japan and South America today. The core range consists of *Singleton of Glendullan*. Previously there has also been a 12 year old in the Flora & Fauna series which was generally available. In May 2010, a *single cask from 1995* was released as part of the Manager´s Choice series.

The Singleton of Glendullan

Glen Elgin

Owner:　　　　　**Region/district:**
Diageo　　　　　　 Speyside

Founded:　**Status:**　**Capacity:**
1898　　　 Active　　　 1 700 000 litres

Address: Longmorn, Morayshire IV30 3SL

Tel:　　　　　　 **website:**
01343 862100　　　 www.malts.com

History:
1898 – The bankers William Simpson and James Carle found Glen Elgin.

1900 – Production starts in May but the distillery closes just five months later.

1901 – The distillery is auctioned for £4,000 to the Glen Elgin-Glenlivet Distillery Co. and is mothballed.

1906 – The wine producer J. J. Blanche & Co. buys the distillery for £7,000 and production resumes.

1929 – J. J. Blanche dies and the distillery is put up for sale again.

1930 – Scottish Malt Distillers (SMD) buys it and the license goes to White Horse Distillers.

1964 – Expansion from two to six stills plus other refurbishing takes place.

1992 – The distillery closes for refurbishing and installation of new stills.

1995 – Production resumes in September.

2001 – A 12 year old is launched in the Flora & Fauna series.

2002 – The Flora & Fauna series malt is replaced by Hidden Malt 12 years.

2003 – A 32 year old cask strength from 1971 is released.

2008 – A 16 year old is launched as a Special Release.

2009 – Glen Elgin 1998, a single cask in the new Manager's Choice range is released.

Glen Elgin 12 year old

GS – A nose of rich, fruity sherry, figs and fragrant spice. Full-bodied, soft, malty and honeyed in the mouth. The finish is lengthy, slightly perfumed, with spicy oak.

DR – Ginger, crystallised barley sweet and a complex array of fruit on the nose, a beautiful balanced taste with light fruit, sweet spice and a zesty freshness and mouth filling finish.

Glen Elgin is not widely known as a single malt, but the spirit has, instead, for a long time been an essential part of the blend whisky White Horse. That brand can trace its roots back to the 1860s when James Logan Mackie, owner of Lagavulin also sold blended whisky through his company. He was later joined by his nephew, Peter Mackie, who registered the brand as a trademark in 1891. White Horse, which used to be one of the big brands, has slipped down to around 20th place on the top list. Despite this, as many as around 800,000 cases are sold worldwide, mainly in the UK, USA, Japan and Brazil. A new, emerging market is Russia.

The distillery, situated in the small village of Fogwatt, a few miles south of Elgin, belongs to the Diageo group of distilleries called Speyside West, with the others being Glen Spey, Benrinnes, Dailuaine, Glenlossie, Mannochmore and Linkwood.

The distillery is equipped with a Steinecker full lauter mash tun, six washbacks made of larch and three pairs of stills. The stills are connected to six wooden worm tubs placed in the yard. They were installed in 2004 replacing six old worm tubs. Spirit from the new production is stored at Glenlossie and Auchroisk, while the older production is stored in dunnage warehouses on site. In 2010, the distillery will be doing 11 mashes per week (four short fermentations and seven long).

In 2001, Glen Elgin was launched as a part of the Flora & Fauna series, but was replaced the year after by a new *12 year old* in what was then called "Hidden Malts". Three limited editions have also been released: a *19 year old* in 2000, a *32 year old* in 2003 and, finally, a *16 year old* was launched in 2008. In autumn of 2009, a *single cask* from *1998* was released as part of the new series *Manager's Choice*. Recent independent bottlings include an 18 year old from Cadenhead.

16 years old

Glenfarclas

Owner:
J. & G. Grant

Region/district:
Speyside

Founded: 1836
Status: Active (vc)
Capacity: 3 000 000 litres

Address: Ballindalloch, Banffshire AB37 9BD

Tel: 01807 500257
website: www.glenfarclas.co.uk

History:

1836 – Robert Hay founds the distillery on the original site since 1797.

1865 – Robert Hay passes away and John Grant and his son George buy the distillery for £511.19s on 8th June. They lease it to John Smith at The Glenlivet Distillery.

1870 – John Smith resigns in order to start Cragganmore and J. & G. Grant Ltd takes over.

1889 – John Grant dies and George Grant takes over.

1890 – George Grant dies and his widow Barbara takes over the license while sons John and George control operations.

1895 – John and George Grant take over and form The Glenfarclas-Glenlivet Distillery Co. Ltd with the infamous Pattison, Elder & Co.

1898 – Pattison becomes bankrupt. Glenfarclas encounters financial problems after a major overhaul of the distillery but survives by mortgaging and selling stored whisky to R. I. Cameron, a whisky broker from Elgin.

In 2011 Glenfarclas will be celebrating their 175th anniversary of licensed distilling. Originally it was founded by Robert Hay and came to the Grant family's ownership in 1865, making it the second oldest family-owned malt distillery in Scotland. Today, the sixth generation of the family is involved in the business through the Brand Ambassador George Grant.

The distillery is equipped with a very large semi-lauter mash tun, which measures ten metres in diameter and holds 16.5 tonnes of grist. From the grist 83,000 litres of wort is obtained. The wort is then allocated to two (out of 12) stainless steel washbacks for a 48 hour fermentation. Each washback will then fill one wash still (there are three pairs of stills) for the first distillation. After that it goes into the spirit still for the second distillation where 4,000 litres of spirit (the heart) is collected and filled into casks. This means that from 16.5 tonnes of malt (83,000 litres of wort) 7,000 litres of spirit is obtained. All the stills at Glenfarclas are directly fired by North Sea gas.

There are 30 dunnage warehouses on-site which hold more than 50,000 casks. Glenfarclas uses an unusually large share of sherry butts, mainly Oloroso. For the single malts, first and second fill casks are used and for blends, refill casks. When bourbon barrels are used they are never first fill.

One of the biggest successes for Glenfarclas was the launch of the first commercially available cask strength whisky of modern age, Glenfarclas 105. The "105" in the name relates to the old way of measuring spirit strength called proof. It was abandoned in Europe in 1980 and replaced by today's system – percentage of alcohol. 105 is 5 overproof indicating a strength of 60%.

The biggest excitement this year in terms of new bottlings was the *40 year old* where 6,000 bottles were released at the end of April 2010. It will also become a permanent member of the core range, which also consists of *10, 12, 15, 21, 25* and *30 years old*. Furthermore, there is *Glenfarclas 105*, a limited version of *105* which is *40 years old* and was released in autumn of 2008 and limited editions of a *50 years old*.

Three years ago, Glenfarclas presented a unique collection of bottlings called *Family Casks*. No less than 43 single casks from 43 different years were launched simultaneously. To add to the uniqueness, it turned out that this was an unbroken series of vintages from 1952 to 1994. The fifth edition of these Family Casks was released in June (1965, 1967, 1981, 1982, 1990, 1993, 1994) and another release was made in the autumn.

History (continued):

1914 – John Grant leaves due to ill health and George continues alone.

1948 – The Grant family celebrates the distillery's 100th anniversary, a century of active licensing. It is 9 years late, as the actual anniversary coincided with WW2.

1949 – George Grant senior dies and sons George Scott and John Peter inherit the distillery.

1960 – Stills are increased from two to four.

1968 – Glenfarclas is first to launch a cask-strength single malt. It is later named Glenfarclas 105.

1972 – Floor maltings is abandoned and malt is purchased centrally.

1973 – A visitor centre is opened.

1976 – Enlargement from four stills to six.

2001 – Glenfarclas launches its first Flower of Scotland gift tin which becomes a great success and increases sales by 30%.

2002 – George S Grant dies and is succeeded as company chairman by his son John L S Grant

2003 – Two new gift tins are released (10 years old and 105 cask strength).

2005 – A 50 year old is released to commemorate the bi-centenary of John Grant's birth.

2006 – Ten new vintages are released.

2007 – Family Casks, a series of single cask bottlings from 43 consecutive years, is released.

2008 – New releases in the Family Cask range. Glenfarclas 105 40 years old is released.

2009 – A third release in the Family Casks series.

2010 – A 40 year old and new vintages from Family Casks are released.

105 Cask Strength
(Duty Free version)

40 years old

105 Cask Strength
40 years

Glenfarclas 10 year old

GS – Full and richly sherried on the nose, with nuts, fruit cake and a hint of citrus fruit. The palate is big, with ripe fruit, brittle toffee, some peat and oak. Medium length and gingery in the finish..

DR – Creamy sherry and bitter oranges on the nose, rich fruit cake and red berries on the palate with a pleasant spice and barley interplay and long and warming finish.

10 years old

12 years old

The Family Casks 1959

Glenfiddich

Owner: **Region/district:**
William Grant & Sons   Speyside

Founded: **Status:**   **Capacity:**
1886   Active (vc)   10 000 000 litres

Address: Dufftown, Keith, Banffshire AB55 4DH

Tel: **website:**
01340 820373 (vc)   www.glenfiddich.com

History:

1886 – The distillery is founded by William Grant, 47 years old, who had learned the trade at Mortlach Distillery. The equipment is bought from Mrs. Cummings of Cardow Distillery. The construction totals £800.

1887 – The first distilling takes place on Christmas Day.

1892 – William Grant builds Balvenie.

1898 – The blending company Pattisons, largest customer of Glenfiddich, files for bankruptcy and Grant decides to blend their own whisky. Standfast becomes one of their major brands.

1903 – William Grant & Sons is formed.

1957 – The famous, three-cornered bottle is introduced.

1958 – The floor maltings is closed.

1963 – Glennfiddich becomes the first whisky to be marketed as single malt in the UK and the rest of the world.

1964 – A version of Standfast's three-cornered bottle is launched for Glenfiddich in green glass.

1969 – Glenfiddich becomes the first distillery in Scotland to open a visitor centre.

1974 – 16 new stills are installed.

2001 – 1965 Vintage Reserve is launched in a limited edition of 480 bottles. Glenfiddich 1937 is bottled (61 bottles).

Until December 2009 there had been only five Master Blenders working for William Grant & Sons since the company's founding in 1887. One can therefore understand the magnitude of the occasion when David Stewart, who held the position for 35 years, handed over the responsibility to his apprentice and successor, Brian Kinsman, who has worked at his side for nine years. David is not leaving the company as he will now concentrate on his new position as Malt Master for Balvenie.

Three years ago, the owners of Glenfiddich launched a giant campaign called Every Year Counts at a cost of £23m. One of the campaign's aims was to become the first single malt brand to reach 1 million cases sold in a year. At that time the goal seemed to be within reach, but then the recession set in. Sales dropped by 6% to 874,000 cases in 2009 in just two years and number two, Glenlivet (which increased during 2009), saw an opportunity. Glenlivet has never been closer to Glenfiddich than now during the last 15 years, even if they still only sell for 70% of the archrival's volume.

Glenfiddich distillery is equipped with two big, stainless steel, full lauter mash tuns (11.2 tonnes), each with copper domes and a capacity of 4 mashes per day, i. e. 56/week. There are 24 Douglas fir washbacks with a fermentation time of 66 hours. One still room holds 5 wash and 10 spirit stills and the other 5 and 8 respectively. The wash stills are all onion-shaped while half of the spirit stills are of the lantern model and the rest have a boiling ball. All the stills are directly fired using gas. Some 90% of the casks are bourbon and the rest first or refill sherry butts. Fortyfour warehouses on site (of which six are dunnage) are shared with Balvenie and Kininvie.

Glenfiddich's core range consists of *12, 15, 18, 21* and *30 years old* and the new member, *Rich Oak 14 year old*. The latter, released in February 2010, was matured in second fill Bourbon barrels for 14 years and then received a finish of 12 weeks in new European Oak and another six in new American Oak. This was probably the first time that new European Oak had been used to mature Scotch whisky. *Caoran Reserve*, the peated version of Glenfiddich introduced in 2002, has disappeared from the range. The *15 year old cask strength* (Distillery Edition), previously a duty free exclusive, can now be found in key markets worldwide. Recent limited bottlings include the *40* (the sixth edition released in 2010) and the *50 year old*. As usual, a *Vintage Reserve* was released in the autumn - distilled in *1978* and it was chosen by a panel of renowned whisky bloggers who made their selection using Twitter.

History (continued):

2002 – Glenfiddich Gran Reserva 21 years old, finished in Cuban rum casks is launched. Sales in the USA are not possible due to the trade embargo between the USA and Cuba. Caoran Reserve 12 years, an attempt to recreate the peaty Glenfiddich produced during the war years, is launched. Glenfiddich Rare Collection 1937 (61 bottles) is launched at a recommended price of £10,000 each and becomes the oldest Scotch whisky on the market.

2003 – 1973 Vintage Reserve (440 bottles) is launched.

2004 – 1991 Vintage Reserve (13 years) and 1972 Vintage Reserve (519 bottles) are launched.

2005 – Circa £1.7 million is invested in a new visitor centre.

2006 – 1973 Vintage Reserve, 33 years (861 bottles) and 12 year old Toasted Oak are released.

2007 – 1976 Vintage Reserve, 31 years is released in September.

2008 – 1977 Vintage Reserve is released.

2009 – A 50 year old and 1975 Vintage Reserve are released.

2010 – Rich Oak, 1978 Vintage Reserve and the sixth edition of the 40 year old are released.

Glenfiddich 12 year old

GS – Delicate, floral and slightly fruity on the nose. Well mannered in the mouth, malty, elegant and soft. Rich, fruit flavours dominate the palate, with a developing nuttiness and an elusive whiff of peat smoke in the fragrant finish.

DR – Classic rich fruit and peerless clean barley nose, fruit bowl and sharp malt palate and pleasant and warming lengthy finish.

30 years old	1978 Vintage Reserve	40 years old

12 years old	Rich Oak	18 years old

Glen Garioch

Owner:
Morrison Bowmore
(Suntory)

Region/district:
Eastern Highlands

Founded: **Status:**
1797 Active (vc)

Capacity:
1 000 000 litres

Address: Oldmeldrum, Inverurie,
Aberdeenshire AB51 0ES

Tel:
01651 873450

website:
www.glengarioch.com

History:

1797 – Thomas Simpson founds Glen Garioch.

1837 – The distillery is bought by John Manson & Co., owner of Strathmeldrum Distillery.

1908 – Glengarioch Distillery Company, owned by William Sanderson, buys the distillery.

1933 – Sanderson & Son merges with the gin maker Booth's Distilleries Ltd.

1937 – Booth's Distilleries Ltd is acquired by Distillers Company Limited (DCL).

1968 – Glen Garioch is decommissioned.

1970 – It is sold to Stanley P. Morrison Ltd.

1973 – Production starts again.

1978 – Stills are increased from two to three.

1982 – Becomes the first distillery to use gas from the North Sea for heating.

1994 – Suntory controls all of Morrison Bowmore Distillers Ltd.

1995 – The distillery is mothballed in October.

1997 – The distillery reopens in August.

2004 – Glen Garioch 46 year old is released.

2005 – 15 year old Bordeaux Cask Finish is launched. A visitor centre opens in October.

2006 – An 8 year old is released.

2009 – Complete revamp of the range - 1979 Founders Reserve (unaged), 12 year old, Vintage 1978 and 1990 are released.

2010 – 1991 vintage is released.

A handful of distilleries have laid claim to be the oldest working distillery in Scotland. It is difficult to independently judge which one actually holds the rights to the claim, but among those who consider themselves worthy of the title are Bowmore, Glenturret and, just recently, Glen Garioch - a charming distillery in the town of Oldmeldrum 20 miles north-west of Aberdeen. The distillery is one of few urban distilleries left in Scotland.

Sales of Glen Garioch single malt decreased by 30% from 2005 to 2008 when 175,000 bottles were sold. After that the entire range of expressions was revamped as four core bottlings were reduced to two with a couple of limited vintages added. Sales continued decreasing during 2009 to 110,000 bottles, but this was hardly surprising since the new range was not launched until September 2009 and the 12 year old as late as the beginning of 2010. Key markets for Glen Garioch are the UK, France, Germany, Netherlands, USA and Taiwan.

Glen Garioch is equipped with a full lauter mash tun, eight stainless steel washbacks and one pair of stills. There is also a third still which has not been in use for a long time, but the owners are now discussing using it for increased production in the future. The spirit is tankered to Glasgow, filled into casks and returned to be stored in the distillery's four warehouses. The current capacity is 1 million litres but in 2010, Glen Garioch are aiming for 520,000 litres (9 mashes per week).

The new core range is *1797 Founder's Reserve* (without age statement) and a *12 year old*, both of them bottled at the rather unusual strength of 48% and non-chill-filtered. There will also be a number of limited cask strength vintages released every year. The first two were *1978* and *1990* and in summer of 2010 came *1991*. Finally, the Founders Reserve is also available in 1 litre bottles reserved for Duty Free.

Glen Garioch 12 years old

GS – Luscious and sweet on the nose, focusing on fresh fruits: peaches and pineapple, plus vanilla, malt and a hint of sherry. Full-bodied and nicely textured, with more fresh fruit on the palate, along with spice, brittle toffee and finally quite dry oak notes.

DR – Surprisingly floral and light on the nose, with fruity sweetness. The taste includes tinned sweet pear, vanilla and caramel with some earthiness as an undercarpet. There is some spice in the finale.

12 years old

Glenglassaugh

Owner: **Region/district:**
Glenglassaugh Distillery Co Speyside
(Scaent Group)

Founded: **Status:**   **Capacity:**
1875   Active   1 100 000 litres

Address: Portsoy, Banffshire AB45 2SQ

Tel: **website:**
01261 842367   www.glenglassaugh.com

History:
1873-75 – The distillery is founded by Glenglassaugh Distillery Company.

1887 – Alexander Morrison embarks on renovation work.

1892 – Alexander Morrison, the sole survivor of the original founders, sells the distillery to Robertson & Baxter. They in turn sell it on to Highland Distilleries Company for £15,000.

1908 – The distillery closes.

1931 – The distillery reopens.

1936 – The distillery closes.

1957-59 – Substantial reconstruction, including acquisition of new stills, takes place. Own maltings are abandoned.

1960 – The distillery reopens.

1986 – Glenglassaugh is mothballed.

2005 – A 22 year old is released.

2006 – Three limited editions are released - 19 years old, 38 years old and 44 years old.

2008 – The distillery is bought by the Scaent Group for £5m. Three bottlings are released - 21, 30 and 40 year old.

2009 – New make spirit and 6 months old are released.

2010 – A 26 year old replaces the 21 year old.

Glenglassaugh 26 year old

GS – Initially, aromas of of marshmallow, then mossy and herbal, with cracked pepper and ginger. Refined and balanced on the palate, with malt, summer berries and a hint of milk chocolate. Medium to long in the finish, with citrus fruit notes.

DR – Rich red berries, sweet vanilla and apple crumble on the nose, toasted almonds, honeyed oats and breakfast bar on the palate and a pleasant sweet and fruity conclusion.

When Scaent Group revived Glenglassaugh distillery after being dormant for 22 years, most of the old equipment could be used again but an investment of £1m, mainly to build a new boiler room, was required in order to be ready for the inauguration in November 2008.

The equipment consists of a rare Porteus cast iron mash tun with rakes, four wooden washbacks and two stainless steel ones (although the last two are not being used) and, finally, one pair of stills. In 2010 there were six mashes per week, which corresponds to just over 200,000 litres of alcohol. The first peated production was done towards the end of 2009 and this was repeated at the end of June 2010. It is vital to build up stock because only 400 casks of maturing Glenglassaugh (from 1963 to 1986) were included in the deal. The owner has received planning permission for a visitor centre which, according to plans, will be built during the winter and be ready to receive visitors around easter-time 2011.

The whisky is matured in a combination of dunnage and racked warehouses. There is no final decision on which casks to use and there is still much experimenting going on.

The first limited releases from the new owner were *21, 30* and *40 year olds*. In 2010 the 21 year old was replaced by a *26 year old*. There is also a triple pack of 200 ml bottles with a *37* and a *43 year old* supplementing the 26 year old. Apart from the whisky, the strategy is to also sell spirit drinks, i. e. new make or slightly older but not matured for the required three years. The first, now called *Clearac*, is the entire output from a single mash released as new make, while *Blushes* is new spirit left to mature for six months in a red wine cask. Two new spirits were released in summer 2010; *Fledgling XB* which is 12 month old spirit from a first fill bourbon barrel and the new make *Peated*.

26 years old

Glengoyne

Owner:
Ian Macleod Distillers

Region/district:
Southern Highlands

Founded: **Status:**
1833   Active (vc)

Capacity:
1 100 000 litres

Address: Dumgoyne by Killearn,
Glasgow G63 9LB

Tel:
01360 550254 (vc)

website:
www.glengoyne.com

History:

1833 – The distillery is licensed under the name Burnfoot Distilleries by the Edmonstone family.

1876 – Lang Brothers buys the distillery and changes the name to Glenguin.

1905 – The name changes to Glengoyne.

1910 – Own floor maltings ceases.

1965-66 – Robertson & Baxter takes over Lang Brothers and the distillery is refurbished. The stills are increased from two to three.

2001 – Glengoyne Scottish Oak Finish (16 years old) is launched.

2003 – Ian MacLeod Distillers Ltd buys the distillery plus the brand Langs from the Edrington Group for £7.2 million.

2004 – A 12 year old cask strength is released.

2005 – Limited editions of a 19 year old, a 32 year old and a 37 year old cask strength are launched.

2006 – Nine "choices" from Stillmen, Mashmen and Manager are released.

2007 – A new version of the 21 year old, two Warehousemen's Choice, Vintage 1972 and two single casks are released.

2008 – A 16 year old Shiraz cask finish, three single casks and Heritage Gold are released.

2009 – A 40 year old, two single casks and a new 12 year old are launched.

2010 – Two single casks, 1987 and 1997, released.

Glengoyne 12 year old

GS – Fresh and well-rounded on the nose, with medium sweet aromas suggesting malt, oak, and a hint of sherry. Smooth and delicate on the palate, slightly oaky, with a suggestion of cooking apples. The finish is pleasingly long, with buttery, vanilla notes.

DR – Tinned pear and peach on the nose, crystallised barley, lemon and grapefruit on the palate, and a fruity and peppery finish.

Glengoyne lies magnificently in the picturesque Trossarchs, at the base of Dumgoyne Hill and right on the border between the Lowlands and the Highlands. As a matter of fact, the A81 road, with the distillery on one side and the warehouses on the other, is the dividing line.

Glengoyne distillery is equipped with a traditional mash tun with rakes, six Oregon Pine washbacks, one wash still and two spirit stills. In 2010, 12 mashes per week are made which entails 750,000 litres of alcohol. Both short (56 hours) and long (110) fermentations are practiced which, together with the exceptionally slow distillation, contributes to a subtle and complex character of Glengoyne single malt. Glengoyne was previously known as one of few distilleries using the old barley variety Golden Promise, but this hasn't been used for several years now. All produce destined for single malt sales is stored in two dunnage warehouses, while the part that goes for blending, is stored in four newly constructed racked warehouses with a capacity of 55,000 casks. Glengoyne are dedicated to filling sherry casks (with exception for the new 12 year old) but have also experimented with different casks made of German, Swedish and Japanese oak. Except for a few casks of the 40 year old saved for future bottlings, the oldest cask in the warehouse is from 1983. Total sales in 2009 was 40,000 cases, but the owners have a five-year objective to reach 70,000 cases. The high quality visitor centre receives 40,000 visitors annually and on offer are no less than five different distillery tours with the most detailed, The Master Class, lasts for five hours and includes the opportunity of creating one's own blend. The core range consists of *10, 12, 12 (cask strength), 17, 21 years old* and a newly introduced wood finish, the first being a *13 year old port finish* released in September 2010. The line-up for duty free consists of the unaged *Burnfoot* and *14 year old Heritage Gold*. Recent limited editions include a *40 year old* released in autumn 2009 followed by two *single casks* (*13 and 23 years old*) launched in summer 2010.

12 years old

Meet the Manager

ROBBIE HUGHES
DISTILLERY MANAGER, GLENGOYNE DISTILLERY

When did you start working in the whisky business and when did you start at Glengoyne?

I began my career in the whisky industry in 1984 at Balblair Distillery and started at Glengoyne Distillery in October 2003.

Have you been working in other lines of business before whisky?

I spent a year after leaving school working in an oil rig fabrication yard training to be a welder/fabricator. That didn't appeal to me and I didn't want make it my career.

What kind of education or training do you have?

I left school at the age of 17, I did OK, got some O grades and Highers but wasn't a great scholar and the thought of further education at that time bored me; I wanted to make some money. I did get some formal qualifications through work in the whisky industry; I have a Diploma in Distilling, Scottish Vocational Qualification (SVQ) in management and I spent a year training to be a Brewer at Tormore Distillery.

Describe your career in the whisky business.

Began rolling casks in 1984 as a warehouse-man at Balblair Distillery, became a Relief Operator and eventually worked as a full time operator there. In 1993 I moved to Tormore Distillery to train as a Brewer. I was a Brewer at Tormore for a couple of years. Started working for Diageo in 2000 as a Site Operations Manager at Glen Elgin/Linkwood/Mannochmore/Glenlossie and in October 2003, moved to Glengoyne Distillery to become the Manager.

What are your main tasks as a manager?

Ensuring the distillery is as efficient as pos-sible is vital. I have a great team working at Glengoyne Distillery and one of the main things I do is to make sure they have every-thing they need to carry out their duties.

What are the biggest challenges of being a distillery manager?

I think keeping the site compliant with all of the legislation that applies to a whisky distil-lery is paramount. We have HM Customs & Revenue, Health & Safety Executive, Scottish Environment Protection Agency etc.

What would be the worst that could go wrong in the production process?

For me it has to be a contamination of the new spirit. Something as simple as some cleaning solution not being fully rinsed from a wash still after a clean can cause contamination. That spirit will never reach the bottle, what a waste, and a mountain of paper work.

How would you describe the character of Glengoyne single malt?

We have lots of fruity notes in the new make often described as green apple but can easily be mistaken for a sour pear drop. This cha-racter is the starting point for everything we do. The whole range of Glengoyne whiskies will give the drinker different flavours and smells, but not lying dormant in them all is the taste and smell of the Glengoyne distil-lery whisky. We have just released a 12 year old, and with some of the whisky maturing in bourbon casks, (we have only ever used sherry and refill casks in the past for our core range whiskies), this is taking the Glengoyne whisky on a completely new road and once again it is so different from the others and yet the Glengoyne character is there.

What are the main features in the process at Glengoyne, contributing to this character?

A balanced system ensures a consistent spirit quality is always achieved. We have a very slow distillation giving us a spirit run that last three hours. We invest a lot of money in our wood, especially the fresh wood such as american bourbon barrels and sherry casks. We have a very high ratio of sherry butts, these are more expensive but they play a key part in all of our core range whiskies.

What is your favourite expression of Glengoyne and why?

I enjoy the Glengoyne 17 year old; to me it ticks all of the boxes. It has just enough sherry influence from the casks to appeal to me but isn't masked by the sherry, it's an all time favourite of mine long before I started working at Glengoyne Distillery.

If it were your decision alone – what new expression of Glengoyne would you like to see released?

Not sure if we need any more new expres-sions at the moment but what i would like to see again is the Scottish Oak. I was particularly fond of that dram.

If you had to choose a favourite dram other than Glengoyne, what would that be?

Never an easy question! If i was to pick just the one then it would be Linkwood 23 year old cask strength from the Rare Malts range.

What are the biggest changes you have seen the past 10-15 years in your profession?

Big whisky companies getting bigger and bigger, legislation is increasing all the time

with regards environmental law and health and safety. We have recently experienced a boom for the whisky industry that resulted in new distilleries being built, independent companies have come on the scene such as Ian Macleod Distillers doing great things and investing big sums of money.

Do you see any major changes in the next 10 years to come?

There will be more of the same and its obvious that environmental issues are going to be a key influence for the industry.

Do you have any special interests/hobbies that you pursue?

I enjoy fishing Lochs for Trout in the remote Highlands. Walking up and down the hills behind Glengoyne Distillery with my dog Meg has become a hobby, walking around record shops to discover music from bands I've never heard of.

You have put a lot of effort into developing a range of distillery tours on different levels. Is educating the customer an important target for you?

We employ a dedicated team of managers; they have achieved the highest training standards and levels of understanding for all their team in the production of Glengoyne whisky. Their reason for doing this is to pass as much of this information on to the visitors as possible in a fun and informative way.

How is it working for one of the few family-owned companies in the business compared to the big conglomerates where you used to work?

When you work for a family owned business there is a more personal feel and a stronger sense of belonging and appreciation. My role is far wider working here than it ever was with the big companies. We don't have the same support set up so if I have a problem then I have to find a solution myself.

Glen Grant

Owner: **Region/district:**
Campari Group   Speyside

Founded: **Status:**   **Capacity:**
1840   Active (vc)   5 900 000 litres

Address: Elgin Road, Rothes,
Banffshire AB38 7BS

Tel: **website:**
01340 832118   www.glengrant.com

History:

1840 – The brothers James and John Grant, managers of Dandelaith Distillery, found the distillery.

1861 – The distillery becomes the first to install electric lighting.

1864 – John Grant dies.

1872 – James Grant passes away and the distillery is inherited by his son, James junior (Major James Grant).

1897 – James Grant decides to build another distillery across the road; it is named Glen Grant No. 2.

1902 – Glen Grant No. 2 is mothballed.

1931 – Major Grant dies and is succeeded by his grandson Major Douglas Mackessack.

1953 – J. & J. Grant merges with George & J. G. Smith who runs Glenlivet distillery, forming The Glenlivet & Glen Grant Distillers Ltd.

1961 – Armando Giovinetti and Douglas Mackessak found a friendship that eventually leads to Glen Grant becoming the most sold malt whisky in Italy.

1965 – Glen Grant No. 2 is back in production, but renamed Caperdonich.

The owner of Glen Grant, Campari Group, feels that its spirits portfolio has a too big exposure towards the Italian consumers (circa 40%) and is determined to expand the markets more. The recent re-launch of Glen Grant single malt on the important US market where it has not been sold for many years, is completely in line with this. The range will be the 10 year old and the new 16 year old and during 2010, seven states will be targeted in anticipation of a wider launch in 2011. Hopefully, long term sales in America can make up for the loss the brand has suffered in Italy which, by tradition, has been the largest market and where Glen Grant has been the number one malt. However, since 2006, Italian sales of all kinds of Scotch whisky have undergone a drastic decline. While blended Scotch decreased by 20%, single malt has decreased by as much as 75%. Glen Grant's decrease (37%) is, in view of that, considerable but not as dramatic. A total of 248,000 cases during 2009 rendered it number 5 on the top list.

The distillery is equipped with a semi-lauter mash tun, ten Oregon pine washbacks and four pairs of stills. The stills are peculiar in that they have vertical sides at the base of the neck and are all fitted with purifiers. This gives an increased reflux and creates a light and delicate whisky. There have been discussions of a possible capacity expansion by adding another four pairs of stills, but these plans have now been put on hold. Production for 2010 is expected to be 4.6 million litres.

Bourbon casks are used for maturation and the share of sherry butts is less than 10% (mainly used for the 10 year old). The previous owner, Chivas Brothers, still owns most of the warehouses but, in 2008, Glen Grant bought eleven warehouses in Rothes. A reconstruction of the visitor centre took place in late 2008 at a cost of £500,000 with The Major's Coachmans House being converted into a new visitor centre.

Some 50% of the production goes into blended whisky, especially Chivas Regal. The Glen Grant core range of single malts consists of *Major's Reserve* with no age statement but probably around 7 years old, a *5 year old* sold in Italy only, a *10 year old* and the recently introduced *16 year old*. Recent limited editions, and available at the distillery only, include two different cask strength, non-chill filtered bottlings at *15* and *17 years* respectively. To celebrate the 170th anniversary, a special limited *170th Anniversary Edition* was released in August 2010. Casks from 1976 to 1999 were selected by Master Distiller, Dennis Malcolm, to mark the occasion.

History (continued):

1972 – The Glenlivet & Glen Grant Distillers merges with Hill Thompson & Co. and Longmorn-Glenlivet Ltd to form The Glenlivet Distillers. The drum maltings ceases.

1973 – Stills are increased from four to six.

1977 – The Chivas & Glenlivet Group (Seagrams) buys Glen Grant Distillery. Stills are increased from six to ten.

2001 – Pernod Ricard and Diageo buy Seagrams Spirits and Wine, with Pernod acquiring the Chivas Group.

2006 – Campari buys Glen Grant for €115 million in a deal that includes the acquisition of Old Smuggler and Braemar for another €15 million.

2007 – The entire range is re-packaged and re-launched and a 15 year old single cask is released. Reconstruction of the visitor centre.

2008 – Two limited cask strengths - a 16 year old and a 27 year old - are released.

2009 – Cellar Reserve 1992 is released.

2010 – A 170th Anniversary bottling is released.

Glen Grant 10 year old

GS – Relatively dry on the nose, with cooking apples. Fresh and fruity on the palate, with a comparatively lengthy, malty finish, which features almonds and hazelnuts.

DR – Sweet banana and toffee, vanilla and pear on the nose, sweet barley, crystallised pineapple on the palate with a touch of honey and finally a cinnamon and spice note at the finish.

16 years old

Cellar Reserve 1992

170th Anniversary

10 years old

The Major's Reserve

Glengyle

Owner:
Mitchell's Glengyle Ltd

Region/district:
Campbeltown

Founded: 2004
Status: Active
Visitor centre:
750 000 litres

Address: 85 Longrow, Campbeltown,
Argyll PA28 6EX

Tel:
01586 552009

website:
www.kilkerran.com

History:

1872 – The original Glengyle Distillery is built by William Mitchell.

1919 – The distillery is bought by West Highland Malt Distilleries Ltd.

1925 – The distillery is closed.

1929 – The warehouses (but no stock) are purchased by the Craig Brothers and rebuilt into a petrol station and garage.

1941 – The distillery is acquired by the Bloch Brothers.

1957 – Campbell Henderson applies for planning permission with the intention of reopening the distillery.

2000 – Hedley Wright, owner of Springbank Distillery and related to founder William Mitchell, acquires the distillery.

2004 – The first distillation after reconstruction takes place in March.

2007 – The first limited release - a 3 year old.

2009 – Kilkerran "Work in progress" is released.

2010 – Kilkerran "Work in progress 2" is released.

Kilkerran Work in Progress 2

GS – A fresh and fruity nose, with tinned pears and fragrant spice. More fruit in the mouth, with quite lively oak and a hint of ginger. Steadily drying in a medium-length finish.

DR – Full, rich and fruity on the nose, oily, intense and savoury on the palate, but with a bewitching and very different fruity heart. Earthy, oily and savoury but blossoming nicely.

When J & A Mitchell bought the closed Glengyle distillery in 2000, they took care to retain as many of the original facilities as possible. The boiler house was the only building that had to be constructed. But the equipment was gone ever since the distillery had closed way back in 1925, so stills (as well as spirit safe and spirit receivers) had to be bought from another closed distillery, Ben Wyvis. To increase the reflux the body of the stills were reshaped and the lye pipes made slightly ascending. The Boby mill was acquired from Craigellachie and the 4 tonnes semi lauter mash tun came from Glenrothes distillery. The four washbacks, with a capacity of 30,000 litres each, are newly made from boat skin larch. The fermentation time is at least 72 hours, sometimes longer.

The owner is now planning short-term for new warehouses and a bottling plant to be constructed and long-term for own maltings. Today the malt is brought over from neighbouring Springbank whose staff also runs operations. Although the capacity is 750,000 litres, two months production is sufficient for the current needs. In 2010 there was production for one month only, in March.

The spirit is filled on a variety of different casks: sherry, bourbon, Madeira, Marsala and Port.

The name Kilkerran is used for the whisky as Glengyle was already in use for a vatted malt produced by Loch Lomond Distillers. In 2007 a limited 3 year old matured in Port pipes was for sale at the distillery. The first more widely available bottling was a 5 year old, named *Kilkerran Work in progress*, released in summer 2009. In June 2010, the *second edition of Kilkerran Work in Progress* appeared as a 6 year old, this time with 50% of the casks being fresh fill bourbon and the remaining casks a split between fresh sherry and refill bourbon. A total of 18,000 bottles were released. The standard Kilkerran 12 years will first be released in 2016.

*Kilkerran
- Work in Progress II*

Glenkinchie

Owner: **Region/district:**
Diageo   Lowlands

Founded: **Status:**   **Capacity:**
1837   Active (vc)   2 350 000 litres

Address: Pencaitland, Trenant,
East Lothian EH34 5ET

Tel: **website:**
01875 342004   www.malts.com

History:

1825 – A distillery known as Milton is founded by John and George Rate.

1837 – The Rate brothers are registered as licensees of a distillery named Glenkinchie.

1853 – John Rate sells the distillery to a farmer by the name of Christie who converts it to a sawmill.

1881 – The buildings are bought by a consortium from Edinburgh.

1890 – Glenkinchie Distillery Company is founded. Reconstruction and refurbishment is on-going for the next few years.

1914 – Glenkinchie forms Scottish Malt Distillers (SMD) with four other lowland distilleries.

1939-45 – Glenkinchie is one of few distilleries allowed to maintain production during the war.

1968 – Floor maltings is decommissioned.

1969 – The maltings is converted into a museum.

1988 – Glenkinchie 10 years becomes one of selected six in the Classic Malt series.

1998 – A Distiller's Edition with Amontillado finish is launched.

2007 – A 12 year old and a 20 year old cask strength are released.

2010 – A cask strength exclusive for the visitor centre, a 1992 single cask and a 20 year old are released.

Glenkinchie 12 year old

GS – The nose is fresh and floral, with spices and citrus fruits, plus a hint of marshmallow. Notably elegant. Water releases cut grass and lemon notes. Medium-bodied, smooth, sweet and fruity, with malt, butter and cheesecake. The finish is comparatively long and drying, initially rather herbal.

DR – The nose is light and flowery, with wet meadow notes and cucumber, the palate is pure barley with a touch of star anise spice and an earthy note.

The Highlands may be considered the heart of Scotch whisky production today, but it was the Lowlands that dominated in the beginning. Grain and fuel supplies were greater, they had better roads for transportation and they were closer to the market. Despite a tax of ten times higher, it was most profitable to produce there. By the time Glenkinchie was founded in 1837, 115 licensed distilleries were listed in the Lowlands. The turning point came with railway expansion northwards, enabling easier transports for Highlands distilleries. Today, only five Lowland distilleries producing malt whisky remain - Glenkinchie, Auchentoshan, Bladnoch and the two newly constructed Daftmill and Ailsa Bay.

Glenkinchie is equipped with a full lauter mash tun, six wooden washbacks and one pair of stills. A cast iron worm tub is used for cooling the spirits. Filling was done on site until 2001 and since then, it has been done centrally. Bourbon barrels are mostly used and of the three dunnage warehouses on site, one has three floors which is quite unusual. They contain around 10,000 casks maturing, the oldest from 1952. Just as in 2009, the distillery runs for full capacity which means 14 mashes per week and 2.5 million litres of alcohol in the year, much of which is used for blended whiskies. Glenkinchie is the one of the six 1988 Classic Malts selling least (circa 200,000 bottles a year). The proximity to Edinburgh is one reason why more than 40,000 visitors find their way to the distillery and its excellent visitor centre each year.

The core range consists of a *12 year old* and a *Distiller's Edition 14 years* old since 2007. In April 2010, a *single cask* from *1992* was released as part of the Manager's Choice series and one month later, Glenkinchie got their first distillery exclusive, available only at the visitor centre. It was a *cask strength without age statement*, matured in ex-bourbon barrels and with a finish in Amontillado casks. In autumn finally, as part of this year's Special Release, a *20 year old cask strength* distilled in 1990 was released.

*20 year old cask strength
distilled 1990*

Glenlivet

Owner:
Chivas Brothers
(Pernod Ricard)

Region/district:
Speyside

Founded: 1824

Status: Active (vc)

Capacity: 10 500 000 litres

Address: Ballindalloch, Banffshire AB37 9DB

Tel: 01340 821720 (vc)

website: www.theglenlivet.com

History:
1817 – George Smith inherits the farm distillery Upper Drummin from his father Andrew Smith who has been distilling on the site since 1774.

1840 – George Smith buys Delnabo farm near Tomintoul and leases Cairngorm Distillery. His son William takes over operations at Upper Drummin.

1845 – George Smith leases three other farms, one of which is situated on the river Livet and is called Minmore.

1846 – William Smith develops tuberculosis and his brother John Gordon moves back home to assist his father. Sales of Smith's Glenlivet increases steadily and neither Upper Drummin nor Cairngorm Distillery can meet demand.

1858 – George Smith buys Minmore farm, which he has leased for some time, and obtains permission from the Duke of Gordon to build a distillery.

1859 – Upper Drummin and Cairngorm close and all equipment is brought to Minmore which is renamed The Glenlivet Distillery.

1864 – George Smith cooperates with the whisky agent Andrew P. Usher and exports the whisky with great success.

1871 – George Smith dies and his son John Gordon takes over.

Glenlivet single malt was number three on the sales list, after Glenfiddich and Glen Grant, when Pernod Ricard bought the distillery. Two years later, Glen Grant had been overtaken but second place was held for just a year as Glenlivet was surpassed by Macallan. Glenlivet has, however, been number two behind Glenfiddich after 2005. But the owners are not satisfied with that and have stated a clear objective of becoming the most sold single malt in the world, even if it will take ten or fifteen years.

This is also the cause for a major capacity expansion in 2009/2010. The original equipment line-up consisted of one mash tun, eight wooden washbacks and four pairs of stills producing 5.8 million litres per year. In 2009, another huge mash tun, eight wooden washbacks and 2 pairs of stills were added and then, in May 2010, yet another pair of stills. This gives the distillery a capacity of no less than 10.5 million litres - bigger than archrival Glenfiddich. The refurbished and expanded distillery, which has cost £10m, was inaugurated on 4th June by HRH The Prince of Wales.

Like most other brands, Glenlivet was hit by the recession that began in 2008 and figures for that year came in 5% lower than in 2007. Last year however, Glenlivet was back on track selling 612,000 cases while Glenfiddich fell 3,2% to 874,000 cases. The unrivalled and most important market for Glenlivet is the USA where 45% of all Glenlivet is sold and where the brand accounts for 27% share of the single malt category. Around 62,000 casks are stored on site in both dunnage and racked warehouses. Glenlivet's core range is the *12 year old*, matured in bourbon casks, the *French Oak 15 years* (with 6-9 months finish in new Limousin Oak casks) and the *18 year old* (matured in ex-sherry casks). Limited editions include the re-launched *21 year old Archive*, *Glenlivet XXV* (launched in 2007) and *1973 Cellar Collection* (released in 2009). The latter is a combination of one sherry butt and two American Oak refill hogsheads. To celebrate the expansion of the distillery, *Glenlivet Founder's Reserve* - a 21 year old - was released in 2010. There were 1824 bottles to mark the year when the distillery received its license.

Three expressions are earmarked for the Duty Free market: *First Fill Sherry Cask 12 years old*, *15 years old* and *Nadurra* (16 years old and non-chill filtered). A *cask strength* version of *Nadurra* was released in the USA in 2006 and in November 2009, yet another variety, *Nadurra Triumph 1991*, appeared. It is 18 years old (two years older than the cask strength version) and the name derives from the Triumph barley that was used in the distillation.

History (continued):

1880 – John Gordon Smith applies for and is granted sole rights to the name The Glenlivet. All distilleries wishing to use Glenlivet in their names must from now hyphenate it with their brand names.

1890 – A fire breaks out and some of the buildings are replaced.

1896 – Another two stills are installed.

1901 – John Gordon Smith dies.

1904 – John Gordon's nephew George Smith Grant takes over.

1921 – Captain Bill Smith Grant, son of George Smith Grant, takes over.

1953 – George & J. G. Smith Ltd merges with J. & J. Grant of Glen Grant Distillery and forms the company Glenlivet & Glen Grant Distillers.

1966 – Floor maltings closes.

1970 – Glenlivet & Glen Grant Distillers Ltd merges with Longmorn-Glenlivet Distilleries Ltd and Hill Thomson & Co. Ltd to form The Glenlivet Distillers Ltd.

1978 – Seagrams buys The Glenlivet Distillers Ltd. A visitor centre opens.

1996/97 – The visitor centre is expanded, and a multimedia facility installed.

2000 – French Oak 12 years and American Oak 12 years are launched

2001 – Pernod Ricard and Diageo buy Seagram Spirits & Wine. Pernod Ricard thereby gains control of the Chivas group.

2004 – This year sees a lavish relaunch of Glenlivet. French Oak 15 years replaces the previous 12 year old.

2005 – Two new duty-free versions are introduced – The Glenlivet 12 year old First Fill and Nadurra. The 1972 Cellar Collection (2,015 bottles) is launched.

2006 – Nadurra 16 year old cask strength and 1969 Cellar Collection are released. Glenlivet sells more than 500,000 cases for the first time in one year.

2007 – Glenlivet XXV is released.

2009 – Four more stills are installed and the capacity increases to 8.5 million litres. Nadurra Triumph 1991 is released.

2010 – Another two stills are commissioned and capacity increases to 10.5 million litres. Glenlivet Founder's Reserve is released.

1973 Cellar Collection

Nadurra Triumph 1991

First Fill Sherry Cask 12 years old

Glenlivet 12 year old

GS – A lovely, honeyed, floral, fragrant nose. Medium-bodied, smooth and malty on the palate, with vanilla sweetness. Not as sweet, however, as the nose might suggest. The finish is pleasantly lengthy and sophisticated.

DR – Freshly chopped apple, rhubarb and crisp barley on the nose, soft rounded and beautiful mouth feel with green fruit and gooseberries and a delicate, rounded and medium long finish.

12 years old

18 years old

15 years old French Oak Reserve

Glenlossie

Owner:
Diageo

Region/district:
Speyside

Founded: 1876
Status: Active
Capacity: 1 800 000 litres

Address: Birnie, Elgin, Morayshire IV30 8SS

Tel: 01343 862000
website: www.malts.com

History:

1876 – John Duff, former manager at Glendronach Distillery, founds the distillery. Alexander Grigor Allan (to become part-owner of Talisker Distillery), the whisky trader George Thomson and Charles Shirres (both will co-found Longmorn Distillery some 20 years later with John Duff) and H. Mackay are also involved in the company.

1895 – The company Glenlossie-Glenlivet Distillery Co. is formed. Alexander Grigor Allan passes away.

1896 – John Duff becomes more involved in Longmorn and Mackay takes over management of Glenlossie.

1919 – Distillers Company Limited (DCL) takes over the company.

1929 – A fire breaks out and causes considerable damage.

1930 – DCL transfers operations to Scottish Malt Distillers (SMD).

1962 – Stills are increased from four to six.

1971 – Another distillery, Mannochmore, is constructed by SMD on the premises. A dark grains plant is installed.

1990 – A 10 year old is launched in the Flora & Fauna series.

2010 – A Manager's Choice single cask from 1999 is released.

Glenlossie 10 year old

GS – Cereal, silage and vanilla notes on the relatively light nose, with a voluptuous, sweet palate, offering plums, ginger and barley sugar, plus a hint of oak. The finish is medium in length, with grist and slightly peppery oak.

DR – Powdery and light, with salt and pepper on the nose, big, earthy and spicy palate; savoury and full, with a long and mouth-coating finish.

Taking care of the residues from whisky making does not just incur costs for the distillery, but can sometimes also generate a profit. Pot ale is what is left after the first distillation in the wash still. When alcohol reaches below 1% the fluids are collected in a special tank which mainly consists of water and dead yeast cells. After reducing it to a syrup, which is rich in proteins and carbohydrates, it can be used for animal feed. It can also be mixed with draff and is then called dark grains, also perfect for feeding livestock. Draff is the cereal residue obtained after the mashing is completed. There is a dark grains plant at Glenlossie, serving not only Glenlossie, but many other Diageo distilleries as well. The volumes are impressive; 110,000 tonnes of draff and 8.5 million litres of pot ale is treated every year. The distillery itself is equipped with a stainless steel full lauter mash tun (8.2 tonnes) installed in 1992, eight washbacks made of larch and three pairs of stills. The spirit stills are also equipped with purifiers between the lyne arms and the condensers to increase the reflux which gives a light and clean spirit.

The workforce used to alternate between Glenlossie and its sister distillery, Mannochmore, with each of them being in production for half a year at a time. In 2007 this was changed and both distilleries are now producing simultaneously. During 2010 a five-day week with 12 mashes was implemented, resulting in 1.8 million litres of alcohol.

The whisky is mainly used for blends, especially Haig, and the only official bottling available today is a *10 year old* in the Distillery Malts (Flora & Fauna) series. In May 2010, 200 bottles were released from a *first fill bourbon cask* distilled in 1999. This was a part of Diageo's Manager's Choice series. A 16 year old distilled in 1993 was recently released by the independent bottler Cadenhead.

Flora & Fauna 10 years old

New Books We Enjoyed

Ian Buxton has spoiled us with reprints of fascinating old whisky books for years. This year he has written several book of his own which was about time. The first one is *101 Whiskies to Try Before You Die* where he has chosen brands that are not only affordable but also available to most drinkers around the world. The language of the book is brilliant, both witty and knowledgeable and the layout is contemporary and slick. One of the best whisky books in recent years. Another book by Ian, *Glenglassaugh - a Distillery Reborn*, deals with the resurrection of a distillery that was closed for decades. It is a fascinating story and even

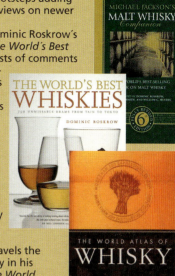

more so since Ian sits on first-hand information about the twists and turns of resurrecting it.
Michael Jackson´s *Malt Whisky Companion* was the obvious guide for many of us when we started to explore the world of whisky back in the 80s. He managed to publish five editions before his untimely death three years ago. This is the sixth, where Gavin D Smith and Dominic Roskrow follow in his footsteps adding their personal views on newer releases.

The bulk of Dominic Roskrow´s latest book, *The World´s Best Whiskies*, consists of comments and tasting notes for whiskies of all sorts and from all corners of the world. But there are also chapters on how whisky is produced, how to combine whisky and food, how to make whisky cocktails and much more.

Dave Broom travels the world of whisky in his latest book *The World Atlas of Whisky* and with the help of flavour charts and more than 300 tasting notes, he presents not only single malts but also blended Scotch, bourbon, rye and other types of whisky.

101 Whiskies to Try Before You Die
ISBN 978-0755360833
Glenglassaugh - a Distillery Reborn
ISBN 978-1906476137

Michael Jackson´s Malt Whisky Companion
ISBN 978-1405319669
The World´s Best Whiskies
ISBN 978-1906417420

The World Atlas of Whisky
ISBN 978-1845335410

Recommended Magazines

Malt Advocate
www.maltadvocate.com

Whisky Magazine
www.whiskymag.com

Whisky Time
www.whiskytime-magazin.com

Der Whisky-Botschafter
www.whiskybotschafter.com

Whisky Passion
www.whiskypassion.nl

Allt om Whisky
www.alltomwhisky.se

Glenmorangie

Owner:
The Glenmorangie Co
(Moët Hennessy)

Region/district:
Northern Highlands

Founded: 1843
Status: Active (vc)
Capacity: 6 000 000 litres

Address: Tain, Ross-shire IV19 1BR

Tel: 01862 892477 (vc)
website: www.glenmorangie.com

History:

1843 – William Mathesen applies for a license for a farm distillery called Morangie, which is rebuilt by them. Production took place here in 1738, and possibly since 1703.

1849 – Production starts in November.

1880 – Exports to foreign destinations such as Rome and San Francisco commence.

1887 – The distillery is rebuilt and Glenmorangie Distillery Company Ltd is formed.

1918 – 40% of the distillery is sold to Macdonald & Muir Ltd and 60 % to the whisky dealer Durham. Macdonald & Muir takes over Durham's share by the late thirties.

1931 – The distillery closes.

1936 – Production restarts in November.

1980 – Number of stills increases from two to four and own maltings ceases.

1990 – The number of stills is doubled to eight.

1994 – A visitor centre opens. September sees the launch of Glenmorangie Port Wood Finish which marks the start of a number of different wood finishes.

1995 – Glenmorangie's Tain l'Hermitage (Rhone wine) is launched.

Glenmorangie has seen large changes during the last three years. The whole range of blended whiskies, save for a few exceptions, was abandoned in order to concentrate on the single malts. The latter was groomed and re-launched in 2007. The head office and bottling plant in Broxburn was sold to Diageo and new facilities were moved into in 2010. The distillery itself was meticulously expanded and raised its capacity as a result. Finally, a number of new expressions, born in designer casks or from varieties of malted barley, have seen the light. Since March 2009 when the expansion was completed, the equipment now consists of a full lauter mash tun, ten stainless steel washbacks and five pairs of stills. The two new stills are exact replicas of the extremely tall gin type of stills that have been in use since 1843. The reconstruction amounted to £4.5m. Glenmorangie has always been very particular with the casks that are used. American oak is preferred and a part of them, known as designer casks, come from slow growth woods in the Ozarks, Missouri. They are air-dried for a minimum of two years and when water content is down to 17% they are dried further through mechanical means. Then the casks are made, heavily toasted using infrared technology and then lightly charred. After having been filled with bourbon for four years, they are emptied and brought to Scotland. This programme started already in 1985 and today designer casks are used mainly for the Astar expression, but for the last couple of years, they have also been used for Original.

The core range consists of *Original* (the former 10 year old), *18 years old* and *25 years old*. The wood finishes have been reduced to three: *Quinta Ruban* (port), *Nectar D'Or* (Sauternes) and *Lasanta* (sherry). They are all non-chill filtered and bottled at 46%. Added to the core range are *Astar* and *Signet*. *Astar* has matured in designer casks and is a follow-up to Artisan Cask which was released in 2004. The *Signet* is an unusual piece of work which has been crafted by the distillery's two whisky creators, Bill Lumsden and Rachel Barrie. A portion of the whisky (20%) has been made using chocolate malt which is normally used to produce porter and stout. The Signet also contains single malts from the seventies, eighties and nineties.

There have been several limited editions throughout the years. The most recent, released in autumn of 2010, was *Finealta*, the second in the Private Collection series which started the year before with *Sonnalta PX*. Finealta is a mix of American oak and European oak Oloroso casks. Finealta will be sold as a Duty Free exclusive for the first three months and will thereafter be released to the public.

History (continued):

1996 – Two different wood finishes are launched, Madeira and Sherry. Glenmorangie plc is formed.

1997 – A museum opens.

2001 – A limited edition of a cask strength port wood finish is released in July, Cote de Beaune Wood Finish is launched in September and Three Cask (ex-Bourbon, charred oak and ex-Rioja) is launched in October for Sainsbury's.

2002 – A Sauternes finish, a 20 year Glenmorangie with two and a half years in Sauternes casks, is launched.

2003 – Burgundy Wood Finish is launched in July and a limited edition of cask strength Madeira-matured (i. e. not just finished) in August.

2004 – Glenmorangie buys the Scotch Malt Whisky Society which has 27,000 members worldwide. The Macdonald family decides to sell Glenmorangie plc (including the distilleries Glenmorangie, Glen Moray and Ardbeg). Bidding is frantic and the buyer is Moët Hennessy (owned by Diageo and LVMH) at £300 million. A new version of Glenmorangie Tain l'Hermitage (28 years) is released and Glenmorangie Artisan Cask is launched in November.

2005 – A 30 year old is launched.

2007 – The entire range gets a complete makeover with 15 and 30 year olds being discontinued and the rest given new names as well as new packaging.

2008 – An expansion of production capacity is started. Astar and Signet are launched.

2009 – The expansion is finished and Sonnalta PX is released for duty free.

2010 – Finealta is released.

Glenmorangie Original

GS – The nose offers fresh fruits, butterscotch and toffee. Silky smooth in the mouth, mild spice, vanilla, and well-defined toffee. The fruity finish has a final flourish of ginger.

DR – Rounded honey and light tangerine on the nose, much weightier on the palate, with vanilla, honey, oranges and lemons nudging alongside some tannins and soft peat, all coming together in a rich and warming finish.

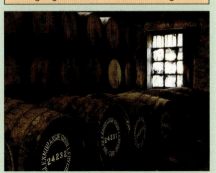

Signet

Astar

Finealta

Nectar D'Or

Original (10 years old)

Quinta Ruban

Glen Moray

Owner:
La Martiniquaise

Region/district:
Speyside

Founded: 1897

Status: Active (vc)

Capacity: 2 200 000 litres

Address: Bruceland Road, Elgin, Morayshire IV30 1YE

Tel: 01343 542577

website: www.glenmoray.com

History:

1897 – West Brewery, dated 1828, is reconstructed as Glen Moray Distillery.

1910 – The distillery closes.

1920 – Financial troubles force the distillery to be put up for sale. Buyer is Macdonald & Muir.

1923 – Production restarts.

1958 – A reconstruction takes place and the floor maltings are replaced by a Saladin box.

1978 – Own maltings are terminated.

1979 – Number of stills is increased to four.

1992 – Two old stills are replaced by new.

1996 – Macdonald & Muir Ltd changes name to Glenmorangie plc.

1999 – Three wood finishes are introduced - Chardonnay (no age) and Chenin Blanc (12 and 16 years respectively).

2004 – Louis Vuitton Moët Hennessy buys Glenmorangie plc for £300 million. A new visitor centre is inaugurated and a 1986 cask strength, a 20 and a 30 year old are released. Wood finishing ceases.

2005 – The Fifth Chapter (Manager's Choice from Graham Coull) is released.

2006 – Two vintages, 1963 and 1964, and a new Manager's Choice are released.

2007 – The second edition of Mountain Oak is released.

2008 – The distillery is sold to La Martiniquaise.

2009 – A 14 year old Port finish and an 8 year old matured in red wines casks are released.

Glen Moray has now spent two years under French ownership and seems like a distillery re-born. The long-term goal is to sell 100,000 cases per year and from 2008 to 2009, the volume has increased by 25% to 50,000 cases. Some new exciting bottlings have been released and the owner is also seriously looking at expanding the distillery by 2011. This is quite a difference compared to the years when it was overshadowed by Glenmorangie and Ardbeg!

The owner, La Martiniquaise, already established in 1934, has had a presence in Scotland since 2004, with its huge maturation, blending and bottling plant called Glen Turner near Bathgate. The company was one of the bidders for Invergordon grain distillery in 2006, but has now expanded the plant in West Lothian with a distillery able to make 5 million litres of malt whisky and 25 million litres of grain whisky. The distillery was commissioned in summer 2010.

Glen Moray distillery is equipped with a stainless steel mash tun, five stainless steel washbacks and two pairs of stills. The capacity is now increased, thanks to a heat recovery project in the still house, and the target for 2010 on a 7-day production is 2.2 million litres of alcohol. The whisky is matured to 99% in bourbon casks. There are also some sherry butts and the odd Madeira, Burgundy and rum casks lying in the eight dunnage and two palletised warehouses. The oldest casks are from 1971 and the rest are from the eighties and forward. In 2009, the distillery also produced a share of whisky from peated malt with around 40ppm phenols. The volume of the first batch amounted to 300,000 litres and it will mainly be used in the owner's Label 5 blended whisky, but some may be used as single malt as well.

The core range consists of *Classic*, *12* and *16 years old*. Recent limited editions include *Signature*, a *30 year old* and from late 2009 - a *14 year old port finish* and an *8 year old matured in red wine casks*. Portwood and Madeira finishes are announced for release in 2011, but a *Chardonnay matured* expression appeared already in 2010.

1995 Manager's Choice

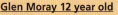

Glen Moray 12 year old

GS – Mellow on the nose, with vanilla, pear drops and some oak. Smooth in the mouth, with spicy malt, vanilla and summer fruits. The finish is relatively short, with spicy fruit.

DR – Maltesers and soft vanilla ice cream on the nose, full and rich sweet malt, a touch of vanilla and hints of tannin on the palate and a pleasant and pleasing finish.

Glen Ord

Owner:　　　　　**Region/district:**
Diageo　　　　　　　Northern Highlands

Founded:　**Status:**　**Capacity:**
1838　　　　Active (vc)　4 000 000 litres

Address: Muir of Ord, Ross-shire IV6 7UJ

Tel:　　　　　　　**website:**
01463 872004 (vc)　www.malts.com

History:

1838 – Thomas Mackenzie founds the distillery and licenses it to Ord Distillery Co. (Robert Johnstone and Donald MacLennan).

1847 – The distillery is put up for sale.

1855 – Alexander MacLennan and Thomas McGregor buy the distillery.

1870 – Alexander MacLennan dies and the distillery is taken over by his widow who eventually marries the banker Alexander Mackenzie.

1877 – Alexander Mackenzie leases the distillery.

1878 – Alexander Mackenzie builds a new still house and barely manages to start production before a fire destroys it.

1882 – Mackenzie registers the name Glenoran to be used for whisky from Glen Ord.

1896 – Alexander Mackenzie dies and the distillery is sold to the blending company James Watson & Co. for £15,800.

1923 – John Jabez Watson, James Watson's son, dies and the distillery is sold to John Dewar & Sons. The name is changed from Glen Oran to Glen Ord.

1925 – Dewar's joins Distillers Company Limited.

1961 – Floor maltings is abandoned in favour of a Saladin box.

1966 – The two stills are increased to six.

1968 – To augment the Saladin box a drum maltings is built.

1983 – Malting in the Saladin box ceases.

1988 – A visitor centre is opened.

2002 – A 12 year old is launched.

2003 – A limited-edition cask strength, 28 years, is launched.

2004 – A 25 year old is launched.

2005 – A 30 year old is launched as a Special Release from Diageo.

2006 – A 12 year old Singleton of Glen Ord is launched.

2010 – A Singleton of Glen Ord 15 year old is released in Taiwan.

Singleton of Glen Ord 12 year old

GS – Honeyed malt and milk chocolate on the nose, with a hint of orange. These characteristics carry over onto the sweet, easy-drinking palate, along with a biscuity note. Subtly drying, with a medium-length, spicy finish.

DR – Red fruits and blackcurrant, mince pies, red apple and sherry on the nose, enjoyable taste of apple, prune and cinnamon, and a delightful and more-ish finish.

In the mid-eighties the brand name Singleton, was invented to help sell the whisky from difficult-to-pronounce Auchroisk Distillery. This was in use until 2001 when Auchroisk became a part of the Flora & Fauna range. Five years later, the brand name was resurrected and used for a range of whiskies from three different distilleries destined for three different markets - Dufftown, Glendullan and Glen Ord. The latter, aimed at the Asian market, became one of the biggest successes for the owners in recent years. The brand reached number 14 on the world sales' list in only four years and is now selling 80,000 cases a year, with more than 90% being sold in Taiwan.

Glen Ord distillery is situated 15 miles west of Inverness in the fertile Black Isle. The buildings are a mix of modern and old, with a new still house with glazed curtain walls built in 1966, to accommodate another four stills. The equipment consists of a new stainless steel full lauter mash tun which in autumn 2010 replaced the old one made of cast iron, eight washbacks made of Oregon Pine and three pairs of stills. There are five dunnage warehouses with a capacity of 15,000 casks.

A major part of the site is occupied by the Glen Ord Maltings. This is one of four maltings owned by Diageo and with a capacity of 36,000 tonnes per year it produces malt for several other Diageo distilleries. The distillery used floor maltings until 1961 when it was replaced by Saladin boxes. The Saladin boxes supplied malt for the distillery until 1984, but already in 1968, the large drum malting with 18 drums was built.

The core expression is the *Singleton of Glen Ord 12 year old*, with a 50/50 mix of sherry and bourbon casks. Other expressions in the range are the *15 year old* (released in June 2010), the *18 year old* and the two extremely limited ones - *32* and *35 year old*. In April 2010, a bourbon-matured *single cask Glen Ord* from *1997* was released in the Manager's Choice series.

The Singleton of Glen Ord

Glenrothes

Owner:
The Edrington Group

Region/district:
Speyside

Founded: **Status:**
1878   Active

Capacity:
5 600 000 litres

Address: Rothes, Morayshire AB38 7AA

Tel:
01340 872300

website:
www.glenrotheswhisky.com

History:
1878 – James Stuart & Co., licensees of Macallan since 1868, begins planning a new distillery in Rothes. Robert Dick, William Grant and John Cruickshank are partners in the company. Stuart has financial problems so Dick, Grant and Cruick-shank terminate the partnership, form William Grant & Co. and continue the building of the distillery in Rothes.

1879 – Production starts in May.

1884 – The distillery changes name to Glenrothes-Glenlivet.

1887 – William Grant & Co. joins forces with Islay Distillery Co. (owners of Bunnahabhain Distillery) and forms Highland Distillers Company.

1897 – A fire ravages the distillery in December.

1898 – Capacity doubles.

1903 – An explosion causes substantial damage.

1963 – Expansion from four to six stills.

1980 – Expansion from six to eight stills.

1989 – Expansion from eight to ten stills.

1999 – Edrington and William Grant & Sons buy Highland Distillers.

2002 – Four single cask malts from 1966 and 1967 are launched.

2005 – A 30 year old is launched together with Select Reserve and Vintage 1985.

2006 – 1994 and 1975 Vintage are launched.

2007 – A 25 year old is released as a duty free item.

2008 – 1978 Vintage and Robur Reserve are launched.

2009 – The Glenrothes John Ramsay, two vintages (1988 and 1998), Alba Reserve and Three Decades are released.

2010 – Berry Brothers takes over the brand while Edrington remains owner of the distillery.

Glenrothes Select Reserve

GS – The nose offers ripe fruits, spice and toffee, with a whiff of Golden Syrup. Faint wood polish in the mouth, vanilla, spicy and slightly citric. Creamy and complex. Slightly nutty, with some orange, in the drying finish.

DR – On the nose, oranges dominating a fruit bowl of flavours that includes berries among the citrus. The palate is wonderfully rounded and complete, a masterclass in fruit, wood and spice balance, and the finish is a total joy, perfectly weighted and balanced.

Single malt from Glenrothes Distillery has been a vital part in the blend Cutty Sark ever since it was invented 87 years ago by Berry Bros & Rudd (BBR). Edrington, the owner of Glenrothes, has continually produced the whisky for BBR. In later years, Glenrothes has become a strong brand in its own right - owned by Edrington but marketed and distributed by BBR. Sales of Cutty Sark have declined since the seventies, when it was the biggest Scotch blend in the US and BBR realised that in the present world of mega brands looking for a global distribution, it was better if Edrington took over Cutty Sark and for BBR, with their strength in premium niche brands, to take over Glenrothes. A deal was agreed upon in spring 2010 when the two brands switched owners but with Edrington still owning Glenrothes distillery.

The distillery is equipped with a stainless steel semi-lauter mash tun. Ten washbacks made of Oregon Pine are in one room, whilst an adjacent modern tun room houses eight new stainless steel washbacks. The still house has five pairs of stills and the spirit is stored in twelve dunnage and four racked warehouses. The core expression of Glenrothes is the *Select Reserve* without age statement, while it is the vintages that have brought fame to Glenrothes. In 2009, *1998* was released as the new core vintage after 1991 and 1994, while a *1988* was earmarked for Taiwan. In August 2009, *Alba Reserve*, matured solely in American Oak refill bourbon casks, was released. This was also the first kosher whisky from the producers. The retiring Master Blender, John Ramsay, presented his legacy in September with *The Glenrothes John Ramsay*. It was a vatting of ex-sherry casks from 1973 to 1987. In 2007 and 2008 two expressions were launched for the Duty Free market - a *25 year old* and *Robur Reserve*. At the end of 2009 came yet another one, *Glenrothes Three Decades*, which held whisky from the seventies, eighties and nineties matured in both ex bourbon and ex sherry casks.

1988 Vintage

Whisky Chronology

continued from page 73
continued from page 73

1960 Edrington Holdings is formed.

1960 Whyte & Mackay merges with Mackenzie Brothers and takes over Dalmore Distillery.

1961 Ind Coope, Tetley Walker and Ansells form Ind Coope Tetley Ansell (later to become Allied Breweries).

1962 United Wine Traders merges with W. A Gilbey and forms United Distillers & Vintners.

1963 Ind Coope Tetley Ansell changes name to Allied Breweries.

1964 Inver House Distillers becomes a subsidiary to Publicker Industries.

1965 Invergordon Distillers is formed.

1969 Allied Breweries buys Alexander Stewart & Son.

1969 Seager Evans changes name to Long John International.

1970 Highland Distilleries Co. buys Matthew Gloag & Son Ltd.

1970 Hill Thomson merges with Glenlivet & Glen Grant Distilleries and form The Glenlivet Distilleries.

1972 International Distillers & Vintners (IDV) is bought by Watney Mann.

1972 Watney Mann is bought by Grand Metropolitan.

1973 House of Fraser buys Whyte & Mackay.

1974 Lonhro buys Whyte & Mackay.

1975 Pernod Ricard buys Campbell Distillers.

1975 Schenley sells Long John International to Whitbread & Company.

1976 Allied Brewers takes over William Teacher & Sons.

1978 Seagram buys the Glenlivet Distillers Limited.

1978 Allied Breweries buys J. Lyons.

1981 Allied Breweries changes name to Allied-Lyons in December.

1983 Grand Met buys International Distillers & Vintners (IDV).

1985 Scottish & Newcastle Breweries sells their whisky division to Invergordon Distillers.

1985 Guinness Group buys Bell's for £356 million.

1986 DCL sells A. & A. Crawford to Whyte & Mackay.

1986 Allied Lyons buys 51% of Hiram Walker Gooderham & Worts.

1987 Guinness buys DCL, who merges with Arthur Bell to become United Distillers, for £2,35 billion.

1987 Louis Vuitton and Moët Hennessy merge into LVMH.

1988 Andrew Symington and his brother Brian found Signatory Vintage Scotch Whisky.

1987 Allied Lyons buys the remaining 49% of Hiram Walker Gooderham & Worts.

1988 Allied Distillers becomes a new subsidiary to Allied Lyons and is made up of Ballantine, Long John International, Stewarts of Dundee and William Teacher.

1988 United Distillers launches 'The Classic Malts'.

1988 Management buy-out of Inver House from Publicker Industries.

1989 Lonhro sells Whyte & Mackay to Brent Walker.

1989 Whitbread's wine & spirits division is acquired by Allied Lyons for £545 million.

1989 Management buys out Invergordon Distillers from Hawker Siddely.

1990 Fortune Brands (then called American Brands) buys Whyte & Mackay from Brent Walker for £165 million.

1990 Guinness and LVMH in 12% cross-shareholding.

1991 Allied Lyons buys Long John from Whitbread.

1993 United Distillers sells Benromach to Gordon & MacPhail.

1993 Whyte & Mackay (Fortune Brands) buys Invergordon Distillers for £382 million.

1994 Allied Lyons acquires Pedro Domecq and changes name to Allied Domecq plc.

1995 Blackadder International is founded by Robin Tucek and John Lamond.

1996 Highland Distilleries buys Macallan-Glenlivet plc.

1996 Whyte & Mackay changes name to JBB (Greater Europe).

1997 Guinness and Grand Metropolitan form Diageo. United Distillers and International Distillers & Vintners (IDV), merge and form United Distillers & Vintners (UDV).

1997 Fortune Brands transfers administration of Whyte & Mackay to Jim Beam Brands.

1997 Glenmorangie plc buys Ardbeg distillery for £7 million.

1998 Diageo sells Dewars and Bombay to Bacardi for £1 150 million.

1998 Highland Distilleries changes

name to Highland Distillers Ltd.

1999 Edrington Group and William Grant & Sons buy Highland Distillers for £601 million. Grant and Edrington form 1887 Company, owned 70% by Edrington and 30% by Grant.

1999 Gordon & MacPhail introduces their 'Rare Old Series'.

2000 Allied Domecq suggests Diageo that they jointly acquire Seagram Spirits & Wine, but Diageo declines.

2001 Pernod Ricard and Diageo buy Seagram Spirits & Wine from Vivendi Universal for £5 710 million (5,7 billion) on 21st December.

2001 Pacific Spirits, owned by Great Oriole Group, buys Inver House Distillers at a price tag of £56 million.

2001 West LB bank and management buy out the Fortune Brands subsidiary JBB (Greater Europe) for £208 million in October. The new company is called Kyndal.

2001 Chivas Brothers and Campbell Distillers form Chivas Brothers.

2001 Murray McDavid buys Bruichladdich from Whyte & Mackay.

2002 Trinidad-based venture capitalists CL Financial buys Burn Stewart Distillers for £50 million.

2003 Kyndal changes name to Whyte & Mackay.

2003 Robert Tchenguiz owns 35% of Whyte & Mackay while West LB holds 21%.

2004 Glenmorangie plc buys Scotch Malt Whisky Society.

2004 Ian Bankier, formerly Burn Stewart Distillers, buys Whisky Shop retail chain for £1,5 million.

2004 Moët Hennessy (owned by Diageo and LVMH) buys Glenmorangie plc for £300 million.

2005 Pernod Ricard buys Allied Domecq.

2005 Pernod Ricard sells Bushmills to Diageo.

2006 Pernod Ricard sells Glen Grant distillery to Campari.

2007 United Spirits buys Whyte & Mackay.

2008 Glenmorangie sells Glen Moray distillery to La Martiniquaise and Pernod Ricard sells Glendronach distillery to BenRiach.

Glen Scotia

Owner: **Region/district:**
Loch Lomond Distillery Co   Campbeltown

Founded: **Status:**   **Capacity:**
1832   Active   750 000 litres

Address: High Street, Campbeltown,
Argyll PA28 6DS

Tel: **website:**
01586 552288   www.lochlomonddistillery.com

History:
1832 – The family Galbraith founds Scotia Distillery (the year 1835 is mentioned by the distillery itself on labels).

1895 – The distillery is sold to Stewart Galbraith.

1919 – Sold to West Highland Malt Distillers.

1924 – West Highland Malt Distillers goes bankrupt and one of its directors, Duncan MacCallum, buys the distillery.

1928 – The distillery closes.

1930 – Duncan MacCallum commits suicide and the Bloch brothers take over.

1933 – Production restarts.

1954 – Hiram Walker takes over.

1955 – A. Gillies & Co. becomes new owner.

1970 – A. Gillies & Co. becomes part of Amalgated Distillers Products.

1979–82 – Reconstruction takes place.

1984 – The distillery closes.

1989 – Amalgated Distillers Products is taken over by Gibson International and production restarts.

1994 – Glen Catrine Bonded Warehouse Ltd takes over and the distillery is mothballed.

1999 – Production restarts 5th May through J. A. Mitchell & Co., owner of Springbank.

2000 – Loch Lomond Distillers runs operations with its own staff from May onwards.

2005 – A 12 year old is released.

2006 – A peated version from 1999 is released.

Glen Scotia 12 year old

GS – Initially floral on the nose, then gummy, with spice, citrus fruit and a faintly phenolic note. Quite full-bodied, peaty and nutty on the palate. Lengthy in the mildly herbal finish, with a whiff of smoke.

DR – The nose is of rich fudge and butter, the palate sliced apricot, walnut and fudge, with a medium finish touched with sweet spice.

When Rieclachan distillery closed in 1934, it left the former whisky capital of Campbeltown with only two operating distilleries. Springbank was one and the other was Glen Scotia, but in recent years Glengyle distillery has made them company. Glen Scotia lies hidden away between modern high-rise buildings and it is only the sign at the gate that reveals malt whisky production, albeit at a lesser scale than in the old times. The owner, also owner of Loch Lomond distillery, used to hire staff from Springbank to run the distillery, but today, the plant is run by the new Distillery Manager since two years, Iain McAlister, the mashman, David Watson and the stillman, Jim Grogan.

Glen Scotia's equipment consists of a traditional cast iron mash tun, six washbacks made of the unusual Corten steel and one pair of stills. In the old days, worm tubs were used for cooling the spirit vapours, but they are now replaced by tube condensers. Fermentation time is usually 48 hours but can be as long as up to five days. The one racked warehouse is proving too small, so the old No. 2 warehouse will probably have to be used in the future. There are usually 3 mashes per week and last year the distillery was producing 126,000 litres which is around 17% of the capacity. Medium peated barley (17ppm) has been used for two periods per year since 1999.

The core range consists of a *12 year old* which replaced the 8 and 14 year olds in 2005. Peated expressions (*6* and *7 year old*) were released in 2006 and 2007 in the owner's Distillery Select range and some single casks of the unpeated version have also been bottled. Older expression include a 17 year old and the occasional vintage.

Quite a few independent bottlings have appeared recently; two old ones from Dewar Rattray (33 years) and Ian MacLeod (32 years), a 1992 from Cadenhead and an 18 year old from 1991 bottled by Duncan Taylor.

12 years old

Glen Spey

Owner: **Region/district:**
Diageo   Speyside

Founded: **Status:**   **Capacity:**
1878   Active   1 390 000 litres

Address: Rothes, Morayshire AB38 7AU

Tel: **website:**
01340 831215   www.malts.com

History:
1878 – James Stuart & Co. founds the distillery which becomes known by the name Mill of Rothes.

1886 – James Stuart buys Macallan.

1887 – W. & A. Gilbey buys the distillery for £11,000 thus becoming the first English company to buy a Scottish malt distillery.

1920 – A fire breaks out.

1962 – W. & A. Gilbey combines forces with United Wine Traders and forms International Distillers & Vintners (IDV).

1970 – The stills are increased from two to four.

1972 – IDV is bought by Watney Mann who is then acquired by Grand Metropolitan.

1997 – Guiness and Grand Metropolitan merge to form Diageo.

2001 – A 12 year old is launched in the Flora & Fauna series.

2010 – A 21 year old is released as part of the Special Releases and a 1996 Manager´s Choice single cask is launched.

Glen Spey distillery was built by James Stuart, miller and grain dealer, who was courageous enough to enter the distilling business. He did not just convert his oatmeal mill into a distillery, he was also the licensee and, later, owner of Macallan Distillery. One of James Stuart's reasons for turning his mill into a distillery was that the project he had devised with three other parties, to build Glenrothes Distillery, had come to a halt. The bank that was intended to finance it withdrew and when construction eventually started, James Stuart was not in the picture.

There are four active distilleries in the town of Rothes, and Glen Spey is definitely the least known of them. Glen Grant is one of the five big single malts in the world, Glenrothes has become a premium malt during the last ten years with devoted followers, not least in Asia, and Speyburn is the seventh best selling malt in the USA. Glen Spey, on the other hand, has functioned as a malt producer for blends and in particular for J & B during this time.

The distillery is equipped with a semi lauter mash tun, eight stainless steel mash tuns and two pairs of stills where the spirit stills are equipped with purifiers. The stills are also operated at a lower pressure than usual (4 pounds per square inch (psi) instead of 8) so there is no need to ever use the release valves on the stills. An odd detail in the equipment is the mill, a Bühler Miag, which was previously used to grind rice. There have been no official bottlings since 2001 when the *12 year old Flora & Fauna* bottling was launched, until now that is. No less than two additional expressions were launched in 2010. In January a *single cask* from new American Oak, distilled in *1996*, was released as a part of the Manager´s Choice series. Six months later a *21 year old* turned up with a maturation in ex-sherry American oak. This was the first time Glen Spey had been represented in the yearly Special Releases.

21 years old from 1988

Glentauchers

Owner:
Chivas Brothers
(Pernod Ricard)

Region/district:
Speyside

Founded: 1897

Status: Active

Capacity: 4 500 000 litres

Address: Glentauchers, Keith,
Banffshire AB55 6YL

Tel: 01542 860272

website: -

History:

1897 – James Buchanan and W. P. Lowrie, a whisky merchant from Glasgow, found the distillery.

1898 – Production starts.

1906 – James Buchanan & Co. takes over the whole distillery and acquires an 80% share in W. P. Lowrie & Co.

1915 – James Buchanan & Co. merges with Dewars.

1923-25 – Mashing house and maltings are rebuilt.

1925 – Buchanan-Dewars joins Distillers Company Limited (DCL).

1930 – Glentauchers is transferred to Scottish Malt Distillers (SMD).

1965 – The number of stills is increased from two to six.

1969 – Floor maltings is decommissioned.

1985 – DCL mothballs the distillery.

1989 – United Distillers (formerly DCL) sells the distillery to Caledonian Malt Whisky Distillers, a subsidiary of Allied Distillers.

1992 – Production recommences in August.

2000 – A 15 year old Glentauchers is released.

2005 – Chivas Brothers (Pernod Ricard) become the new owner through the acquisition of Allied Domecq.

Glentauchers 1991 Gordon & MacPhail

GS – Fresh and floral aromas, with sweet fruits and peppery peaches. Medium to full-bodied in the mouth, with cereal and sweet spice. The finish is medium to long.

DR – Deep plum and sherry on the nose, then cocoa and blackcurrant. The palate is soft, with plum, raisin and green banana, and the finish is banana and date cake.

Glentauchers single malt has never enjoyed an honourable life as a brand bottled on its own merits. In the early years, it was a part of Buchanan´s Black & White and, in more recent years, it has become one of the cornerstones in Ballantine´s and Teacher´s. On the other hand, being an integral part of two of the most famous blended Scotch in the world, entails both tender care and financial investments from the owner's side. Pernod Ricard spent a substantial amount of money in the distillery which was closed during part of 2006 for an upgrade of the still house, and then, in summer 2007, the old cast iron mash tun (installed in 1966) was replaced. Today, the distillery is equipped with a stainless steel semi-lauter mash tun with the copperdome from the old mash tun fitted on top. There are six washbacks made of European larch and three pairs of stills. The washbacks are among the biggest in the industry holding 60,000 litres each. The fact that they are made of wood and not stainless steel has, according to some people in the industry, an impact on the taste of the spirit. Especially the malolactic fermentation, which takes place after 48 hours of fermentation, is benefited by the wood bacteria. Others are of the opinion that the taste is not affected at all by the material of the washbacks.

The spirit is filled in bourbon casks and part of them mature in the two racked warehouses on site holding a total of 6,000 casks, while the rest is taken to Chivas' central warehouses in Keith by road tanker. The capacity of Glentauchers is generally considered to be 3.4 million litres but that is with a six-day production cycle. With 19 mashes, the full capacity is more in the range of 4.5 million litres.

An official *15 year old* was released by Allied Domecq some years ago but has recently been difficult to obtain.

*Gordon & MacPhail
Glentauchers 1990*

Glenturret

Owner:
The Edrington Group

Region/district:
Eastern Highlands

Founded: **Status:**   **Capacity:**
1775   Active (vc)   340 000 litres

Address: The Hosh, Crieff, Perthshire PH7 4HA

Tel: **website:**
01764 656565   www.thefamousgrouse.com

History:
1775 – Whisky smugglers establish a small illicit farm distillery named Hosh Distillery.

1818 – John Drummond is licensee until 1837.

1826 – A distillery in the vicinity is named Glenturret, but is decommissioned before 1852.

1852 – John McCallum is licensee until 1874.

1875 – Hosh Distillery takes over the name Glenturret Distillery and is managed by Thomas Stewart.

1903 – Mitchell Bros Ltd takes over.

1921 – Production ceases and the buildings are used for whisky storage only.

1929 – Mitchell Bros Ltd is liquidated, the distillery dismantled and the facilities are used as storage for agricultural needs.

1957 – James Fairlie buys the distillery and re-equips it.

1959 – Production restarts.

1981 – Remy-Cointreau buys the distillery and invests in a visitor centre.

1990 – Highland Distillers takes over.

1999 – Edrington and William Grant & Sons buy Highland Distillers for £601 million. The purchasing company, 1887 Company, is a joint venture between Edrington (70%) and William Grant (30%).

2002 – The Famous Grouse Experience, a visitor centre costing £2.5 million, is inaugurated.

2003 – A 10 year old Glenturret replaces the 12 year old as the distillery´s standard release.

2007 – Three new single casks are released.

Glenturret 10 year old

GS – Nutty and slightly oily on the nose, with barley and citrus fruits. Sweet and honeyed on the full, fruity palate, with a balancing note of oak. Medium length in the sweet finish.

DR – Full and rich honeyed nose, oily and fruity palate with some appealing rootsy savouriness. Something of the farmyard about it. Charming finish.

Glenturret is the spiritual home of the Famous Grouse blended Scotch - a brand that has been established on the top 8 list for a decade now and which is number one in the UK. During the last couple of years the range has been expanded by the peated and hugely successful Black Grouse and the grain whisky Snow Grouse - an attempt to attract the younger consumers. Another extension of the range was the introduction of Famous Grouse Blended Malt around 2000. At the beginning it was a success and it soon established itself as the second most sold in the category after Johnnie Walker Green Label. The last couple of years though, have been a disappointment with sales dropping by 60% and both Glen Turner and Ballantine blended malts have now overtaken it.

Glenturret Distillery is equipped with an open stainless steel mash tun dressed in wood and it is perhaps the only one in Scotland where the mash is still turned manually by large wooden spades. There are also eight Douglas Fir washbacks, one pair of stills and 10,500 casks maturing in six warehouses on site. Eight mashes a week result in 156,000 litres of spirit per year. Peated whisky, destined for the Black Grouse blend, has been distilled since 2009.

Recent focus has been on a groundbreaking project where CO_2 is captured and re-cycled into protein and animal feed. The recycling is made through algae reactors and these also eliminate chemicals and captured copper from the wastewater.

"The Famous Grouse Experience" is the distillery´s visitor centre. Opened in 2002, it has since been expanded continuously.

There is only one official bottling in the core range, the *10 year old*. An 8 year old that used to be produced, has now been discontinued. A limited edition of three single casks was released in spring 2007: a *14 year old* from 1991, a *15 year old* from 1992 and a *29 year old* from 1977.

10 years old

Highland Park

Owner:
The Edrington Group

Region/district:
Highlands (Orkney)

Founded: 1798

Status: Active (vc)

Capacity: 2 500 000 litres

Address: Holm Road, Kirkwall, Orkney KW15 1SU

Tel: 01856 874619

website: www.highlandpark.co.uk

History:
1798 – David Robertson founds the distillery. The local smuggler and businessman Magnus Eunson previously operated an illicit whisky production on the site.

1816 – John Robertson, an Excise Officer who arrested Magnus Eunson, takes over production.

1826 – Highland Park obtains a license and the distillery is taken over by Robert Borwick.

1840 – Robert's son George Borwick takes over but the distillery deteriorates.

1869 – The younger brother James Borwick inherits Highland Park and attempts to sell it as he does not consider the distillation of spirits as compatible with his priesthood.

1876 – Stuart & Mackay becomes involved and improves the business by exporting to Norway and India.

1895 – James Grant (of Glenlivet Distillery) buys Highland Park.

1898 – James Grant expands capacity from two to four stills.

1937 – Highland Distilleries buys Highland Park.

1979 – Highland Distilleries invests considerably in marketing Highland Park as single malt which increases sales markedly.

Highland Park distillery, one of Scotland's oldest distilleries and built in the late 18th century, lies on the outskirts of Kirkwall overlooking both the town and Scapa Bay and reminds of how village churches were placed in the old days.

Highland Park's single malt has become extremely popular in recent years. Sales have increased with 175% the last ten years and the brand finds itself just below the Top Ten now. Highland Park is one of few distilleries malting part (20%) of their barley themselves, with the balance coming from Simpson's in Berwick-upon-Tweed. There are five malting floors with a capacity of almost 36 tonnes of barley. The malt is dried for 18 hours using peat and the final 18 hours using coke. The phenol content is 30-40 ppm in own malt while the externally sourced malt is unpeated. The two varieties are always mixed before mashing, but recently test distillations with just the peated malt have been made. Experiments are also ongoing with a new strain of barley (Tartan), which is grown on Orkney.

The distillery equipment consists of one full lauter mash tun, twelve Oregon Pine washbacks and two pairs of stills. The whisky matures in 19 dunnage and four racked warehouses holding a total of 44,000 casks. The part that is sold as single malt (amounting to ca 60%) has always matured in sherry casks (20% first fill and 80% refill) while the whisky destined for blending (Famous Grouse and Cutty Sark) has been filled into bourbon barrels. Highland Park distillery is extremely particular about the wood it uses. The oak is left to air dry for four years in Spain and thereafter filled with sherry for 2-3 years. The owners spend £10m every year on wood alone.

The core range of Highland Park consists of *12, 15, 18, 25, 30* and *40 years old*. Travel retail exclusives since 2010 are four different vintages - *1973, 1990, 1994* and *1998*. Recent limited editions include the *15 year old Earl Magnus* which in autumn of 2010 was followed by *Saint Magnus* (12 years) and in spring of 2011 by *Haakon* (18 years). They are all bottled at cask strength and the names celebrate the Viking heritage of Orkney. Another limited range, *Orcadian Vintages*, started in 2008 with *1968*, followed by *1964* and (in 2010) *1970*. A *10 year old single cask* was also released for Whisky Live London and Tokyo in spring of 2010. The biggest thrill of they year from Highland Park, however, was the *50 year old* which was released in autumn 2010. This, the oldest ever bottling of Highland Park, is a vatting of five casks filled in 1960. There is a total of 275 bottles which will be released over a period of 4 years and the price is set to £10,000 per bottle.

History (continued):

1986 – A visitor centre, considered one of Scotland's finest, is opened.

1997 – Two new Highland Park are launched, an 18 year old and a 25 year old.

1999 – Highland Distillers are acquired by Edrington Group and William Grant & Sons.

2000 – Visit Scotland awards Highland Park "Five Star Visitor Attraction". The distillery has spent over £2 million on the visitor centre and distillery.

2005 – Highland Park 30 years old is released, first in the US and in the autumn in the UK. A 16 year old for the Duty Free market and Ambassador's Cask 1984 are released.

2006 – The second edition of Ambassador's Cask, a 10 year old from 1996, is released. New packaging is introduced.

2007 – The Rebus 20, a 21 year old duty free exclusive, a 38 year old and a 39 year old are released.

2008 – A 40 year old and the third and fourth editions of Ambassador's Cask are released.

2009 – Two vintages and Earl Magnus 15 year are released.

2010 – A 50 year old, Saint Magnus 12 year old, Orcadian Vintage 1970 and four duty free vintages are released.

Highland Park 12 year old

GS – The nose is fragrant and floral, with hints of heather and some spice. Smooth and honeyed on the palate, with citric fruits, malt and distinctive tones of wood smoke in the warm, lengthy, slightly peaty finish.

DR – Honey, peat and marmalade fruit in balance on the nose, then on the palate a big mouth feel with dark chocolate, chilli, sharp barley and honey, concluding with a monster pot pouri of a finish.

St Magnus

50 years old

Orcadian Vintage 1970

12 years old

18 years old

25 years old

Jura

Owner: **Region/district:**
Whyte & Mackay   Highlands (Jura)
(United Spirits)

Founded: **Status:**   **Capacity:**
1810   Active (vc)   2 200 000 litres

Address: Craighouse, Isle of Jura PA60 7XT

Tel: **website:**
01496 820240   www.isleofjura.com

History:

1810 – Archibald Campbell founds a distillery named Small Isles Distillery.

1853 – Richard Campbell leases the distillery to Norman Buchanan from Glasgow.

1867 – Buchanan files for bankruptcy and J. & K. Orr takes over the distillery.

1876 – The licence is transferred to James Ferguson & Sons.

1901 – The distillery closes and Ferguson dismantles the distillery.

1960 – Charles Mackinlay & Co. embarks on reconstruction and extension of the distillery. Newly formed Scottish & Newcastle Breweries acquires Charles Mackinlay & Co.

1962 – Scottish & Newcastle forms Mackinlay-McPherson for the operation of Isle of Jura.

1963 – The first distilling takes place.

1978 – Stills are doubled from two to four.

1985 – Invergordon Distilleries acquires Charles Mackinlay & Co., Isle of Jura and Glenallachie from Scottish & Newcastle Breweries.

1993 – Whyte & Mackay (Fortune Brands) buys Invergordon Distillers.

1996 – Whyte & Mackay changes name to JBB (Greater Europe).

2001 – The management of JBB (Greater Europe) buys out the company from the owners Fortune Brands and changes the name to Kyndal.

2002 – Isle of Jura Superstition is launched.

2003 – Kyndal reverts back to its old name, Whyte & Mackay. Isle of Jura 1984 is launched.

2004 – Two cask strengths (15 and 30 years old) are released in limited numbers.

2006 – The 40 year old Jura is released.

2007 – United Spirits buys Whyte & Mackay. The 18 year old Delmé-Evans and an 8 year old heavily peated expression are released.

2008 – A series of four different vintages, called Elements, is released.

2009 – The peated Prophecy and three new vintages called Paps of Jura are released.

2010 – Boutique Barrels and a 21 year old Anniversary bottling are released.

Jura 10 year old

GS – Resin, oil and pine notes on the delicate nose. Light-bodied in the mouth, with malt and drying saltiness. The finish is malty, nutty, with more salt, plus just a wisp of smoke.

DR – The nose is sweet condensed milk, the palate an intriguing mix of earthy malt and tangy spice, with a medium sweet and spice finish.

Although the distillery is lovely and the Isle of Jura, with its 197 people and 4,000 deer is breathtakingly beautiful, the whisky produced rarely used to be very exciting. The turning point came five years ago, even if the cause of it dates back to 1999. That was when it was established that too many casks in the warehouses were not up to standard. Re-racking into high quality bourbon casks was commenced and that, together with Master Blender Richard Paterson's experienced nose, has resulted in a number of exciting releases. In 1999, Jura started to produce peated whisky four weeks per year and this has now added an interesting twist to some of the traditionally unpeated bottlings.

Jura distillery is equipped with one semi-lauter mash tun, six stainless steel washbacks and two pairs of stills. The stills are extremely high, second only to the ones at Glenmorangie, which are Scotland's tallest at over 26 feet. During 2010 the distillery is working a five-day week producing 1,750,000 litres of alcohol. Almost 40% of that is destined to become single malt and is matured in the five racked warehouses on site with the oldest cask being from 1973. The rest is taken to Invergordon on the mainland. The spirit is matured mainly in bourbon casks and with 5% maturing in sherry casks.

The core range consists of *Origin* (10 years), *Diurach's Own* (16 years), *Superstition* (13% peated Jura and various casks from 13 to 21 years of age) as well as the peated *Prophecy* which was released in 2009 and is the only unchillfiltered of the four. There have been plenty of limited releases during the last few years and for 2010, it is the *Boutique Barrels* - all bottled at cask strength, matured in re-fill bourbon and with an added finish; *1993* Oloroso finish, *1995* first fill bourbon finish and *1999*, same as 1995, but heavily peated. To celebrate the 200th anniversary of the distillery, a *21 year old* which had matured in a Vintage 1963 Gonzales Byass cask was released in autumn.

16 years old

Meet the Manager

WILLIE COCHRANE
DISTILLERY MANAGER, JURA DISTILLERY

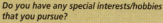

When did you start working in the whisky business and when did you start at Jura?

I started work at Jura Distillery 33 years ago in July 1977.

Had you been working in other lines of business before whisky?

I worked as a mechanical engineer in Glasgow.

What kind of education or training do you have?

I left school at 16 to start an engineering apprenticeship which I successfully completed 5 years later. Further qualifications since then have been gained through Institute of Management courses.

Describe your career in the whisky business.

I was first introduced to the whisky industry in 1977 when I became a mash/still operator at Jura Distillery. A few years later my engineering background was called upon when I was asked to take on the role of distillery engineer. That was when I really got into the guts of the distillery. It would be safe to say that I know every nut and bolt in the plant. I was then asked to take on the dual role of brewer/engineer, which I did for many years, before becoming Distillery Manager.

What are your main tasks as a manager?

My tasks include overseeing all aspects of production, ensuring we continuously maintain the same high quality product, complying with customs and excise and SEPA regulations, ensuring safe working practices, organising delivery of raw materials, man management and PR, meeting and greeting members of the trade and the public and whenever possible taking distillery manager tours.

What are the biggest challenges of being a distillery manager?

The challenges are many and varied but I would say the biggest challenge would be maintaining the high standard expected on a week to week basis.

What would be the worst that could go wrong in the production process?

We have controls in place that should avoid any major incidents arising in the production process but my worst nightmare would be losing any of our valuable mature stock as this could never be replaced.

How would you describe the character of Jura single malt?

Gently spiced, soft peaches and honey, with a hint of citrus and marzipan would describe the character of the original Jura malts. Obviously older expressions would have different characters.

What are the main features in the process at Jura, contributing to this character?

The water on Jura is very soft and peaty. Combine this with our balanced production system and the unique shape and height of our stills to ensure a continuity of character and flavours carrying over to our filling vat. The sprit is then put into first fill bourbon casks and dispatched to our warehouse where the unique Jura climate provided by the Gulf stream, enhances the maturation. Throw a dedicated, enthusiastic work team into the mix and these would be the contributing features to this character.

What is your favourite expression of Jura and why?

My absolute favourite expression of Jura would be the islander's favourite, Jura 16 year old. The light, fruity, spicy element of this dram is perfect just before an evening meal. Prophecy is a contrasting dram but it is my second favourite. It is a heavily peated malt with a hint of cinnamon and it goes down very nicely on a cold winter evening.

If it were your decision alone – what new expression of Jura would you like to see released?

Actually I am proud to say I have just selected some special casks from our warehouse which will be released over the next few years as our Boutique Barrel range. Each bottle in this range will have its own unique expression.

If you had to choose a favourite dram other than Jura, what would that be?

I have no hesitation in answering that question. It would have to be the Dalmore 12 year old closely followed by a Bruichladdich.

What are the biggest changes you have seen the past 10-15 years in your profession?

There are more environmental issues and legislation compliances. Marketing has become a huge part of the profession but on the production side of things, the process at Jura has remained the same. A huge variety of casks have been introduced over the past 10-15 years which have given us a large range of great new styles and finishes.

Do you see any major changes in the next 10 years to come?

There will be new emerging markets but who can predict the next 10 years? Industry will have to change to accommodate the environment.

Do you have any special interests/hobbies that you pursue?

I love gardening. It helps me unwind after a days work. I am a big football fan and although I no longer play for the Jura Football Club, I enjoy nothing more than watching a good game on the telly. I also like to travel, especially to the Far East.

Running a whisky distillery on a remote island like Jura must sometimes be challenging. What are the main difficulties you have to deal with?

The Jura ferry is our link with Islay and carries all our supplies from the mainland. It is virtually the island's lifeline. It can stop sailing for days at a time either through bad weather or breakdowns and unless we have at least 3 days of essential supplies i.e. yeast, barley and oil in reserve, our production would come to a standstill. I must also be able to adapt when there is a breakdown in the plant. All of our parts are shipped from the mainland therefore I often have to improvise until the required part arrives.

The distillery was reconstructed in the early sixties when many Diurachs had left the island. What does the distillery mean to the Jura community today?

The distillery supports the community on a daily basis and in return is supported by the community. We are involved with or sponsor most of the events that take place on the island such as sheep dog trials, fell race and regatta to name but a few. We are also the largest employer on the island employing 14 locals. I think the Distillery is a vital part of the island and considered to be a friend of the community.

Inchgower

Owner: **Region/district:**
Diageo   Speyside

Founded: **Status:**   **Capacity:**
1871   Active   2 800 000 litres

Address: Buckie, Banffshire AB56 5AB

Tel: **website:**
01542 836700   www.malts.com

History:
1871 – Alexander Wilson & Co. founds the distillery. Equipment from the disused Tochieneal Distillery, also owned by Alexander Wilson, is installed.

1936 – Alexander Wilson & Co. becomes bankrupt and Buckie Town Council buys the distillery and the family's home for £1,600.

1938 – The distillery is sold on to Arthur Bell & Sons for £3,000.

1966 – Capacity doubles to four stills.

1985 – Guinness acquires Arthur Bell & Sons.

1987 – United Distillers is formed by a merger between Arthur Bell & Sons and DCL.

1997 – Inchgower 1974 (22 years) is released as a Rare Malt.

2004 – Inchgower 1976 (27 years) is released as a Rare Malt.

Inchgower 14 year old

GS – Ripe pears and a hint of brine on the light nose. Grassy and gingery in the mouth, with some acidity. The finish is spicy, dry and relatively short.

DR – Rootsy, fresh cut grass and hay nose, light grassy and hay-like palate, and incredibly delicate barley-like nose, with a very delicate dusting of spice.

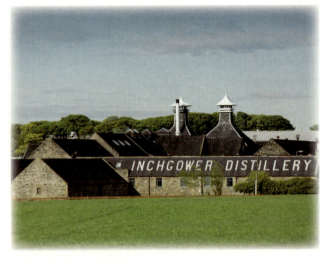

When Inchgower was built in 1871, it was supposed to replace a distillery called Tochieneal, a few miles to the south east. The latter had been founded already in 1824 by John Wilson, but closed in 1867 as the water source had started to drain. The owner at that time was John´s son, Alexander, and he moved most of the equipment to use it for his new Inchgower distillery.

The distillery is difficult to miss as it is situated just by the A98, only 10 miles west of Glenglassaugh distillery, near the small fishing port of Buckie on the Moray Firth. If one is driving from Elgin towards Banff it is even easier to spot as the name appears on the roof.

The distillery is equipped with a stainless steel semi-lauter mash tun, six washbacks made from Oregon Pine and two pairs of stills. Most of the production is matured elsewhere, but there are also 13 warehouses on site with room for 60,000 casks, a large part of which come from other distilleries within the Diageo group. Despite being situated only a few miles from the Greencore Maltings in Buckie, the malt is not acquired from there. Diageo is self-sustaining when it comes to malted barley through its facilities in Port Ellen, Glen Ord, Roseisle and Burghead which thus deliver to Inchgower as well.

The absolutely greater part of production is used for Bell´s blended whisky. Besides the official *Flora & Fauna 14 years old* there have been two *Rare Malt* bottlings: *1974 (22 years)* and *1976 (27 years)*. In April 2010 a new bottling appeared - a *single sherry cask* distilled in *1993* and part of the Manager´s Choice series was introduced in autumn of 2009.

*Flora & Fauna
14 years old*

Kilbeggan

Owner: **Region/district:**
Cooley Distillery plc   Ireland

Founded: **Status:**   **Capacity:**
1757   Active (vc)   80 000 litres

Address: Kilbeggan, Co. Westmeath

Tel:
+353 (0)57 933 2183

website: www.kilbegganwhiskey.com

History:
1757 – The distillery is founded by the McManus family.

1794 – The Codd family takes over and capacity is doubled.

1843 – John Locke & Sons buy the distillery.

1954 – Production stops.

1957 – The distillery is officially closed.

1988 – Cooley Distillery plc buys the brand Kilbeggan as well as the old distillery to use it for warehousing.

2007 – The first distillation in the refurbished distillery takes place on 19 March.

2010 – The first single malt since the resurrection is released.

Kilbeggan Distillery Reserve

GS – Highly individualistic on the nose. Oily and herbal, with tarragon, warm leather, paper gum, and even violets. The palate is quite delicate, yet far from fragile, with gentle leather and developing fruity spices. Drying in a medium-length finish.

Kilbeggan Distillery's re-opening in 2007 was nothing less than a sensation. Suddenly a distillery that could lay claim to being the oldest in the world was producing whiskey again. The distillery, which lies in the town Kilbeggan on the N6 and just an hour's drive west of Dublin, was bought by John Teeling and his Cooley Distillery way back in 1988. By that time it had not been producing for 35 years and it is uncertain whether it was Teeling's plan to start again, as he used it for storing the production from his other distillery, Cooley, north-east of Dublin. The distillery and its equipment was in fairly good condition, however, thanks to some locals who had maintained it and even ascertained that its distilling licence was still valid. Eventually, the new owner decided to reinstate the distillery to its former glory and to start distilling again. Meanwhile, a blended Kilbeggan whiskey, a brand taken over simultaneously with the distillery, was selling with great success.

In March 2007, 250 years after Kilbeggan was built, the first spirit ran from the still under supervision of descendants of the four families that had been involved with the distillery - the McManus', the Codd's, the Locke's and the Teeling's.

At first, the mashing, fermentation and first distillation were made at Cooley distillery while the final distillation took place at Kilbeggan. In 2009/2010, however, another still was installed as well as four Oregon pine washbacks and a wooden mash tun so now the whole production takes place at Kilbeggan and with an option to also practice classical Irish triple distillation. There are even plans for setting up a column still, last used by Tullamore distillery, to produce grain spirit. The capacity of Kilbeggan is 250,000 bottles per year. There is also a visitor centre at the distillery - The Old Kilbeggan Distillery Experience.

The first single malt whiskey release (a *3 year old* bottled at 40%) from the new production came in June 2010, but previously, spirit from the distillery had been launched at one month, one year and two years of age. The blended range of Kilbeggan includes a no age statement, a 15 year old and a soon to be introduced 18 year old.

*Kilbeggan
Distillery Reserve*

Kilchoman

Owner:
Kilchoman Distillery Co.

Region/district:
Islay

Founded:
2005

Status:
Active (vc)

Capacity:
110 000 litres

Address: Rockside farm, Bruichladdich,
Islay PA49 7UT

Tel:
01496 850011

website:
www.kilchomandistillery.com

History:
2002 – Plans are formed for a new distillery at
Rockside Farm on western Islay.

2005 – Production starts in June.

2006 – A fire breaks out in the kiln causing a
few weeks' production stop but malting has to
cease for the rest of the year.

2007 – The distillery is expanded with two new
washbacks.

2009 – The first single malt, a 3 year old, is
released on 9th September followed by a second
release.

2010 – Three new releases and an introduction
to the US market. John Maclellan from
Bunnahabhain joins the team as General
Manager.

Kilchoman Third Release

GS – The nose offers sweet smoke, buttery
fish, toasted oats and berries. Sweet on the
palate, with spicy, youthful oak notes, more
berries and vanilla fudge. Medium length in
the warming, gently spiced, finish.

DR – Amazingly integrated for one so young,
with the peat and sweet toffee nose reflected
on the palate by steam train smoke and rich
berried fruits. The finish is long and balanced.
This is pioneering modern malt travelling in
to unchartered territory.

In 2005 Kilchoman opened as the first distillery on Islay since
1908. Five years later the distillery has completed four releases
of bottlings which all sold out instantaneously. It has started
exports to the lucrative US market and count on selling 50,000
bottles in 2010. All in all, a great start for Islay's smallest distillery!

Kilchoman is one of few distilleries in Scotland with own floor
maltings. What makes it even more special is the fact that as
much as a third of barley requirements come from fields surrounding the distillery. The malt is peated to 20 to 25 ppm and
the remaining malt, with the same specification as for Ardbeg
(50 ppm), is bought from Port Ellen. Other equipment include
a stainless steel semi-lauter mash tun, four stainless steel washbacks and one pair of stills. The distillery is currently running
at full capacity. The average fermentation time is 100 hours
and the average spirit yield for Ardbeg specification malt is
385 litres per tonne and for their own malted barley 365 litres.
The spirit is filled into fresh and refill bourbon casks (80%)
and fresh oloroso sherry butts (20%,) but there is also room
for experiments like Madeira casks and ex
bourbon octaves (50 litres). Maturation
takes place in a dunnage warehouse which
Kilchoman grew out of many years ago.
Bruichladdich, which is nearby, has assisted
with space, but in late 2010, a new dunnage warehouse with room for 6,000 casks,
will be ready at Port Charlotte.

The *first expression*, bourbon matured for
3 years with a six months Oloroso finish,
was released in September 2009. The
second release had only 2.5 months
sherry finish and *the third* (in April
2010) was finished for 3 months,
but four non-finished bourbon
barrels were also added to the
batch. *Release number four* in July
was the first all-bourbon expression and the first to be sold in
the US, while *release number 5* is
planned for November. Starting in
2010 there will also be single cask
releases for 10-12 selected
markets. The first bottling from
own maltings (Kilchoman 100%
Islay) is due in 2011.

Inaugural Release

Kininvie

Owner:
William Grant & Sons

Region/district:
Speyside

Founded: **Status:**
1990 Active

Capacity:
4 800 000 litres

Address: Dufftown, Keith,
Banffshire AB55 4DH

Tel:
01340 820373

website:
-

History:
1990 – Kininvie distillery is inaugurated on 26th June and the first distillation takes place 18th July.

2006 – The first expression of a single malt Kininvie is released as a 15 year old limited edition under the name Hazelwood.

2008 – In February a 17 year old Hazelwood Reserve is launched at Heathrow´s Terminal 5.

If you plan to visit Kininvie distillery in the hope of seeing a typical and pretty Scottish distillery you are in for a surprise. That is, if you even manage to find the distillery where it is, tucked away behind Balvenie. Kininvie actually only consists of one still house constructed in white, corrugated metal. It has always been a distillery that the owners, William Grant & Sons, rarely talk about. Instead, they have kept it as it was planned for - a working distillery producing malt whisky for the increasingly popular Grant´s blended whiskies.

The still house, visible from the Balvenie tun room, was erected in 1990 and the distillery came on stream in July the same year. Kininvie is equipped with a stainless steel full lauter mash tun which is placed next to Balvenie´s in the Balvenie distillery. The tun is filled with 10.8 tonnes of malted barley and can run 28 mashes per week. Ten Douglas fir washbacks (six large and four small) can be found in two separate rooms next to the Balvenie washbacks. Three wash stills and six spirit stills are all heated by steam coils. The only piece of equipment that Kininvie shares with Balvenie is the mill.

Kininvie malt whisky is frequently sold to other companies for blending purposes under the name Aldundee. To protect it from being sold as Kininvie single malt, the whisky is always "teaspooned", i. e. a small percentage of Balvenie whisky is blended with the make.

As mentioned, Kininvie malt is mainly used for the Grant´s blend but is also a major part of the blended malt Monkey Shoulder.

The first time that Kininvie appeared as an official single malt bottling was in August 2006 when a *15 year old* was launched to celebrate the 105th birthday of Janet Sheed Roberts, the last surviving grandchild of the founder of the company, William Grant, and who opened the distillery in 1990. Since 1933 she had lived at Hazelwood House, close to the distillery. A two year older version of this, aged in ex sherry casks, was released in February 2008 as *Hazelwood Reserve* and was sold at Heathrow´s Terminal 5. No other bottlings are planned.

Hazelwood Reserve 17 year old

GS – New leather and creamy nougat on the nose. Developing molasses notes with time. Rich, leathery and spicy on the palate, with oranges and milk chocolate. Lengthy and elegant in the finish.

*Hazelwood Reserve
17 years old*

Knockando

Owner:
Diageo.

Region/district:
Speyside

Founded: 1898

Status: Active

Capacity: 1 300 000 litres

Address: Knockando, Morayshire AB38 7RT

Tel: 01340 882000

website: www.malts.com

History:

1898 – John Thompson founds the distillery. The architect is Charles Doig.

1899 – Production starts in May.

1900 – The distillery closes in March and J. Thompson & Co. takes over administration.

1904 – W. & A. Gilbey purchases the distillery for £3,500 and production restarts in October.

1962 – W. & A. Gilbey merges with United Wine Traders (including Justerini & Brooks) and forms International Distillers & Vintners (IDV).

1968 – Floor maltings is decommissioned.

1969 – The number of stills is increased to four.

1972 – IDV is acquired by Watney Mann who, in its turn, is taken over by Grand Metropolitan.

1978 – Justerini & Brooks launches a 12 year old Knockando.

1997 – Grand Metropolitan and Guinness merge and form Diageo; simultaneously IDV and United Distillers merge to United Distillers & Vintners.

2010 – A Manager's Choice 1996 is released.

Knockando 12 year old

GS – Delicate and fragrant on the nose, with hints of malt, worn leather, and hay. Quite full in the mouth, smooth and honeyed, with gingery malt and a suggestion of white rum. Medium length in the finish, with cereal and more ginger.

DR – Beeswax, honey and gentle peat on the nose, the palate is altogether bolder, with pepper and earthy peat in evidence mixing it with very sweet crystallised barley and a sweet and rounded finish.

The majority of the Scottish single malts experienced a decrease in sales' volumes after the global recession in 2008. Knockando was one of the worst affected with a 20% decrease between 2007 and 2008. The reason for this brand being so vulnerable was that the lion's share of sales for many years, went to Spain and France. Demand for Scotch decreased significantly in those two countries; over 50% in Spain between 2007 and 2009, while France fared a bit better with just 27%.

Knockando is equipped with a semi-lauter mash tun, eight Douglas fir washbacks and two pairs of stills. Knockando's heavy, nutty character, a result of the cloudy worts coming from the mash tun, has given it its fame. However, in order to balance the taste, the distillers also wish to produce the typical Speyside floral notes by using boiling balls on the spirit stills in order to increase reflux. On site filling stopped six years ago and, in common with most Diageo distilleries in Speyside, the spirit is tankered to either Glenlossie or Auchroisk.

Knockando has always worked a five-day week with 16 mashes per week, 8 short (48 hours) and 8 long (104 hours). The spirit is filled mainly into bourbon barrels, although sherry butts are also used, and matures in two dunnage and two racked warehouses. The heavy snowfall in January 2010 caused damage to one of the warehouses, which eventually will have to be demolished and rebuilt. Since the 1970s, Knockando has bottled its whisky according to vintage and without any age statement, but lately bottles on all markets show both vintage and age on the label. The core range consists of a *12 year old* (90% bourbon and 10% sherry), an *18 year old Slow Matured* (20% sherry), mainly reserved for the French market and a *21 year old Master Reserve* (30% sherry casks). In May 2010, a *Knockando 1996*, matured in a sherry cask, was released in the Manager's Choice series. Independent bottlings are virtually impossible to find.

1991 12 years old

Knockdhu

Owner:
Inver House Distillers
(Thai Beverages plc)

Region/district:
Speyside

Founded: 1893

Status: Active

Capacity: 1 500 000 litres

Address: Knock, By Huntly,
Aberdeenshire AB54 7LJ

Tel: 01466 771223

website: www.ancnoc.com

History:

1893 – Distillers Company Limited (DCL) starts construction of the distillery.

1894 – Production starts in October.

1930 – Scottish Malt Distillers (SMD) takes over production.

1983 – The distillery closes in March.

1988 – Inver House buys the distillery from United Distillers.

1989 – Production restarts on 6th February.

1990 – First official bottling of Knockdhu.

1993 – First official bottling of An Cnoc, the new name to avoid confusion with Knockando.

2001 – Pacific Spirits (Great Oriole Group) purchases Inver House Distillers at a price of $85 million.

2003 – Reintroduction of An Cnoc 12 years, with new, contemporary packaging.

2004 – A 14 year old from 1990 is launched.

2005 – Two limited editions, a 30 year old from 1975 and a 14 year old from 1991 are launched.

2006 – International Beverage Holdings acquires Pacific Spirits UK.

2007 – anCnoc 1993 is released.

2008 – anCnoc 16 year old is released.

An Cnoc 12 year old

GS – A pretty, sweet, floral nose, with barley notes. Medium bodied, with a whiff of delicate smoke, spices and boiled sweets on the palate. Drier in the mouth than the nose suggests. The finish is quite short and drying.

DR – Complex and layered nose, with delicate peat, green fruits and pear. On the palate there's a full savoury peatiness then tingling yellow fruity follow through and fairydust finale.

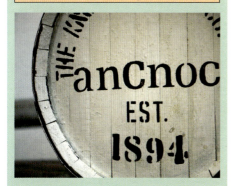

This beautiful distillery near Huntly in the Highlands, is one that the owner, Inver House, has made great investments in the last couple of years when it comes to technical refurbishing. 2010 was no exception, with a new draff discharge system and a new malt intake.

The distillery is equipped with a stainless steel lauter mash tun installed (but retaining the old copper canopy) in 2009, six washbacks made of Oregon Pine and one pair of stills. The spirit is condensed using a cast iron worm tub. The owners made a smart move when they replaced the old cast iron mash tun. The new tun has the same diameter, but is deeper than the previous one, which made it possible to increase the capacity by 100,000 litres per year. In similarity with last year, Knockdhu is running 24/7 doing 19-20 mashes per week. Around 15% of production is destined to be used for single malts. These are filled on site while the rest is tankered away to Airdrie.

In general, a mix of bourbon and sherry casks are used, but some interesting experiments with rum casks have been made, the results yet to be seen. The casks are stored in one racked and four dunnage warehouses. In similar with a lof of other distilleries, Knockdhu was hit by the massive snowfall in January 2010 and two dunnage warehouses were more or less destroyed. Fortunately the losses of casks were low. anCnoc is traditionally an unpeated malt, but for the last few years Knockdhu has also produced a more peated variety (22ppm) each year. During 2010, 700 tonnes of peated malt were bought, which means almost 20% of the production is peated. It has until now, been destined for use in Inver House's blended whiskies, but the first single malt expressions may be released in 2011/2012. UK, USA, Sweden and Germany are the biggest markets and close to 14,000 cases were sold in 2009.

The core range consists of *12* and *16 year old* and the *1975 Vintage*. The only new bottling for 2010 was a limited *vintage 1995* of which 50% of the release went to the German market.

16 years old

Lagavulin

Owner:		Region/district:
Diageo		Islay
Founded:	Status:	Capacity:
1816	Active (vc)	2 200 000 litres

Address: Port Ellen, Islay, Argyll PA42 7DZ

Tel: website:
01496 302749 (vc)   www.malts.com

History:

1816 – John Johnston founds the distillery.

1825 – John Johnston takes over the adjacent distillery Ardmore founded in 1817 by Archibald Campbell and closed in 1821.

1835 – Production at Ardmore ceases.

1837 – Both distilleries are merged and operated under the name Lagavulin by Donald Johnston.

1852 – The brother of the wine and spirits dealer Alexander Graham, John Crawford Graham, purchases the distillery.

1867 – The distillery is acquired by James Logan Mackie & Co. and refurbishment starts.

1878 – Peter Mackie is employed.

1889 – James Logan Mackie passes away and nephew Peter Mackie inherits the distillery.

1890 – J. L. Mackie & Co. changes name to Mackie & Co. Peter Mackie launches White Horse onto the export market with Lagavulin included in the blend. White Horse blended is not available on the domestic market until 1901.

1908 – Peter Mackie uses the old distillery buildings to build a new distillery, Malt Mill, on the site.

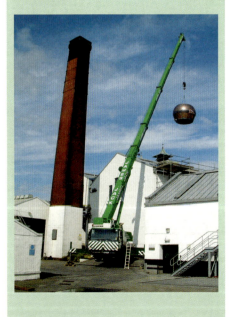

Two disitilleries were in the lead as peated single malt raved through the whisky world in the 1990s - Laphroaig and Lagavulin. Each with their devoted followers arguing about which one was the peatiest and most pungent. If any of the two attracted more popularity, it would have been Lagavulin which had already sold 160,000 cases in 1998 and which gave it place 7 on the world sales' list. Volumes had decreased considerably halfway into the first decade of the 21th century due to limited supplies, caused by a temporary, lower production pace in the mid-eighties. Sales have picked up since then, even if Laphroaig has passed Lagavulin when it comes to volumes.

Operations have run 24 hours a day, seven days a week, for some time now to avoid getting into the same troublesome situation again. This means 28 mashes per week and 2.25 million litres of spirit.

The distillery is equipped with a stainless steel full lauter mash tun, ten washbacks made of larch and two pairs of stills. Unusually, the spirit stills are slightly larger than the wash stills. The former are filled to 95% of its capacity during distillation which is very unconventional. The result is that the spirit vapour's diminished contact with the copper produces a more robust spirit. The tough production scheme causes wear and tear on the stills and in summer 2009, the body of No. 1 wash still and the head of No. 2 had to be replaced. Diageo has its own company of coppersmiths to do this kind of work. The company, based in Alloa, dates back to 1790 and was taken over by Diageos predecessor in 1948. The name of the company today is Diageo Abercrombie. Bourbon hogsheads are used almost without exception for maturation and all of the new production is stored on the mainland. There are only around 16,000 casks on Islay, split between warehouses at Lagavulin, Port Ellen and Caol Ila.

The core range of Lagavulin consists of *12 years old cask strength*, *16 years* and the *Distiller´s Edition*, a Pedro Ximenez sherry finish. As in recent years, a new *12 year old* was released in autumn 2010 as a Special Release, but before that, there were three new bottlings the same year. All were released in May; a *cask strength distillery exclusive* with no age statement, matured in ex bourbon with a finish in Pedro Ximenez sherry cask, then an *ex sherry single cask* distilled in *1993* as part of the Manager's Choice series and, finally, this year's *Feis Isle* bottling, a *single cask* also from *1993* and bottled at cask strength.

History (continued):

1924 – Peter Mackie passes away and Mackie & Co. changes name to White Horse Distillers.

1927 – White Horse Distillers becomes part of Distillers Company Limited (DCL).

1930 – The distillery is administered under Scottish Malt Distillers (SMD).

1952 – An explosive fire breaks out and causes considerable damage.

1960 – Malt Mills distillery closes and today it houses Lagavulin's visitor centre.

1974 – Floor maltings are decommisioned and malt is bought from Port Ellen instead.

1988 – Lagavulin 16 years becomes one of six Classic Malts.

1998 – A Pedro Ximenez sherry finish is launched as a Distillers Edition.

2002 – Two cask strengths (12 years and 25 years) are launched.

2006 – A 30 year old is released.

2007 – A 21 year old from 1985 and the sixth edition of the 12 year old are released.

2008 – A new 12 year old is released.

2009 – A new 12 year old appears as a Special Release.

2010 – A new edition of the 12 year old, a single cask exclusive for the distillery and a Manager´s Choice single cask are released.

Lagavulin 12 year old

GS – Soft and buttery on the nose, with dominant, fruity, peat smoke, grilled fish and a hint of vanilla sweetness. More fresh fruit notes develop with the addition of water. Medium-bodied, quite oily in texture, heavily smoked, sweet malt and nuts. The finish is very long and ashy, with lingering sweet peat.

DR – A monster truck nose with rich smoke, lychee and unripe pear, with prickly smoke and banana skin notes on the palate, and a superb long dark chocolate and smoky finish.

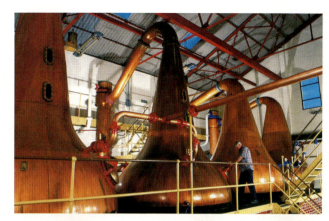

30 years old   Distiller´s Edition

16 years old   12 years old (9th ed.)   Distillery Exclusive no age

Laphroaig

Owner:
Beam Global
Spirits & Wine

Region/district:
Islay

Founded: 1810
Status: Active (vc)
Capacity: 2 900 000 litres

Address: Port Ellen, Islay, Argyll PA42 7DU

Tel: 01496 302418
website: www.laphroaig.com

History:

1810 – Brothers Alexander and Donald Johnston found Laphroaig.

1815 – Official year of starting.

1836 – Donald buys out Alexander and takes over operations.

1837 – James and Andrew Gairdner found Ardenistiel a stone's throw from Laphroaig.

1847 – Donald Johnston is killed in an accident in the distillery when he falls into a kettle of boiling hot burnt ale. The Manager of neighbouring Lagavulin, Walter Graham, takes over.

1857 – Operation is back in the hands of the Johnston family when Donald's son Dugald takes over.

circa 1860 – Ardenistiel Distillery merges with Laphroaig.

1877 – Dugald, being without heirs, passes away and his sister Isabella, married to their cousin Alexander takes over.

1907 – Alexander Johnston dies and the distillery is inherited by his two sisters Catherine Johnston and Mrs. William Hunter (Isabella Johnston).

1908 – Ian Hunter arrives in Islay to assist his mother and aunt with the distillery.

Laphroaig is still the best-selling of all Islay single malts, but from 2008 to 2009 sales slipped by 8% to 171,000 cases. The number two on Islay, Bowmore, on the other hand, had increased sales by 12% to 164,000 cases and this is the closest it has been to Laphroaig since 1999. It remains to be seen, though, if this is just temporary. According to the owners, Laphroaig has been on allocation for some time now due to low stock and they expect to be able to deliver more volume in 2010.

Laphroaig is one of very few distilleries with their own maltings. Four malting floors hold 7 tonnes each and together account for 15% of requirements, another 70% comes from Port Ellen maltings on Islay, while 15% are imported from the mainland. Malt from different suppliers is always blended before mashing. Only on one occasion (at least in modern times), in 2003, was there a batch made just from the floor maltings. There is a stainless steel full lauter mash tun and six washbacks that are also made of stainless steel. The distillery uses an unusual combination of three wash stills and four spirit stills.

With Laphroaig single malt being in such a high demand, Distillery Manager, John Campbell, last year changed the distilling regime in order to increase production. The mash tun is now filled with 5.5 tonnes of grist instead of 8.5 tonnes. With two of these new mashes the washbacks can be filled fuller (52,750 litres instead of 42,000 litres). 30 mashes per week will result in 2.85 million litres of alcohol in 2010. A new lift system was set up in 2009 so that the three dunnage and five racked warehouses now hold 60,000 casks.

The core range consists of *10 year old, 10 year old cask strength, Quarter Cask* and *18 year old*. Since 2009 the cask strength is bottled in one batch each year. For 2010 it took place in January and at 58.3%. A *20 year old Double Cask* was released exclusively for French Duty Free retailer Aelia in May 2010. It is the 18 year old with another two years in quarter casks. In connection with Feis Isle a new limited version of *Cairdeas* called *Master Edition* was released. This combination of whiskies from 11 to 19 years of age was later offered on the Laphroaig website and on the Swedish market.

Previous limited releases include *Cairdeas 12* and *Cairdeas 30 year old, 25 year old cask strength* and *Laphroaig Triple Wood* with maturation first in ex-bourbon barrels, then in Quarter Casks and finally in European Oak.

History (continued):

1924 – The two stills are increased to four.

1927 – Catherine Johnston dies and Ian Hunter takes over.

1928 – Isabella Johnston dies and Ian Hunter becomes sole owner.

1950 – Ian Hunter forms D. Johnston & Company

1954 – Ian Hunter passes away and management of the distillery is taken over by Elisabeth "Bessie" Williamson, who was previously Ian Hunters PA and secretary. She becomes Director of the Board and Managing Director.

1967 – Seager Evans & Company buys the distillery through Long John Distillery, having already acquired part of Laphroaig in 1962. The number of stills is increased from four to five.

1972 – Bessie Williamson retires. Another two stills are installed bringing the total to seven.

1975 – Whitbread & Co. buys Seager Evans (now renamed Long John International) from Schenley International.

1989 – The spirits division of Whitbread is sold to Allied Distillers.

1991 – Allied Distillers launches Caledonian Malts. Laphroaig is one of the four malts included.

1994 – HRH Prince Charles gives his Royal Warrant to Laphroaig. Friends of Laphroaig is founded.

1995 – A 10 year old cask strength is launched.

2001 – 4,000 bottles of a 40 year old, the oldest-ever Laphroaig, are released.

2004 – Quarter Cask, a mix of different ages with a finish in quarter casks (i. e. 125 litres) is launched.

2005 – Fortune Brands becomes new owner.

2007 – A vintage 1980 (27 years old) and a 25 year old are released.

2008 – Cairdeas, Cairdeas 30 year old and Triple Wood are released.

2009 – An 18 year old is released.

2010 – A 20 year old for French Duty Free and Cairdeas Master Edition are launched.

Laphroaig 10 year old

GS – Old-fashioned sticking plaster, peat smoke and seaweed leap off the nose, followed by something a little sweeter and fruitier. Massive on the palate, with fish oil, salt and plankton, though the finish is quite tight and increasingly drying.

DR – Salt, peat, seawood and tar in a glorious and absorbing nose, then structured and rock like barley with waves of tarry peat washing over them, then a long phenolic and peaty finish.

18 years old

Cairdeas Master Edition

Triple Wood

10 years old

10 years old cask strength

Quarter Cask

Linkwood

Owner: Diageo

Region/district: Speyside

Founded: 1821

Status: Active

Capacity: 3 500 000 litres

Address: Elgin, Morayshire IV30 3RD

Tel: 01343 862000

website: www.malts.com

History:

1821 – Peter Brown founds the distillery.

1868 – Peter Brown passes away and his son William inherits the distillery.

1872 – William demolishes the distillery and builds a new one.

1897 – Linkwood Glenlivet Distillery Company Ltd takes over operations.

1902 – Innes Cameron, a whisky trader from Elgin, joins the Board and eventually becomes the major shareholder and Director.

1932 – Innes Cameron dies and Scottish Malt Distillers takes over in 1933.

1962 – Major refurbishment takes place.

1971 – The two stills are increased by four. Technically, the four new stills belong to a new distillery sometimes referred to as Linkwood B.

1985 – Linkwood A (the two original stills) closes.

1990 – Linkwood A is in production again for a few months each year.

2002 – A 26 year old from 1975 is launched as a Rare Malt.

2005 – A 30 year old from 1974 is launched as a Rare Malt.

2008 – Three different wood finishes (all 26 year old) are released.

2009 – A Manager´s Choice 1996 is released.

Linkwood 12 year old

GS – Floral, grassy and fragrant on the nutty nose, while the slightly oily palate becomes increasingly sweet, ending up at marzipan and almonds. The relatively lengthy finish is quite dry and citric.

DR – Sweet and squidgy with over-ripe melon and soft pear on the nose, and a delightful palate of marzipan, vanilla, green apples and a touch of spice. The finish is balanced, pleasant and very enticing.

The Blender´s List from 1974 categorizes malts from different distilleries in different classes based on how useful and important they are from a blending perspective. Only twelve qualify as Top Class and Linkwood is one of them. This still holds true today and is shown by how important this single malt is for the character of major blends like Johnnie Walker and White Horse. It is therefore not surprising how much money Diageo spends on keeping it in an excellent condition. Six old washbacks were refurbished and put back into production in 2008. In 2009 the lye pipes of both wash stills and the bottom of spirit still number 1 were replaced. In 2011 finally, the distillery will be closed between January and May when a new stainless steel mash tun is installed, botch wash stills will be replaced from the bottom up to the swan necks and new control systems will be installed in both the mash house and the still house. No wonder that the distillery will be operating at full steam during 2010, producing 3.5 million litres of alcohol.

Linkwood has been renovated and expanded several times over the years and is divided into one old and one new still house, the latter having been built in 1971. The old still house has not been used since 1996. When it was operational, a cast iron worm tub was used to cool the spirit vapours. Currently the distillery is equipped with a full lauter cast iron mash tun, five wooden washbacks (plus six smaller ones in the old building) with a fermentation time of 75 hours, and two pairs of stills. The beautiful dam by the distillery is used for condensing only; the process water comes from springs near Millbuies Loch.

As mentioned above, most of the production goes into Diageo´s blended whiskies, but around a million litres are sold to other companies each year.

The core expression is a *12 year old Flora & Fauna*. In autumn 2008 a limited edition of three *26 year old* bottlings were released, all of them finished for the last 14 years in three different types of casks - *port, rum* and *sweet red wine*. The most recent expression was a *Manager´s Choice* from *1996*, released in autumn 2009.

12 years old

Loch Lomond

Owner:
Loch Lomond
Distillery Co.

Region/district:
Western Highlands

Founded: **Status:**   **Capacity:**
1965   Active   4 000 000 litres

Address: Lomond Estate, Alexandria G83 0TL

Tel: **website:**
01389 752781   www.lochlomonddistillery.com

History:
1965 – The distillery is built by Littlemill Distillery Company Ltd owned by Duncan Thomas and American Barton Brands.

1966 – Production commences.

1971 – Duncan Thomas is bought out and Barton Brands reforms as Barton Distilling (Scotland) Ltd.

1984 – The distillery closes.

1985 – Glen Catrine Bonded Warehouse Ltd buys Loch Lomond Distillery.

1987 – The distillery resumes production.

1993 – Grain spirits are also distilled.

1997 – A fire destroys 300,000 litres of maturing whisky.

1999 – Two more stills are installed.

2005 – Inchmoan and Craiglodge are officially launched for the first time. Both are 4 years old from 2001. Inchmurrin 12 years is launched.

2006 – Inchmurrin 4 years, Croftengea 1996 (9 years), Glen Douglas 2001 (4 years) and Inchfad 2002 (5 years) are launched.

2010 – A peated Loch Lomond with no age statement is released as well as a Vintage 1966, exclusively for the German market.

Inchmurrin 12 year old

GS – Malt and spicy oranges on the nose; newly-opened glossy magazines. The palate is lively and spicy with notes of caramel, fudge and honey. Fudge and spice persist in the medium-length finish.

Loch Lomond Distillery does not look like any other distillery in Scotland. The former dye factory lies in a rather run-down industrial area in Alexandria at the southern tip of Loch Lomond, but it is the unusual equipment set-up which makes this distillery special. First of all, there are two traditional copper pot stills (soon to be augmented by another pair). Then there are four copper stills where the swan necks have been exchanged with rectifying columns which enables making different types of spirit in the same stills. Furthermore, there is one Coffey still for continuous distillation where, for example, the Old Rhosdhu single malt is produced. As this was not enough, an additional distillery with continuous stills producing grain whisky is housed in the same building. There are also ten stainless steel washbacks with another eight that are currently not in use, but which will be replaced with new ones. The distillery has its own cooperage and there are 30 palletised and racked warehouses on site.

Loch Lomond is currently producing 4 million litres of malt spirit and 15 million litres of grain spirit which is at full capacity. Peated malt is produced one month every year. Half of the production is intended for own bottlings and the rest is sold to other companies.

The company, which includes the largest independent bottler of spirit in Scotland, Glen Catrine Bonded Warehouse, is family-owned and headed by 83 year old Sandy Bulloch.

Loch Lomond produces a broad range of whiskies. While there were three different single malt brands in the range previously, another five surfaced in 2005/2006. There are now eight, from unpeated Glen Douglas to heavily peated (40ppm) Croftengea.

Single malt: Loch Lomond no age and 18 years, Loch Lomond Peated (no age), Loch Lomond 1966 (for Germany), Old Rhosdhu 5 years, Old Rhosdhu 1967 32 years, Inchmurrin 4 and 12 years, Inchmoan 2001 4 years, Craiglodge 2001 4 years, Croftengea 2003 4 years, Glen Douglas 2002 5 years, Inchfad 2002 5 years.

Single blended: Loch Lomond

Blended: Scots Earl **Single grain:** Loch Lomond

Inchmurrin 12 years old

Longmorn

Owner:
Chivas Brothers
(Pernod Ricard)

Region/district:
Speyside

Founded: 1894 **Status:** Active **Capacity:** 3 500 000 litres

Address: Longmorn, Morayshire IV30 8SJ

Tel: 01343 554139 **website:** -

History:

1893 – John Duff & Company, which founded Glenlossie already in 1876, starts construction. John Duff, George Thomson and Charles Shirres are involved in the company. The total cost amounts to £20,000.

1894 – First production in December.

1897 – John Duff buys out the others and founds Longmorn Distillery.

1898 – John Duff builds another distillery next to Longmorn which is called Benriach (at times aka Longmorn no. 2). Duff declares bankruptcy and the shares are sold by the bank to James R. Grant.

1970 – The distillery company is merged with The Glenlivet & Glen Grant Distilleries and Hill Thomson & Co. Ltd. Own floor maltings ceases.

1972 – The number of stills is increased from four to six. Spirit stills are converted to steam firing.

1974 – Another two stills are added.

1978 – Seagrams takes over through The Chivas & Glenlivet Group.

1994 – Wash stills are converted to steam firing.

2001 – Pernod Ricard buys Seagram Spirits & Wine together with Diageo and Pernod Ricard takes over the Chivas group.

2004 – A 17 year old cask strength is released.

2007 – A 16 year old is released replacing the 15 year old.

Longmorn 16 year old

GS – The nose offers cream, spice, toffee apples and honey. Medium bodied in the mouth, with fudge, butter and lots of spice. The finish is quite long, with oak and late-lingering dry spices.

DR – Cut flowers and mixed fruit on the nose, rounded and full fruit and honey with some wood and spice adding complexity, long and rich finish.

When Chivas Bros repackaged Longmorn back in 1994 and introduced it, together with Glen Keith, Benriach and Strath-isla, as the Heritage Selection, the single malt became more known to the consumer but it never really took off. Until a few years ago, the 15 year old was selling just around 5,000 cases per year. Things started to change when the 16 year old was released as a super-premium malt three years ago and the bottle was given a completely new, contemporary look. Sales started to increase and the brand now has devoted followers in mainly Taiwan, France, the US and Canada. Aside from its success as a single malt, Longmorn still is one of the most important parts of Chivas Regal 18 years old and Royal Salute. The distillery is equipped with a stainless steel traditional mash tun with rakes and the wooden washbacks were replaced some years ago by eight stainless steel ones. The four wash stills and the four spirit stills are separated in their own still houses, actually the same building, but with a sliding door in-between. On two of the spirit stills the furnace is still visible in the bottom, a reminder of the time when the stills were coal-fired. The spirit safe is probably the most eye-catching in the industry and each spirit still has its own receiver, which means that technically four different kinds of malt could be made if desired. On site there are six dunnage and six palletised warehouses, of which three are placed with neighbouring BenRiach Distillery. The distillery used to be powered by a steam engine, which is still on display in the still room, although it has not been used since 1979. The engine was made by G. Chrystal in Perth who also made similar engines for Ardmore and Auchroisk. The *16 year old* was released in 2007 and there is also a *17 year old cask strength* for sale at Chivas´s visitor centres.

16 years old

Meet the Manager

NEAL CORBETT
OPERATIONS MANAGER, LONGMORN, GLENBURGIE AND
MILTONDUFF DISTILLERIES

When did you start working in the whisky business and when did you start at Longmorn?

I started at Burghead Maltings with United Distillers in 1995 and have been responsible for Longmorn since 2005.

Had you been working in other lines of business before whisky?

I was a Maintenance Electrician at Burghead for 4 years, before moving to Distilling.

What kind of education or training do you have?

I joined the Royal Navy with 3 "O" Levels straight from school. During my 11 years in the Navy I trained as an Electrical Technician, with a Diploma in Marine Engineering, and was an Engineering Officer of the Watch when I left in 1994. Whilst working in the whisky industry I have passed the Distilling Diploma and NEBOSH Certificate for Health and Safety.

Describe your career in the whisky business.

After 4 years at Burghead Maltings as a Maintenace Electrician I was accepted onto Diageo's Malt Distillers program. After spending time training at various sites I started at Dailuaine Distillery as Site Operations Manager. In 2000 I moved to Talisker and a year later I joined Allied Distillers as Brewer at Glenburgie Distillery where I was involved in the building of the new distillery. I was then moved to Miltonduff Distillery to work as part of the compliance team. In July 2005 Allied Distillers were taken over by Pernod Ricard and became part of Chivas Brothers Ltd. I then became Operations Manager for Miltonduff, Glenburgie and Longmorn.

What are your main tasks as a manager?

Managing the day to day production, ensuring we produce the highest quality spirit and the best possible price, while adhering to all the legislative regulations such as HM Customs and Revenue, Health, Safety and Environment.

What are the biggest challenges of being a distillery manager?

Ensuring that all the sites under my control comply with all the relative controls, which can change from time to time, whilst still maintaining good relations with all our customers, suppliers and most importantly the technicians that actually operate the plant, as we are always looking to improve and attain higher standards.

What would be the worst that could go wrong in the production process?

Until recently I would have thought it would have been a large loss of spirit, however we recently had major problems with our boiler plant for main steam generation, you can deal with issues and problems as they occur with the process, but without steam your dead in the water.

How would you describe the character of Longmorn single malt?

Sweet Creamy Slight Toffee

What are the main features in the process at Longmorn, contributing to this character?

Longmorn uses plain unpeated malt, through a traditional mash tun, a relatively short fermentation time of 48 hours. the wash and spirit stills are traditional shaped Speyside, with automated cut points giving a very consistent spirit quality. We mature Longmorn in Butts, Hogsheads (American oak) and Barrels as the stock is required for Single Malt and for blending in both Ballantines and Chivas.

What is your favourite expression of Longmorn and why?

I actually prefer the most recent expression of Longmorn, the 16 year old. it's not only because the package has been upgraded to a more deluxe style, the whisky really is something special. Longmorn has always been a very smooth spirit, but the 16 year old is one to savour with good company.

If it were your decision alone – what new expression of Longmorn would you like to see released?

I think the 16 year old already typifies the sweet creamy character of Longmorn and would be hard to beat.

If you had to choose a favourite dram other than Longmorn, what would that be?

I still have a soft spot for Talisker when I'm looking for something a little different, however I can't really see past The Glenlivet. The 18 year old is fantastic and Nadurra is also a fine dram.

What are the biggest changes you have seen the past 10-15 years in your profession?

The automation of plants has been one of the biggest changes. Not that there were many operators at the sites when I started anyway, but now with single manning, the skills required to do the job and the extra responsibility require a different type of person.

Do you see any major changes in the next 10 years to come?

The major changes and challenges I see is the continued drive to be more energy efficient. We have seen many various initiatives come along, such as renewable power etc. It will be interesting to see how the industry embraces these changes.

Do you have any special interests/hobbies that you pursue?

I am a keen fisherman and I also enjoy riding motorbikes and watching rugby.

The stills at Longmorn were direct fired using coal until 1994. How has the change to indirect firing influenced the flavour of the spirit?

The spirit stills were converted to steam in 1972/3, so any changes would really have been back then, as only the wash stills were direct fired up until 1994, and the company carried out extensive trials to ensure the character remained the same after conversion. If any change has had an affect on character it would be the automation of the spirit cut points, as the spirit is much more consistent now.

You are also responsible for Miltonduff and Glenburgie distilleries. Are there any differences between the three in terms of how the production is run?

Longmorn has a traditional tumbler rake mash tun, Miltonduff and Glenburgie both have full lauters. Longmorn is based around a 6 hour cycle for mashing and distillation, which most Chivas sites work around, and has a relatively short fermentation time of 48 hours. Glenburgie was rebuilt as a new production facility in 2004, Miltonduff was modernised in 1999. All plants are computer controlled sites, however Glenburgie still has manual operation of still cuts. Glenburgie and Miltonduff both have heat recovery and thermo compression on the wash stills with external heat exchangers, making them the most energy efficient sites we have within the Chivas Group.

Macallan

Owner: | **Region/district:**
Edrington Group | Speyside

Founded: | **Status:** | **Capacity:**
1824 | Active (vc) | 8 750 000 litres

Address: Easter Elchies, Craigellachie,
Morayshire AB38 9RX

Tel: | **website:**
01340 871471 | www.themacallan.com

History:

1824 – The distillery is licensed to Alexander Reid under the name Elchies Distillery.

1847 – Alexander Reid passes away and James Shearer Priest and James Davidson take over.

1868 – James Stuart takes over the licence. He founds Glen Spey distillery a decade later.

1886 – James Stuart buys the distillery.

1892 – Stuart sells the distillery to Roderick Kemp from Elgin. Kemp expands the distillery and names it Macallan-Glenlivet.

1909 – Roderick Kemp passes away and the Roderick Kemp Trust is established to secure the family's future ownership.

1965 – The number of stills is increased from six to twelve.

1966 – The trust is reformed as a private limited company.

1968 – The company is introduced on the London Stock Exchange.

1974 – The number of stills is increased to 18.

1975 – Another three stills are added, now making the total 21.

1979 – Allan Schiach, descendant of Roderick Kemp, becomes the new chairman of the board after Peter Schiach.

1984 – The first official 18 year old single malt is launched.

1986 – Japanese Suntory buys 25% of Macallan-Glenlivet plc stocks.

Edrington Group, the owner of Macallan (and Highland Park, GlenRothes and Glenturret Distilleries), is controlled by The Robertson Trust. It is a charitable trust founded by the three granddaughters of the founder of Robertson & Baxter, the origin of today's Edrington. Foreign companies have tried to acquire the company on at least two occasions (Seagram in 1947 and Hiram Walker in 1979) and, as a result, the company structure surrounding Edrington is probably one of the most complicated and impenetrable in Scotland.

In September 2008 the old Macallan still room with another six stills was recommissioned and, therefore, the production is now taking place in two separate plants. The number one plant holds one full lauter mash tun, 16 stainless steel washbacks, five wash stills and ten spirit stills. The recommissioned number two plant is comprised of one semi-lauter mash tun, six new wooden washbacks, two wash stills and four spirit stills. Macallan was one of very few distilleries in Scotland that were still heating some of their stills by direct fire (using gas). However, after the summer closure 2010, all stills are indirectly fired using steam. In August 2009 the working week was reduced from seven to five days, but starting in April 2010 a seven-day week is reinstated which results in 8.75 million litres produce a year. Warehouse capacity was expanded towards the end of 2008 when two of six planned warehouses were completed, each holding 20,000 casks.

The *Macallan 1824 Collection*, the Duty Free range that was introduced in 2009, expanded in July 2010 with *Oscuro*, containing whiskies distilled from 1987 to 1997. September 2009 saw the release of the third in the *Lalique* decanter collection, a *57 year old* including one cask going back to 1949. Another exclusive bottling was presented in April 2010, *Cire Perdue* 64 years old. There is just one decanter and it will be auctioned off in November 2010, with proceeds of the auction donated to charity. November 2010, finally, saw the release of the yearly *Easter Elchies Cask Selection*, a distillery exclusive.

The current range can be divided into:
Sherry Oak: 10 and 12 years, Cask Strength (US only), 18, 25 and 30 years
Fine Oak: 10, 12, 15, 17, 18, 21, 25 and 30 years old.
Travel retail: Elegancia 12 years, Cask Strength 10 years, 1824 Collection (Select Oak, Whisky Maker's Edition, Estate Reserve, 1824 Limited Reserve), Oscuro, 40 years
Distillery exclusives: Woodland Estate, Estate Oak
Fine and Rare: A range of vintages from 1926 to 1989.

History (continued):

1996 – Highland Distilleries buys the remaining stocks and terminate the Kemp family's influence on Macallan. 1874 Replica is launched.

1999 – Edrington and William Grant & Sons buys Highland Distilleries (where Edrington, Suntory and Remy-Cointreau already are shareholders) for £601 million. They form the 1887 Company which owns Highland Distilleries with 70% held by Edrington and 30% by William Grant & Sons (excepting the 25% share held by Suntory).

2000 – The first single cask from Macallan (1981) is named Exceptional 1.

2001 – A new visitor centre is opened.

2002 – Elegancia replaces 12 year old in the duty-free range. 1841 Replica, Exceptional II and Exceptional III, from 1980, are also launched.

2003 – 1876 Replica and Exceptional IV, single cask from 1990 are released.

2004 – Exceptional V, single cask from 1989 is released as well as Exceptional VI, single cask from 1990. The Fine Oak series is launched.

2005 – New expressions are Macallan Woodland Estate, Winter Edition and the 50 year old.

2006 – Fine Oak 17 years old and Vintage 1975 are launched.

2007 – 1851 Inspiration and Whisky Maker's Selection are released as a part of the Travel Retail range. 12 year old Gran Reserva is launched in Taiwan and Japan.

2008 – Estate Oak and 55 year old Lalique are released.

2009 – Capacity increased by another six stills. The Macallan 1824 Collection, a range of four duty free expressions, is launched. A 57 year old Lalique bottling is released.

2010 – Oscuro is released for Duty Free.

Macallan 12 year old Sherry Oak

GS – The nose is luscious, with buttery sherry and Christmas cake characteristics. Rich and firm on the palate, with sherry, elegant oak and Jaffa oranges. The finish is long and malty, with slightly smoky spice.

DR – Unmistakenly the sherried version of The Macallan, with a classic red berry and orange mix. The palate is plummy, with intense sherry and some toffee and cocoa notes. The finish is medium long sweet and fruity.

Macallan 12 year old Fine Oak

GS – The nose is perfumed and quite complex, with marzipan and malty toffee. Expansive on the palate, with oranges, marmalade, milk chocolate and oak. Medium in length, balanced and comparatively sweet.

DR – Vanilla, butterscotch, satsumas and orange candy on the nose, mixed grapefruit, orange and other fruits on the palate and then a big dash of spice, and a reasonably long and balanced mix of fruit and spice in the finish.

Oscuro   Whisky Maker's Edition   Select Oak

Fine Oak 17 yo   1949 vintage   Cask Strength

12 years old   18 years old   25 years old   Elegancia

Macduff

Owner:
John Dewar & Sons Ltd
(Bacardi)

Region/district:
Highlands

Founded: **Status:**   **Capacity:**
1962   Active   3 340 000 litres

Address: Banff, Aberdeenshire AB45 3JT

Tel: **website:**
01261 812612   -

History:
1962 – The distillery is founded by Marty Dyke, George Crawford and Brodie Hepburn (who is also involved in Tullibardine and Deanston). Macduff Distillers Ltd is the name of the company.

1963 – Production starts.

1965 – The number of stills is increased from two to three.

1967 – Stills now total four.

1972 – William Lawson Distillers buys the distillery from Glendeveron Distilleries.

1980 – William Lawson is bought by Martini Rossi through the subsidiary General Beverage Corporation.

1990 – A fifth still is installed.

1992 – Bacardi buys Martini Rossi (including William Lawson) and transfers Macduff to the subsidiary John Dewar & Sons.

Glen Deveron 10 year old

GS – Sherry, malt and a slightly earthy note on the nose. Smooth and sweet in the mouth, with vanilla, spice and a hint of smoke. Sweet right to the finish.

DR – The nose is a mix of crisp barley, orange, hay and a trace of smoke, and on the palate an oily and fruity combination beautifully coats the mouth before giving way to a pepper, savoury and astringent finish.

To be the best selling malt of five within Dewar´s does not say so much. In MacDuff's case, or Glen Deveron as it is known when bottled, it entails 27,000 cases last year and a ranking of around 30 on the sales list. But Dewar's is virtually only about blended Scotch and there are two to chose from; Dewar´s (3.5 million cases sold in 2009) and William Lawson´s (1.6 million cases). It is as an ingredient in the latter that Macduff plays its important role. William Lawson was one of few blended Scotch whiskies that increased in volumes in 2009. As it is found in the lower price segment, it was not so badly affected by the financial downturn and the brand also managed to enter The Power 100 list from Intangible Business. A number of variables (among them market share, brand growth, brand perception and price positioning) were measured and William Lawson ended up in 27th place.

Macduff distillery is equipped with a stainless steel semi-lauter mash tun, nine washbacks made of stainless steel and the rather unusual set-up of five stills (two wash stills and three spirit stills). For maturation, a mix of sherry and bourbon casks is used. Parts of the distillery were rebuilt in 1990 and 2000 and new boilers were installed in 2007. In 2010 the distillery is running at full capacity, which means 3.34 million litres.

The above mentioned Glen Deveron is an official bottling from Macduff Distillery, while if the name on the label is Macduff, it is an independent bottling. The most common Glen Deveron today is a 10 year old but there is also a *15 year old*. Older versions of *8* and *12 year olds* are also available.

One recent independent bottling is from Berry Brothers - a 25 year old distilled in 1984.

10 years old

Mannochmore

Owner: **Region/district:**
Diageo   Speyside

Founded: **Status:** **Capacity:**
1971   Active   3 450 000 litres

Address: Elgin, Morayshire IV30 8SS

Tel: **website:**
01343 862000   www.malts.com

History:
1971 – Scottish Malt Distillers (SMD) founds the distillery on the site of their sister distillery Glenlossie. It is managed by John Haig & Co. Ltd.

1985 – The distillery is mothballed.

1989 – In production again.

1992 – A Flora & Fauna series 12 years old becomes the first official bottling.

1997 – United Distillers launches Loch Dhu – The Black Whisky which is a 10 year old Mannochmore. A 22 year old Rare Malt from 1974 and a sherry-matured Manager's Dram 18 years are also launched.

2009 – An 18 year old is released.

2010 – A Manager's Choice 1998 is released.

Mannochmore 12 year old

GS – Perfumed and fresh on the light, citric nose, with a sweet, floral, fragrant palate, featuring vanilla, ginger and even a hint of mint. Medium length in the finish, with a note of lingering almonds.

DR – Buttery, with lemon, sweet dough and floral notes on the nose, oily, malty and floral on the palate and with a relatively short finish.

There are another seven distilleries within five miles from Mannochmore i Speyside. While the others were constructed in the 19th century, Mannochmore can be considered a newcomer. The distillery was erected when the interest for whisky boomed, but experienced a rough patch just ten years later. It survived, however, and is today mainly a reliable supplier of malt whisky for Diageo's blended brands, like its sister, on the same site, Glenlossie.

Mannochmore is equipped with a large cast iron lauter mash tun (11.1 tonnes and due for replacement in a couple of years), eight washbacks made of larch and three pairs of stills, which strangely enough are larger than the wash stills. The side panels on two of the wash stills and one spirit still were replaced last year and in August 2010, the swan neck of one of the wash stills was replaced. The production is running on a five-day week with 12 mashes which amounts to 2.8 million litres in the year. Mannochmore and Glenlossie share the warehouses which hold 250,000 casks in total, a large part coming from other distilleries within Diageo. There is also a huge dark grains plant on site which processes draff and pot ale from 21 different distilleries. Reducing carbon footprint is very much in fashion among Scottish distilleries these days and a project is running at the moment to install a biomass burner producing energy for the two distilleries. It is expected to be completed in 2012.

The core range of Mannochmore is just a *12 year old Flora & Fauna* and has been so for a long time. It was therefore encouraging to see the distillery represented in Diageo Special Releases in 2009 for the first time with a limited *18 year old* matured in re-charred sherry casks, bourbon casks and new American Oak casks. It did not take long until the next expression was released (April 2010), this time as part of the *Manager's Choice* range, a sherry matured single cask from *1998*. An independent bottling of a 27 year old with a claret finish was released by Cadenhead in 2010.

Flora & Fauna 12 years old

Miltonduff

Owner:
Chivas Brothers
(Pernod Ricard)

Region/district:
Speyside

Founded: 1824

Status: Active

Capacity: 5 500 000 litres

Address: Miltonduff, Elgin,
Morayshire IV30 8TQ

Tel: 01343 547433

website: -

History:

1824 – Andrew Peary and Robert Bain obtain a licence for Miltonduff Distillery. It has previously operated as an illicit farm distillery called Milton Distillery but changes name when the Duff family buys the site it is operating on.

1866 – William Stuart buys the distillery.

1895 – Thomas Yool & Co. becomes new part-owner.

1936 – Thomas Yool & Co. sells the distillery to Hiram Walker Gooderham & Worts. The latter transfers administration to the newly acquired subsidiary George Ballantine & Son.

1964 – A pair of Lomond stills is installed to produce the rare Mosstowie.

1974-75 – Major reconstruction of the distillery.

1981 – The Lomond stills are decommissioned and replaced by two ordinary pot stills, the number of stills now totalling six.

1986 – Allied Lyons buys 51% of Hiram Walker.

1987 – Allied Lyons acquires the rest of Hiram Walker.

1991 – Allied Distillers follow United Distillers´ example of Classic Malts and introduce Caledonian Malts in which Tormore, Glendronach and Laphroaig are included in addition to Miltonduff. Tormore is later replaced by Scapa.

2005 – Chivas Brothers (Pernod Ricard) becomes the new owner through the acquisition of Allied Domecq.

Miltonduff 10 year old (Gordon & MacPhail)

GS – Fresh and fruity on the nose, with toasted malt and a mildly herbal note. Soft fruits and mild oak on the palate, while the finish is subtly drying, with a touch of ginger.

DR – Clean, honeyed and deceptively gentle on the nose, chunky malt and clean vanilla on the plate, pleasant and warming finish.

Together with Glenburgie, Miltonduff is considered the most important malt whisky in the Ballantine´s blended whisky. Like most of the big brands, Ballantine's managed to increase volumes during 2008 as the recession did not hit until rather late in the autumn. As anticipated, 2009 would prove to be a much tougher challenge. All of the top five blended Scotch brands saw decreased sales. Worst affected was J&B which, with its great exposure to Spain, decreased by 17%. Ballantine´s experienced an identical decrease as category leader Johnnie Walker, i. e. 11%, and managed to sell 5.8 million cases.

Miltonduff is a high-capacity distillery, in fact, one of the ten biggest in Scotland in this respect. It is equipped with a full lauter mash tun and, when producing at full capacity, performs 40 mashes a week. There are no less than 16 stainless steel washbacks and three pairs of stills. A balanced distillation similar to that of, for example, Glenburgie, incorporating one wash and one spirit still working in tandem and served by a designated feints and low wines receiver, was introduced in autumn 2009. In summer of 2010, a new boiler was installed and a heat recovery upgrade took place. Several racked warehouses on the site hold 54,000 casks. Evidence of this distillery's strong position with Pernod Ricard is that the company recently moved its headquarters for Northern Division from Strathisla to Miltonduff. From 1964 to 1981 Lomond stills were also used at Miltonduff. The malt from these stills was named Mosstowie and is still available. An official Miltonduff *1991, 18 years old*, was recently released in Chivas Brothers cask strength series. Otherwise Gordon & MacPhail are more or less responsible for "official" bottlings from Miltonduff. A 10 year old and a cask strength from 1996 are the current ones. Another recent bottling is a 23 year old from 1987 released by Ian MacLeod.

*Gordon & MacPhail
1993 Cask Strength*

Mortlach

Owner: **Region/district:**
Diageo   Speyside

Founded: **Status:**   **Capacity:**
1823   Active   3 600 000 litres

Address: Dufftown, Keith,
Banffshire AB55 4AQ

Tel: **website:**
01340 822100   www.malts.com

History:
1823 – The distillery is founded by James Findlater.

1824 – Donald Macintosh and Alexander Gordon become part-owners.

1831 – The distillery is sold to John Robertson for £270.

1832 – A. & T. Gregory buys Mortlach.

1837 – James and John Grant of Aberlour become part-owners. No production takes place.

1842 – The distillery is now owned by John Alexander Gordon and the Grant brothers.

1851 – Mortlach is producing again after having been used as a church and a brewery for some years.

1853 – George Cowie joins and becomes part-owner.

1867 – John Alexander Gordon dies and Cowie becomes sole owner.

1895 – George Cowie Jr. joins the company.

1897 – The number of stills is increased from three to six.

1923 – Alexander Cowie sells the distillery to John Walker & Sons.

1925 – John Walker becomes part of Distillers Company Limited (DCL).

1930 – The administration is transferred to Scottish Malt Distillers (SMD).

1964 – Major refurbishment.

1968 – Floor maltings ceases.

1996 – Mortlach 1972 (23 years) is released as a Rare Malt. The distillery is renovated at a cost of £1.5 million.

1998 – Mortlach 1978 (20 years) is released as a Rare Malt.

2004 – Mortlach 1971, a 32 year old cask strength is released.

2009 – Mortlach 1997, a single cask in the new Manager´s Choice range is released.

Dufftown is undoubtedly the whisky capital of Scotland with its six working distilleries. The oldest of them all is Mortlach which predates the second, Glenfiddich, by more than 60 years. The founder of Glenfiddich, William Grant, actually worked at Mortlach for many years before founding his own distillery. Mortlach lies on historic ground, for it was here that the Scottish king, Malcolm II, won over invading Danish Vikings which had succeeded in sailing their ships up the Spey river. This was in 1010 and in July this year the victory was celebrated through re-enactments of that battle.

The distillery is equipped with a 12 tonnes full lauter mash tun, six washbacks made of larch and six stills in various sizes. The distillation process at Mortlach, sometimes called partial triple distillation, is unique in Scotland. There are three wash stills and three spirit stills where the No. 3 pair act as a traditional double distillation. The stronger parts (some 80%) of the low wines from wash stills No. 1 and 2 go into spirit still No. 2, while the weaker parts go into the smallest spirit still, No. 1, also known as "Wee Witchie". Before the final spirit run in the "Wee Witchie", some of the spirit has already been distilled both once or even twice, resulting in a fraction being quadruple distilled. The spirit vapours are cooled using wooden worm tubs on the outside. There are also five dunnage warehouses with a total of 21,000 casks maturing.

Many consider the whisky from Mortlach the most powerful in Speyside, a character derived from the long fermentation time, the distillation with as little reflux as possible and the cooling using worm tubs.

Mortlach is important to the Johnnie Walker blends and especially Black Label. The only official bottling used to be the 16 year old Flora & Fauna. In autumn of 2009, however, a Mortlach 1997 single cask was released in the new range Manager´s Choice.

Flora & Fauna 16 years old

Mortlach 16 year old

GS – A rich, confident and spicy, sherried nose, with sweet treacle and pepper. Complex, elegant, yet masterful. Sherry, Christmas cake, gunpowder, black pepper on the palate. A long, relatively dry, and slightly smoky, gingery finish.

DR – Christmas cake and rich sherry nose, and a rich full plum-fruit and soft summer fruit palate. The finish is rich, full and long, with the wood making its presence felt.

Oban

Owner:
Diageo

Region/district:
Western Highlands

Founded: **Status:** **Capacity:**
1794 Active (vc) 670 000 litres

Address: Stafford Street, Oban, Argyll PA34 5NH

Tel: **website:**
01631 572004 (vc) www.malts.com

History:

1793 – John and Hugh Stevenson found the distillery on premises previously used for brewing.

1794 – Start of operations.

1820 – Hugh Stevenson dies.

1821 – Hugh Stevenson's son Thomas, having recently returned from Buenos Aires, takes over.

1829 – Bad investments force Thomas Stevenson into bankruptcy. His eldest son John takes over operations at the distillery.

1830 – John buys the distillery from his father's creditors for £1,500.

1866 – Peter Cumstie buys the distillery.

1883 – Cumstie sells Oban to James Walter Higgins who refurbishes and modernizes it.

1898 – The Oban & Aultmore-Glenlivet Co. takes over with Alexander Edwards at the helm.

1923 – The Oban Distillery Co. owned by Buchanan-Dewar takes over.

1925 – Buchanan-Dewar becomes part of Distillers Company Limited (DCL).

1930 – Administration is transferred to Scottish Malt Distillers (SMD).

1931 – Production ceases.

1937 – In production again.

1968 – Floor maltings ceases and the distillery closes for reconstruction.

1972 – Reopening of the distillery.

1979 – Oban 12 years is on sale.

1988 – United Distillers launches Classic Malts. Oban 14 year is selected to represent Western Highlands.

1989 – A visitor centre is built.

1998 – A Distillers' Edition is launched.

2002– The oldest Oban (32 years) so far is launched in a limited edition of 6,000 bottles.

2004 – A 20 year old cask strength from 1984 (1,260 bottles) is released.

2009 – Oban 2000, a single cask in the new Manager's Choice range is released.

2010 – A no age distillery exclusive is released.

Oban 14 year old

GS – Lightly smoky on the honeyed, floral nose. Toffee, cereal and a hint of peat. The palate offers initial cooked fruits, becoming spicier. Complex, bittersweet, malt, oak and more gentle smoke. The finish is quite lengthy, with spicy oak, toffee and discreet, new leather.

DR – A mixed nose of heather, honey, pineapple and nuts, a perfectly balanced mix of grapey fruit, pineapple chunks, roast nuts and smoky undertow, and a rounded and fruity finish, drying and more-ish.

Oban distillery is the second smallest in the Diageo group (Royal Lochnagar is the smallest) but, at the same time, it is the fifth best selling single malt in the company and the biggest seller in the US of all the Diageo malts. Enhancing capacity, though, is easier said than done, even if it is high on the wish list. Oban is situated in the city centre surrounded by buildings on three sides and a steep hill on the fourth side. Most buildings are listed so chances for expansion seem slim.

The distillery is equipped with a traditional stainless steel mash tun with rakes, four washbacks made of European Larch and one pair of stills. Attached to the stills is a rectangular, double worm tub to condensate the spirit vapours. The tub is not so striking and pretty as the wooden ones at Glen Elgin and Dalwhinnie, but made of stainless steel, built into the roof and hidden under metal covers. A brand new wash worm was installed in 2010 as well as part of the spirit worm. The distillery is running at full capacity, i.e. 700,000 litres. The size of the stills could allow for more, but the bottleneck is the washbacks. All of the production is used for single malts.

Oban is one of the original six Classic Malts and has a very nice visitor centre and well-stocked shop.

Caol Ila, Talisker and Clynelish all have it - a distillery exclusive bottling that can be found only at the distilleries' visitor centres. Now another four Diageo distilleries, among them Oban, can offer their visitors a rare treat. In Oban's case, it is *bourbon-matured* with a finish in Pedro Montilla Fino sherry cask *without age statement*, released in May 2010.

The core range just consists of two expressions - a *14 year old* and a *Distiller's Edition* with a montilla fino finish. In autumn 2010 a *limited bottling*, available only at the distillery, was released. It is finished in Fino sherry casks and has no age statement. Older limited editions include a *32 year old*, a *20 year old* and, exclusive for the American market (8,700 bottles), an *18 year old* released in 2008.

*Distillery Exclusive
no age*

Meet the Manager

BRENDAN MCCARRON
DISTILLERY MANAGER, OBAN DISTILLERY

When did you start working in the whisky business and when did you start at Oban?

I joined Diageo in September 2006 as part of the company's graduate trainee scheme. I completed 3 one-year secondments in that time, the first being in malt distilling. I started at Oban in July 2009.

Have you been working in other lines of business before whisky?

When I left University I spent almost 2 years with GlaxoSmithKline, the global pharmaceutical company. I really enjoyed my time there but it was impossible to say no when the offer to work in the whisky industry came through.

What kind of education or training do you have?

I went to the University of Strathclyde where I studied Chemical Engineering. I left Uni in 2003. There are many different routes into distillery operations management!

Describe your career in the whisky business.

In my first year with Diageo I was originally posted to Burghead Maltings where I worked on a project to save energy in the Malt Kilns. After 2 months I was given the opportunity to work in the project team planning and designing Roseisle Distillery.

What are your main tasks as a manager?

The first priority is Safety, always. That aside my work is quite varied; I am responsible for both production in the distillery and for the visitor centre. I also get involved in projects which encompass all of our plants in Malt distilling, not just Oban distillery. There are also plenty of ViP visits - this is a famous distillery!

What are the biggest challenges of being a distillery manager?

This is my first year in the job so there are lot of challenges for me. I have no previous experience of visitor centres so that was one of the first places I wanted to learn and understand. On the process side, we're geographically isolated from the other distilleries in our group so all our support functions are 3 hours away. Simply keeping the plant running is a big challenge for the team.

What would be the worst that could go wrong in the production process?

Assuming no harm to people, my next biggest fear is for the quality of our spirit not meeting the standard. Oban is a hugely popular whisky and demand far outstrips supply. Since we only produce for Oban Single malt, losing the spirit character would have a huge impact on our future supply.

How would you describe the character of Oban single malt?

It's a very balanced malt, but totally avoids being bland. The nose has lots of fruits – oranges, lemons and pears, with a signature touch of sea-salt and peaty smokiness. I can taste all the same things I pick up in the nose of the whisky. Its my favourite malt and has been for some time.

What are the main features in the process at Oban, contributing to this character?

During mashing we deliberately produce very clear wort, which we then ferment for over 4 days. This long fermentation produces the orange aromas present in the nose of the matured spirit. We also have large worm tub condensers to provide our required spirit character.

What is your favourite expression of Oban and why?

Due to the massive demand for Oban 14 year old there are very few other expressions of Oban available. We do have the Distillers Edition, finished in a Montilla Fino sherry cask and this year we have started to stock a cask strength Distillery Own bottling, which is only available in the Visitor centre shop.

If it were your decision alone – what new expression of Oban would you like to see released?

If there was enough to spare then I would like to try a 10 year old. I've tried Oban 14, 18 and 32 years old. All of these expressions have their unique characteristics. I'd like to see what difference 4 years less in the cask makes to the final spirit.

If you had to choose a favourite dram other than Oban, what would that be?

Caol Ila 18 year old and Mortlach are both current favourites of mine.

What are the biggest changes you have seen the past 10-15 years in your profession?

I've only worked in Whisky for 3 years and the big changes since then have been in the focus on environmental goals. There is real speed at which new environmental projects are being completed, and its increasing year on year.

Do you see any major changes in the next 10 years to come?

I believe the investment at Roseisle and Cameronbridge into bio-energy will really shape the technology used in the whisky industry over the next 10 years. Conserving the environment is the key challenge facing the whisky industry in Scotland and I think more innovations like bio-energy will arrive in the next 10 years.

Do you have any special interests/hobbies that you pursue?

I played a lot of football up until this year, but moving locations every year has put paid to that plus I don't like playing in the rain, which there's plenty of in Oban. I love playing golf though it's a sport I just cannot get the hang of no matter how hard I try. Maybe this summer will be the breakthrough...

You are the manager of one of the few urban distilleries left in Scotland. Does that have any implications, for example when it comes to transports, waste treatment, expansion etc?

We are in the centre of Oban, and are surrounded on all sides by buildings except for at the back of site where there is a sheer cliff. So we can't expand, despite the huge demand. At present our relatively low volume of production means we have little impact on the waste treatment plant, and there is a low number of transportation movements in and out of Oban.

You were involved in planning Roseisle - the newest distillery in Scotland and now you are the manager of a distillery built in the 1700s. What are the similarities and the differences when you compare?

Although there are many innovations at Roseisle, the process of making malt whisky is exactly the same there as it is here at Oban. Mashing, fermentation and distillation happens in exactly the same way at both distilleries. The main difference is just the scale of Roseisle. It can make in a week what Oban makes in a year.

Pulteney

Owner:
Inver House Distillers
(Thai Beverages plc)

Region/district:
Northern Highlands

Founded: 1826
Status: Active (vc)
Capacity: 1 500 000 litres

Address: Huddart St, Wick, Caithness KW1 5BA

Tel: 01955 602371
website: www.oldpulteney.com

History:
1826 – James Henderson founds the distillery.

1920 – The distillery is bought by James Watson.

1923 – Buchanan-Dewar takes over.

1925 – Buchanan-Dewar becomes part of Distillers Company Limited (DCL).

1930 – Production ceases.

1951 – In production again after being acquired by the solicitor Robert Cumming.

1955 – Cumming sells to James & George Stodart Ltd, a subsidiary to Hiram Walker & Sons.

1958 – The distillery is rebuilt.

1959 – The floor maltings close.

1961 – Allied Breweries buys James & George Stodart Ltd.

1981 – Allied Breweries changes name to Allied Lyons after the acquisition of J Lyons in 1978.

1994 – Allied Lyons acquires Pedro Domecq and changes name to Allied Domecq plc.

1995 – Allied Domecq sells Pulteney to Inver House Distillers.

1997 – Old Pulteney 12 years is launched.

2001 – Pacific Spirits (Great Oriole Group) buys Inver House at a price of $85 million.

2004 – A 17 year old is launched (4,200 bottles).

2005 – A 21 year old is launched (3,000 bottles).

2006 – International Beverage Holdings acquires Pacific Spirits UK.

2009 – A 30 year old is released.

2010 – WK499 Isabella Fortuna is released.

Old Pulteney 12 year old

GS – The nose presents pleasingly fresh malt and floral notes, with a touch of pine. The palate is comparatively sweet, with malt, spices, fresh fruit and a suggestion of salt. The finish is medium in length, drying and decidedly nutty.

DR – Honey and lemon lozenges on the nose, sweet citrus fruits, chunky malt and some traces of sea brine on the palate, an amusing sweet and sour two step at the finish.

Pulteney is the most northerly distillery on the Scottish mainland and is situated in the small town of Wick (c 7,000 inhabitants). Once, this was the busiest herring port in Europe. Old Pulteney (as the whisky from Pulteney distillery is called) is, together with Speyburn, the best-selling of Inver House´s single malts.

The semi-lauter mash tun is made of cast iron and for the six washbacks, with an average fermentation time of 54 hours, Corten steel has been used. Few distilleries (Glen Scotia is one) still use this type of washbacks. Pulteney is equipped with one pair of stills. The wash still is large (21,700 litres) with a huge ball creating added reflux. Its top is quaintly chopped off as the still was apparently too tall for the stillroom when it was instal-led. The spirit still (17,300 litres) is equipped with a purifier and both stills use stainless steel worm tubs for condensing the spirit. The capacity is 1.5 million litres but for 2010, there will be 15 mashes per week, which is the equivalent of 1.32 million litres of spirit. New roofs were laid on the five warehouses in 2008/2009, which can hold 24,000 casks. The biggest markets for Old Pulteney are the UK, the US and Sweden. The core range is a *12 year old* with limi-ted editions of a *17 year old* and a *21 year old*. In July 2009 a *30 year old*, the oldest Old Pulteney ever, was released. Matured in ex-bourbon casks, it is non-chill filtered and without colouring. 2010 saw the first release of a Duty Free exclusive from Pulteney. The bottling is called *WK499 Isabella Fortuna* and has its name after one of Wick´s two remaining herring drifters. It is non-aged, matured in ex bourbon casks and bottled at 52%. Old Pulteney is, since 2007, included in Barrogill, a blended malt released by the owner, Inver House.

An 18 year old from 1990 by Caden-heads, a 1982 from Dewar Rattray and a 1990 released by Blackadder are among the most recent indepen-dent releases.

1991 15 years old

Royal Brackla

Owner:
John Dewar & Sons
(Bacardi)

Region/district:
Highlands

Founded: **Status:** **Capacity:**
1812   Active   3 900 000 litres

Address: Cawdor, Nairn, Nairnshire IV12 5QY

Tel: **website:**
01667 402002   -

History:

1812 – The distillery is founded by Captain William Fraser.

1835 – Brackla becomes the first of three distilleries allowed to use 'Royal' in the name.

1852 – Robert Fraser & Co. takes over the distillery.

1898 – The distillery is rebuilt and Royal Brackla Distillery Company Limited is founded.

1919 – John Mitchell and James Leict from Aberdeen purchase Royal Brackla.

1926 – John Bisset & Company Ltd takes over.

1943 – Scottish Malt Distillers (SMD) buys John Bisset & Company Ltd and thereby acquires Royal Brackla.

1966 – The maltings closes.

1970 – Two stills are increased to four.

1985 – The distillery is mothballed.

1991 – Production resumes.

1993 – A 10 year old Royal Brackla is launched in United Distillers' Flora & Fauna series.

1997 – UDV spends more than £2 million on improvements and refurbishing.

1998 – Bacardi–Martini buys Dewar's from Diageo.

2004 – A new 10 year old is launched.

Royal Brackla 10 year old

GS – An attractive malty, fruity, floral nose, with peaches and apricots. Quite full-bodied, the creamy palate exhibits sweet malt, spice and fresh fruit. The finish is medium to long, with vanilla and gently-spiced oak.

DR – Pineapple and citrus fruits on the nose, candy barley, melon and pleasant sweet spice on the palate, medium sweet finish with a trace of green melon.

In the hands of Dewar's, Royal Brackla is not a single malt brand much heard of, in contrast to when it was owned by Diageo and had a short period of relative fame. This happened a few years before Diageo had to sell off Dewar's, with Royal Brackla and a few other distilleries, for competitive reasons. At that time Diageo decided to niche Royal Brackla as a low-priced whisky. The decision was caused by supermarkets starting to work with own labels, sold at favourably, low prices. Diageo's response was to bottle Royal Brackla without age statement and sell it at supermarket prices. Since the distillery had been closed during 1983-1991 the whisky was actually around 12 years old and quite a bargain.

When Bacardi bought Dewar's (and the distillery) from Diageo ten years ago no stock was included in the deal. That is why the oldest Brackla cask in the central warehouses in Glasgow is from as recently as 1998. On a few occasions older casks have been bought back, such as when the 25 year old was released a few years ago.

Royal Brackla was the first of three distilleries to receive a Royal Warrant by William IV in 1835. In those days the honour of holding a Royal Warrant was much greater than it is today and until the reign of Queen Victoria the warrant holders totalled as few as 25. The distillery, beautifully situated just south of Nairn and Moray Firth, is equipped with a big (12 tonnes) full lauter mash tun from 1997. There are six wooden washbacks (but with stainless steel tops!) and another two made of stainless steel which are insulated because they are placed outside and the fermentation time is quite long (72 hours). Finally, there are two pairs of stills. At the moment the distillery is running at full capacity, which means 17 mashes per week and 4 million litres of alcohol per year. This makes it the biggest distillery in the Dewar's group.

Today's core range consists of a *10 year old* and a limited edition of a *25 year old*.

10 years old

Royal Lochnagar

Owner: Diageo

Region/district: Eastern Highlands

Founded: 1845

Status: Active (vc)

Capacity: 450 000 litres

Address: Crathie, Ballater, Aberdeenshire AB35 5TB

Tel: 01339 742700

website: www.malts.com

History:

1823 – James Robertson founds a distillery in Glen Feardan on the north bank of River Dee.

1826 – The distillery is burnt down by competitors but Robertson decides to establish a new distillery near the mountain Lochnagar.

1841 – This distillery is also burnt down.

1845 – A new distillery is built by John Begg, this time on the south bank of River Dee. It is named New Lochnagar.

1848 – Lochnagar obtains a Royal Warrant.

1882 – John Begg passes away and his son Henry Farquharson Begg inherits the distillery.

1896 – Henry Farquharson Begg dies.

1906 – The children of Henry Begg rebuild the distillery.

1916 – The distillery is sold to John Dewar & Sons.

1925 – John Dewar & Sons becomes part of Distillers Company Limited (DCL).

1963 – A major reconstruction takes place.

2004 – A 30 year old cask strength from 1974 is launched in the Rare Malts series (6,000 bottles).

2008 – A Distiller's Edition with a Moscatel finish is released.

2010 – A Manager's Choice 1994 is released.

Royal Lochnagar 12 year old

GS – Light toffee on the nose, along with some green notes of freshly-sawn timber. The palate offers a pleasing and quite complex blend of caramel, dry sherry and spice, followed by a hint of liquorice before the slightly scented finish develops.

DR – Rich fruit and honey on the nose, sophisticated mix of crystal barley, chunky fruit and delicious peat base and a warming and rounded finish.

Royal Lochnagar is by far the smallest in terms of production in the Diageo-family of distilleries. It is also the most traditionally managed distillery too. The nine hour mashing is done in an open, traditional cast-iron mash tun using rakes. Fermentation takes place in two wooden washbacks, with a short fermentation of 75 hours and a longer one of 126 hours. There is one pair of stills with slightly descending lyne arms and the cooling of the spirit vapours takes place in cast iron worm tubs. The whole production is filled on site with around 1,000 casks stored in the only warehouse (which previously was used for the maltings) and the rest is sent to Glenlossie for maturation. For 2010 four mashes per week will be made, resulting in 375,000 litres of alcohol per year, which is close to the maximum capacity. The winter of 2009/2010 was unusually hard with snowfall starting in December and lasting until April and Royal Lochnagar had its share of snow damage, but avoided serious trouble such as collapsing warehouses. The distillery normally closes in October, but this time the closure will not be until January 2011 instead.

The pretty visitor centre attracts 10,000 visitors a year, a figure that could easily be quadrupled if it had been more accessible by way of one of the main roads.

The founder of the new distillery in 1845, John Begg, was a close friend of the creator of VAT 69 blended whisky, William Sanderson, and for many years Lochnagar made up an important part of it. Today, however, its whisky is reserved for more exclusive Johnnie Walker expressions like Blue Label.

The core range consists of the *12 year old* which sells around 60,000 bottles a year and the more unusual expression *Selected Reserve*. The latter is a vatting of selected casks, usually around 18-20 years of age. In April 2010 a *single cask* distilled in 1994 was released as part of the *Manager's Choice* series. In the shop at neighbouring Balmoral Castle, a whisky branded as Balmoral Whisky can be found. It used to be produced by Springbank distillery, but nowadays has its origins at Royal Lochnagar.

One recent independent bottling is a 23 year old from Duncan Taylor.

Selected Reserve

Scapa

Owner: Chivas Brothers (Pernod Ricard)

Region/district: Highlands (Orkney)

Founded: 1885   **Status:** Active   **Capacity:** 1 500 000 litres

Address: Scapa, St Ola, Kirkwall, Orkney KW15 1SE

Tel: 01856 876585   **website:** www.scapamalt.com

History:

1885 – Macfarlane & Townsend founds the distillery with John Townsend at the helm.

1919 – Scapa Distillery Company Ltd takes over.

1934 – Scapa Distillery Company goes into voluntary liquidation and production ceases.

1936 – Production resumes.

1936 – Bloch Brothers Ltd (John and Sir Maurice) takes over.

1954 – Hiram Walker & Sons takes over.

1959 – A Lomond still is installed.

1978 – The distillery is modernized.

1994 – The distillery is mothballed.

1997 – Production takes place a few months each year using staff from Highland Park.

2004 – Extensive refurbishing takes place at a cost of £2.1 million. Scapa 14 years is launched.

2005 – Production ceases in April and phase two of the refurbishment programme starts. Chivas Brothers becomes the new owner.

2006 – Scapa 1992 (14 years) is launched.

2008 – Scapa 16 years is launched.

Scapa 16 year old

GS – The nose offers apricots and peaches, nougat and mixed spices. Pretty, yet profound. Medium-bodied, with caramel and spice notes in the mouth. The finish is medium in length and gingery, with fat, buttery notes emerging at the end.

DR – Sweet baked banana in cream with shortbread on the nose. The taste is a delightful mix of sweet and sour, with sugar and salt sparring but kept apart by green and orange fruit. There's a late sharper note towards lengthy fruit finish.

Scapa Distillery is magnificently situated by the sandy beach at the interior of Scapa Bay. Orkney's second, and considerably more well-known, distillery, Highland Park, is clearly visible if looking in the direction of the city Kirkwall. One would have thought that two distilleries so close to each other would produce similar whiskies, but the difference cannot be larger. While Highland Park's whisky is more or less peated and matured on sherry casks, Scapa is completely unpeated and all the new make is filled into first fill bourbon barrels. Allied Distillers and, later, Pernod Ricard, started investing heavily in Scapa in 2005, and after several years' closure, gave it a new lease of life. A new mash tun was installed and the stills were moved to a new stillhouse with a spectacular view over Scapa Bay.

The equipment consists of a semi-lauter mash tun and eight washbacks. Four of them (installed in 1968) are made of stainless steel, while the old ones (1955) are made of Corten steel. Scapa probably has the longest fermentation time of any distillery in Scotland. All the washbacks are filled and left for a week before distillation begins. The wash still is of Lomond type with a cylindrical neck, but has had the typical rectification plates removed. The spirit still is of a traditional onion design, but both stills have peculiar bends on the end of the lye pipe leading to purifiers. For the last couple of years, distillation has taken place from Monday to Wednesday, resulting in a production of circa 400,000 litres of alcohol. The entire output is destined for single malts. There are three dunnage and three racked warehouses, but only the latter are in use today.

For many years the core expression of Scapa was a 12 year old. In 2004 this was changed to a 14 year old and at the end of 2008 to a 16 year old. The reason for all this is small stock of mature whisky due to the fact that production was more or less intermittent (at best) for several years.

The Scapa core range is just the *16 year old*, while limited editions include a *25 year old* from 1980 and a *Vintage 1992*.

16 years old

Speyburn

Owner:
Inver House Distillers
(Thai Beverages plc)

Region/district:
Speyside

Founded: 1897
Status: Active
Capacity: 2 000 000 litres

Address: Rothes, Aberlour,
Morayshire AB38 7AG

Tel: 01340 831213
website: www.speyburn.com

History:

1897 – Brothers John and Edward Hopkin and their cousin Edward Broughton found the distillery through John Hopkin & Co. They already own Tobermory. The architect is Charles Doig. Building the distillery costs £17,000 and the distillery is transferred to Speyburn-Glenlivet Distillery Company.

1916 – Distillers Company Limited (DCL) acquires John Hopkin & Co. and the distillery.

1930 – Production stops.

1934 – Productions restarts.

1962 – Speyburn is transferred to Scottish Malt Distillers (SMD).

1968 – Drum maltings closes.

1991 – Inver House Distillers buys Speyburn.

1992 – A 10 year old is launched as a replacement for the 12 year old in the Flora & Fauna series.

2001 – Pacific Spirits (Great Oriole Group) buys Inver House for $85 million.

2005 – A 25 year old Solera is released.

2006 – Inver House changes owner when International Beverage Holdings acquires Pacific Spirits UK.

2009 – The un-aged Bradan Orach is introduced for the American market.

Speyburn 10 year old

GS – Soft and elegant on the spicy, nutty nose. Smooth in the mouth, with vanilla, spice and more nuts. The finish is medium, spicy and drying.

DR – Sweet malt nose, then one of the sweetest and most easy-drinking of all malts, with the faintest touch of smoke in the mix. Like eating a bag of sugar.

Three years before Speyburn distillery was bought, Inver House Distillers had already changed hands when five persons from management bought out the company from its American owners. They paid £8.2m and sold it, 12 years later, to Pacific Spirits för £56m. The owners could split no less than £37m among them but the 130 staff did not go unrewarded as £5.6 was shared among them. Inver House is currently owned by ThaiBev which controls 60% of Thailand's beer and spirits consumption. The company is listed on the Singapore Stock Exchange and Thailand's richest man, Charoen Sirivadhana-bhakdi, worth $2.6bn is the main owner.

The distillery is equipped with a stainless steel mash tun which replaced the old cast iron tun in 2008. There are six washbacks of which two were changed to Oregon Pine during 2010, while the others are made of larch. Finally, there is one wash still (17,300 litres) and one spirit still (13,200 litres) using stainless steel worm tubs with 104 metre long copper tubes for cooling. There are three dunnage warehouses with 5,000 casks where the spirit intended for bottling as single malt is maturing. The distillery was producing 1.8 million litres of spirit in 2009 , i. e. 90% of the capacity.

In 1900, Speyburn was the first distillery to abandon floor malting in favour of a new method - drum malting. In the late sixties, the maltings closed and ready malt was bought instead, but the drum maltings are still there to see, protected by Historic Scotland.

For a long time now, Speyburn single malt has been known by its *10 year old* apart from a few limited expressions (*21, 25* and *25 year old Solera*). In late 2008 a decision was made to introduce yet another expression in the core range of the American market. This was *Bradan Orach* (golden salmon in Gaelic) without age statement. Bradan Orach has also been launched in other markets since then, including Duty Free.

10 years old

Speyside

Owner:
Speyside Distillers Co.

Region/district:
Speyside

Founded: **Status:** **Capacity:**
1976 Active 600 000 litres

Address: Glen Tromie, Kingussie
Inverness-shire PH21 1NS

Tel: **website:**
01540 661060 www.speysidedistillery.co.uk

History:
1956 – George Christie buys a piece of land at Drumguish near Kingussie.

1957 – George Christie starts a grain distillery near Alloa.

1962 – George Christie (founder of Speyside Distillery Group in the fifties) commissions the drystone dyker Alex Fairlie to build a distillery in Drumguish.

1986 – Scowis assumes ownership.

1987 – The distillery is completed.

1990 – The distillery is on stream in December.

1993 – The first single malt, Drumguish, is launched.

1999 – Speyside 8 years is launched.

2000 – Speyside Distilleries is sold to a group of private investors including Ricky Christie, Ian Jerman and Sir James Ackroyd.

2001 – Speyside 10 years is launched.

Speyside 12 year old

GS – A nicely-balanced nose of herbs and toasted barley. Medium-bodied, with a suggestion of peat, plus hazelnuts and oak. Toffee and orange notes in the lingering finish.

DR – Rootsy damp straw nose, a sharp and clean barley delivery on the palate with an earthy, peaty undertow, and a willowy, nutty savoury finish.

Low key and set in beautiful surroundings, it was no wonder that the production people from BBC chose Speyside Distillery to feature Lagganmore distillery in their television series Monarch of the Glen from the early 2000. Speyside distillery is the brainchild of whisky business veteran, George Christie, who now in his mid nineties still lives up the road from the distillery. The distillery is equipped with a semi-lauter mash tun, four stainless steel washbacks and one pair of stills. The head, swan neck and ogee (the bent part between the shoulder and the swan neck) on the wash still were changed in 2010, which means that production will be slightly lower than last year, around 450,000 litres of alcohol. There are no warehouses on site. Instead, the spirit is tankered away to the company's bonded warehouses in Glasgow.

Since December 2006 a peated spirit is produced one week per year. The first of the peated production legally became whisky at the end of 2009, but according to Distillery Manager, Andrew Shand, Speyside will probably wait another couple of years before releasing it.

Speyside produces three brands of single malt: *Speyside* (360,000 bottles) with the core range of *12* and *15 year old*, *Drumguish* (600,000) and the quaint and almost black *Cu Dubh* (60,000 bottles). The release of a special bottling of the first batch of distillation from 1990 was planned for 2010.

Aside from the distillery at Drumguish, there is a diverse range of activities at the company's base in Rutherglen, Glasgow. Cask warehousing, a bottling plant and a blending operation are all found there. There is a range of 20 brands of blended whiskies and two ranges of single malts from other distilleries - Scott's Selection and Private Cellar. The total number of staff is 80 and exports go to more than 100 countries with the US and the Far East as top markets.

12 years old

Springbank

Owner:
Springbank Distillers
(J & A Mitchell)

Region/district:
Campbeltown

Founded: 1828

Status: Active

Capacity: 750 000 litres

Address: Well Close, Campbeltown,
Argyll PA28 6ET

Tel:
01586 552085

website:
www.springbankdistillers.com

History:

1828 – The Reid family, in-laws of the Mitchells (see below), founds the distillery.

1837 – The Reid family encounters financial difficulties and John and William Mitchell buy the distillery.

1897 – J. & A. Mitchell Company Ltd is founded..

1926 – The depression forces the distillery to close.

1933 – The distillery is back in production.

1960 – Own maltings ceases.

1969 – J. & A. Mitchell buys the independent bottler Cadenhead.

1979 – The distillery closes.

1985 – A 10 year old Longrow is launched.

1987 – Limited production restarts.

1989 – Production restarts.

1992 – Springbank takes up its own maltings again.

1997 – First distillation of Hazelburn.

1998 – Springbank 12 years is launched.

1999 – Dha Mhile (7 years), the world's first organic single malt, is released.

2000 – A 10 year old is launched.

2001 – Springbank 1965 'Local barley' (36 years), 741 bottles, is launched.

2002 – Number one in the series Wood Expressions is a 12 year old with five years on Demerara rum casks. Next is a Longrow sherry cask (13 years). A relaunch of the 15 year old replaces the 21 year old.

Production-wise, it has been fairly quiet from Springbank the last two years. After deciding on a temporary closure in early summer 2008, distillation only took place a few months in spring 2009. In May and June of 2010, production was resumed and from August it was back to normal. This does, however, not mean that distilling can take place all year round, since the workforce alternates between Springbank and neighbouring Glengyle. The intermittent whisky production does not imply idling though. A lot of refurbishing has taken place, among it, installing an expanded bottling line.

Springbank got a new Distillery Manager when Gavin McLachlan took over from Stuart Robertson, who had been at Springbank since 2006 in summer 2010. Robertson is moving to Huntly to oversee the building of Duncan Taylor´s distillery. McLachlan, who is the first locally-born man to take charge in over 60 years and who has been Assistant Manager for the past four years, will also be managing Glengyle distillery.

Springbank produces three distinctive single malts with different phenol contents in the malted barley; Springbank is distilled two and a half times (12-15ppm), Longrow is distilled twice (50-55 ppm) and Hazelburn is distilled three times (unpeated). Currently, Springbank makes up 60% of production, while the remaining part is split between Longrow and Hazelburn.

All whisky is matured on site in nine dunnage and two racked warehouses. The distillery is equipped with an open cast iron mash tun, six washbacks made of Scandinavian larch, one wash still and two spirit stills. The wash still is unique in Scotland, as it is fired by both an open oil-fire and internal steam coils. Ordinary condensers are used to cool the spirit vapours, except in the first of the two spirit stills, where a worm tub is used. Springbank are unique in Scotland as they malt their whole need of barley using own floor maltings. The peat comes from a bog at the nearby Machrihanish and from Tomintoul in the Highlands.

The core range of Springbank distillery is *Springbank 10, 15* and *18 years* (second edition released in 2010), *Springbank 12 year old cask strength* (new for 2010 and replacing 100 proof), *Springbank CV, Longrow 10 year old cask strength* (will be released in 2010/2011 to replace the 100 proof), *Longrow 14 year old, Longrow CV, Hazelburn 12 years old and Hazelburn CV (new for 2010)*. The *Longrow 10 year old* has been discontinued. Limited release for 2010 was a S*pringbank 12 year old claret wood* expression. A *Sauternes wood* expression of *Hazelburn* will be released in January 2011 and there is also talk about an *8 year old cask strength*.

History (continued):

2004 – J. & A. Mitchell's main owner, Hedley Wright, reopens Glengyle Distillery. Springbank 10 years 100 proof is launched as well as Springbank Wood Expression bourbon, Longrow 14 years old, Springbank 32 years old and Springbank 14 years Port Wood.

2005 – 2 400 bottles of Springbank 21 years old are released in March. The first version of Hazelburn (8 years old) is released. Longrow Tokaji Wood Expression is launched.

2006 – Longrow 10 years 100 proof, Springbank 25 years (1,200 bottles), Springbank 9 years Marsala finish, Springbank 11 years Madeira finish and a new Hazelburn 8 year old are released.

2007 – Springbank Vintage 1997 and a 16 year old rum wood are released.

2008 – The distillery closes temporarily. Three new releases of Longrow - CV, 18 year old and 7 year old Gaja Barolo.

2009 – Springbank Madeira 11 year old, Springbank 18 year old, Springbank Vintage 2001 and Hazelburn 12 year old are released.

2010 – Springbank 12 year old cask strength and a 12 year old claret expression together with new editions of the CV and 18 year old are released. Longrow 10 year old cask strength and Hazelburn CV are also new.

Springbank 10 year old 100 proof

GS – Fresh and briny on the nose, with toffee and fruit notes following through. Sweet and smooth on the palate, with developing brine, wood smoke and vanilla toffee. The finish is lengthy, with more salt and a suggestion of coconut oil.

DR – The nose is full, sweet and full of barley but with some oak and spice, the palate is rich full and savoury, with a long, full and spicy finish.

Longrow 10 year old 100 proof

DR – Subtle lemon and daffodil nose with traces of phenols, sweet, fruity and oily palate covered in a smattering of charcoal dust, lengthy, subtle and fragrant finish.

Hazelburn 12 year old

GS – A highly aromatic nose, featuring nutty toffee, sherry, dried fruits and dark chocolate. The palate is rich and spicy, with cocoa, coffee, ginger and sweeter notes of caramel and orange marmalade. Long and spicy in the finish, with more caramel, coffee, chocolate and oak notes.

DR – Rich and fruity nose of nectarine, peach, plums and some nuttiness. On the palate rich plums, red berries, dry sherry and drying tannins, with an intense rich and fruity finish.

Springbank 12 year old cask strength

Hazelburn 12 years old

Springbank Claret 12 years old

Springbank CV

Longrow CV

Strathisla

Owner:
Chivas Brothers
(Pernod Ricard)

Region/district:
Speyside

Founded: 1786

Status: Active (vc)

Capacity: 2 400 000 litres

Address: Seafield Avenue, Keith,
Banffshire AB55 5BS

Tel: 01542 783044

website: www.maltwhiskydistilleries.com

History:

1786 – Alexander Milne and George Taylor found the distillery under the name Milltown, but soon change it to Milton.

1825 – MacDonald Ingram & Co. purchases the distillery.

1830 – William Longmore acquires the distillery.

1870 – The distillery name changes to Strathisla.

1880 – William Longmore retires and hands operations to his son-in-law John Geddes-Brown. William Longmore & Co. is formed.

1890 – The distillery changes name to Milton.

1940 – Jay (George) Pomeroy acquires majority shares in William Longmore & Co. Pomeroy is jailed as a result of dubious business transactions and the distillery goes bankrupt in 1949.

1950 – Chivas Brothers buys the run-down distillery at a compulsory auction for £71,000 and starts restoration.

1951 – The name reverts to Strathisla.

1965 – The number of stills is increased from two to four.

1970 – A heavily peated whisky, Craigduff, is produced but production stops later.

2001 – The Chivas Group is acquired by Pernod Ricard.

Strathisla 12 year old

GS – Rich on the nose, with sherry, stewed fruits, spices and lots of malt. Full-bodied and almost syrupy on the palate. Toffee, honey, nuts, a whiff of peat and a suggestion of oak. The finish is medium in length, slightly smoky and a with a final flash of ginger.

DR – Rich, full and fruity nose with lots of barley, then barley, currants and a touch of oak, peat and pepper, concluding with a complex and intriguing finish.

Strathisla Distillery is one of the most picturesque distilleries in Scotland and its excellent visitor centre was recently awarded Five Star status by Visit Scotland. The centre, however, is more focussed on the blend Chivas Regal than the single malt Strathisla. This is the spiritual home of the famous Scotch blend in which the single malt produced here plays an increasingly important role. Chivas Regal is number five on the top list of blended Scotch and sold 4.5 million cases in 2008. In 2009 the numbers slipped to 4.2 million. This was the first time since 2002 that sales decreased but, on the other hand, the competitors also decreased with between 5 and 15% in 2009 due to the recession.

Strathisla is equipped with a traditional stainless steel mash tun with a raised copper dome, ten washbacks of Oregon Pine (formerly eleven, but one has been remade into a pot ale tank) and two pairs of stills. The spirit produced at Strathisla is piped to nearby Glen Keith distillery (mothballed since 2000) for filling or to be tankered away. A small amount is stored on site in two racked and one dunnage warehouse. Chivas Brothers also hold large warehousing, filling and blending facilities in Keith called Keith Bond 1 & 2. The roofs of two warehouses collapsed due to the heavy snowfall in early 2010. This pales in significance compared to what happened a few miles to the west in Mulben where Chivas Bros have their largest facilities. The roofs on no less than 29 warehouses caved in. Moray Council granted permission in early June 2010 to build new warehouses, with the wall 6 feet beyond the existing ones, and first thereafter remove the demolished buildings. An unconfirmed source says the whole project will cost around £10m.

Pernod Ricard has only released two official bottlings - the *12 year old* and a *15 year old cask strength*.

12 years old

Strathmill

Owner:
Diageo

Region/district:
Speyside

Founded: **Status:** **Capacity:**
1891 Active 2 300 000 litres

Address: Keith, Banffshire AB55 5DQ

Tel:
01542 883000

website:
www.malts.com

History:
1891 – The distillery is founded in an old mill from 1823 and is named Glenisla-Glenlivet Distillery.

1892 – The inauguration takes place in June.

1895 – The gin company W. & A. Gilbey buys the distillery for £9,500 and names it Strathmill.

1962 – W. & A. Gilbey merges with United Wine Traders (including Justerini & Brooks) and forms International Distillers & Vintners (IDV).

1968 – The number of stills is increased from two to four and purifiers are added.

1972 – IDV is bought by Watney Mann which later the same year is acquired by Grand Metropolitan.

1993 – Strathmill becomes available as a single malt for the first time since 1909 as a result of a bottling (1980) from Oddbins.

1997 – Guinness and Grand Metropolitan merge and form Diageo.

2001 – The first official bottling is a 12 year old in the Flora & Fauna series.

2010 – A Manager's Choice single cask from 1996 is released.

Strathmill 12 year old

GS – Quite reticent on the nose, with nuts, grass and a hint of ginger. Spicy vanilla and nuts dominate the palate. The finish is drying, with peppery oak.

DR – Butterscotch and summer flowers mixed with lemon flu powder, and some powdery, talc-like notes on the nose, the palate has some apricot and peach fruits before a wave of salt and pepper and a spicy conclusion.

Almost all the distilleries owned today by Diageo were previously owned by Distillers Company Limited (DCL), a company already established in 1877 and which was taken over by Guinness in 1987. But when Diageo was finally formed in 1997, it was through a merger between Guinness and another, at that time, giant player in the drinks business - Grand Metropolitan Plc. When Guinness brought more than 20 whisky distilleries and the icon Scotch blend Johnnie Walker into the deal, mega brands like Smirnoff and J&B came from the Grand Met side. J&B had been acquired in 1972 when they bought International Distillers & Vintners and, included in that deal, were four Scotch whisky distilleries including Strathmill. The distillery's traditional ties to the J&B blend are still strong today (as they are for the three other distilleries) and virtually all of production goes into blending. Strathmill distillery, beautifully embedded in the greenery along the river Isla on the outskirts of Keith, is equipped with a stainless steel semi-lauter mash tun, six stainless steel washbacks and two pairs of stills. Strathmill is one of a few select distilleries using a facility called purifier on the spirit stills. This device is mounted between the lyne arm and the condenser and acts as a mini-condenser allowing the lighter alcohols to travel towards the condenser and forcing the heavier alcohols to go back into the still for another distillation. The result is a lighter and fruitier spirit.

The spirit is tankered away to Auchroisk for filling and some of the casks find their way back for storage in six on-site warehouses.

The only official bottling was a *12 year old* in the Flora & Fauna series until January 2010, when a new, American oak, *single cask* distilled in *1996* was released as part of the Manager's Choice series.

Flora & Fauna 12 years

Talisker

Owner: **Region/district:**
Diageo   Highlands (Skye)

Founded: **Status:**   **Visitor centre:**
1830   Active (vc)   2 600 000 litres

Address: Carbost, Isle of Skye,
Inverness-shire IV47 8SR

Tel: **website:**
01478 614308 (vc)   www.taliskerwhisky.com

History:
1830 – Hugh and Kenneth MacAskill, sons of the local doctor, found the distillery.

1848 – The brothers transfer the lease to North of Scotland Bank and Jack Westland from the bank runs the operations.

1854 – Kenneth MacAskill dies.

1857 – North of Scotland Bank sells the distillery to Donald MacLennan for £500.

1863 – MacLennan experiences difficulties in making operations viable and puts the distillery up for sale.

1865 – MacLennan, still working at the distillery, nominates John Anderson as agent in Glasgow.

1867 – Anderson & Co. from Glasgow takes over.

1879 – John Anderson is imprisoned after having sold non-existing casks of whisky.

1880 – New owners are now Alexander Grigor Allan and Roderick Kemp.

1892 – Kemp sells his share and buys Macallan Distillery instead.

1894 – The Talisker Distillery Ltd is founded.

1895 – Allan dies and Thomas Mackenzie, who has been his partner, takes over.

1898 – Talisker Distillery merges with Dailuaine-Glenlivet Distillers and Imperial Distillers to form Dailuaine-Talisker Distillers Company.

Nowadays it is easy to reach the Isle of Skye as a bridge has been constructed. It takes an hour from the bridge along winding, but beautiful, roads to arrive at Talisker distillery. The location is perfect, sheltered from the Atlantic storms as it is situated furthest in the bay at Carbost. No less than 52,000 visitors find their way to Talisker each year, which makes it Diageo's most visited distillery. It is probably not just the picturesque surroundings that cause this stream of visitors, but also the fact that recent years have seen Talisker single malt become one of Diageo's biggest sellers (with only Cardhu selling more). The malt comes from Glen Ord maltings peated at 18-20ppm which gives a phenol content of 5-7 ppm in the new make. The distillery is equipped with a stainless steel lauter mash tun with a capacity of 8 tonnes. Two new washbacks were installed in September 2008 which forced reconstruction of the whole tun room. The increased capacity means that eight washbacks now serve the unusual combination of two wash stills and three spirit stills. This is a leftover from the time when Talisker was triple distilled, a practice which stopped in 1928. Some of the stills at Talisker are equipped with purifiers, a device between the still and the lyne arm which is intended to increase the reflux during distillation. At Talisker there is an old style purification using the colder outside air and a u-bend in the lyne arm, instead of a water jacket. Also, the purifiers are attached to the wash stills instead of the spirit stills. The fermentation time is quite long (65-75 hours) and the middle cut from the spirit still is collected between 76% and 65%. The clear wort from the mashing, the long fermentation, the unusual set-up of the stills and the cooling using worm tubs, contribute to a complex and delicate whisky which, in combination with the peatiness, has attracted many followers. Only a small part of the produce (mostly refill bourbon) is matured on the island while the rest is tankered and taken to the mainland for storage. The distillery is currently running at full capacity.

Talisker's core range consists of *10 year old, 18 year old,* a *Distiller's Edition* with an Amoroso sherry finish and *Talisker 57° North.* The name alludes to both the latitude of the distillery and its alcohol content. It was initially launched as a duty-free item but is now available across the UK. A *12 year old cask strength* is sold at the distillery only. Limited releases for 2010 were the fifth edition of the *30 year old* and a *single sherry cask* distilled in *1994* and part of the Manager's Choice series.

History (continued):

1916 – Thomas Mackenzie dies and the distillery is taken over by a consortium consisting of, among others, John Walker, John Dewar, W. P. Lowrie and Distillers Company Limited (DCL).

1928 – The distillery abandons triple distillation.

1930 – Administration of the distillery is transferred to Scottish Malt Distillers (SMD).

1960 – On 22nd November the distillery catches fire and substantial damage occurs.

1962 – The distillery reopens after the fire with five new identical copies of the destroyed stills.

1972 – Malting ceases and malt is now purchased from Glen Ord Central Maltings.

1988 – United Distillers introduce Classic Malts, Talisker 10 years included. A visitor centre is opened.

1998 – A new stainless steel/copper mash tun and five new worm tubs are installed. Talisker is launched as a Distillers Edition with an amoroso sherry finish.

2004 – Two new bottlings appear, an 18 year old and a 25 year old.

2005 – To celebrate the 175th birthday of the distillery, Talisker 175th Anniversary is released (60 000 bottles). The third edition of the 25 year old cask strength is released (15 600 bottles).

2006 – A 30 year old and the fourth edition of the 25 year old are released.

2007 – The second edition of the 30 year old and the fifth edition of the 25 year old are released.

2008 – Talisker 57° North, sixth edition of the 25 year old and third edition of the 30 year old are launched.

2009 – New editions of the 25 and 30 year old are released.

2010 – A 1994 Manager´s Choice single cask and a new edition of the 30 year old are released.

Talisker 10 year old

GS – Quite dense and smoky on the nose, with smoked fish, bladderwrack, sweet fruit and peat. Full-bodied and peaty in the mouthy; complex, with ginger, ozone, dark chocolate, black pepper and a kick of chilli in the long, smoky tail.

DR – Grilled oily fish in lemon oil, on the nose, dry salt and pepper on the palate, peat and pepper in a tastebud treat of a finish.

57° North   25 years old 7th edition   30 years old 5th edition

10 years old   18 years old   Distiller's Edition 1992

Tamnavulin

Owner:
Whyte & Mackay
(United Spirits)

Region/district:
Speyside

Founded: **Status:**
1966 Active

Capacity:
4 000 000 litres

Address: Tomnavoulin, Ballindalloch,
Banffshire AB3 9JA

Tel:
01807 590285

website:
-

History:
1966 – Tamnavulin-Glenlivet Distillery Company,
a subsidiary of Invergordon Distillers Ltd, founds
Tamnavulin.

1993 – Whyte & Mackay buys Invergordon
Distillers.

1995 – The distillery closes in May.

1996 – Whyte & Mackay changes name to JBB
(Greater Europe).

2000 – Distillation takes place for six weeks.

2001 – Company management buy out
operations for £208 million and rename the
company Kyndal.

2003 – Kyndal changes name to Whyte &
Mackay.

2007 – United Spirits buys Whyte & Mackay.
Tamnavulin is opened again in July after having
been mothballed for 12 years.

Tamnavulin 12 year old

GS – Delicate and floral on the nose, with
light malt and fruit gums. Light to medium
bodied, fresh, malty and spicy on the palate,
with a whiff of background smoke. The finish
is medium in length, with lingering spice,
smoke, and notes of caramel.

DR – Wet hay, celery and cucumber on the
nose and a delightful exotic fruit and citrus
taste and a satisfying and pleasant finish.

During the 12 years of closure, Tamnavulin was close to being
sold several times and the owners looked at re-opening it on
four different occasions. When it finally started producing
again in 2007, it did not come as a surprise, for two reasons.
First of all, the new owner, Indian United Spirits, needed Scotch
single malt to be used in their Indian blends. Secondly, Whyte &
Mackay has for a long time been the leading supplier of whisky
for the own label market with most of the clients being the
chains of super-markets. It still means 2 million cases per year,
even if the supermarket share has halved since the Indians took
over.

The distillery is equipped with a full lauter mash tun, eight
washbacks (four of them made of stainless steel and the rest
of Corten steel) and three pairs of stills. The wash stills were all
replaced in summer 2008, and in 2010 it is time to exchange
the three spirit stills, as well as the condensers. Two racked
warehouses (10 casks high) on site have a
capacity of 34,250 casks with the oldest ones
dating back to 1967. Two hundred casks are
filled every week on site, while the rest of the
production is tankered to Invergordon for
filling. 3.5 million litres (85% of production
capacity) was already reached in 2008, but
15 mashes per week and 2.6 million litres are
planned for 2010.

Tamnavulin is situated in a very scenic part
of the Highlands with Glenlivet, Tomintoul
and Braeval as its closest neighbours.
There used to be a visitor centre run by
the local community, but it closed at the
end of the nineties.

The only standard release of Tamnavulin,
for quite some time now, has been a *12
year old*. A number of aged *Stillman's
Dram* have also been launched, the most
recent being a 30 year old.

Independent bottlings occur now and
then. A 16 year old distilled in 1992 was
recently released by Speciality Drinks.

12 years old

Teaninich

Owner:
Diageo

Region/district:
Northern Highlands

Founded: 1817

Status: Active

Capacity: 4 400 000 litres

Address: Alness, Ross-shire IV17 0XB

Tel: 01349 885001

website: www.malts.com

History:

1817 – Captain Hugh Monro, owner of the estate Teaninich, founds the distillery.

1831 – Captain Munro sells the estate to his younger brother John.

1850 – John Munro, who spends most of his time in India, leases Teaninich to the infamous Robert Pattison from Leith.

1869 – John McGilchrist Ross takes over the licence.

1895 – Munro & Cameron takes over the licence.

1898 – Munro & Cameron buys the distillery.

1904 – Robert Innes Cameron becomes sole owner of Teaninich.

1932 – Robert Innes Cameron dies.

1933 – The estate of Robert Innes Cameron sells the distillery to Distillers Company Limited.

1970 – A new distillation unit with six stills is commissioned and becomes known as the A side.

1975 – A dark grains plant is built.

1984 – The B side of the distillery is mothballed.

1985 – The A side is also mothballed.

1991 – The A side is in production again.

1992 – United Distillers launches a 10 year old Teaninich in the Flora & Fauna series.

1999 – The B side is decommissioned.

2000 – A mash filter is installed.

2009 – Teaninich 1996, a single cask in the new Manager´s Choice range is released.

There are three whisky distilleries in the vicinity of the town of Alness on The Cromarty Firth. Two of them belong to Whyte & Mackay – Dalmore, producer of premium single malts and Invergordon, a grain distillery producing 36 million litres of alcohol per year. The third distillery, Teaninich, lies in an industrial estate on the outskirts of the town and has a fairly anonymous existence. This has not always been the case though. At one time, back in the seventies, Teaninich was one of the largest distilleries in Scotland with a capacity of 6 million litres. And if we go back to the early 1900s, the owner of the distillery was one Robert Innes Cameron, an influential whisky business person with interests in Benrinnes, Tamdhu and Linkwood distilleries and for 10 years he was the chairman of Malt Distillers´ Association of Scotland.

One interesting feature distinguishes Teaninich from all other distilleries; in 2000 a Meura 2001 mash filter was installed in place of a traditional mash tun. Many breweries already use a mash filter and the advantages are that a mash can be made in half the time and a more efficient extraction of sugars is obtained which results in a higher spirit yield. In order to operate the mash filter, the malt needs to be ground into a very fine flour without husks, so an Asnong hammer mill capable of this, was installed at Teaninich instead of a traditional roller mill. The mash filter itself required a staggering £3m investment.

Besides the mash filter the distillery is equipped with 10 washbacks - eight made of larch and two of stainless steel - and six stills. There are no warehouses on site; instead 4-5 tankers leave the distillery each week for filling elsewhere. Twenty mashes are done per week corresponding to 4.4 million litres which is more or less at capacity.

Teaninich is mainly produced to be a component of Johnnie Walker blended whiskies. The only official bottling was a *10 year old* in the *Flora & Fauna* series until autumn of 2009 when a Teaninich *1996 single cask* was released in the new range Manager´s Choice.

Flora & Fauna 10 years old

Teaninich 10 year old

GS – The nose is initially fresh and grassy, quite light, with vanilla and hints of tinned pineapple. Mediumbodied, smooth, slightly oily, with cereal and spice in the mouth. Nutty and slowly drying in the finish, with pepper and a suggestion of cocoa powder notes.

DR – All about the barley this one, with clean, sweet ginger barley on the nose, and a clean and crealy palate with some orange and other citrus notes. Pleasant, clean and impressive with a wave of spices late on.

Tobermory

Owner:
Burn Stewart Distillers
(C L Financial)

Region/district:
Highland (Mull)

Founded: 1798

Status: Active (vc)

Capacity: 1 000 000 litres

Address: Tobermory, Isle of Mull,
Argyllshire PA75 6NR

Tel: 01688 302647

website: www.burnstewartdistillers.com

History:

1798 – John Sinclair founds the distillery.

1837 – The distillery closes.

1878 – The distillery reopens.

1890 – John Hopkins & Company buys the distillery.

1916 – Distillers Company Limited (DCL) takes over John Hopkins & Company.

1930 – The distillery closes.

1972 – A shipping company in Liverpool and the sherrymaker Domecq buy the buildings and embark on refurbishment. When work is completed it is named Ledaig Distillery Ltd.

1975 – Ledaig Distillery Ltd files for bankruptcy and the distillery closes again.

1979 – The estate agent Kirkleavington Property buys the distillery, forms a new company, Tobermory Distillers Ltd and starts production.

1982 – No production. Some of the buildings are converted into flats and some are rented to a dairy company for cheese storage.

1989 – Production resumes.

1993 – Burn Stewart Distillers buys Tobermory for £600,000 and pays an additional £200,000 for the whisky supply.

2002 – Trinidad-based venture capitalists CL Financial buys Burn Stewart Distillers for £50m.

2005 – A 32 year old from 1972 is launched.

2007 – A Ledaig 10 year old is released.

2008 – A limited edition Tobermory 15 year old is released.

Tobermory 10 year old

GS – Fresh and nutty on the nose, with citrus fruit and brittle toffee. A whiff of peat. Medium-bodied, quite dry on the palate with delicate peat, malt and nuts. The finish is medium to long, with a hint of mint and a slight citric tang.

DR – Barley and crystal ginger on the nose, but the palate carries this, with a nice oily mouth feel, and creamed fruits giving way to a sharper spicier conclusion.

Ledaig 10 year old

GS – The nose is profoundly peaty, sweet and full, with notes of butter and smoked fish. Bold, yet sweet on the palate, with iodine, soft peat and heather. Developing spices. The finish is medium to long, with pepper, ginger, liquorice and peat.

DR – Peat and smoke on the nose, more fruity and malty on the palate but with a definite tarry heart, and then gristly smoke in the finish.

The only distillery on the island of Mull, Tobermory, lies beautifully tucked in by the harbour of Tobermory village. The distillery was called Ledaig for some time, which is the name of the part of the village where it is situated, but that name is now reserved for the peated production.

Production of Ledaig did not start until 1996 and the malted barley today (30-40ppm) comes from Port Ellen. There is a 50/50 split in total production between peated Ledaig and unpeated Tobermory and to ensure there is no cross contamination of distillates, additional feints vessels have been installed. Mashing and fermentation of Ledaig is similar to Tobermory's, but the spirit run has a lower cut off point (59% compared to Tobermory's 63%) in order to collect the rich, peaty flavours.

Tobermory whisky is produced in an artisan way and one has to look hard to find a computer on the premises. The cast iron mash tun is traditionally equipped with rakes and there are four wooden washbacks and two pairs of stills with unusual S-shaped lyne arms to increase the reflux. Storage space is small and most produce is sent to Deanston distillery on the mainland for maturation. However, in 2007 a part of the old tun room was converted into a small warehouse.

During 2010 there will be four mashes per week resulting in 500,000 litres of alcohol. The capacity is 1 million litres but the big stills could easily double that. The bottleneck is instead the washbacks.

When Burn Stewart bought Tobermory in 1993 they also bought some stock produced between 1972-1989, but found that much of it was of inferior quality. The best casks by far were the ones from 1972 and some of them were released as a *32 year old* in 2005. There are still four casks of 1972 left on Mull and a few more at Deanston. The *10 year old* Tobermory was supplemented in 2008 by a *15 year old* non chill-filtered edition. The current expression of *Ledaig* is a *10 year old*.

10 years old

Meet the Manager

IAN MACMILLAN
MASTER BLENDER AND GENERAL DISTILLERIES MANAGER
– BUNNAHABHAIN, DEANSTON, TOBERMORY DISTILLERIES

When did you start working in the whisky business and when did you start at Tobermory?

My career in the whisky industry started in 1972 at Glengoyne Distillery. I first encountered Tobermory early 1993 when I was asked to provide a full report on the plant prior to the purchase by Burn Stewart Distillers.

Have you been working in other lines of business before whisky?

I had been studying in college when I took up a summer job at Glengoyne and became intrigued with the whisky production process. When I was offered a full-time position I was delighted to accept much to the dismay of my parents at the time.

What kind of education or training do you have?

I have been extremely fortunate that I have received the most in depth informative training covering every aspect from malting, mashing, distilling, maturation and blending from some of the most highly regarded and experienced people in the industry over the last 37 years to whom I will always be indebted.

Describe your career in the whisky business.

Lang Brothers – Glengoyne Distillery 1972 – 1976, DCL – Port Dundas Distillery, Caledonian Distillery, John Watney Distillery – London plus a spell at Gordons & Booths Gin Distilleries 1976 - 1989, Highland Distillers – Glenturret Distillery 1989 – 1991, Burn Stewart Distillers Ltd – 1991 to date.

What are your main tasks as a manager?

I have the overall responsibility to ensure the production of consistent quality of spirit at all our distilleries. To ensure compliance with all legislation and to meet all budget and fiscal objectives across the sites.

What are the biggest challenges of being a distillery manager?

It is key to have experienced and passionate managers who hold the same values as myself in ensuring that their respective distilleries are run efficiently, produce consistent high quality spirit and that any visitors to the distillery have a memorable experience.

What would be the worst that could go wrong in the production process?

The absolute worst occurance would be any accident resulting in the tragic loss of life or any serious injury. We operate with very hot liquids and high pressure steam and great care and attention must always be observed even by the most experienced operators.

How would you describe the character of Tobermory single malt?

We create a west highland style of malt. The Tobermory being earthy and malty with coastal overtones. The Ledaig is rich and peaty but with a sweet character without the recognised antiseptic overtones of the peaty Islays.

What are the main features in the process at Tobermory, contributing to this character?

Like the other BSD distilleries Tobermory is traditionally operated without any automation. The main contributing factor to the unique style of both Tobermory distillates is the unique unusual "S" shaped lye pipes on all the stills which encourage a heavier reflux resulting in a less oily spirit full of flavour.

What is your favourite expression of Tobermory and why?

The Tobermory whiskies are very approachable at a young age but also age extremely well. My current favourite expressions are the Tobermory 15yo and the Ledaig 10yo. But look out in a few years for an astonishing Ledaig 40yo that will be released in 2012.

If you had to choose a favourite dram other than Tobermory, what would that be?

I have many favourite drams that I enjoy not only from our own range but from other companies as well. Whisky is a mood and location choice of drink. It would be fair to say that I also enjoy drinking blended whiskies around 50% of the time.

What are the biggest changes you have seen the past 10-15 years in your profession?

By far the biggest change that I have experienced over my 37 years in Malt Whisky production has been the introduction of automation resulting in the reduction of distillery workforce. I am a traditionalist at heart and believe that moving to almost total automation will destroy the myth of what consumers still believe to be a hand crafted product. If we totally remove the human element from the production processes I believe this may in time lead to a blandness across the different regions.

Do you see any major changes in the next 10 years to come?

The consumer will become far more informed and ultimately more selective. I believe if the versatility of blended whiskies across the world markets is emphasised far more along with the uniqueness of all the single malts, Scotch Whisky sales will continue to grow.

Do you have any special interests/hobbies that you pursue?

As well as enjoying all whiskies, I also appreciate fine wines from around the world. The main sport that I enjoy is rugby but sadly only from the sidelines these days.

Why did you decide to make two distinctively different whiskies at the distillery – Tobermory and Ledaig?

Originally Tobermory would have produced a typical Island peaty whisky and I wanted to re-create this style. When I first distilled the Ledaig expression the main view was to use this in blending. However as I watched this product mature I knew we had a very special single malt in the making and always envisaged that we would bottle this expression at 10 years old.

You are not only the General Distilleries Manager responsible for three distilleries but also the Master Blender. Could you tell me a little more about that part of your job?

As Master blender for BSD I have overall responsibility for all bottled and bulk products produced by the company. Ensuring consistent quality of our major blended brands - Scottish Leader and Black Bottle as well as all expressions of our single malts. Development of new brands and new expressions of existing bottled products. Maintain strict wood quality programme for all maturation and development requirements. I also carry out worldwide ambassadorial duties presenting our brands to our distributors and customers in major markets.

Tomatin

Owner:
Tomatin Distillery Co
(Takara Shuzo Co. Ltd., Kokubu & Co., The
Marubeni Corporation)

Region/district:
Highland

Founded: **Status:** **Capacity:**
1897   Active (vc) 5 000 000 litres

Address: Tomatin, Inverness-shire IV13 7YT

Tel: **website:**
01463 248144 (vc)   www.tomatin.com

History:
1897 – The Inverness businessmen behind
Tomatin Spey Distillery Company found Tomatin.

1906 – Production ceases.

1909 – Production resumes through Tomatin
Distillers Co. Ltd.

1956 – Stills are increased from two to four.

1958 – Another two stills are added.

1961 – The six stills are increased to ten.

1964 – One more still is installed.

1974 – The stills now total 23 and the maltings
closes.

1985 – The distillery company goes into
liquidation.

1986 – Two long-time customers, Takara Shuzo
Co. and Okara & Co., buy Tomatin through
Tomatin Distillery Co. Tomatin thus becomes
the first distillery to be acquired by Japanese
interests.

1997 – Tomatin Distillery Co buys J. W. Hardie
and the brand Antiquary.

1998 – Okura & Co, owners of 20% of Tomatin
Distillery, is liquidated and Marubeni buys out
part of their shareholding.

2004 – Tomatin 12 years is launched.

2005 – A 25 year old and a 1973 Vintage are
released.

2006 – An 18 year old and a 1962 Vintage are
launched.

2008 – A 30 and a 40 year old as well as several
vintages from 1975 and 1995 are released.

2009 – A 15 year old, a 21 year old and four
single casks (1973, 1982, 1997 and 1999) are
released.

2010 – The first peated release - a 4 year old
exclusive for Japan.

Tomatin 12 year old

GS – Barley, spice, buttery oak and a floral
note on the nose. Sweet and medium-bodied,
with toffee apples, spice and herbs in the
mouth. Medium-length in the finish, with
sweet fruitiness.

DR – Strawberry cream and raspberry ripple
ice cream and pecan on the nose, delicate
zesty barley on the palate, with a sweet citrus
and powdery spice mix contributing to a very
welcoming finish. More-ish.

For many years Tomatin was a low-profile distillery below radar
coverage of the whisky-dedicated consumer. This has changed
quite dramatically in the past few years and the single malt
from the distillery is now mentioned with respect by the
aficionados. The brand is selling around 200,000 bottles per
year and the three biggest markets, Sweden, Japan and the US
are geographically very diverse! It is also popular in Germany
and Portugal and the owners are now targeting new markets
like Brazil, Argentina and India.

Due to heavy expansion in the 60s and 70s, Tomatin was
Scotland's largest distillery in 1974 with a production of 12
million litres of alcohol (cf Glenfiddich which makes 10 million
litres today). However, it only ran at full capacity between 1975
and 1980. Today, the capacity is lower with 5 million litres
(actual production in 2010 is 2.5 million) as 11 of the original
stills were dismantled in 2002.

The distillery is equipped with two stainless
steel mash tuns (one is not being used), 12
stainless steel washbacks and six pairs of stills,
all the same size (almost 17,000 litres). There
are 12 racked and two dunnage (where single
malts are maturing) warehouses holding
170,000 casks. The distillery also has a cooperage with two coopers working. Normally the
whisky produced by Tomatin is unpeated, but
since 2004 a peated spirit (12ppm) has been
produced during the last week of every
year.

Tomatin single malt is used in the owners
blended whiskies such as Antiquary
(10,000 cases/year) and Talisman (45,000
cases). The core range of single malts
consists of *12 year old* (80% of sales), *15
year old, 18 year old* and *25 year old*. All
of them are sherry matured, except for
the 15 year old (released in August 2009)
which has been matured in ex bourbon
casks. Limited editions in 2009 and early
2010 included a *21 year old*, a *1999 single
cask* with a *Tempranillo finish*, as well as
single casks from 1973, 1982 and *1997*. In
2010, the first bottling from the *peated*
production was released as a *4 year old*
exclusive for Japan and there was also a
single cask released in Belgium.

15 years old

Tomintoul

Owner:		Region/district:
Angus Dundee Distillers		Speyside
Founded:	**Status:**	**Capacity:**
1964	Active	3 300 000 litres

Address: Ballindalloch, Banffshire AB37 9AQ

Tel: **website:**
01807 590274   www.tomintouldistillery.co.uk

History:

1964 –The distillery is founded by Tomintoul Distillery Ltd, which is owned by Hay & MacLeod & Co. and W. & S. Strong & Co.

1965 – On stream in July.

1973 – Scottish & Universal Investment Trust, owned by the Fraser family, buys the distillery. It buys Whyte & Mackay the same year and transfers Tomintoul to that company.

1974 – The two stills are increased to four and Tomintoul 12 years is launched.

1978 – Lonhro buys Scottish & Universal Investment Trust.

1989 – Lonhro sells Whyte & Mackay to Brent Walker.

1990 – American Brands buys Whyte & Mackay.

1996 – Whyte & Mackay changes name to JBB (Greater Europe).

2000 – Angus Dundee plc buys Tomintoul.

2002 – Tomintoul 10 year is launched as the first bottling after the change of ownership.

2003 – Tomintoul 16 years is launched.

2004 – Tomintoul 27 years is launched.

2005 – A young, peated version called Old Ballantruan is launched.

2008 – 1976 Vintage and Peaty Tang are released.

2009 – A 14 year old and a 33 year old are released.

2010 – A 12 year old Port wood finish is released.

Tomintoul 10 year old

GS – A light, fresh and fruity nose, with ripe peaches and pineapple cheesecake, delicate spice and background malt. Medium-bodied, fruity and fudgy on the palate. The finish offers wine gums, mild, gently spiced oak, malt and a suggestion of smoke.

DR – Toffee and fruit on the nose then an easy, pleasant rounded and sweet barley taste before a gently fading finish.

TOMINTOUL
DISTILLERY
Angus Dundee Distillers Plc
Licensed Distillers

The owner of Tomintoul, Angus Dundee Distillers, is one of the biggest exporter of Scotch whisky with customers all over the world. It has even managed to get a foothold on the expanding Chinese market over the last couple of years.

Tomintoul distillery itself, even though not the prettiest of Scottish distilleries, lies in some of the most beautiful surroundings in Scotland, with Tomintoul village being the highest situated village in the Highlands. In 2009 more fame was brought to the village when the distillery produced the world's largest whisky bottle to be displayed by the village square. The bottle, earning a Guinness Book of Records entry, is 144 cm tall and holds the equivalent of 150 standard bottles.

The distillery is equipped with one mash tun and six washbacks, all made of stainless steel, and two pairs of stills heated by steam kettles. There are currently 15 mashes per week which means that capacity is used to the full, and the six racked warehouses have a storage capacity of 116,000 casks. The malt used for mashing is slightly peated but two weeks per year, heavily peated (55 ppm) malt is used for the peated range. A blend centre was built in 2003 with ten blend vats varying in size from 10,000 bulk litres to 100,000 bulk litres.

A major part of the production is used in different blended whiskies, but the last five years has seen the range of single malts expand considerably. The core range consists of *10 year old, 14 year old* (released in 2009), *16 year old* and *Old Ballantruan*, a peaty expression distilled in 2001. A new limited edition of a *12 year old portwood finish* was launched in 2010, finished for 20 months and non-chill filtered. Previous limited editions include *1976 Vintage*, the oldest official Tomintoul so far, a *12 year old* with the 18 last months in *Oloroso* sherry butts, *Peaty Tang*, a vatting of 4-5 year old peated Tomintoul and 8 year old unpeated Tomintoul and finally, a *33 year old* released in August 2009 which replaced the 27 year old.

14 years old

Tormore

Owner:
Chivas Brothers
(Pernod Ricard)

Region/district:
Speyside

Founded: 1958
Status: Active
Capacity: 4 100 000 litres

Address: Tormore, Advie, Grantown-on-Spey, Morayshire PH26 3LR

Tel: 01807 510244
website: www.tormore.com

History:
1958 – Schenley International, owners of Long John, founds the distillery.

1960 – The distillery is ready for production.

1972 – The number of stills is increased from four to eight.

1975 – Schenley sells Long John and its distilleries (including Tormore) to Whitbread.

1989 – Allied Lyons (to become Allied Domecq) buys the spirits division of Whitbread.

1991 – Allied Distillers introduce Caledonian Malts where Miltonduff, Glendronach and Laphroaig are represented besides Tormore. Tormore is later replaced by Scapa.

2004 – Tormore 12 year old is launched as an official bottling.

2005 – Chivas Brothers (Pernod Ricard) becomes new owners through the acquisition of Allied Domecq.

Tormore 12 year old

GS – Caramel on the nose, with hints of lemon and mint, mildly spicy, gentle and enticing. Good weight of body, and a creamy, honeyed mouth feel. Fudge and mixed spices, notably ginger, dry in the increasingly complex finish.

DR – A perfumey and delicate smell on the nose and soft but pleasant palate with macaroni cake and toasted almond in the mix, and a soft fading finish.

The historic owners of Scottish distilleries have more or less always been hard-working industrialists, leaving behind no trace of scandals. When American companies entered the stage in the first part of the 19th century, more colourful personalities appeared, such as at Tormore. The distillery was built by Schenley industries, owned by Lewis Rosenstiel, known for his close relations with the mafia. He built his fortune by cheaply acquiring competitors during Prohibition. He sold his company to Meshulam Riklis and the company Rapid-American in 1968. Riklis was the first to act as a corporate raider when taking over companies and also introduced junk bond transactions in the 70s and 80s. One of his closest friends was Michael Milken, The Junk Bond King of Wall Street, who had to serve two years in prison for fraud. Reportedly, Riklis left his creditors unpaid with over $2.9 billion in debt.

The architecture of Tormore is unique among Scottish distilleries. The famous architect, Sir Albert Richardson, was contracted and the distillery cost £600,000 in total to build, which in today's currency would correspond to £10m. Tormore became the first distillery in the 20th century to be constructed from scratch (Tullibardine and Glen Keith both made use of existing buildings).

The equipment at Tormore is made up of one stainless steel lauter mash tun from Newmill Ironworks in Elgin and eight stainless steel washbacks serving four pairs of stills. All the stills are fitted with purifiers resulting in a lighter spirit. The spirit is tankered away to Keith Bonds or another Chivas Bros facilities for filling in ex-bourbon casks and part of it returns to the distillery for maturation in a combination of six palletised and racked warehouses.

There is only one official bottling, a *12 year old* introduced in 2004/05. A *15 year old* was released several years ago but has been difficult to obtain lately.

12 years old

Tullibardine

Owner:
Tullibardine Distillery Ltd

Region/district:
Highlands

Founded: 1949
Status: Active (vc)
Capacity: 2 700 000 litres

Address: Blackford, Perthshire PH4 1QG

Tel: 01764 682252
website: www.tullibardine.com

History:
1949 – The architect William Delmé-Evans founds the distillery.

1953 – The distillery is sold to Brodie Hepburn.

1971 – Invergordon Distillers buys Brodie Hepburn Ltd.

1973 – The number of stills increases to four.

1993 – Whyte & Mackay (owned by Fortune Brands) buys Invergordon Distillers.

1994 – Tullibardine is mothballed.

1996 – Whyte & Mackay changes name to JBB (Greater Europe).

2001 – JBB (Greater Europe) is bought out from Fortune Brands by management and changes name to Kyndal (Whyte & Mackay from 2003).

2003 – A consortium including Michael Beamish buys Tullibardine in June for £1.1 million. The distillery is in production again by December. The first official bottling from the new owner is a 10 year old from 1993.

2004 – Three new vintage malts, from 1964, 1973 and 1988 respectively, are launched.

2005 – Three wood finishes from 1993, Port, Moscatel and Marsala, are launched together with a 1986 John Black selection.

2006 – Vintage 1966 (plus a special World Cup version), Sherry Wood 1993 and a new John Black selection are launched.

2007 – Five different wood finishes are released as well as a couple of single cask vintages.

2008 – A Vintage 1968 40 year old is released.

2009 – Aged Oak is released.

Tullibardine Aged Oak

GS – The nose exhibits barley, light citrus fruits, pear drops, marzipan and cocoa. Oily in the mouth, slightly earthy, with Brazil nuts and developing vanilla and lemon on the palate. The finish is drying and slightly woody, with lingering spices.

DR – Syrupy fruit and honey-filled lemon lozenges on the nose, a light and creamy ginger barley core on the palate, with some wood. Oak and fruit dominate a medium finish.

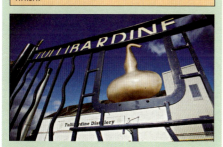

Tullibardine is a prime example of the ingenuity required when managing a "new" distillery. The new owners took over in 2003 and, by that time, Tullibardine had not been on stream since 1994, so there was just a small supply amounting to only 3,000 casks of mature whisky to rely on. While waiting for the new make to mature, the owners ascertained that a large commercial outlet was constructed in the village of Blackford on the A9 between Perth and Stirling next to the distillery. 130,000 visitors are received at Tullibardine each year and that has contributed to a well-needed cash flow. A profit of £512,000 was reported in the fiscal year ending May 2008, which decreased to £131,000 the following year when the recession set in. The biggest growth for the brand has been in Canada, but the whisky is in high demand also in France and The Netherlands. Around 7,000 cases were sold last year.

The distillery is equipped with a stainless steel mash tun, nine stainless steel washbacks and two pairs of stills. Last summer a Byworth Yorkshireman 2, one of the most fuel-efficient boilers on the market, was installed. In the first year of operation 100,000 litres of alcohol were produced. In 2008 full capacity, i. e. 2.7 million litres, was reached but the year after it was down to 1.2 million litres and for 2010 the projection is 1.4 million. Up until now, the current range of malts from Tullibardine has been built on produce from the previous owner. Late 2009, however, saw the first release where post re-opening whisky played a part. The new bottling is called Aged Oak and consists mainly of whisky distilled in 2004, with an additional small amount of Tullibardine older than 15 years.

It is difficult to identify a core range of bottlings from Tullibardine, as the general aim is to bottle vintages and various wood finishes. Apart from *Aged Oak*, the current range consists of *vintages* from *1988* and *1993*, as well as several *wood finishes* - *Port, Sauternes, Oloroso* and *PX sherry*. A *rum finish* is also expected during 2010. An unexpected move was the release of *Pure Pot Spirit*, new spirit distilled in 2008.

Aged Oak

The really new ones!

Daftmill

Owner:	Region/district:	
Cuthbert family	Lowlands	
Founded:	**Status:**	**Capacity:**
2005	Active	c 65 000 litres
Address:	**Tel:**	**website:**
By Cupar, Fife KY15 5RF	01337 830303	www.daftmill.com

Permission was granted in 2003 for a steading at Daft-mill Farmhouse in Fife to be converted into a distillery. Contrary to most other new distilleries selling shares in their enterprise, Hazel and Francis Cuthbert together with Francis' brother Ian, have quietly established the distillery. The distilling license was granted on St Andrews Day 2005 and the first distillation was on 16th December that same year. It is run as a typical farmhouse distillery. The barley is grown on the farm and malted without peat at commercial maltsters. The equipment consists of a one tonne semi-lauter mash tun, two stainless steel washbacks with a 90 hour fermentation and one pair of stills with slightly ascending lyne arms. The wash still has a capacity of 3,000 litres and the spirit still 1,600 litres. The owner fill the spirit into ex-bourbon casks from Heaven Hill but also uses casks from Makers Mark and Jack Daniels. There are also a few sherry butts in the warehouse.

The establishment of Daftmill increased the number of Lowland distilleries from three to four, and with Ailsa Bay there are now five. It could have been possible to launch a 3 year old whisky already in December 2008 but the owner has not decided a launch year yet, preferring to make the launch when the whisky is considered mature enough. Daftmill Farm is not just about whisky. Besides distilling, the Cuthberts also grow potatoes and have a fine herd of beef cattle. Distilling has been irregular recently as taking care of the rest of the business on the farm (which is what is bringing in the money at the moment) takes its time.

Abhainn Dearg

Owner:	Region/district:	
Mark Tayburn	Islands (Isle of Lewis)	
Founded:	**Status:**	**Capacity:**
2008	Active	c 20 000 litres
Address:		
Carnish, Isle of Lewis, Outer Hebrides HS2 9EX		
Tel:	**website:**	
01851 672429	www.abhainndearg.co.uk	

When Kilchoman Distillery opened on Islay in 2005 it became the westernmost distillery in Scotland. This did not last for long though three years later, in September 2008, spirit flowed from a newly constructed distillery in Uig on the island of Lewis in the Outer Hebrides. The Gaelic name of this distillery is Abhainn Dearg which means Red River, and the founder and owner is Mark "Marko" Tayburn who was born and raised on the island. Very little was known about Abhain Dearg until it was suddenly ready and producing. Part of the distillery was converted from an old fish farm while some of the buildings are new. There are two 500 kg mash tuns made of stainless steel and two 7,500 litre washbacks made of Douglas fir. The two stills are modelled after an old, illicit still which is now on display at the distillery. The wash still has a capacity of 2,112 litres and the spirit still 2,057 litres. Both have very long necks and steeply descending lye pipes leading out into two wooden worm tubs. To start with Marko is using ex-bourbon barrels for maturation but

is planning for ex-sherry butts as well. The malted barley is imported from North of Scotland but he plans on using local barley in the future. This year over ten acres of the Golden Promise variety were planted.

According to plans the first whisky will be called The Spirit of Lewis with a limited launch in October 2011. However, already in early 2010, an 18 months old spirit was bottled at 65% and apart from being sold through the distillery it could also be found in Glasgow and in Germany.

Roseisle

Owner:	Region/district:	
Diageo	Highlands	
Founded:	**Status:**	**Capacity:**
2009	Active	10 000 000 litres
Address:		**Tel:**
Roseisle, Morayshire IV30 5YP		01343 832100

The planning for a new mega distillery at Roseisle, a few miles west of Elgin, commenced in early 2006, and in October 2007 it was approved by Moray Council. Commissioning was planned in early 2009 with production starting in spring. The work was slightly delayed, however, and the distillery was commissioned first in spring 2009 with production commencing in early autumn. The location makes sense as the distil-lery was built on the same grounds as the already existing Roseisle maltings. The cost was £40m and the size is huge. The equipment consists of two mash tuns, 14 stainless steel washbacks and 14 stills. The stills were manufactured by Diageo´s own coppersmiths at Abercrombies, Alloa.

But Roseisle is not only state of the art when it comes to distilling. Green technology has been in the focus and it only emits 15% of the carbon dioxide an ordinary, same-sized distillery does. The pot ale from the distillation will be piped into anaerobic fermen-ters to be transformed into biogas and the dried solids will act as a biomass fuel source. Furthermore, the waste water from the distillery will be re-used in the adjacent maltings. Around 25 people work at the dis-tillery and the output has increased Diageo´s whisky production by 10-12%.

Ailsa Bay

Owner:	Region/district:	
William Grant & Sons	Lowlands	
Founded:	**Status:**	**Capacity:**
2007	Active	6 000 000 litres
Address:		**Tel:**
Girvan, Ayrshire KA26 9PT		01465 713091

It was not haphazardly that William Grant constructed its new, large malt distillery at Girvan near Ayr on Scotland´s west coast. Girvan Distillery, one of seven Scottish grain distilleries with a capacity of 75 million litres, was already located there and the site also holds a giant warehousing (39 warehouses to be exact) and blending complex. It was the perfect place bearing in mind that the produce from Ailsa Bay is destined for blended whisky. There has been malt whisky distil-lation at Girvan before by the much smaller Ladyburn Distillery (from 1968 to 1975).

It only took nine months to build the distillery which was commissioned in September 2007. It is equipped with a 15 tonne full lauter mash tun and the eight stills are made according to the same standards as Balvenie´s. A unique feature is the octangular spirit safe which sits between the two rows of stills. Each side corresponds to one specific still. Another feature is the preheater for the wash. This is in common use in Cognac where wine heaters let steam pass through the wine tank for the next distillation in order to save heat and speed up the distillation.

Using this technique at Ailsa Bay the wash enters the still preheated at 60° C.

There will be three different kinds of whisky made: a light, a more heavy and oilier and one heavily pea-ted (responsible for circa 2% of the production).

Photo: © Erkin Tuzmuhamedov

Closed distilleries

The following distilleries are either mothballed, closed, dismantled or demolished and the chances of any of them producing whisky again are minute. A couple of words for those of you who are of the opinion that these distilleries receive less space in the newer editions of Malt Whisky Yearbook: you are, of course, absolutely right but the reason is, obviously, that not much happens to them in between editions. Even new bottlings are rare and these formerly hard-working distilleries give way for more recent news. The excellent *Scotch Missed - Scotland's Lost Distilleries* by Brian Townsend is recommended for those readers who wish to know more.

Banff

Owner:	Region:	Founded:
Diageo	Speyside	1824

Status:
Closed in 1983, partly demolished in 1985, destroyed in a fire 1991.

Facts & Bottlings:
Banff Distillery's history is lined with disaster. In 1877 most of the distillery was devastated in a fire, in 1941 a German Junkers plane bombed one of the warehouses and in 1991 another fire destroyed it totally. Diageo has released it in the Rare Malts series once. Independent bottlings sometimes occur, the most recent being a 34 year old distilled in 1975 and released by Dewar Rattray.

Brora

Owner:	Region:	Founded:
Diageo	N Highlands	1819

Status:
Closed in 1983.

Facts & Bottlings:
This is probably the most popular of the closed distilleries with lots of dedicated followers. Since 2002, Diageo has released a new bottling every year with a 30 year old coming out in autumn of 2010. However, stocks are now becoming very low. Douglas Laing is known among the independents for some exceptional Broras. In autumn of 2008 one distilled in 1981 was released. Other recent independent bottlings include a Signatory, a Duncan Taylor and one from Ian MacLeod - all distilled in 1981.

Caperdonich

Owner:	Region:	Founded:
Chivas Brothers	Speyside	1897

Status:
Mothballed in 2002. Buildings sold to Forsyth's in 2010.

Facts & Bottlings:
Caperdonich was constructed as a sister distillery to Glen Grant and was named Glen Grant 2 for some time. It closed in 1902 and did not open until 1965. Chivas Bros has put Caperdonich up for sale and in 2010 it was sold to the manufacturer of, among other, copper pot stills Forsyth's in Rothes who already have business adjacent to it. The only official bottling was a cask strength released in 2005. Duncan Taylor recently released two old bottlings - 1972 (37 years) and 1968 (41 years).

Coleburn

Owner:	Region:	Founded:
Diageo	Speyside	1897

Status:
Closed in 1985, dismantled in 1996.

Facts & Bottlings:
This closed distillery between Rothes and Elgin was bought by Dale and Mark Winchester in 2004, with the purpose of rebuilding it into a hotel and conference centre. The plans have been opposed by other hoteliers in the area and construction has not yet begun. Coleburn single malt has appeared once in the Rare Malts series. Independent bottlings are also extremely rare. The latest was a 36 year old released by Signatory in 2006.

Convalmore

Owner:	Region:	Founded:
Diageo	Speyside	1894

Status:
Closed in 1985, dismantled and buildings sold to William Grant in 1990.

Facts & Bottlings:
This is one of the few of the closed distilleries that are still more or less intact, save the equipment. It can easily be sighted when visiting Balvenie distillery. W Grant bought the buildings to use for warehousing but Diageo kept the rights to the brand. The latest official bottling was a 28 year old Special Release from 2005. Independent bottlings are rare. The latest was a 32 year old from 1975 released by Douglas Laing.

Dallas Dhu

Owner:	Region:	Founded:
Diageo	Speyside	1898

Status:
Closed in 1983, sold to Historic Scotland in 1986 which now runs it as a museum.

Facts & Bottlings:
Dallas Dhu distillery was built with one purpose in mind - to supply its owners with malt whisky for the famous blend Roderick Dhu. This was hugely popular in India and Australia in the late 1800s. Diageo has released a couple of bottlings as Rare Malts and a few for Historic Scotland, the current owners of the distillery. One of the most recent bottlings from independents was distilled in 1981 and released as a 29 year old by Duncan Taylor.

Glen Albyn

Owner:	Region:	Founded:
Diageo	N Highlands	1844

Status:
Closed in 1983, demolished in 1986.

Facts & Bottlings:
Another Inverness distillery, which, like Glen Mhor, was completely demolished in the mid 1980s. Never really famous for its whisky, the site made its contribution during World War II when anti-submarine boom defences for Scapa Flow were constructed in the buildings. Glen Albyn has been released as a Rare Malt by the owners on one occasion. The most recent independent bottling appeared in 2009 - a 28 year old released by Signatory.

Glen Esk

Owner: Diageo
Region: E Highlands
Founded: 1897

Status:
Closed in 1985, dismantled in 1996, now used as maltings.

Facts & Bottlings:
This distillery has been called many names, such as Highland Esk, Montrose, North Esk and Hillside. In 1968 a drum maltings was built on the site and it now belongs to Greencore Malt. In August 2010 a fire broke out when 27 tons of grain ignited. The single malt has been bottled on three occasions in the Rare Malts series by the owner. Independent bottlings have only turned up sporadically in recent years.

Glen Keith

Owner: Chivas Brothers
Region: Speyside
Founded: 1957

Status:
Mothballed in 2000.

Facts & Bottlings:
Even though it is not distilling, Glen Keith plays an important role for nearby Strathisla's business. The spirit from Strathisla is pumped to Glen Keith for filling and the boiler at Glen Keith is also used by them. The site also accommodates a laboratory and a technical centre. The official 10 year old has become hard to find while independent bottlings are easier to come by. Recent ones include a 20 year old from Speciality Drinks, a 17 year old from Dewar Rattray and 15 year old from Ian MacLeod.

Glenlochy

Owner: Diageo
Region: W Highlands
Founded: 1898

Status:
Closed in 1983, demolished in 1992 except for the kiln and the malt barn.

Facts & Bottlings:
Parts of this distillery can still be seen despite having been closed for 30 years. The kiln with the pagoda roof is a listed building and other parts have been reconstructed into a guest house. Official bottlings have occurred twice in the Rare Malts series. Douglas Laing released a 49 year old in 2003 and both Signatory and Duncan Taylor released 24 years olds in 2005.

Glen Mhor

Owner: Diageo
Region: N Highlands
Founded: 1892

Status:
Closed in 1983, demolished in 1986.

Facts & Bottlings:
In the 1980s there were only three distilleries left in Inverness and they were all closed within a couple of years. It did not take long before Glen Mhor was demolished and today there is a supermarket on the site. Glen Mhor appeared twice in Diageo's Rare Malts series. Independent bottlings, however, still occur. The most recent are two 27 year olds distilled in 1982 and released by Cadenheads and Signatory.

Glenury Royal

Owner: Diageo
Region: E Highlands
Founded: 1825

Status:
Closed in 1983 and later demolished.

Facts & Bottlings:
The distillery was one of only three allowed to use Royal in its name (the others being Royal Lochnagar and Royal Brackla). The non-demolished buildings have been converted into flats. A couple of spectacular official bottlings were released during 2003-2007 - a 50 year old and two 36 year olds. In addition to them, Glenury Royal occurred three times in the Rare Malts series. Independent bottlings are few. Among recent ones is a 32 year old from 1976 by Douglas Laing.

Imperial

Owner: Chivas Brothers
Region: Speyside
Founded: 1897

Status:
Mothballed in 1998.

Facts & Bottlings:
Production at this distillery was already erratic from the beginning and, in all, it has been closed for 60% of its existence. Virtually all the equipment is still in place but the owners show no sign of starting production again. The latest official bottling, a 15 year old, is difficult to obtain today. Independent bottlers release more though, among them Gordon & MacPhail and Duncan Taylor. The latter recently released a 13 year old distilled in 1997.

Littlemill

Owner: Loch Lomond Distillery Co.
Region: Lowlands
Founded: 1772

Status:
Closed in 1992, dismantled in 1996, later demolished.

Facts & Bottlings:
Until 1992, Littlemill was Scotland's oldest working malt distillery, its roots possibly dating back to the 1750s. A deliberate fire in 2004 destroyed most of the buildings, which were then demolished. There is plenty of Littlemill still in stock and the owner bottles a 12 year old (which now is closer to 18 years old). One recent independent bottling is a 19 year old distilled in 1991 and released by Cadenheads.

Lochside

Owner: Chivas Brothers
Region: E Highlands
Founded: 1957

Status:
Closed in 1992, demolished in 2005.

Facts & Bottlings:
Lochside became the first and so far the only Scottish distillery to be owned by a Spanish company when DYC bought the distillery in 1973. Thereafter most of the whisky went to Spain to be a part of a local blended whisky. There are no contemporary official bottlings of Lochside and independent ones are also rare. Some of the most recent ones come from Dewar Rattray, Blackadder and Cadenheads - all distilled in the 1980s.

Millburn

Owner: Diageo **Region:** N Highlands **Founded:** 1807

Status:
Closed in 1985, dismantled in 1988.

Facts & Bottlings:
This is the only of the three Inverness distilleries that closed in the 1980s where you can still see the buildings, some of which have been turned into a restaurant. It was also the oldest of the three and the last one to close. Diageo has released just a couple of Rare Malts Millburn and there is not much more to obtain from the independents. A few of the most recent ones are Cadenhead 1974 (31 years), Douglas Laing 1969 (36 years), Signatory 1979 (26 years) and Blackadder 1974 (33 years).

North Port

Owner: Diageo **Region:** E Highlands **Founded:** 1820

Status:
Closed in 1983, demolished in 1993.

Facts & Bottlings:
Nothing remains to be seen of this distillery. Instead, a supermarket has taken its place. The only distillery operating in Brechin today is Glencadam. The names North Port and Brechin are used interchangeably on the whisky labels. Diageo has released two official bottlings in the Rare Malts series and on one occasion (2005), it appeared as a Special Release as a 28 year old. Independent bottlings are now very rare, the latest coming from Duncan Taylor in 2008.

Pittyvaich

Owner: Diageo **Region:** Speyside **Founded:** 1974

Status:
Closed in 1993, demolished in 2002.

Facts & Bottlings:
Pittyvaich distillery did not even last 20 years before being closed. At one time it served as a test plant for gin distillation before the production of Gordon´s Gin moved from England to Cameronbridge. The only activity left on the site is a bio-plant. The owners bottle a 12 year old Flora & Fauna and in autumn of 2009 a 20 year old was released. One of the most recent independent bottlings was a 23 year old rum finish by Cadenheads.

Port Ellen

Owner: Diageo **Region:** Islay **Founded:** 1825

Status:
Closed in 1983, dismantled in the 1990´s.

Facts & Bottlings:
The distillery may have been closed but on the site remains Port Ellen maltings which produce malted barley for several of the Islay distilleries. Port Ellen competes with Brora for being the most popular distillery on these three pages among whisky aficionados. Diageo bottles new expressions annually and for 2010 it was a 31 year old. Independents are also fond of the whisky and recent releases include a 28 year old by Ian MacLeod, a 27 year old from Signatory and a 26 year old from Duncan Taylor.

Rosebank

Owner: Diageo **Region:** Lowlands **Founded:** 1798

Status:
Closed in 1993. Buildings sold to British Waterways and Westpoint Homes.

Facts & Bottlings:
At one time a contender to become the Classic Malt representing the Lowlands, its fate was sealed when Glenkinchie was chosen instead. Most of the equipment was in place, until a year ago, when it was stolen to be sold as metal scrap. The official Flora & Fauna 12 years is still released and in 2007 a 25 year old appeared in the Special Release series. Independent bottlings from 2010 include a 20 year old from Ian MacLeod.

St Magdalene

Owner: Diageo **Region:** Lowlands **Founded:** 1795

Status:
Closed in 1983, most of the buildings converted into flats in the mid 1990´s

Facts & Bottlings:
At one time no less than seven distilleries were active in the small town of Linlithgow, one of them St Magdalene. It fell victim in the big closure of 1983 when eight Scottish distilleries were closed. Diageo have released four bottlings during the last couple of years, three as Rare Malts and a 30 year old Linlithgow from 1973. Two 26 year olds from Ian MacLeod and Douglas Laing were released in 2008.

Tamdhu

Owner: Edrington **Region:** Speyside **Founded:** 1896

Status:
Mothballed in 2010.

Facts & Bottlings:
There was much surprise at the news in November 2009 that Tamdhu would close, at least temporarily. Running parallel with the distillery were maltings which have supplied Edrington´s distilleries with malted barley. The whisky has mainly been used as a part in the Famous Grouse blended whisky but the owners have also sold a non-aged single malt, as well as a couple of limited old expressions (18 and 25 year olds). One recent independent bottling is a 16 year old from Ian MacLeod.

The extremely rare ones
Bottlings from these distilleries are very hard to find.

Ben Wyvis - opened in 1965 and closed in 1977
The latest release was an official 37 year old in 2002.

Glen Flagler - opened in 1964 and closed in 1985
The latest release (in 2003) was a 1973 from Inver House.

Glenugie - opened in 1831 and closed in 1983
The latest release was a 30 year old Ian MacLeod from 1980.

Inverleven - opened in 1938 and closed in 1991
The latest release was a 30 year old from 1977 by Signatory.

Killyloch - opened in 1964 and closed in 1975
In 2003 InverHouse released a bottling from 1967.

Kinclaith - opened in 1957 and closed in 1975
Most recent bottlings from Signatory and Duncan Taylor.

Ladyburn - opened in 1966 and closed in 1975
Two official and a couple of independent bottlings.

Distilleries per owner

c = closed, d = demolished, mb = mothballed, dm = dismantled

Diageo
Auchroisk
Banff (d)
Benrinnes
Blair Athol
Brora (c)
Bushmills
Caol Ila
Cardhu
Clynelish
Coleburn (dm)
Convalmore (dm)
Cragganmore
Dailuaine
Dallas Dhu (c)
Dalwhinnie
Dufftown
Glen Albyn (d)
Glendullan
Glen Elgin
Glenesk (dm)
Glenkinchie
Glenlochy (d)
Glenlossie
Glen Mhor (d)
Glen Ord
Glen Spey
Glenury Royal (d)
Inchgower
Knockando
Lagavulin
Linkwood
Mannochmore
Millburn (dm)
Mortlach
North Port (d)
Oban
Pittyvaich (d)
Port Ellen (dm)
Rosebank (c)
Roseisle
Royal Lochnagar
St Magdalene (dm)
Strathmill
Talisker
Teaninich

Pernod Ricard
Aberlour
Allt-a-Bhainne
Braeval
Caperdonich (mb)
Glenallachie
Glenburgie
Glen Keith (mb)
Glenlivet
Glentauchers
Imperial (c)
Inverleven (d)
Lochside (d)
Longmorn
Miltonduff
Scapa

Strathisla
Tormore

Edrington Group
Glenrothes
Glenturret
Highland Park
Macallan
Tamdhu (mb)

Inver House (Thai Beverage)
Balblair
Balmenach
Glen Flagler (d)
Knockdhu
Pulteney
Speyburn

John Dewar & Sons (Bacardi)
Aberfeldy
Aultmore
Craigellachie
Macduff
Royal Brackla

Whyte & Mackay (United Spirits)
Dalmore
Fettercairn
Jura
Tamnavulin

William Grant & Sons
Ailsa Bay
Balvenie
Glenfiddich
Kininvie
Ladyburn (dm)

**Glenmorangie Co.
(Moët Hennessy)**
Ardbeg
Glenmorangie

Morrison Bowmore (Suntory)
Auchentoshan
Bowmore
Glen Garioch

**Burn Stewart Distillers
(CL Financial)**
Bunnahabhain
Deanston
Tobermory

Loch Lomond Distillers
Glen Scotia
Littlemill (d)
Loch Lomond

Angus Dundee Distillers
Glencadam
Tomintoul

Long John Whitbread
Glenugie (dm)
Kinclaith (d)

J & A Mitchell
Glengyle
Springbank

Beam Global Spirits & Wine
Ardmore
Laphroaig

Benriach Distillery Co.
Benriach
Glendronach

Campari Group
Glen Grant

Isle of Arran Distillers
Arran

**Signatory Vintage
Scotch Whisky Co.**
Edradour

Ian Macleod Distillers
Glengoyne

**Tomatin Distillery Co.
(Marubeni Europe plc)**
Tomatin

J & G Grant
Glenfarclas

**Bruichladdich Distillery Co.
(Murray McDavid)**
Bruichladdich

**Co-ordinated
Development Services**
Bladnoch

Gordon & MacPhail
Benromach

**Glenglassaugh Distillery Co Ltd
(Scaent Group)**
Glenglassaugh

La Martiniquaise
Glen Moray

Ben Nevis Distillery Ltd (Nikka)
Ben Nevis

Tullibardine Distillery Ltd
Tullibardine

Speyside Distillers Co.
Speyside

Cooley Distillery plc
Cooley
Kilbeggan

Kilchoman Distillery Co.
Kilchoman

Cuthbert family
Daftmill

Mark Tayburn
Abhainn Dearg

Single malts from Japan

by Chris Bunting

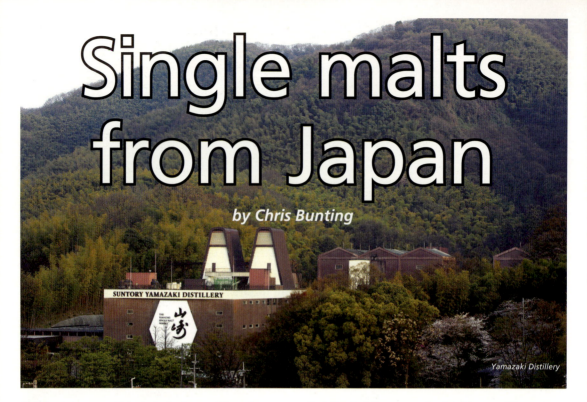

Yamazaki Distillery

The Japanese whisky industry has got its mojo back. It has been a while. The last time the Japanese distillers saw a sustained increase in domestic whisky drinking, in 1988, Ben Jonson was beating Carl Lewis in the Olympic 100m final and Rick Astley was topping the U.S. pop charts with "Never gonna give you up." Since then, with the exception of a brief blip in 1998, it has all been down hill. Sales in 2008 were about a quarter of the whisky soaked early 1980s.

But the nightmare may have ended. The latest full year's figures we have are for 2009 and show a 10.3% increase in whisky drinking over the previous year, the first double digit increase in 26 years. The indications are that the revival picked up pace in 2010. In the first six months of the year, Suntory, Japan's biggest whisky maker, saw a 30 percent increase in sales of its Japanese-made brands compared with 2009. Nikka and Kirin, Suntory's two major rivals, are both predicting a 10% increase in shipments in 2010 and believe the growth will be sustained into 2011.

The resurgence can be attributed quite specifically to a Suntory advertising campaign featuring the actress and model Koyuki (of "The Last Samurai" fame), which revives the idea of drinking Suntory's mass market blended whisky, Kakubin, in highballs.

The highball was extremely popular during the golden age of whisky drinking in Japan, between the 1960s and 80s, and for that reason had become very unfashionable, associated with sweaty old salarymen with drinking problems and wandering hands. The genius of the Suntory campaign is that it successfully mixes a pinch of post-war nostalgia with a big dollop of cutting edge cool. It seems to have caught the imagination of younger drinkers. I found it telling

that the first time I saw Apple's hip new iPhone 4 "smart phone" in Japan, it was being held by a sleek woman with a Kakubin highball in her other hand.

The "highball boom" has not just boosted Suntory's profits but the whole blended whisky sector. Nikka says its standard Black Nikka Clear Blend sold 10% more in 2009 than in 2008 and looks set to sell even more in 2010. Kirin's standard Fuji Sanroku increased its sales by 25% in 2009. But what does this new found health in the mass-market mean for Japanese single malts?

The quick answer is: "Not a great deal". Drinking blended whisky in highballs is really about rediscovering whisky as a bubbly, mouth-cleaning drink that can compete with the crisp, light lager beers that dominate much of Japanese drinking culture. It has little to do with appreciating single malts and it remains to be seen whether the highball trend will lead significant numbers of drinkers to crossover into premium whisky drinking.

What is important, however, is that the whisky industry is no longer an obvious basket case. In the end, that fact probably matters more to single malt drinkers than to fashion following highball quaffers. We started 2010 worrying about a proposed merger between Suntory and Kirin. From the whisky drinker's perspective, at least, it looked like a classic example of retrenchment in a declining market. The chances of all four of the merged company's distilleries - Yamazaki, Hakushu, Fuji-Gotemba and the already mothballed Karuizawa - surviving looked slight.

As the year wore on, however, the gloom seemed to lift. In February, the merger was called off. In March, we had the first of the now routine announcements of success in international competitions by

the Japanese distillers: Nikka's Taketsuru 21 year old pure malt won the "World's Best Blended Malt Whisky" title for the second year in a row at the 2010 World Whiskies Awards and Suntory's Hibiki 21 year old bagged the "World's Best Blended Whisky" prize. The independent White Oak distillery in Eigashima, Hyogo Prefecture continued its emergence on the single malt whisky scene and, in July, we got the exciting news that Hombo spirits, which owns the long silent Shinshu distillery in Nagano Prefecture, was repairing its stills and planned to start distilling again in 2011. Ichiro Akuto's Chichibu distillery in Saitama Prefecture is still the flagship of the craft whisky scene in Japan but 2010's developments raised the hope, if not yet the reality, of real diversity in the sector.

The fashion for whisky highballs will almost certainly last no more than a few years. Japan's alcohol sales are notoriously faddish. Before highballs, it was shochu, Japan's indigenous spirit. Shochu's sales are now declining again. But, in the meantime, the upward sloping graphs are likely to make it a lot easier to convince investors and boards to invest in whisky. This window of prosperity may leave a lasting mark on the industry.

Scottish whisky has been defined by its export trade since the 19th Century, but Japanese export sales are still tiny compared to the domestic market. Despite the Japanese makers' continuous success in international competitions over the last decade, some still seem loath to lift a finger in foreign markets. One European distributor approached a large Japanese distillery this year, only to be told flatly that not only were they not interested in the deal but they had no interest in exporting at all. Such attitudes may, however, soon become a thing of the past. Suntory, which often seems to be in the vanguard of innovation, added a commitment to increasing whisky exports to its 2009 company strategy document and has released major bottlings (Hibiki 12, Yamazaki 1984) not only in Europe, where the Japanese whisky market is already mature, but in the previously neglected United States market. It saw its exports hit 106,000 cases in 2009, an increase of 17% from 2008. Nikka enjoyed an 11% increase in exports to Europe in 2009 and the company was planning to export 25,000 cases in 2010, up 40% from the previous year.

Nikka's European success can largely be put down to the furious innovation of its distributor, La Maison du Whisky in Paris, who, together with the British-based Number One Whisky Company, have ensured that European whisky drinkers have access to a startling variety of premium bottlings, not only from Suntory and Nikka's big distilleries but also from distilleries such as Hanyu, Karuizawa, Chichibu and, soon, I understand, Eigashima.

For Marcin Miller, of Number One Drinks, the days of being able to sell Japanese whisky largely on its novelty value are gone:

"You could argue that getting Japanese whisky noticed was the easy bit, because of the good quality and interesting provenance. The difficult bit, sustaining growth and interest, comes now and it will require budgets. The US, as the world's biggest premium spirits market, must be the next target."

Chichibu

Owner: Venture Whisky   **Founded**: 2008
Capacity: 90,000
Malt whisky range: The first Chichibu malt whiskies will be released in 2011. The "Newborn" series of new spirit bottlings has given a glimpse of what is to come.

Eight years after the old Hanyu distillery stopped production, Ichiro Akuto put himself firmly back on the Japanese whisky map with the opening of the new Chichibu distillery in Saitama Prefecture in Spring 2008. The first proper Chichibu whisky will be released in Spring 2011. If the surprisingly good taste of the 2009 "Chichibu Newborn" new spirit bottlings are anything to go by, there is some excellent whisky waiting for us in Chichibu's casks.

The distillery, housed in a utilitarian factory unit given a romantic lift by a pagoda roof and the forested hills in which its sits, uses a pair of stills manufactured by Forsyths in Scotland, with whom Akuto worked very closely during design and construction. There are five washbacks made of Japanese oak. Most Japanese distillers rely almost entirely on imported malt but, from the start of the Chichibu adventure, Akuto has wanted to produce his own malt. Over the last year, they have been experimenting with in-house malting, which Akuto says has been a success. "There has also been an effort to train people in coopering. It has really been a year of training and that has been our major area of achievement," he says.

White Oak Distillery

Owner: Eigashima Shuzo **Founded**: 1919
Capacity: 60,000
Malt whisky range: Akashi Single Malt 8 years old, Akashi Single Malt 5 years old, Akashi single Malt 12 years old (due July 2010).

White Oak is Japan's most maritime whisky distillery. The Akashi strait, one of Japan's most famous coastal fishing areas, is just a hundred metres down the road. Its owner, Eigashima Shuzo, is not a specialist whisky maker. The old wooden buildings at the centre of the Eigashima site, are used for brewing sake, while a rickety corrugated-iron tower across the road produces the indigenous distilled spirit

Fuji Gotemba

Owner: Kirin Holdings   *Founded*: 1973
Capacity: 12,000,000 litres (including grain whisky)
Malt whisky range: Fuji-Gotemba Single Malt 18 year old, Fuji-Sanroku Single Malt 18 year old, a range of Fuji-Gotemba single casks, most easily available at the distillery.

Kirin do things there own way. The Fuji Gotemba site, hidden in forest at the foot of Mount Fuji, must be one of the world's most iconic distillery locations. It takes its water from rain and melted snow running off Mount Fuji itself and its elevation, at more than 2,000 feet above sea level, means that, while much of Japan's swelters in summer, Fuji Gotemba's temperatures are only a few degrees higher than the Scottish distilleries on average. Despite all its advantages, Kirin seem more reluctant that the rest of the Japanese whisky to build Fuji Gotemba's profile as a single malt whisky distillery.

The distillery is equipped with two pairs of pot stills and a continuous still for grain whisky production. Its blended Fuji Sanroku brand enjoyed a 25% increase in sales in 2009 because of the highball boom. However, Kirin do not offer a full Fuji Gotemba single malt range to rival those of Nikka and Suntory's distilleries. Only the elegant and well poised 18 year old Fuji Sanroku, receives any kind of publicity and, at 14,000 yen (125 euros/161 dollars) a bottle, it is more of a luxury range-topper than a serious attempt to grab a slice of the premium whisky market.

shochu. The whisky operation is housed in a modern white painted structure and boasts a semi-lauter mash tun, four stainless steel washbacks, a 4,500 litre wash still and a 3,000 litre spirit still.

After tentatively dipping their toes into the single malt whisky market in 2007, with the release of their 8 year old Akashi Single Malt, Eigashima Shuzo committed to premium malt production in 2010, with the their 5 year old Akashi Single Malt. "The 4,500 bottles of the 8 year old had sold out as of September 2009," says Mikio Hiraishi, president of the company. "The idea is that the 5 year old will serve as our regular single malt. Although it is shorter in maturation (than the 8 year old), we see it as just right for our single malt's light, clear style."

A very limited 2,000 bottle, 12 year old Spanish oak matured expression was scheduled for the second half of 2010, but Haraishi says it will take a number of years for the distillery to build up the stocks to sustain regular bottlings of older single malts because the company previously concentrated on short maturation for cheap blends. A small amount of Akashi 5 year old will be available to European consumers, courtesy of Number One Drinks and La Maison du Whisky.

Tasting note:
Akashi Single Malt Whisky 5 year old
II have never encountered a whisky with such a marked honey smell. This one, like the 8-year-old before it, is extremely mild on the palate but there is even more sweetness here: honey and butter, cereal and the memory of treacle at the finish. Not a complicated whisky but very drinkable.

The company is also far more cautious about the idea of raising its profile internationally than either of its rival conglomerates. Asked about the possibility of exporting its best malts, a spokesperson said: "While we regard exports as very important, and though we would be able to appeal to Fuji Gotemba's distinctive character, our first priority is to create a steady market domestically. We are currently not exporting." When Kirin does make that move it is likely to make a splash. We will just have to keep our fingers crossed in the meantime.

Hakushu

Owner: Suntory **Founded**: 1973
Capacity: 3,000,000 litres
Malt whisky range: Hakushu Single Malt 10,12,18 and 25 years old and a wide range of limited bottlings.

Suntory's second distillery at Hakushu receives a little less attention than its famous sibling at Yamazaki, but quietly produces some excellent single malts. The Hakushu site actually encompasses two separate distilleries. The original distillery was opened in 1973 and a second, Hakushu Higashi (Hakushu East) came on line in 1981. For a time in the 1980s, when all 36 stills in both distilleries were working, it was the biggest distillery in the world. Now, all of the malt making is done by the 12 stills at Hakushu East. Suntory's announcement in January 2010 that it was building a mineral water plant on part of the Hakushu site seemed to symbolise how times had changed since the height of Japanese whisky drinking. But, who knows, the highball boom might call for some greater distilling capacity after all?

A notable feature of Hakushu Higashi's stillroom, as Ulf Buxrud explains in detail in his book "Japanese Whisky: Facts, Figures and Taste," is the variety in the stills' design, size and heating methods. That diversity allows Hakushu to produce a surprising range of styles. The 12 year old official bottling is popular for its light, spicy style, but as you go up the range you can find whiskies of great complexity and depth. The whole range enjoyed a very successful year in international competition in 2009, with the 12 and 25 year olds grabbing gold medals at the International Wine and Spirits Competition and the 18 year old winning gold at the International Spirits Challenge.

Tasting note:
Hakushu 12 year old
A restrained nose with grapes, caramel and a floral flourish. Light and playful in the mouth with dried apricot sweetness and a well-controlled pepperiness. A very slight medicinal note emerges at the finish.

Hanyu

Owner: Toa Shuzo **Founded**: 1941
Capacity: Dismantled
Malt whisky range: Ichiro's Malt 15 and 20 years old and a wide variety of Ichiro's Malt "card series" and other bottlings; Full Proof Europe's 1988 and 1990 Hanyu single casks; Toa Shuzo's Golden Horse 8 year old.

For a distillery that went silent a decade ago and was completely dismantled four years later, Hanyu exercises an extraordinarily powerful grip on the imagination of contemporary Japanese malt lovers. That is thanks mainly to Ichiro Akuto, who opened the new Chichibu distillery in 2008, but continues to release his celebrated Ichiro's Malt bottlings from a stock of 400 casks of Hanyu whisky saved from the wreckage of the bankrupt business.

Akuto's range is such a whirl of activity that it can be hard to keep up, but basically there are two mainstay single malts, the Ichiro's Malt 15 and 20 year olds, both of which have recently had new bottlings, and a constant stream of single casks released under the "Card series." Recent additions to the deck are the malty, slightly waxy 19 year old Jack of Hearts (finished in a barrel made partly of red oak!), the Japanese oak matured 10 year old Four of Spades, the rich, syrupy 23 year old King of Hearts, a fruity 19 year old Queen of Spades, an 18 year old Eight of Diamonds and the 9 year old Six of Clubs. In 2010, Ichiro also "celebrated" the decade since the Hanyu's demise with the 10 year old Final Vintage of Hanyu. As if the continual new arrivals in Ichiro's range were not enough, Full Proof Europe (www.fullproof.eu) brought out a couple cheekily labeled 1988 and 1990 Hanyu single casks in 2009. The British-based importer Number One Drinks Company's 1988 Hanyu Noh Series whisky came from the same cask as the 1988 Full Proof.

Tasting note:
Ichiro's Malt 8 of Hearts Bottle 2008. Cask 9303
A fudgy almost cheesy nose. The palate is more austere than many Ichiro's Malt bottlings with dry chewing stick and ginger tastes and a bitter sweetness emerging in a medium-length finish.

Karuizawa

Owner: Kirin Holdings   **Founded**: 1956
Capacity: Mothballed
Malt whisky range: Karuizawa 12 years old, Karuizawa 17 years old, Karuizawa Vintage bottlings, the Noh Series bottlings and other independent bottlings in Europe.

Karuizawa stopped distilling in 2001 and, apart from a few distilling runs for maintenance purposes, has not been active since. The latest word from Kirin, which took over the distillery's owner Mercian in 2007, is that the distillery is inactive. The most recent new official bottling was a 2007 12 year old Karuizawa Wine Cask, to mark the 12th anniversary of the museum on the site of the distillery.

And that would be the rather sad ending to 45 years of whisky distilling in this beautiful Nagano Prefecture mountain resort if it were not for the phenomenal energy of the Japanese single malt scene in Europe, and, in particular, of the Number One Drinks Company. A string of new bottlings under Number One's Vintage and Noh series brands have recently brought unprecedented attention to Karuizawa. Marcin Miller at Number One, says: "When we bottle a whisky in the 'official' Vintage series it should be true to the distillery's character. For example, the 1985 #7017 was, for me, archetypal Karuizawa; big, bold, uncompromising, complex and reminiscent of an autumnal forest walk (pine, mushroom, truffle) with plenty of sherry and mixed nuts. The same applies to classics like the Karuizawa 1967 and 1971. Occasionally we come across a cask that doesn't fit in with the traditional Karuizawa flavour profile and we felt they needed to be presented differently. (Those whiskies come under the Noh banner)." There have been six Karuizawa Noh whiskies so far, each carrying a beautiful label illustrated with a Noh mask. Miller says another 1977 bottling is in the works.

Tasting note:
Karuizawa Noh 1976
A powerful nose, with loads of sweet sherry. Even with a generous splash of water, this is an uncompromising drink, with delicious fruit jam, prune and faint wood notes developing. A long finish with mustier old wood and tobacco flavours.

Miyagikyo

Owner: Nikka Whisky   **Founded**: 1969
Capacity: 5,000,000 litres
Malt whisky range: Miyagikyo Single Malt (no age statement), Miyagikyo Single Malt 10,12, and 15 years old and an annual 20 year old limited release named after the year it was distilled.

Miyagikyo distillery, also known as the Sendai distillery, opened in 1969, just before Suntory's Hakushu. Its location, sandwiched between the Hirosegawa and Nikkawagawa rivers and surrounded by mountains, was chosen by the founder of Nikka Masataka Taketsuru. Nowadays, its Coffey stills and eight pot stills provide much of the malt and grain whisky that goes into Nikka's mass market blends.

It also makes some some elegant single malt whisky, but the charisma and excellence of Nikka's much older Yoichi distillery in Hokkaido has sometimes overshadowed its southern sibling. As Minoru Miake, manager of the production section at Miyagikyo, put it:

"Naturally there is some friendly rivalry with Yoichi. Yoichi has done so brilliantly in these competitions."

It was therefore a fillip to Miake and others in Sendai that, in the 2009 World Whiskies Awards (Japan section), Miyagikyo topped Yoichi and the other Japanese distilleries with two nominations: the Miyagikyo 12 year old won the best Japanese single malt category and the Miyagikyo (no age statement) was adjudged the best young single malt. The 2010 nominations did not bring any more joy but the rich character of the Single Malt Miyagikyo 1988 and 1989 bottlings show there is plenty more to come from this distillery.

Tasting note:
Miyagikyo 10 year old
A restrained, butter and vanilla nose. Starts out mild and sweet in the mouth but opens out with big oaky, dark chocolate and tobacco gestures. Miyagikyo has a reputation for relatively quiet malts but this young bottling shows the danger of type casting

Shinshu

Owner: Hombo Shuzo **Founded**: 1960
Capacity: Not yet operational but Hombo expects 600 litres per day.
Malt whisky range: Mars Maltage Komagatake Single Malt 10 years old and Mars Single Cask Vintage Malt Whisky Komagatake 1988, 1989 and 1992.

Perhaps this would have been the year to call it a day on the Malt Whisky Yearbook's entry on the Shinshu distillery. It had not distilled any whisky since 1992 and like Hombo Shuzo's other long defunct distillery at Kagoshima (they still sell a Kagoshima 1984 single malt and a Maltage 8 vatting of Kagoshima and Shinshu malts), there might have been an argument for consigning Shinshu to the great pot still scrapyard in the sky. A visitor in January 2010 reported that one of Shinshu's two stills was too damaged to be operated safely. Stocks in the warehouse were dwindling.

Then, in July, we got some startling and wonderful news from Makoto Kawaida at Hombo's headquarters. Hombo had decided to invest in a complete overhaul of its whisky equipment - a full lauter mash tun, five cast iron washbacks and a pair of stills - and planned to start distillation again in 2011. He said the company's new whisky strategy was still under discussion but that producing single malts was definitely on the agenda.

Shinshu's stills have an important place in Japanese whisky history. According to Ulf Buxrud's "Japanese Whisky: Facts, Figures and Taste," they have a straight head similar to those at Yoichi and were designed by Kiichiro Iwai, who was one of the men who decided to send Nikka Whisky founder Masataka Taketsuru on his historic journey to Scotland in 1918 and received Taketsuru's detailed report on whisky making on his return. It is good to have them back.

Yoichi

Owner: Nikka Whisky **Founded**: 1934
Capacity: 5,000,000 litres
Malt whisky range: Yoichi Single Malt (no age statement); Yoichi Single Malt 10, 12, 15 and 20 years old and an annual 20 year old limited release named after the year it was distilled.

Yoichi distillery, also known as the Hokkaido distillery, is Japan's second oldest distillery. It was built by the father of Japanese' whisky Masataka Taketsuru when he split from Suntory in 1934. High up on the north coast of Japan's northern Island of Hokkaido, it spends much of the year deep in snow. Taketsuru chose the location because he felt it was similar to the maritime distilleries in which he worked during his studies in Scotland in 1919 and 1920. Yoichi still uses old coal-fired pot stills, a method which Taketsuru learned in Scotland but which has now died out in that country, and they are also unusual in their concentration on charred, unused casks rather than barrels seasoned in the manufac-

ture of other wines and spirits.

It is obviously a winning formula because Yoichi has made a habit of breakthrough victories in international competitions. In 2001, it was a 10 year old Yoichi whisky that won the "Best of the Best" award at Whisky Magazine's World Whiskies Awards, and started to draw attention to Japanese whisky. A 2008 World Whiskies Award for best single malt in the world dealt a hammer blow to diehards maintaining that Japanese whiskies were not world class. The last two years have been relatively quiet for Yoichi on the awards front, with the 20 year old Yoichi winning the Japanese category in the 2010 World Whiskies Awards and the 15 year old earning a gold medal at the 2009 International Spirits Challenge, but Taketsuru 21 year old pure malt, which contains malts from both Yoichi and Miyagikyo, has continued to bang home Nikka's excellence by winning back-to-back World Whiskies Awards (2009, 2010) in the vatted malt category and the overall whisky prize at the International Spirits Challenge in October 2009.

Tasting note:
Yoichi 12 year old
Plump squashy dried apricots on the nose. Sweet and mild on first tasting but then becomes more assertive and complex, with earthy themes developing. Yoichi has a reputation for providing some of the more "masculine" of Japanese malts. This is a good example.

Yamazaki

Owner: Suntory **Founded**: 1924
Capacity: 3,500,000 litres
Malt whisky range: Yamazaki Single Malt 10,12,18,
25, 35 and 50 years old and a range of limited edition
bottlings.

Yamazaki is the oldest Japanese malt whisky distillery. It was set up in 1924 by Shijiro Torii, the founder of Suntory, who employed Masataka Taketsuru following his return from his studies of whisky distilling in Scotland. It is nestled up against forested hills between Kyoto and Osaka and at the confluence of the Katsura, Kizu and Uji rivers, an area famous for its superb water since the 16th Century. Yamazaki has 12 pot stills in a variety of designs and can make whisky in a wide variety of styles. Most of the pot stills are indirectly heated but three wash stills are directly fired with gas.

The Yamazaki malts have been at the forefront of Suntory's recent export drive. The Yamazaki 12 and 18 year olds have long been the only Japanese single malts commonly available in the United States, but the new push was heralded in 2009 by the export of 500 bottles of the wonderfully complex, Japanese oak-aged Yamazaki 1984 and 8,000 bottles of Sherry Cask Yamazaki to both the U.S. and Europe. The blended Hibiki 12 is now being shipped to both markets. In the long term, Suntory has its eye on potentially huge rewards in countries such as India and China, but its medium term aim is to establish its name in the mature European and American markets. That effort was helped by a "double gold" medal for the Yamazaki 1984 at the 2010 World Spirits Competition (WSC) in the U.S and a gold at the 2009 International Spirits Competition in the U.K. The Yamazaki 18 year old won double gold at the WSC for the third year in a row.

Tasting note:
Yamazaki 25 year old
Cereal and rich jammy, port soaked smells. In the mouth: jam, red wine, vanilla and treacle overlaid on woods and tannins. The finish is slightly drying.

The Grain distilleries

One of the more interesting subplots in the Japanese whisky narrative over the past few years has been the emergence of quality single grain whiskies.

Nikka's single Coffey grains from their now defunct distillery in Nishinomiya have been around for some time now, but La Maison du Whisky plan to bring two single casks of Nikka Coffey Grain 2000 to Europe in the latter half of 2010 to celebrate the 10th anniversary of the start of grain distilling at Miyagikyo. The stills are the same ones we have already drunk from at Nishinomiya, but we will now get the chance to see whether their move to Miyagikyo affected the product. Suntory's continuous stills at Chita have kept a low profile but a Chita Distillery Special Grain bottling gained a mention in the 2009 World Whisky Awards as the best Japanese grain whisky. There are plans afoot to bring Chita to Europe too.

But the biggest news has been the discovery by Ichiro Akuto (see Hanyu and Chichibu distilleries) of grain whiskies from the long-closed Kawasaki distillery. The distillery at Kawasaki, an industrial city between Yokohama and Tokyo, had several incarnations but it was originally built by the old Showa Brewery company, which is believed to have produced some malt whisky in the late 1950s. Grain whisky was made from about 1969, by which time Kawasaki was part of the Sanraku Ocean company. Through a contact at Karuizawa distillery, which also used to be part of Sanraku Ocean, Akuto was able to uncover some 1976, 1981 and 1982 grain casks at a winery in Katsunuma, Yamanashi Prefecture and bottled them in 2009 under his "Ichiro's Choice" brand. The real surprise has been that these neglected casks actually seem to contain some good whisky. Nicholas Sikorski at La Maison du Whisky in Paris describes the 1976 grain as "one of the best Japanese whisky finds of the year" and says the quality of 120 bottles of Kawasaki 1982 which La Maison are bringing to into Europe is such that they plan to feature it prominently in their 2010/2011 catalogue.

Tasting note:
Ichiro's Choice 1982 Single Grain Whisky Kawasaki
Not a particularly appealing nose: alcohol. Surprisingly soft on the palate for its 65.4% alcohol content. With a good splash of water, notes of sweet Demerara sugar, coffee and stewed black tea.

Chris Bunting is a British journalist living in Japan since 5 years. He works for a Japanese newspaper and his guide to Japanese alcohol culture, titled "Drinking Japan", is due to be published at the end of the year. He is currently working on a book about Japanese whisky and writes on that subject at www.nonjatta.com.

Masataka Taketsuru - the father of Japanese whisky production

竹鶴政孝翁

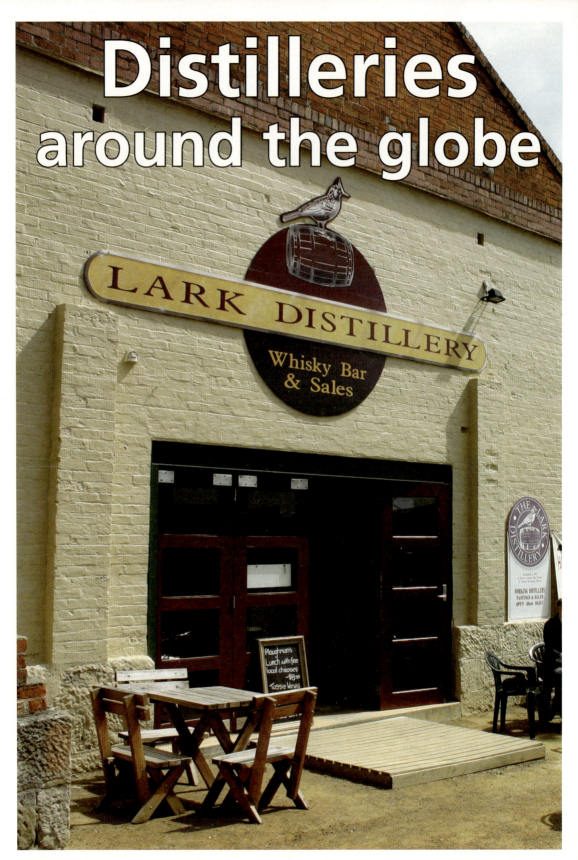

Distilleries
around the globe

The increase in the number of malt whisky distilleries outside of Scotland, Ireland and Japan is continuing with no signs of weakening. Enterprises combining beer brewing and distilling, or distilling of a variety of different spirits where malt whisky is just one of them, are still dominating, although distilleries built for the sole purpose of distilling malt whisky are becoming increasingly common.

In Denmark, Braunstein released its first whisky in March 2010 and another Danish distillery, Fary Lochan, started distilling the same year. The pot is really brewing in Sweden; the third dedicated whisky distillery came on stream in Smögen in August and during the summer of 2010 no less than four would-be distilleries had their copper stills delivered - Ådalen Whisky (BOX), Grythyttan Whisky, Gotland Whisky and Gammelstilla. All four of them report that they will start distilling during autumn of 2010. Staying in Sweden, there are two other projects where whisky has already been produced - Norrtelje Brenneri, where the emphasis is on other spirits, filled its first cask in late 2009 and Wannborga on the island of Öland, a combination of restaurant, brewery and distillery, already made its first distillation in late 2007.

Another country where the interest in whisky production is virtually booming is the USA. No less than nine new entries have been included in this year's edition of the Yearbook and more are in the pipeline. A difference between Old World and US producers is that the latter often release their products at a very young age (sometimes just a couple of months old) and this is, in many cases, due to differences in legislation. Still, it is possible to find distillers in the US that wait three years and more for their first releases.

Across the border, in Canada, two new distilleries started production in 2009/2010 - Victoria Spirits and Pemberton distillery, both in British Columbia and now we are waiting for another one, Shelter Point distillery, to come on stream any day.

In Taiwan, last year's new entry, Yuanshan distillery, has already enjoyed much interest from malt whisky drinkers around the world, even though its whisky is only available in Taiwan and China so far. Capacity though is huge, so it probably is just a matter of time before we see Kavalan whisky on European shelves as well. The people at Kavalan have recently seen competition from state-owned Taiwanese Tobacco & Liquer Co (TTL) which started to distil malt whisky two years ago. Nothing has been released from TTL so far however.

In Europe, Switzerland is one of the most active countries when it comes to malt whisky production. There are currently at least ten active distilleries with one of them, Brennerei Stadelmann, releasing their first official bottlings in summer of 2010. Not far from Switzerland lies Lichtenstein and that small country can add itself to the whisky producing countries since Brennerei Telser already launched their very first single malt in 2009, with two more releases to be expected during 2010.

The first, and so far the only, whisky distillery in England for over a hundred years, St. George's in Norfolk launched their first whisky in late 2009 and several more expressions followed in 2010.

From Australia we can report on yet another distillery, this time in Timboon, Victoria. It actually already started distilling in 2007 and the first bottling was released in summer of 2010 as was the first expression from Nant distillery in Tasmania.

And just to show how exciting and full of surprises the world of malt whiskies can be, at the beginning of August 2010, Stock Spirits announced the release of Hammer Head, a 21 year old single malt Czech whisky, distilled in the old Prádlo Distillery way back in 1989.

EUROPE

Austria

DISTILLERY: Waldviertler Roggenhof,
Roggenreith
FOUNDED: 1995
OWNER/MANAGER: Johann & Monika Haider
www.roggenhof.at

In the small village of Roggenreith in northern Austria, Johann and Monika Haider have been distilling whisky since 1995. In 2005, they opened up a Whisky Experience World with guided tours, a video show, whisky tasting and exhibitions. Four years later, more than 70,000 visitors have found their way to the distillery. Roggenhof was the first whisky distillery in Austria and over the years production has increased to currently reach 30,000 litres. The capacity is at 100,000 litres annually.

The wash is allowed to ferment for 72 hours before it reaches either of the two 450 litre Christian Carl copper stills. The desired strength is reached in one single distillation, thanks to the attached column.

The new make is filled in casks made of the local Man-hartsberger Oak adding a slight vanilla flavour and left to mature for three years. When the casks are used a second time, the whisky matures for five years. The casks are used a third time, but only after dismantling, shaving and charring before filling. Spirit on third fill casks is expected to mature for 12-18 years. A new warehouse was commissioned in June 2009 so there is now storage capacity for almost 3,000 barrels. Two single malts made of barley are available: Gersten Malzwhisky J. H. (light malt) and Gersten Malzwhisky J. H. Karamell (dark, roasted malt). There are also three different rye whiskies. New expressions are planned for 2011 when two peated, dark roasted varieties (one rye and one single malt) will be launched.

DISTILLERY: Reisetbauer, Kirchberg-Thening
FOUNDED: 1994 (whisky since 1995)
OWNER/MANAGER: Julia & Hans Resisetbauer
www.reisetbauer.at

This is a family-owned farm distillery near Linz in northern Austria specialising in brandies and fruit schnapps. Since 1995, a range of malt whiskies are also produced. The distillery is equipped with five 350 litre stills. All stills are heated, using hot water rather than steam, which, according to Hans Reisetbauer, allows for a more delicate and gentle distillation. The 70 hour-long fermentation takes place in stainless steel washbacks. Approximately 20,000 litres of pure alcohol destined for whisky making are produced annually, using local barley to make the unpeated malt. Casks are sourced locally from the best Austrian wine producers. The whisky is filled the same day the wine casks have been emptied in order to save aromas from oxidation and to avoid the use of SO_2.

In 2002, the first whisky was released. The current range includes a 7 year old single malt which consists of a vatting of whiskies aged in casks that have previously contained Chardonnay and Trocken-beerenauslese. There is also a 10 year old cask strength aged exclusively in Trockenbeeren-auslese and a 12 year old (the first for Austria) which has also undergone maturation in Trockenbeerenauslese barrels. The whisky is currently exported to Germany, Switzerland, France, the Netherlands, Denmark, Russia, the United Kingdom and the USA.

DISTILLERY: Destillerie Weutz,
St. Nikolai im Sausal
FOUNDED: 2002
OWNER/MANAGER: Michael & Brigitte Weutz
www.weutz.at

This family distillery, initially producing schnapps and liqueur from fruits and berries, is situated in Steiermark in the south of Austria. In 2004 Michael Weutz started cooperation with the brewer Michael Löscher and since then Weutz has added whisky to its produce based on the wash from the brewery. The business grew quickly and in 2006 the distillery moved to a bigger location. Since 2004, 14 different malt whiskies have been produced. Some of them are produced in the traditional Scottish style: Hot Stone, St.Nikolaus and the peated Black Peat. Others are more unorthodox, for example Green Panther, in which 5% pumpkin seeds are added to the mash, and Franziska based on elderflower. Apart from barley wheat, corn and spelt are also used for some expressions.

Annual production is currently at approximately 14,000 litres and for maturation casks made of French Limousin and Alliere oak are used. So far the whisky is only available for purchase in Austria.

DISTILLERY: Wolfram Ortner Destillerie,
Bad Kleinkirchheim
FOUNDED: 1990
OWNER/MANAGER: Wolfram Ortner
www.wob.at

Fruit brandies of all kinds make up the bulk of Wolfram Ortner´s produce, as well as cigars, coffee and other luxuries. For the last few years he has also been producing malt whisky. New oak of different kinds (Limousin, Alolier, Nevers, Vosges and American) is used for the maturation process. His first single malt, WOB DÖ MALT Vergin, began selling in 2001 and an additional product line, in which Ortner mixes his whisky with other distillates such as orange/moscatel, is called WOB Marriage. Ortner practices an unconventional technique during fermentation as the draff and not only the liquids from the mashing is used.

Belgium

DISTILLERY: The Owl Distillery, Grâce Hollogne
FOUNDED: 1997
OWNER/MANAGER: Etienne Bouillon (manager),
Luc Foubert and Pierre Roberti
www.belgianwhisky.com
www.thebelgianowl.com

In October 2007, Belgium's first single malt 'The Belgian Owl', was released. The next bottling came in June 2008 but was exclusively reserved for private customers. The first commercial bottling was introduced in November 2008, and in February 2009 another 2,766 bottles were released. Bouillon expects to produce around 24,000 bottles annually with five releases per year. A limited cask strength expression, 44 months old, was released end of 2009.

The distillery is equipped with a mash tun holding 4.1 tonnes per mash, one washback where the wash is fermented for 60-100 hours and finally one wash still (550 litres) and one spirit still (450 litres). Every step of production (including malting) is carried out at the distillery near Liege and maturation takes place in first fill bourbon casks from Kentucky. The whisky is neither coloured nor chill-filtered.

At the moment, The Belgian Owl is sold in Belgium, The Netherlands and France.

DISTILLERY: Het Anker Distillery, Blaasfeld
FOUNDED: 1369 (whisky since 2003)
OWNER/MANAGER: Charles Leclef (owner),
www.hetanker.be

Seven years ago the producer of the quality beer Gouden Carolus, Brouwerij Het Anker, and its owner, Charles Leclef, decided to find out how whisky, distilled from the brewery's wash, would taste. Distillation of the spirits was tasked to nearby genever distiller, Filliers, and was done in a genever column still. The result was Gouden Carolus Single Malt - the third Belgian malt whisky to reach the market after Belgian Owl and Goldlys. The first 3,000 bottles were released in January 2008.

No new releases were made in 2009. Instead, Leclef concentrated on the next step in the project, namely, building a distillery of his own with pot stills. The location chosen was not at the brewery in Mechelen, but at Leclef's family estate, Molenberg, at Blaasfeld. Leclef is the fifth generation of a family that long since has been involved in distilling genever and brewing beer. The distillery will be commissioned during 2010 and the owner hopes to start distilling before the end of the summer. The stills have been made by Forsyth's in Scotland with a wash still of 3,000 litres' capacity and a spirit still of 2,000 litres. It will be possible to make 100,000 litres of alcohol per year. According to Paul Verbruggen from the brewery, the first batches of Gouden Carolus Single Malt that have been launched are to be considered as experiments, with the first distillations from the new distillery being the real test of the product.

Czech Rebublic

DISTILLERY: Gold Cock Distillery
FOUNDED: 1877
OWNER/MANAGER: Rudolf Jelinek a.s
www.rjelinek.cz

The distilling of Gold Cock whisky started already in 1877. Gold Cock was originally a malt whisky made from abundunt local barley. Now it is produced in two versions – a 3 year old blended whisky and a 12 year old malt. Production was stopped for a while but after the brand and distillery were acquired by R. Jelinek a.s, the leading Czech producer of plum brandy, the whisky began life anew. The malt whisky is double distilled in 500 litre traditional pot stills. The new owner has created a small whisky museum which is also home to the club Friends of Gold Cock Whisky with private vaults, where any enthusiast can store his bottlings of Gold Cock.

Denmark

DISTILLERY: Stauning Whisky, Stauning
FOUNDED: 2006
OWNER/MANAGER:
www.stauningwhisky.dk

The first Danish purpose-built malt whisky distillery entered a more adolescent phase in May 2009, after having experimented with two small pilot stills bought from Spain. Two new, Portugese-made stills of 1,000 and 600 litres respec-

tively were installed and the distillery could try its wings. Only the new stills are currently used, but it is possible that the smaller stills will be used for special distillations in the future.

The aim has always been to be self-sustaining and Danish barley is bought and turned into malt on an own malting floor. The germinating barley usually has to be turned 6-8 times a day, but Stauning has constructed an automatic "grain turner" to do the job. Two core expressions were decided on - Peated Reserve and Traditional Reserve - and the peat for the first one is acquired from one of few remaining peat bogs in Denmark. A further variety, a rye whisky, has also entered production. The whisky is made from 100% malted rye, like e. g. Old Potrero Single Malt from USA. Most of production is stored in first fill ex-bourbon barrels from Makers Mark. There is also opportunity for some experimenting with sherry butts, Port pipes and casks made of new French oak.

A first, limited edition of 750 bottles each of the two expressions will be released in May 2012. The annual production is roughly 7,000 litres, but is expected to be increased.

An official opening and at the same time tasting, was held on 12th March 2010 led by, among others, the well-known whisky authority, Jim Murray.

DISTILLERY: Ørbæk Bryggeri, Ørbæk
FOUNDED: 1997 (whisky since 2007)
OWNER/MANAGER: Niels and Nicolai Rømer
www.oerbaek-bryggeri.nu

Niels Rømer and his son, Nicolai, have run Ørbæk Brewery since 1997 on the Danish island of Fyn. It is now one of many combinations of a micro-brewery and a micro-distillery where the wash from the brewery is used to produce whisky. Aspirations to start distilling whisky already appeared in 2007, but it took another two years to get the final approvals from Health and Safety authorities. In June 2009 the first barrels of Isle of Fionia single malt were filled and the first release is planned for 2012. The whisky, in common with Ørbæk's beer, will be ecological and two different expressions are planned - Isle of Fionia and the peated Fionia Smoked Whisky.

It is matured in ex-bourbon barrels from Jack Daniels and ex-sherry casks. Within five years the estimated yearly production will amount to 10-20,000 bottles.

DISTILLERY: Braunstein, Køge
FOUNDED: 2005 (whisky since 2007)
OWNER/MANAGER: Michael & Claus Braunstein
www.braunstein.dk

Denmark's first micro-distillery was built in an already existing brewery in Køge, just south of Copenhagen. Unlike many other brewery/whisky distillery enterprises around the world, the owners consider the whisky production to be on

From the official opening of Stauning distillery in March 2010

equal terms with beer production, even in financial terms. The wash, of course, comes from the own brewery. A Holstein type of still, with four plates in the rectification column, is used for distillation and the spirit is distilled once. For five winter months, peated whisky (+60ppm) is produced, while the rest of the year is devoted to unpeated varieties. Peated malt is bought from Port Ellen, unpeated from Simpsons, but as much as 40% is from ecologically grown Danish barley. The lion's share of the whisky is stored on ex- bourbon (peated version) and first fill Oloroso casks (unpeated) from 190 up to 500 litres. The long-term aspirations are to produce a 100% Danish whisky.

The Braunstein brothers filled their first spirit casks in March 2007 and have produced 50,000 litres annually since then. Their first release and the first release of a malt whisky produced in Denmark was on 22nd March 2010 - a 3 year old cask strength called Edition No. 1. For the future, Braunstein will be releasing two parallel series, where Edition series is bottled at cask strength and the Library Collection is bottled at 46%. The first 500 bottles in the Library Collection, called 10:1, were launched in May. The next release, slightly peated, appeared in September and 10:3, unpeated and Oloroso matured will appear in December 2010.

DISTILLERY: Fary Lochan Destilleri, Give
FOUNDED: 2009
OWNER/MANAGER: Jens Erik Jørgensen
www.farylochan.dk

This is the second, purpose-built whisky distillery in Denmark to come on stream and just like the first, Stauning, it is situated in Jutland. The first cask was filled on 31st of December 2009 and the owner plans to produce 3,000 bottles per year, although its capacity is 12,000 bottles.

Jørgensen imports most of the malted barley from the UK, but he also malts some Danish barley by himself. After mashing, it is fermented for five days in a 600 litre stainless steel washback. Distillation is performed in two traditional copper pot stills from Foryth's in Scotland - a 300 litre wash still and a 200 litre spirit still. The spirit is matured in ex-bourbon barrels, some of which have been remade into quarter casks. Jørgensen is aiming for a soft and mellow character of the whisky, but some of it will also be lightly or medium peated. The first release (750 bottles very lightly peated) is expected to take place in autumn 2013.

England

DISTILLERY: St. George´s Distillery, Roudham, Norfolk
FOUNDED: 2006
OWNER/MANAGER: The English Whisky Co.
www.englishwhisky.co.uk

St. George´s Distillery near Thetford in Norfolk was started by father and son, James and Andrew Nelstrop, and came on stream on 12th December 2006. This made them the first English malt whisky distillery for over a hundred years. Customers, both in the UK and abroad, have had the opportunity to follow the development of the whisky via releases of new make as well as 18 months old spirit, both peated and unpeated. These were called Chapters 1 to 4. Finally, in December 2009, it was time for the release of the first whisky called Chapter 5 - unpeated and without chill filtering or colouring. This was a limited release but soon afterwards Chapter 6 was released in larger quantities. The next expression (Chapter 8) was a limited release of a lightly peated 3 year old, followed in June 2010 by Chapter 9 (with the same style but more widely available). Chapter 7, a 3 year old with 6 months finish in a rum cask, was planned for a spring 2010 launch, but will be available in autumn of 2010, as will Chapter 10, with a sherry cask finish. Chapter 7 and 10 will be limited to 600 bottles each and will only be available in the UK.

60,000 bottles are estimated to make up sales in 2010 and important markets are Benelux, France, Scotland, Japan, Singapore and England.

The distillery is equipped with a stainless steel semi-lauter mash tun with a copper top and three stainless steel washbacks with a fermentation of 85 hours. There is one pair of stills, the wash still with a capacity of 2,800 litres and the spirit still of 1,800 litre capacity. First fill bourbon barrels are mainly used for maturation but the odd sherry, Madeira and Port casks have also been filled. The casks are stored in a dunnage warehouse on site which is now slowly filling up, but the construction of another warehouse will start in August 2010. Non-peated malt is bought from Crisp Malting Group and peated malt from Simpson´s Malt in Berwick-

The third edition from Braunstein and Fary Lochan's New Spirit

The visitor centre at St George´s Distillery

upon-Tweed. Around 60% of production is unpeated and the rest is peated. Recently, a bottling line was installed, giving St. George's the possibility to bottle with its own water source. The capacity is 800 bottles per day. Around 150,000 bottles will be produced during 2010.

Finland

DISTILLERY: Teerenpeli, Lahti
FOUNDED: 2002
OWNER/MANAGER: Anssi Pyysing
www.teerenpeli.com

The first Teerenpeli Single Malt was sold as a 3 year old in late 2005, though solely at the owner's restaurant in Lahti. Four years later, the first bottles of a 6 year old were sold in the Teerenpeli Restaurants and later that year also in the state owned ALKO-shops. Pyysing will keep on bottling the 6 year old during 2010, with the introduction of an 8 year old version in 2011. A limited edition, for sale only at the restaurants, is due by the end of 2010 and will be a vatted expression with Teerenpeli and an undisclosed Speyside malt.

Teerenpeli is equipped with one wash still (1,500 litres) and one spirit still (900 litres) and the average fermentation time in the washback is 70 hours. Lightly peated malt obtained locally is used and the whisky matures in ex-sherry and ex-bourbon casks. 7,500 bottles are produced annually. In August 2010 a new mash tun was installed and later that month a new visitor centre was opened.

France

DISTILLERY: Distillerie Guillon, Louvois, Champagne
FOUNDED: 1997
OWNER/MANAGER: Thierry Guillon
www.whisky-guillon.com

Thierry Guillon, originally a wine man, decided in 1997 to begin distilling whisky. Not perhaps a novel idea if it was not for the fact that the distillery is located in the heart of the Champagne district. But besides champagne this area is also known as a major barley producer in France. In fact, several Scotch maltsters buy barley from this region. Guillon has increased his production steadily and now makes 140,000 bottles a year and has 1,200 casks maturing on site.

The range of single malts is quite large and vary in age between 4 and 10 years. Guillon No. 1, has a particularly interesting maturation process. It is a 5 year old matured in a new oak cask the first year, a whisky barrel the second year, then white wine, red wine and finally the last year in a Port pipe. Apart from single malts there is also a blend in the range, Le Premium Blend, consisting of 50% malt and 50% grain whisky and a whisky liqueur. The whisky is exported to several European countries, as well as to China. There is also a visitor centre, which attracts 15,000 visitors per year.

DISTILLERY: Distillerie Bertrand, Uberach, Alsace
FOUNDED: 1874 (whisky since 2002)
OWNER/MANAGER: Affiliate of Wolfberger
www.distillerie-bertrand.com

Distillerie Bertrand is an independent affiliate of Wolfberger, the large wine and eaux-de-vie producer. The manager, Jean Metzger, gets his malt from a local brewer and then distils it in Holstein type stills. Two different types of whisky are produced. One is a single malt at 42.2%, non-chill filtered and with maturation in both new barrels and barrels

St George's lightly peated Chapter 9, released in June 2010

A 6 year old single malt from Teerenpeli in Finland

which have previously contained the fortified wine Banyuls. The other is a single cask at 43.8% matured only in Banyuls barrels. The first bottles, aged 4 years, were released in late 2006 and the annual production is around 7,000 bottles with currently 5,000 bottles being sold per year. In late 2008 Jean Metzger released a limited Single Cask Collection from six different Banyuls barrels. In June 2009 the next expression came - a double matured whisky with a 12 months finish in a Vin Jaune barrel. New releases for 2010 include a 6 year old with three months´ finish in a Pinot Gris vendange tardive cask from Alsace and a 7 year old matured in a Banyuls cask. There are also plans for future releases of whisky matured in cognac and champagne barrels.

At the moment, Uberach Single Malt Alsace, a name taken from the village, is only sold in France, Germany, Switzerland, Luxembourg and Andorra.

DISTILLERY: Glann ar Mor, Pleubian, Bretagne
FOUNDED: 1999
OWNER/MANAGER: Jean Donnay
www.glannarmor.com

Glann ar Mor Distillery in Brittany ("Glann ar Mor" literally means "By the Sea" in Breton language) reached one of its goals in 2008: the first official bottling was launched - a 3 year old unpeated version. The next release came in September 2009, this time a peated version under the name Kornog ("West Wind") and bottled from a bourbon barrel at cask strength. February 2010 saw the second editions of both versions (which sold out in a fortnight) and this time bottled at 46%. The next bottling is due for November and from 2011, larger quantities will become available.

The owner, Jean Donnay, already started his first trials back in 1999. He then made some changes to the distillery and the process and regular production commenced on 12th June 2005. The distillery is very much about celebrating the traditional way of distilling malt whisky. The two small stills are directly fired and Donnay uses worm tubs for condensing the spirit. He practises a long fermentation in wooden washbacks and the distillation is very slow. For maturation, first fill bourbon barrels and ex-Sauternes casks are used and when the whisky is bottled, there is neither chill filtration nor caramel colouring. The full capacity will be 50,000 bottles per year.

Apart from the Glann ar Mor venture, Jean Donnay has also specialised in double maturation Single Malts. The "Celtique Connexion" range includes whiskies originally distilled and matured in Scotland, then further matured at the company's seaside warehouse. The casks used for this are from Sauternes, Vin de Paille du Jura, Armagnac, Champagne and Coteau du Layon, amongst others.

In 2008 the company opened its new premises, including a larger warehouse and a visitor centre, a couple of miles away from the distillery's location, still by the seaside. The whiskies can be found at www.tregorwhisky.com

DISTILLERY: Distillerie Warenghem, Lannion, Bretagne
FOUNDED: 1900 (whisky since 1994)
OWNER/MANAGER: Warenghem
www.distillerie-warenghem.com

Leon Warenghem founded the distillery at the beginning of the 20th century but Armorik, the first malt whisky, was not distilled until 1994 and released in 1999. Since 1983 Gilles Leîzour has run the distillery. The Armorik single malt now exists in two versions; a 4 year old that is bottled at 40%, matured in bourbon barrels and finished in sherry casks, and a 7 year old (42%) with a double maturation in fresh oak and sherry butts. Three blended whiskies supplement the range; Whisky Breton W. B., a 3 year old with 25% share of malt, Breizh matured in fresh oak and with a 50% malt content, as well as Galleg, matured in both sherry and bourbon casks and also with a 50% malt content. Armorik is available in several European countries and is also exported to Japan.

Germany

DISTILLERY: Slyrs Destillerie, Schliersee
FOUNDED: 1928 (whisky since 1999)
OWNER/MANAGER: Florian Stetter
www.slyrs.de

Lantenhammer Destillerie in Schliersee, Bavaria was founded in 1928 and was producing mainly brandy until 1999 when

Kornog - the peated expression from Glann ar Mor distillery and the owner, Jean Donnay

whisky came into the picture, and in 2003 Slyrs Destillerie was founded. The malt, smoked with beech, comes from locally grown grain, and the spirit is distilled twice at low temperatures in the 1,500 litre stills. Maturation takes place in charred 225-litre casks of new American White Oak from Missouri. Recently the owner decided to double the capacity of the distillery. Investments in three new fermentation tanks (washbacks) and a malt silo during 2009/2010 will increase the capacity to 60,000 bottles in 2011.

The non chill-filtered whisky is called Slyrs after the original name of the surrounding area, Schliers. Around 30,000 bottles were released in 2008 and every year 3,000-5,000 bottles are kept for later release. Florian Stetter has plans for releasing a cask strength in 2010 and a 12 year old in 2015. Slyrs whisky is available in several European countries and is also exported to the USA and Australia.

DISTILLERY: Whisky-Destillerie Blaue Maus, Eggolsheim-Neuses
FOUNDED: 1980
OWNER/MANAGER: Robert Fleischmann
www.fleischmann-whisky.de

This is the oldest single malt whisky distillery in Germany and it celebrated its 25th anniversary in February 2008. The first distillate, never released on the market, was made in 1983. It took 15 years until the first whisky, Glen Mouse 1986, appeared. Fleischmann uses unpeated malt and the whisky matures for approximately eight years in casks of fresh German Oak. All whisky from Blaue Maus are single cask and with the release of two new expressions in 2010, Elbe 1 and Otto´s Uisge Beatha, there are currently eight single malts, the others being Blaue Maus, Spinnaker, Krottentaler, Schwarzer Pirat, Grüner Hund and Old Fahr. Some of them are released at cask strength while others are reduced to 40%. The oldest bottlings are more than 20 years old. A new expression was introduced quite recently; Austrasier is the first grain whisky from the distillery. In 2006 a new distillery was built solely for whisky production while mostly new types of malt will be produced in the older distillery.

DISTILLERY: Hammerschmiede, Zorge
FOUNDED: 1984 (whisky since 2002)
OWNER/MANAGER: Karl-Theodor and Alexander Buchholz
www.hammerschmiede.de

In common with many other small whisky producers on mainland Europe, Hammerschmiede´s main products are liqueurs, bitters and spirits from fruit, berries and herbs. But whisky distilling was embarked on in 2002 and production has now increased to 15%.

Unpeated malt is acquired in Germany and mature the spirit in a variety of casks - German Oak, sherry, cognac, port, bordeaux, bergerac, marsala, malaga and madeira casks, as well as Dornfelder barriques (German red wine).

The first 278 bottles were released in early 2006 under the name Glan Iarran. Today, all whisky produced has changed name to Glen Els after the small river Elsbach which flows past the premises. So far, the owners have specialized in single cask releases and this will continue. In autumn 2010, however, the first "distillery edition" of Glen Els was launched - 5,000 bottles mostly from ex-sherry casks. Distillery editions will continue to be released in 2011 (mostly port casks) and in 2012 (predominantly Madeira casks).

So far the whisky has been matured for 3-4 years, but older expressions can be expected in the future. 2010 also saw experiments involving one fifth of the total production, when several new barley strains and especially alternative malting techniques were used. This resulted in quite a different type of aromatic spirit, with, e. g., notes of chocolate.

DISTILLERY: Bayerwald-Bärwurzerei und Spezialitäten-Brennerei Liebl, Kötzting
FOUNDED: 1970 (whisky since 2006)
OWNER/MANAGER: Gerhard Liebl Jr.
www.bayerischer-whisky.de

In 1970 Gerhard Liebl started spirit distillation from fruits and berries. The distillery was rebuilt and expanded on several occasions until 2006, when his son, Gerhard Liebl Jr. ,

Slyrs from Slyrs distillery

Otto´s Uisge Beatha from Blaue Maus

Glen Els Pale Cream Sherry from Hammerschmiede

built a completely new whisky distillery nearby. Leibl Jr uses 100% Bavarian malt and the wash is left to ferment for 3-5 days. It is then double distilled in Holstein stills (wash still 400 litres and spirit still 150 litres). Assisted by the attached rectification columns, completely different levels of alcohol compared to a Scottish distillery are obtained. The low wines from the wash still are at 40% and the middle cut from the spirit still at 85%. Maturation takes place in first or second fill ex-bourbon barrels, except for whisky destined to be bottled as single casks. Sherry, Port, Bordeaux and Cognac casks are used here. The whisky is non chill-filtered and non-coloured. About 10,000 litres of whisky are produced per year and in spring and summer 2009 the first 1,500 bottles bearing the name Coillmór were released in three different expressions - American White Oak, Sherry single cask and Bordeaux single cask. New expressions followed in July 2010 with a Bordeaux single cask and in August a sherry single cask and a peated version.

DISTILLERY: Spreewälder Feinbrand- & Likörfabrik, Schlepzig
FOUNDED: 2004 (whisky production)
OWNER/MANAGER: Torsten Römer
www.spreewaldbrennerei.de

This distillery with attached brewery lies in Spreewald, circa 100 km south-east of Berlin. The main product range consists of different kinds of beers, eau-de-vie and rum, and since 2004 also malt whisky.

So far a 100 litre still with an attached column still has been used, but in late summer of 2010, a new still will be in place. This 650 litre still has eight trays in the fractioning column, is fired using gas and has been specially designed by the famous still manufacturer, Christian Carl. The annual production of whisky and rum will now increase to 15,000 litres per year.

French Oak casks, that have previously contained wine made of Sylvaner and Riesling grapes, are used for maturation, as well as new medium toasted Spessart Oak casks. Torsten Römer is also looking for other casks in Germany (Sylvaner), France (Sauternes) and Spain (Manzanilla). Before filling into casks the spirit is left for six months in stainless steel tanks. The whisky, which was first released in December 2007 as a 3 year old, is called Sloupisti, which is the ancient Sorbic name of the village Schlepzig. At the moment, it is bottled at 40%, but the next cask strength bottling is due in autumn 2010. Some barrels are also reserved for a 12 year old to be released in 2016.

DISTILLERY: Brennerei Höhler, Aarbergen
FOUNDED: 1895 (whisky since 2001)
OWNER/MANAGER: Holger Höhler
www.brennerei-hoehler.de

The main produce from this distillery in Hessen consists of different distillates from fruit and berries. In November 2000, a new 390 litre still with four rectifying plates from Firma Christian Carl was installed. Whisky production commenced thereafter. The first whisky, a bourbon variety, was distilled in 2001 and released in 2004. Since then, Holger Höhler has experimented with different types of grain (rye, barley, spelt and oat). There was a limited release of a single malt in July 2007 and a very limited amount of whisky has been released since then. Until recently, all casks were made from Sessart oak with a storage capacity of between 30 and 75 litres. In spring 2007 Höhler started filling 225 litres barriques. He aims to increase production and eventually launch older whisky.

Liechtenstein

DISTILLERY: Brennerei Telser, Triesen
FOUNDED: 1880 (whisky production since 2006)
OWNER/MANAGER: Telser family
www.brennerei-telser.com

The first distillery in Liechtenstein to produce whisky is not a new distillery. It has existed since 1880 and is now run by the fourth generation of the family. Traditions are strong and Telser is probably the only distillery in Europe still using a wood fire to heat the stills. Like so many other distilleries on mainland Europe, Telser produces mainly spirits from fruits and berries, including grappa and vodka. For whisky, the distillery uses a mixture of different malts (some peated) that are also used by local breweries. The first bottling of Telsington was distilled in May 2006 and released in July 2009. After an extremely long fermentation (10 days), the spirit was triple distilled, filled into a Pinot Noir barrique and left to mature for three years in a 500 year old cellar with an earth floor resembling the dunnage warehouses of Scotland. The second release of Telsington (distilled in 2007) consisted of 200 bottles released in June 2010, with another 200 bottles due in November. The whisky is non chill-filtered

Marcel and Sebastian Telser from Telser distillery in Liechtenstein and their single malt - Telsington

and bottled at 42%, but a cask strength has already been planned for 2012. According to the owner and head distiller, Marcel Telser, there are no plans of using other casks than Pinot Noir. An interesting side effect of that particular maturation is that grappa-drinkers not previously interested in whisky have come to appreciate it.

The Netherlands

DISTILLERY: Us Heit Distillery, Bolsward
FOUNDED: 2002
OWNER/MANAGER: Aart van der Linde
www.usheitdistillery.nl

This is one of many examples where a beer brewery also contains a whisky distillery. Frysk Hynder, as the whisky is called, was the first Dutch whisky and made its debut in 2005 at 3 years of age. The barley is grown in surrounding Friesland and malted at the distillery. The owner of the brewery and distillery, Aart van der Linde, has even developed a malting technique which he describes on a separate website - *www.mouteryfryslan.nl*. Some 10,000 bottles are produced annually and the whisky is matured in various casks - sherry, bourbon, red wine, port and cognac.

DISTILLERY: Vallei Distilleerderij, Leusden
FOUNDED: 2002 (officially opened 2004)
OWNER/MANAGER: Bert Burger
www.valleibieren.nl

This is the latest addition to Dutch whisky distilleries. Bert Burger buys barley from a local farmer but apart from that he is very much in control of the whole process from malting to bottling. The whisky is double distilled in pot stills and he produces some 2,500 litres per year. The first trials were in 2002 but in 2004 the distillery was officially opened. After a while Burger started bottling his 2 year old spirit as Valley single malt spirit in 40 ml bottles for customers to try. Finally, on 1st December 2007, the first bottles of single malt whisky reached the market as a 3 year old. Other products include whisky liqueur and two kinds of beer.

DISTILLERY: Zuidam Distillers, Baarle Nassau
FOUNDED: 1974 (whisky since 1998)
OWNER/MANAGER: Zuidam family
www.zuidam-distillers.com

Zuidam Distillers was started in 1974 as a traditional family distillery producing liqueurs, genever, gin and vodka. The first attempts to distil malt whisky took place in 1998, but according to one of the owners, Patrick van Zuidam, the result is not fit for bottling. Instead, the first release was from the 2002 production and it was bottled in 2007 as a 5 year old.

In 2009 there were two limited editions of 8 year olds, one matured in new American Oak and one in new French Oak. This year also saw the first bottling of a 5 year old 100% potstill rye whisky. A heavily peated expression first to be released in 2009, was postponed and will be launched during 2010.

The whisky is double distilled in two 1,000 litre pot stills made by Kothe & Holstein in Germany. For distillation of other spirits, the distillery is also equipped with two more stills of 500 and 2,000 litres respectively. The malt is sourced both locally and abroad and mashing takes place in three stainless steel mash tuns. Fermentation is slow (five days) and takes place at a low temperature. Maturation takes place in new barrels made of American White Oak, but ex bourbon and ex Oloroso sherry casks are also used. At the moment 20,000 litres per year are produced.

Russia

DISTILLERY: Kizlyarskoye, Mirny, Kizlyar, Republic of Dagestan
FOUNDED: 2003
OWNER/MANAGER: Nauchno-Proizvodstvenoye Predpriyatie Whisky Rossii

In 1948 a winery called Kizlyarski was founded on the outskirts of Kizlyar in Dagestan. Most of the wines are sold locally but some brandy is produced which has become fairly well-known in other parts of Russia.

In 2003 a group of enthusiasts led by Alibek Irazi-hanov, current CEO and distillery manager, ventured into an experiment in the field of whisky. Today the equipment consists of four copper pot stills (5,000 litres each) and a stainless steel column still. Capacity is 3,000 litres of malt whisky per day and 6,000 litres of grain whisky. The spirit is matured on American oak as well as Russian oak from Maikop.

So far production has been very scarce and most of the time the stills are used for distillation of brandy. No official volumes of maturing whiskies are disclosed, nor is it clear when the company will start a consistent regular whisky distillation. But the company receives state support and is listed in prospective Dagestan state plan of Wine and Vineyards development, so it should be just a matter of time for all bureaucratic issues to be resolved.

Spain

DISTILLERY: Distilerio Molino del Arco, Segovia
FOUNDED: 1959
OWNER/MANAGER: Distilerias y Crianza del Whisky (DYC)
www.dyc.es

Spain's first whisky distillery is definitely not a small artisan distillery like so many others on these pages. Established by Nicomedes Garcia Lopez already in 1959 (with whisky distilling commencing three years later), this is a distillery with capacity for producing eight million litres of grain whisky and two million litres of malt whisky per year. In addition to that, vodka and rum are produced and there are in-house maltings which safeguard malted barley for the full production. The distillery is equipped with six copper pot stills and there are about 250,000 casks maturing on site. The blending and bottling plant which used to sit beside the distillery is now relocated to the Anis Castellana plant at Valverde del Majano.

The big seller when it comes to whiskies is a blend simply called DYC which is around 4 years old. It is currently the third most sold whisky in Spain and is supplemented by an 8 year old blend and, since 2007, also by DYC Pure Malt, i. e. a vatted malt consisting of malt from the distillery and from selected Scottish distilleries. It can safely be assumed that two of these Scottish single malts come from Laphroaig and Ardmore, as Beam Global owns both, as well as DYC. A brand new expression was also launched in 2009 to commemorate the distillery's 50th anniversary - a 10 year old single malt, the first single malt from the distillery. In 2006, Beam Global introduced DYC blended whisky on the Indian market. It was launched as an IMFL brand (Indian Made Foreign Liquor) which means that the variety of DYC sold in India is produced from imported malt and grain whisky

produced in India. In spring of 2010 the brand was revamped and positioned with a lower price. Obviously, sales in the premium segment were not as well as expected. Total, worldwide, sales of the brand was 1.2 million cases in 2009.

DYC has an interesting liaison with a Scottish distillery which dates back to the early seventies. It bought Lochside Distillery north of Dundee in 1973 to safeguard malt whisky requirements and retained it until it stopped production in 1992. During that time DYC was acquired by Pedro Domecq, which, in turn, was acquired by Allied Lyons, which eventually changed its name to Allied Domecq. When the latter was bought by Pernod Ricard in 2005, a small share, including DYC, went to Beam Global.

Sweden

DISTILLERY: Mackmyra Svensk Whisky, Valbo
FOUNDED: 1999
OWNER/MANAGER: Mackmyra Svensk Whisky AB
www.mackmyra.se

The first single malt from Sweden has already during its short lifetime been praised both in Sweden and abroad. Inspired by this positive feed-back, the company in March 2009 revealed plans to build a brand new facility in Gävle, a few miles from the present distillery at Mackmyra.

The first stage, estimated at almost £5 million, consists of a visitor distillery and storage. Thereafter 'Mackmyra Whisky-by' (Mackmyra Whisky Village) will expand in different phases over the next ten years. The total investments are expected to amount to approximately £50 million and the capacity of the two distilleries will be approximately 6 million bottles per year, which is ten times that of today. Building permission was granted in April 2010 and funding is now sought in order to have everything ready sometime in 2011/2012.

Mackmyra whisky is based on two basic recipes, one resulting in fruity and elegant whisky, the other being more peaty. The peatiness does not stem from peat, but from juniper wood and bog moss. The first release in 2006/2007 was a series of six called Preludium.
The first "real" launch was in June 2008 – 'Den Första Utgåvan' (The First Edition). It is still a fairly young whisky and 95% bourbon casks and 5% casks made from Swedish Oak have been used. Circa 45% of the mix is stored in 100 litre casks. A second release of First Edition was made in October.

In 2009, Special:02 and Special :03 were launched, the second and third in a new series of limited editions. The fourth release in that series, also known as Double Dip Bourbon, was released in spring 2010. A core expression has also been launched, Mackmyra Brukswhisky, with a maturation in first fill bourbon casks, spiced up with sherry casks and Swedish oak and bottled at 41.4%. The casks for The First Edition have all matured at a depth of 50 metres in the Archean rock in an abandoned mine in northern Sweden. Mackmyra has another three storage sites: an island in the archipelago of Stockholm, on the west coast and at a castle in the southernmost part of Sweden. About 15% of Mackmyra's production is exported and the goal is to increase that to 50%. An introduction of the whisky in the USA is next on the agenda.

DISTILLERY: Spirit of Hven, Ven
FOUNDED: 2007
OWNER/MANAGER: Backafallsbyn AB
www.hven.com

The second Swedish distillery to come on stream, after Mackmyra, was Spirit of Hven, a distillery situated on the island of Ven right between Sweden and Denmark. The first distillation took place on 7th May 2008.

Henric Molin, founder and owner, is a trained chemist but this is not the only similarity with Bill Lumsden, Head of Whisky Creation at Glenmorangie. Henric is equally concerned about choosing the right oak for his casks and, like Lumsden, he sources his oak mainly in Missouri. The oak is left to air dry for three to five years before the casks are loaned to, especially, wine producers in both the USA and Europe. It is mostly sweet wines that are filled in the casks but dry white wines and bourbon could also be used. Around 70% of the casks are made of American White Oak while the rest are of Spanish Red Oak (*Quercus falcata*) and (a few percent) of Japanese Mizunara Oak (*Quercus mongolica*). Henric is not afraid of trying out new, more unusual kinds of oak and experiments with South American, Russian and Slovenian oak too.

Henric's initial objective was to keep the whole process of whisky-making on the distillery premises. Starting in autumn of 2009 some 10% of the barley is malted on site, but more and more will come from own maltings as time passes. Peat was initially bought from Islay for the peated varieties, but nowadays, he sources his peat from mainland Sweden. During malting, the peat is spiced up with local seaweed and sea-grass. The malt is dried for 48 hours using peat smoke and the final 30 hours in hot air. The distillery is

The limited Special:04, also called Double Dip Bourbon, from Mackmyra

Henric Molin - owner of Spirit of Hven

equipped with a 500 kilogram mash tun, six washbacks made of stainless steel and one pair of stills - wash still 2,000 litres and spirit still 1,500 litres. There is also one very small still known as the Essence Still. Here, experiments can be made with small batches and essences to be used in the gins and vodkas that are produced. Since last year, Henric has made arrangements in the still house where he can easily divert certain, unwanted parts of the middle cut, hence creating the exact flavour profile he desires. A new feature is also a solera vat holding 10,800 litres to which part of the whisky production will be moved after three years.

A long fermentation time of 90-120 hours is used in order to achieve a more fully flavoured product with high citric notes and a nutty character. The spirit yield at the distillery, 410-420 litres per tonne of malted barley, is quite impressive given the fact that the distillery is small and part of the production is peated whisky. The yield from his own malted barley is 390 litres.

Henric is (to use his own words) obsessed with being able to trace the exact origin of every bottle of whisky down to the field of barley and the specific oak used for the cask. One batch from the spirit still fills exactly one cask and only one cask is made from each oak tree. The plans are to produce four different types of malt whisky - organic, unpeated, lightly peated and heavily peated. The latter has an astonishing level of phenolic compounds in the new make - 94ppm! The first release (without age statement) will be of the lightly peated version in December 2011. Around 60,000 litres of whisky are hoped to be produced during 2010, but also 10,000 litres of rum made from sugar beet and 100,000 litres of vodka, gin and aquavit are expected to be distilled. A new member of the product range since last year is calvados. Much of Henric´s time is now spent being a consultant for Swedish and, in particular, foreign distilling companies. For example, he was recently involved in launching a new vodka in Vietnam.

DISTILLERY: Smögen Whisky AB, Hunnebostrand
FOUNDED: 2010
OWNER/MANAGER: Pär Caldenby
www.smogenwhisky.se

In the 2010 edition of the Malt Whisky Yearbook, I posed the question which the third distillery in Sweden to come on stream would be - BOX or Grythyttan. A year later the answer is neither! In August 2010, at the same time that the two competitors both announced that they were going to start distilling in the autumn, Smögen Whisky on the west coast of Sweden, produced their first spirit. This project has

Smögen distillery - Pär Caldenby is filling his first cask

quietly progressed since last year without any drum banging and thus became Sweden's third whisky distillery, following Mackmyra and Spirit of Hven. Pär Caldenby - lawyer, whisky enthusiast and the author of Enjoying Malt Whisky is behind it all. He has designed the facilities himself and much of the equipment is constructed locally. The three washbacks, for example, carry 1,600 litres each and are rebuilt milk tanks. The wash still (900 litres), spirit still (600 litres), spirit safe and the horizontal condensers have all been made by Forsyths in Scotland. The maturation will, to a large extent, take place in casks made of French Oak, but ex bourbon barrels will also be used. The cask size ranges from 28 to 500 litres. Heavily peated malt is imported from Scotland and the vision is to produce an Islay-type of whisky. The volume for the first year will be around 10,000 litres.

Switzerland _____

DISTILLERY: Bauernhofbrennerei Lüthy, Muhen, Aargau
FOUNDED: 1997 (whisky since 2005)
OWNER/MANAGER: Urs Lüthy
www.swiss-single-malt.ch

The farm distillery, Lüthy, in the north of Switzerland, started in 1997 by producing distillates from fruit, as well as grappa, absinthe and schnapps. The range was expanded to include whisky in 2005 which was distilled in a mobile pot still distillery. Lüthy´s ambition is to only use grain from Switzerland in his production. Since it was impossible to obtain peated malt from Swiss barley, he decided to build his own floor maltings in autumn 2009.

The first single malt expression to be launched in December 2008, was Insel-Whisky, matured in a Chardonnay cask. It was followed by Wyna-Whisky from a sherry cask in April 2009 and Lenzburg-Whisky, another Chardonnay maturation and bottled in September 2009. The most recent bottling was Swiss Spelt UrDinkel Whisky, made from spelt and matured in a Pinot Noir cask. The selection is so far limited as only 500-1000 bottles are filled per year.

DISTILLERY: Whisky Brennerei Hollen, Lauwil, Baselland
FOUNDED: 1999 (for whisky distillation)
OWNER/MANAGER: The Bader family.
www.swiss-whisky.ch, www.single-malt.ch

Since WW1 Switzerland has had a law forbidding the use of staple foods such as potatoes and grain for making alcohol. On 1st July 1999 this was abolished and the spirit streamed through the stills of Holle the very same day making it the first Swiss producer of malt whisky. The whisky is stored on French oak casks, which have been used for white wine (Chardonnay) or red wine (Pinot Noir). There are currently circa 100 casks in the warehouse. Most bottlings are 4 years old and contain 42% alcohol. A 5 year old has also been released, which has had three years in Pinot Noir casks followed by two years in Chardonnay casks. Other expressions include a peated version and a cask strength Chardonnay-matured.

In Spring 2008, an Easter bottling having had six years on two different casks - American Oak bourbon and French Oak which previously had contained Chardonnay - was released. Bader also recently launched what he calls a dessert whisky from a white wine cask as well as his first single grain whisky, and July 2009 saw the release of a 10 year old. Annual production amounts to roughly 30,000 bottles. The main production of the distillery consists of schnapps distilled from a variety of fruit.

DISTILLERY: Whisky Castle, Elfingen, Aargau
FOUNDED: 2002
OWNER/MANAGER: Ruedi Käser
www.whisky-castle.com

The first whisky from this distillery in Elfingen in the north of Switzerland reached the market in 2004. It was a single malt under the name Castle Hill. Since then the range of malt whiskies has been expanded and today include Castle Hill Doublewood (3 years old matured both in casks made of chestnut and oak), Whisky Smoke Barley (at least 3 years old matured in new oak), Fullmoon (matured in casks from Hungary) and Terroir (4 years old made from Swiss barley and matured in Swiss oak). All these are bottled at 43%. Adding to these are Cask Strength (5 years old and bottled at 58%) and Edition Käser (71% matured in new oak casks from Bordeaux). For a year now, Käser has also made three special single malts for the cruise ship company, Hapag Lloyd. The very latest addition to the range is Vintage, which is a bourbon-style whisky made from 60% corn and 40% malted barley. Future releases will include whisky aged in rum, port and wine casks. All released whiskies are unpeated, but some of them have a smoky flavour which derives from the beech wood used to dry the malt.

A new distillery was built in 2005 and commissioned in 2006, hence the annual production has increased from 5,000 to 25,000 bottles. Ruedi Käser has also constructed a complete visitor's experience, including a restaurant and a shop. The whisky can be bought in Germany, The Netherlands and Austria apart from Switzerland and has also recently been exported to China.

DISTILLERY: Spezialitätenbrennerei Zürcher,
Port, Bern
FOUNDED: 1954 (whisky from 2000)
OWNER/MANAGER: Daniel & Ursula Zürcher
www.lakeland-whisky.ch

The first in the Zürcher family to distil whisky was Heinz Zürcher in 2000, who released the first 1,000 bottles of Lakeland single malt in 2003.

Daniel and Ursula Zürcher took over in 2004. They continued their uncle's work with whisky and launched a second release in 2006. The main focus of the distillery is specialising in various distillates of fruit, absinth and liqueur. The latest barrel of Lakeland single malt was released in 2009 as a 3 year old, but the Zürchers are working on the release of older whiskies in the future. The wash for the whisky is bought from Rugenbräu brewery in Interlaken and matura-

Ruedi Käser outside his Whisky Castle distillery

tion takes place in Oloroso sherry casks.

Cooperation with the brewery has developed in recent years in that Zürcher sometimes distils the wash and then sends back the new make to the brewery for it to be filled into casks to mature. Two expressions from Rugenbräu exist, both of which have matured in American Oak Oloroso casks - Swiss Highland Single Malt Classic (46% and released for the first time in 2007) and Swiss Highland Single Malt Ice Label (cask strength and released for the first time in 2008). The latter is an interesting novelty; it has matured for almost 4 years at 3,454 metres altitude in the ice of Jungfraujoch with a constant temperature of minus 4 degrees Celsius. In April 2010 a new edition of the Ice Label was released and there are now around 70 casks maturing.

DISTILLERY: Brennerei Hagen,
Hüttwilen, Thurgau
FOUNDED: 1999
OWNER/MANAGER: Ueli Hagen
www.distillerie-hagen.ch

A triple distilled malt whisky is, since a few years, produced by Ueli Hagen in the small village of Hüttwilen in the northernmost part of Switzerland. The spirit is matured in bourbon barrels and the first produce was sold in 2002 as a 3 year old. Ueli Hagen produces mainly schnapps and absinth and distills around 300 bottles of malt whisky a year, a number he expects to double. He has recently been experimenting; four years ago when he was building a new cow shed, he found a 1700 year old oak tree in the ground so he put pieces of the oak into a maturing barrel of spirit and he says it gives the whisky a slightly peated touch. Ueli has plans for expansion and in 2010 a new still room will be built.

DISTILLERY: Destillatia AG (Olde Deer),
Langenthal, Bern
FOUNDED: 2005
OWNER/MANAGER: Hans Baumberger
www.olde-deer.ch

The distillery was built in 2005 under the same roof as the brewery Brau AG Langenthal (already established in 2001). The reason for this co-habitation was to access a wash for distillation and thereby avoiding investments in mashing equipment. The wash (in which both peated and unpeated malt is used) is fermented for five days and after that distilled three times, using a Holstein type of still. The casks are all 225 litres and Swiss oak (Chardonnay), French oak (Chardonnay and red wine) and ex sherry casks are used. The first whisky was produced in 2005 and released in 2008 under the name, Olde Deer. Since then a new 3 year old has been released every year. From June 2010, the whisky can be bought using their on-line shop. Apart from whisky, the distillery also produces rum, whisky liqueur and schnapps.

DISTILLERY: Burgdorfer Gasthausbrauerei,
Burgdorf, Bern
FOUNDED: 1999
OWNER/MANAGER: Thomas Gerber
www.burgdorferbier.ch

The Burgdorfer Single Malt Whisky is an excellent example of the kind of cross-fertilization that more and more breweries are choosing. When a wash is made for beer brewing, it is an excellent opportunity to use the batch (without adding hops) to distil spirit which can be made into whisky. The first whisky from Burgdorfer was released as a five year old in 2006 and it is sold using a kind of subscription system. The customer pays 50 swiss francs for a 50 cl bottle and receives it 5 years later. They produce around 300 bottles annually.

DISTILLERY: Brennerei Stadelmann, Altbüron, Luzern
FOUNDED: 1932 (whisky since 2003)
OWNER/MANAGER: Hans Stadelmann
www.schnapsbrennen.ch

Established in the 1930s this distillery was mobile for its first 70 years. The current owner's grandfather and father would visit farmers and distil local fruits and berries. Hans Stadelmann took over in 1972 and in 2001 decided to build a stationary distillery which would also be suitable for crop distilling. The distillery was equipped with three Holstein-type stills (150-250 litres) and the first whisky was distilled for a local whisky club in 2003. In 2005 the first Luzerner Hinterländer Single Malt was released, although not as a whisky since it was just 1 year old. A year later the first 3 year old was bottled for the whisky club under the name Dorfbachwasser and finally, in 2010, the first official bottling from the distillery in the shape of a 3 year old single malt whisky was released. The distillery has a visitor centre, where groups can tour the distillery and sample the whisky and other spirits from the range. Stadelmann's produce is available both at the distillery, as well as from a webshop.

DISTILLERY: Brauerei Locher, Appenzell, Appenzell Innerrhoden
FOUNDED: 1886 (whisky since 1998)
OWNER/MANAGER: Locher family
www.säntisspirits.ch, www.saentismalt.ch

This old, family-owned brewery started to produce whisky in 1998 when the Swiss government changed laws, which had been applicable since WWII, and allowed spirit to be distilled from grain. The whole production of the whisky takes place in the brewery where there is a Steinecker mash tun holding 10,000 litres. The spirit ferments in stainless steel vats and, for distillation, Holstein stills are used. Brauerei Locher is unique in using old (70 to 100 years) beer casks for the maturation.

The production amounts to a couple of thousand bottles per year and at the moment there are three expressions; Säntis, bottled at 40%, Dreifaltigkeit which is slightly

peated having matured in toasted casks and bottled at 52% and, finally, Sigel which has matured in very small casks and is bottled at 40%. In Jim Murray's Whisky Bible 2010, Dreifaltigkeit was awarded European Whisky of the Year. Säntis malt is mainly sold in Switzerland.

Wales

DISTILLERY: Penderyn Distillery, Penderyn
FOUNDED: 2000
OWNER/MANAGER: Welsh Whisky Company Ltd
www.welsh-whisky.co.uk

In 1998 four private individuals started The Welsh Whisky Company and two years later, the first Welsh distillery in more than a hundred years started distilling.

A new type of still, developed by David Faraday for Penderyn Distillery, differs from the Scottish and Irish procedures in that the whole process from wash to new make takes place in one single still. But that is not the sole difference. Every distillery in Scotland is required by law, to do the mashing and fermenting on site. At Penderyn, though, the wash is bought from a regional beer brewer and transported to the distillery on a weekly basis. The normal procedure at a brewery is to boil the wash to clear it from any lactic acid which can make it appear cloudy. This was a problem for Penderyn as lactic acid creates a second fermentation which is beneficial in a whisky context and adds more taste. Penderyn has solved this by pumping the wash to a heated tank where lactic acid is added before distillation is commenced. The first year 60,000 bottles were produced and now production has increased to 100,000 bottles.

The first single malt was launched in March 2004. The core range consists of Penderyn Madeira Finish, Penderyn Sherrywood and Penderyn Peated. Recent limited releases include

Säntis Malt from Brauerei Locher

The odd-looking still at Penderyn distillery

Rich Madeira (in 2008) and Portwood Single Cask (2009). Two single casks were released in summer and early autumn 2010 - one was a 2000 Vintage bourbon-matured and the other an Oloroso sherry maturation. A special version selected for La Maison du Whisky and the French market is Penderyn 41, bourbon matured with a light Madeira finish and bottled at 41%. During the past year, sales have increased by 30% and they are now selling around 120,000 bottles in a year in Europe, North America, Japan and Australia.

The increased sales have led to a higher pace of production and Penderyn has now reached the capacity ceiling of the current equipment. There are long-term plans for one more still or even another distillery, but the timing for this expansion has not yet been announced. A visitor centre was officially opened by HRH, The Prince of Wales, in June 2008 at a total cost of £850,000 and in the first year it welcomed 15,000 visitors.

NORTH AMERICA

USA

DISTILLERY: Stranahans Whiskey Distillery, Denver, Colorado
FOUNDED: 2003
OWNER/MANAGER: Jess Graber et al
www.stranahans.com

Since the start in 2003, demand for Stranahans Colorado Whiskey increased so much that Jess Graber simply had to find a solution to keep up with demand. Until 2009, wash has been purchased from a couple of local breweries, but now he wanted to bring it up one step by producing wash in-house. The equipment required was found in the closed Heavenly Daze Brewery in Denver, but instead of just buying the mash tun and fermenters, he ended up buying the entire 60,000 square foot building. The whole operation was moved to the new location on 6th May 2009.

The plan is to make up to 16 barrels per week. The first distillation takes place in a 2,800 litre Vendome combined pot still/column still, while the second distillation is in a 950 litre pot still. The whiskey is filled into heavily charred barrels of new American White Oak and left to mature for a minimum of two years. Up to 20 barrels with ages between 2 and 5 years are married together when bottling.

The first three barrels were bottled in April 2006 and 60 different batches have been produced so far. In spring 2009 different wood finishes named Snowflakes were released. The first were port and cabernet franc and, in March 2010, a finish in Hungarian White Oak which had previously contained red wine from Sonoma was released.

In April 2009 the 100,000th bottle was bottled, thus making Stranahans one of the American micro distilleries achieving the most successful sales. From exclusively selling locally in Colorado, the whiskey can now be found in 38 states, as well as in Japan and Europe.

STILLERY: Clear Creek Distillery, Portland, Oregon
FOUNDED: 1985
OWNER/MANAGER: Stephen McCarthy
www.clearcreekdistillery.com

Steve McCarthy in Oregon was one of the first to produce malt whiskey in the USA and his 3 year old single malt has earned a reputation as a high-quality whiskey fully com-

parable to the best Scotch whiskies. Like many other small distilleries, Clear Creek started by distilling eau-de-vie from fruit, especially pears, and then expanded the product line into whiskey. It began making whiskey in 1996 and the first bottles were on the market three years later.

There is only one expression at the moment, McCarthy's Oregon Single Malt 3 years old. Steve has for a long time hoped to launch an 8 year old, but so far it has simply not been possible to save adequate quantities due to high demand.

The whiskey is reminiscent of Islay and, in fact, the malt is purchased directly from Islay with a phenol specification of 30-40 ppm. It is then made into wash at the Widmer Brothers Brewery in Portland and distilled in Holstein pot stills. Steve expanded the number of pot stills to four last year to try and catch up with demand. Maturation takes place in ex-sherry butts with a finish in new Oregon White Oak hogsheads.

Steve has doubled the production of whiskey every year since 2004 which does not, however, seem to be enough to satisfy demand. The procedure used to be one release in March and one in August with both of them selling out quickly and 2008 was no exception. In 2009 he changed it to one release per year, with the August one being the biggest ever - 700 cases. The next release will be November 2010. Unlike many of the single malts from the USA, McCarthy's Oregon Single Malt is available in several European countries.

DISTILLERY: Charbay Winery & Distillery, St. Helena, California
FOUNDED: 1983
OWNER/MANAGER: Miles and Marko Karakasevic
www.charbay.com

Charbay has a wide range of products: vodka, grappa, pastis, rum, port and since 1999 also malt whiskey. That was the year when Miles and Marko decided to take 20,000 gallons of Pilsner and double distil it in their Charentais pot still, normally used for distilling for example cognac. From this distillation, a 4 year old called Double-Barrel Release One (two barrels) was launched in 2002. There were 840 bottles at cask strength and non-chill filtered. The whiskey is quite unique since a ready beer, hops and all, rather than wash from a brewery is used.

It took six years before Release II appeared in 2008, this time with 22 barrels. It was matured for six years in heavily charred new American White oak. After six years, five barrels were picked out and the whiskey received another three

Jess Graber and Jake Norris from Stranahans Whiskey Distillery

years of maturation in stainless steel tanks. Release III in the series will probably be bottled in summer 2010. In January 2010 a different type of whiskey was launched, Charbay's Doubled & Twisted Light Whiskey. It was distilled from bottle-ready IPA beer (India Pale Ale) and consists of both aged and white (unaged) whiskies.

DISTILLERY: The Ellensburg Distillery,
Ellensburg, Washington
FOUNDED: 2008
OWNER/MANAGER: Berle Wilson Figgins Jr.
www.theellensburgdistillery.com

Former winemaker Berle "Rusty" Figgins Jr. decided to leave the wine-making business after 10 years to open a distillery instead. The distilled produce will include malt whiskey, rye whiskey, cream liqueur and brandy. The malt whiskey is made from an all-malt mash, incorporating a proprietary blend of pale ale, crystal and chocolate malts, while the wort is fermented with native yeast.

The distillation process is a bit unusual. Rusty uses two alambic pot stills of a design which originates in Armagnac. Both stills, which are united with a T-shaped lyne arm, are simultaneously filled with equal volumes and the spirit is distilled twice. The character is aromatic and full-flavoured from the very beginning and, according to Rusty, this is achieved by the distilling technique where the spirit vapour from each still is manifolded together, to afford a degree of back pressure which increases the degree of reflux. The new make is filled into new American Oak barrels of 112.5 litres and after six months it is re-racked to 225 litre ex sherry casks for another six months. The first Gold Buckle Club malt whiskey (300 bottles) was bottled on 1st September 2009. The second release (another 300 bottles) is due in September 2010, but this time both the mix of malt and the maturation will differ from the first release. The mashbill for the second edition (and for future editions) will be 75% pale-ale malt, 15% crystal malt and 10% high-Lovibond chocolate malt. Furthermore, maturation will start in an ex sherry cask and finish in new American oak. In February 2010, Rusty made an experiment distilling a whiskey made from Washington-grown spelt and apart from whiskey, he is also doing a Peruvian-style grape brandy called El Chalán.

The stills arrive at Eades distillery

DISTILLERY: Eades Distillery,
Lovingston, Virginia
FOUNDED: 2008
OWNER/MANAGER: The Virginia Distillers Co.
(Chris Allwood, Joe Hungate, Brian Gray)
www.eadeswhisky.com

Chris Allwood and his partners spent the first two years of this project to find funding of around $5m to complete their plans for a distillery in Nelson County, Virginia. The plan was originally to start distilling in spring 2009, but it was not until in spring 2010 that funds were secure enough for fuelling hopes to be making whisky by the end of 2010. In early 2011 Eades will also be offering cask sales of the whisky to be.

All equipment has been made in Scotland by Northern Fabricators: a 2 tonne mash tun, a 10,000 litre wash still and an 8,000 litre spirit still. The construction is designed and supervised by Harry Cockburn with over 40 years' experience in the business, which includes a past at Morrison Bowmore. The malting of locally grown barley will be done on-site and they are cooperating with Virginia Tech University to test around six strains in order to find the best variety.

Initial production volumes are expected to be around 2,500 barrels of 200 litres each per year and the spirit will mature mainly in bourbon barrels, but port pipes and wine barrels from local wineries will also be used. It will probably take at least four years before the first bottlings of matured whiskey are for sale.

Meanwhile, the owners have created a series of vatted malt whiskies called "Eades Anticipation Series". In association with Jim McEwan of Bruichladdich, single malts from various Scottish producers have been selected. The idea is to select two different malts aged anything between 10 and 18 years for each bottling, marry them and then let them go through a second maturation in wine barrels. The second edition of the series was released in spring 2010 with the following combinations: Eades Highland, a combination of Ben Nevis and Clynelish, Eades Speyside with Dufftown and Mortlach and, finally, Eades Islay where Bowmore and Caol Ila have been married.

DISTILLERY: Triple Eight Distillery,
Nantucket, Massachusetts
FOUNDED: 2000
OWNER/MANAGER: Cisco Brewers
www.ciscobrewers.com

In 1995 Cisco Brewers was established and five years later it was expanded with Triple Eight Distillery. The base of the whiskey production is, of course, wash from the brewery where Maris Otter barley is used. The first distillation took place as early as ten years ago and the first 888 bottles (5 barrels) were released on 8th August 2008 as an 8 year old. To keep in line, the price of these first bottles was $888. The whiskey is named Notch (as in "not Scotch").

Annual production is approximately 5,000 bottles and the storage is on ex-bourbon casks from Brown Forman (Woodford Reserve) and finished in French Oak. The next release of Notch was due for summer 2010, this time as a 10 year old.

The Nantucket facility consists of a brewery, winery and distillery. Triple Eight also produces vodka and rum that are already available on the market. Whiskey production was moved to a new distillery in May 2007.

DISTILLERY: Tuthilltown Spirits,
Gardiner, New York
FOUNDED: 2003
OWNER/MANAGER: Ralph Erenzo & Brian Lee
www.tuthilltown.com

This is the first whiskey distillery in the State of New York since Prohibition. Just 80 miles north of New York City,

Ralph Erenzo and Brian Lee, with the help of six employees produce bourbon, single malt whiskey, rye whiskey, rum and vodkas distilled from local apples. Erenzo bought the 18th century property in 2002 with the intention of turning it into a camping ground, but neighbours objected. A change in the law in New York State made it possible to start a micro-distillery; paying $1,450 for a licence. Erenzo thus changed direction and started distilling instead. Erenzo and Lee built the distillery, acquired licences and learned the basic craft over the following two years.

The first products came onto the shelves in 2006 in New York and the range now consists of Hudson Baby Bourbon (made from 100% New York corn), Hudson 4-Grain Bourbon (corn, rye, wheat and malted barley), Hudson Single Malt Whiskey (aged in small, new, charred American Oak casks), Hudson Manhattan Rye, Hudson River Rum, Tuthilltown New York Whiskey and Tuthilltown Government Warning Rye.

A cooperative venture was announced between Tuthill-town and William Grant & Sons (Grants, Glenfiddich, Balve-nie et al) in June 2010, in which W Grants acquired the Hud-son Whiskey brand line in order to market and distribute it around the world. Tuthilltown Spirits remains an indepen-dent company that will continue to produce the different spirits. The produce from Tuthilltown currently sells in 17 US states, seven European countries and in Australia.

In July 2009 the distillery crew hand-harvested the first crop of rye grown at the distillery, and opened for its first public house tours. Tuthilltown´s new whiskey tasting room and shop are in the barrel room, the first at a distillery in New York since 1919. Private single cask bottling of whiskey is also available to consumers at the distillery.

DISTILLERY: St. George Distillery,
Alameda, California
FOUNDED: 1982
OWNER/MANAGER: Jörg Rupf/Lance Winters
www.stgeorgespirits.com

The distillery is situated in a hangar at Alameda Point, the old naval air station on the San Fransisco Bay. It was found-ed by Jörg Rupf, a German immigrant who came to California in 1979 with a Holstein pot in tow. Several of his ancestors had preceded him in the trade as distillers of eau-de-vie and Rupf became one of the forerunners when it came to craft distil-ling in America. In 1996, Lance Winters joined him and today he is Distiller as well as co-owner.

The main produce is based on eau-de-vie from locally grown fruit, and vodka under the brand name Hangar One. Whiskey production was picked up in 1996 and the first single malt appeared on the market in 1999. Like in so many other craft distilleries, the wash is not produced in-house. St George´s obtain their from Sierra Nevada Brewery. One advantage of cooperating with a brewery is that brewer´s yeast can be used, something Scottish producers had to give up on in 2005 when it became unavailable. Lance Winters, in common with many other craft distillers, claims that the fruity character of the whiskey is a result of using brewer´s yeast rather than distiller´s yeast. Some of the malt used has been dried with alder and beech but is non-peated. Maturation is in bourbon barrels (80%), French Oak (15%) or port pipes (5%). St. George Single Malt used to be sold as three years old, but nowadays comes to the market as a blend of whis-keys aged from 4 to 12 years.

DISTILLERY: Nashoba Valley Winery,
Bolton, Massachusetts
FOUNDED: 1978 (whiskey since 2003)
OWNER/MANAGER: Richard Pelletier
www.nashobawinery.com

Nashoba Valley Winery lies in the heart of Massachusetts' apple country, just 40 minutes from Boston and is owned by Richard Pelletier since 1995. Although mainly about wines

the facilities have in recent years expanded with a brewery (producing ten different kinds of ales and lagers) and Mas-sachusetts' first distillery, which holds a farmer's distiller's license. Here Pelletier produces a wide range of spirits inclu-ding vodka, brandy and grappa.

Since 2003 malt whiskey is also distilled. The malt is imported from England, France and Canada and the wash is produced in his own brewery. The whiskey is matured in a combination of ex bourbon barrels and American and French Oak casks, which previously have contained wine from the estate. Richard Pelletier produces around 9,000 bottles per year.

In autumn 2009, Stimulus, the first single malt was relea-sed. Getting approval of the name turned out to be more difficult than anticipated. The Bureau of Alcohol was of the opinion that the name indicated a positive effect on health. After Pelletier explained that the name was more about the current political climate, it was finally approved. The two casks of Stimulus were distilled in 2004. In the warehouse lies another 5 casks distilled in 2005, which will be bottled some time in 2010. A further 20 casks were distilled in 2006 and the goal is to put aside 20 casks annually for maturation.

DISTILLERY: Woodstone Creek Distillery,
Cincinnati, Ohio
FOUNDED: 1999
OWNER/MANAGER: Donald Outterson
www.woodstonecreek.com

Since the start in 2003, Don and Linda Outterson have run this winery/distillery part-time keeping their full-time jobs. The reason for focussing primarily on the winery is that Ohio state laws are considerably more lenient when it comes to wine than whiskey. Still, in 2008 a change came through allowing sales of whiskey directly from the distillery premi-ses. The next step the Outtersons (and other distillers in the state) are lobbying for, is that tastings of the spirit will be allowed on the site.

The first whiskey, a five grain bourbon (white and yellow corn, malted barley, malted rye, and malted wheat), was released as Barrel #2 on 4th July 2008 to celebrate the change in Ohio's regulations. The second release, Barrel #1, was launched on 25th November to celebrate Thanksgiving Day. Both bourbons were made of malted grains (no enzymes), 51% corn, sweet mash and without chill-filtering and colouring. In 2010, the Outtersons will be releasing several different spirits - 10 year old single malt (both peated and unpeated), corn whiskey, gin, 100 proof vodka, rum, honey brandy from their own mead and bierschnaps, as well as more bourbon.

Don Outterson opened a farm winery in Lebanon, Ohio in 1999 and relocated to the present facilities in 2003. The malted barley is imported from Scotland and port and sherry casks of own production are used for maturation. The capa-city for single malts in the future is planned to be 10 barrels per year.

DISTILLERY: Edgefield Distillery,
Troutdale, Oregon
FOUNDED: 1998
OWNER/MANAGER: Mike and Brian McMenamin
www.mcmenamins.com

Brothers Mike and Brian McMenamin started their first pub in Portland, Oregon in 1983. It has now expanded to a chain of more than 50 pubs and hotels in Oregon and Washington. Over 20 of the pubs have adjoining microbreweries (the first opened in 1985) and it is now the fourth-largest chain of brewpubs in the United States.

The chain's first and so far only distillery opened in 1998 at their huge Edgefield property in Troutdale and their first whiskey, Hogshead Whiskey (46%), was bottled in 2002. Annual production is now 10,000 litres, thanks to a

newly installed second washback. In the past, ex bourbon casks were used for maturation, but now only charred, new American White Oak barrels are used. There are plans to open up another distillery in Hillsboro, Oregon. An Alembic still has been acquired and the building permits have been approved, but the final decision is yet to be taken.

Hogshead Whiskey is the top seller (3,600 bottles in 2007) but Head Distiller, James Whelan, has a goal of producing four to eight barrels of "specialty" whiskies that differ from the Hogshead. Most of these specialty whiskies are destined to become Devil´s Bit, a limited bottling released every year on St. Patrick´s Day. In 2010 it was an 8 year old whiskey made of 51% red winter wheat and 49% barley. A peated version from 100% barley is designated to become Devil´s Bit in the future and in 2010 Whelan also barrelled a whiskey from organic, floor-malted Maris Otter pale malt imported from Thomas Fawcett in the UK.

Recently he has also introduced a programme for making 5-10 barrels per year of a rye whiskey, based on a recipe given to him by the legendary Booker Noe of Jim Beam fame. Whelan has developed his own technique to quickly cool the rye mash from 65 degrees to 30 degrees before adding yeast. He simply throws 250 pounds of dry ice into the mash.

DISTILLERY: Copper Fox Distillery,
Sperryville, Virginia
FOUNDED: 2000
OWNER/MANAGER: Rick Wasmund
www.copperfox.biz

Copper Fox Distillery was founded in 2000 by Rick Wasmund using the premises and licence of an old, existing distillery. The first whiskey, Copper Fox Whiskey, was made in cooperation with the distillery which they were about to buy, but after a disagreement over the contract the project came to a halt. In 2005 they moved to another site, built a new distillery and began distilling in January 2006.

Rick Wasmund has become one of the most unorthodox producers of single malt. The malted barley is dried using smoke from selected fruitwood but variations of that concept are also used in other places, for example Sweden. It is the maturation process that Rick takes one step further thereby differing from common practice. In every barrel of new make spirit, he adds plenty of hand chipped and toasted chips of apple and cherry trees, as well as oak wood. Adding to the flavour, Wasmund also believes that this pro-

James Whelan, Edgefield distillery, cooling the mash using dry ice

cedure drastically speeds up the time necessary for maturation. In fact, he bottles his Wasmund´s Single Malt after just four months in the barrel. Every batch ranging from 250 to 1,500 bottles tastes a little different and the distillery is now producing around 2,500 bottles every month. 37 different batches have been launched up to the spring of 2010. Other expressions in the range are Copper Fox Rye Whiskey with a mash bill of 2/3 Virginia rye and 1/3 malted barley and two unaged spirits - Rye Spirit and Single Malt Spirit.

DISTILLERY: High Plains Distillery,
Atchison, Kansas
FOUNDED: 2004
OWNER/MANAGER: Seth Fox
www.highplainsinc.com

Former process engineer, Seth Fox, is mainly known for his Most Wanted Vodka of which he sells over 13,000 cases a year in Kansas, Missouri and Texas. The product range was expanded in late 2006 also to include a Most Wanted Kansas Whiskey (reminiscent of a Canadian whisky) and Kansas Bourbon Mash. Fox continued in 2007 to produce his first single malt whiskey made from malted barley but it has not been released yet. He also produces Pioneer Whiskey and a premium vodka called Fox Vodka which is filtered five extra times. The two stills were bought second-hand from Surrey in England. When High Plains opened, it was the first legal distillery in Kansas since 1880. In 2009 he expanded the facility in order to accommodate a production of 70-80,000 cases per year, compared to previous 20,000.

DISTILLERY: Dry Fly Distilling, Spokane,
Washington
FOUNDED: 2007
OWNER/MANAGER: Don Poffenroth
& Kent Fleischmann
www.dryflydistilling.com

Dry Fly Distilling began distilling in autumn 2007 and became the first grain distillery to open in Washington since Prohibition. To ensure a positive cash flow from the start, in common with many other distilleries, vodka and gin were produced and since October 2007, circa 60 batches each of vodka and gin have been released. The first batch of malt whisky was distilled on 4th January 2008. The owners expect to make 200-300 cases of malt whisky annually, but the first bottling will probably not be released until 2013/2014. However, there are a couple of other whiskies in production and one of them is quite unusual - Washington Wheat Whiskey. It was first released in August 2009 and, at that time, it was only the second of this style following Heaven Hill's launch of Bernheim Straight Wheat Whiskey in 2005. In November 2010, Dry Fly Distilling will also launch the first bourbon ever made in Washington State.

The original equipment consisted of one still, a Christian Carl manufactured in Germany. In autumn 2008 another still was installed, as well as two additional fermenters, which raised capacity to 10,000 cases per annum. Dry Fly Distilling is currently sold in 20 states and in Canada.

DISTILLERY: St. James Spirits,
Irwindale, California
FOUNDED: 1995
OWNER/MANAGER: Jim Busuttil
www.saintjamesspirits.com

Peregrine Rock is the name of the 3 year old single malt Jim Busuttil produces in Irwindale, east of Los Angeles. The malt comes from Baird Malts in the UK and is medium peated. Heavy charred new American Oak barrels, but also ex-bourbon barrels from Jim Beam and Jack Daniels are used.

DISTILLERY: New Holland Brewing Co., Holland, Michigan
FOUNDED: 1996 (whiskey since 2005)
OWNER/MANAGER: Brett VanderKamp, David White, Fred Bueltmann
www.newhollandbrew.com

This company started as a beer brewery, but after a decade, it opened up a microdistillery as well and the wash used for the beer is now also used for distilling whiskey. There is a variety of malts for mashing and the house ale yeast is used for fermentation. The spirit is double distilled in a 225 litre, self-constructed pot still. There is also a 2,250 litre copper still built in 1913 and which probably has not been used since prohibition. According to Dennis Downing, the new distiller, a metal worker has been hired to restore the old still. About 4,000 litres of spirit is produced yearly.

The first cases of New Holland Artisan Spirits were released in December 2008 and among them were Zeppelin Bend, their 3 year old straight-malt whiskey. As Michigan laws did not allow a small distiller to produce grain-based spirits until July 2008, the owner, Brett Vanderkamp, took quite a risk when he laid down a few barrels of Zeppelin Bend already in 2005. The next bottling (three 53 gallon barrels) took place in 2010, but a new series of "small barrel" whiskies having matured for a minimum of six months on 5 gallon charred American White Oak barrels were also launched. The expressions include Barley, Wheat, Rye and one called Smoked whiskey, which has been distilled from malted barley. At the moment the whiskey is sold in Michigan and Illinois, but it will soon be found in Kentucky and Wisconsin as well.

DISTILLERY: DownSlope Distilling, Centennial, Colorado
FOUNDED: 2008
OWNER/MANAGER: Mitch Abate, Matt & Andy Causey
www.downslopedistilling.com

The three founders were brought together by their interest and passion for craft-brewing when they started the distil-

Dennis Downing, head distiller of New Holland Artisan Spirits

lery in 2008 and in 2009 they finally got their licence to start distilling. The distillery is equipped with two stills - one very elegant, copper pot still made by Copper Moonshine Stills in Arkansas and a vodka still of an in-house design. The first products to be launched in August 2009 were a vodka made from sugar cane and a white rum. More vodkas and rums were to follow and in April 2010 the first whiskey, Double-Diamond Whiskey, was released. It is made from malted barley and a fraction of rye and matured in small, medium-toasted casks. A whiskey from 100% malted barley (a small percentage of which is peated) has also been produced, but has yet to be released. The barley used was Maris Otter, a strain that has not been used in Scotland for ages due to its low yield. The owners of DownSlope prefer it to others because of the flavour they consider it adds to the spirit.

DISTILLERY: Ballast Point Brewing & Distilling, San Diego, California
FOUNDED: 1996 (whiskey since 2008)
OWNER/MANAGER: Jack White
www.ballastpointspirits.com

Building on Jack White's Home Brew Mart, he and Yuseff Cherney started Ballast Point Brewing Company in 1996. The two decided that, when the beer brewing business had increased to 10,000 barrels per year, a distillery would be added to the operation. Distilling started in 2008 and became the first craft distillery in San Diego. The first product to see the light of day was Old Grove gin in August 2009, followed by Three Sheets rum in April 2010. That same month their malt whiskey, Devil's Share Whiskey, was presented at the American Distilling Institute's annual conference.

DISTILLERY: Green Mountain Distillers, Stowe, Vermont,
FOUNDED: 2001
OWNER/MANAGER: Harold Faircloth III, Tim Danahy
www.greenmountaindistillers.com

Tim Danahy and Howie Faircloth, previously in the beer brewing business, started Green Mountain Distillers in 2001. It is an unusual distillery in the respect of being Certified Organic. The first product to hit the shelves was Sunshine Vodka in 2004, which became a huge success and was followed in summer 2009 with two new versions - Organic Lemon and Organic Orange. Two years earlier, Green Mountain Distillers had also released Maple Syrup Liqueur. However, a 100% organic malt whiskey has always been on their minds. The first batches were already distilled in September 2004, but unlike many other distillers in the USA, Tim and Howie decided to let it mature for quite a number of years. The first release (less than 1000 bottles) can be expected in autumn 2011 and will by then, probably, be the first certified organic malt whisky produced in USA.

DISTILLERY: Lexington Brewing & Distilling Co., Lexington, Kentucky
FOUNDED: 1999
OWNER/MANAGER: Pearse Lyons
www.kentuckyale.com

Most of the producers of malt whiskey in the USA have a background in brewing, winemaking or distilling other spirits. This only applies partly to Lexington Brewing & Distilling Company, as whiskey production is derived from their production of Kentucky Ale. Pearse Lyons' background is interesting – being the owner, the founder and a native of Ireland, he used to work for Irish Distillers in the 1970s. In 1980 he changed direction and founded Alltech Inc, a biotechnology company specializing in animal nutrition and feed supplements. Today, Alltech has 2000 employed and is represented in 120 countries.

Alltech purchased Lexington Brewing Company in 1999, with the intent to produce an ale that would resemble both an Irish red ale and an English ale. Dr Lyons, holding a PhD in brewing and distilling, obviously knew what he was doing, as the ales became an instant success. In 2008, two traditional copper pot stills from Scotland were installed with the aim to produce Kentucky's first malt whiskey. North American 2-row malted barley is mashed in a lauter mash tun and fermented using a yeast designed by Alltech. The capacity of the distillery part is 450,000 litres of pure alcohol per year and the first whiskey was released in August 2010 under the name Pearse Lyons Reserve. In 2009, Lexington also started producing bourbon that will be launched in 2012.

DISTILLERY: RoughStock Distillery,
Bozeman, Montana
FOUNDED: 2008
OWNER/MANAGER: Kari & Bryan Schultz
www.montanawhiskey.com

Unlike many other American micro distilleries relying on obtaining mash from a nearby brewery, RoughStock buys its 100% Montana grown and malted barley and mash themselves in a 1,500 gallon mash cooker. The mash is not drained off into a wash, but fermented directly from the mash tun in open top fermenters for 72 hours before double distillation in a 250 gallon Vendome copper still. Maturation is on a mix of quarter casks and 225 litre barrels made from new American oak. Bryan Schultz also has spirit ageing in French oak and in casks that have contained fortified wine.

In September 2009, the first bottles of RoughStock Montana Whiskey, the first legally made whiskey in Montana's history since Prohibition, were released. Since then, another 15 or so batches have been released, with each batch consisting of between 35 and 60 cases. A limited Distiller's Select Release bottled at 60% has also been launched. Total capacity is around 35,000 bottles per year. In order to keep increasing the capacity, Bryan has recently ordered an additional still (750 gallons).

Pearse Lyons Reserve and RoughStock Montana Whiskey

DISTILLERY: The Solas Distillery,
La Vista, Nebraska
FOUNDED: 2009
OWNER/MANAGER: Zac Triemert, Brian McGee,
Jason Payne
www.solasdistillery.com

The Solas Distillery, the first licensed distillery in Nebraska since prohibition, can trace its origins back to 2005, when Zac Triemert, at that time master brewer of Upstream Brewing Company in Omaha, persuaded his colleagues, Brian McGee and Jason Payne, to set up their own brewery. At first they brewed out of another Omaha brewery. In 2008 their own Lucky Bucket brewery was ready to roll and a year later, at the same premises, a distillery was built. The two units, which are housed in the same building, are separated by a 12 foot fence for legal reasons. The first product to hit the market in November 2009 was Joss Vodka, with the Cuban-style Chava Rum next to be released (due in autumn 2010). In February 2010 single malt whiskey was distilled but it will not be ready to bottle in at least three years. Zac Triemert, who has a Master's Degree in distilling from Herriot-Watt University in Edinburgh, lets the wash ferment for seven days and then distills it in two copper pot stills from Forsyth's in Scotland. The wash still holds 500 gallons, the spirit still 300 gallons and the whiskey is matured in a variety of casks that have previously contained wine or bourbon. A few, charred, new casks are used as well. The plan is to fill 100 barrels during 2010 and then doubling each subsequent year.

DISTILLERY: Prichard's Distillery, Kelso, Tennessee
FOUNDED: 1999
OWNER/MANAGER: Phil Prichard
www.prichardsdistillery.com

Phil Prichard's original intentions were to construct a distillery in Manchester, Tennessee, but religious-fuelled opposition became too strong. He turned to an old schoolhouse in Kelso instead. When he started in 1999, it became the first legal distillery for 50 years in Tennessee. Eleven years later, it is the third largest in the state after giants Jack Daniel's and George Dickel.

Prichard produces around 20,000 cases per year with different kinds of rum as the main track. The biggest seller, however, is a bourbon-based liqueur called Sweet Lucy which is responsible for 50% of sales. Bourbon and single malt whisky has recently started to be produced. The latter is not released yet, but a double-barrel bourbon has hit the market. Prichard's Distillery's range is sold in 44 states and in eight European countries.

DISTILLERY: House Spirits Distillery,
Portland, Oregon
FOUNDED: 2004
OWNER/MANAGER: Lee Medoff, Christian Krogstad
www.housespirits.com

This distillery was started in Corvallis in 2004 by two former brewers from Portland, Lee Medoff and Christian Krogstad. A year later, operations was moved to its present location in Portland. Bearing in mind the brewing past, it is perhaps not so surprising that local breweries are used to produce the wash for the whiskey. It is all organic certified and un-peated. For the double distillation, a 1,500 litre still is used and the spirit is filled into new charred American oak. The three first expressions were released in December 2009. Two of them had been matured for 2 years and 8 months with one bottled at 45% and the other a cask strength at 56.8%. The third bottling was a white dog bottled at 50%. White dog is the non-matured spirit and corresponds roughly to what is called new make in Scotland and poitín in Ireland. The next whiskey release is due for summer 2010.

Other products and the ones that so far have given the distillery a reputation, include Aviation Gin, Krogstad Aquavit and Medoyeff Vodka.

DISTILLERY: Rogue Ales & Spirits,
Newport, Oregon
FOUNDED: 2009
OWNER/MANAGER: Jack Joyce
www.rogue.com

The company started in 1988 as a combined pub and brewery. Over the years the business expanded and now consists of one brewery, two combined brewery/pubs, two distillery pubs (Portland and Newport) and five pubs scattered over Oregon, Washington and California. The main business is still producing Rogue Ales, but apart from whiskey, rum and gin are also distilled.

Two malt whiskies have been released so far. The first, Dead Guy Whiskey, was launched in December 2009 and is based on five different types of barley. Distillers yeast is added to the wort and after fermentation it is distilled twice in a 150 gallon Vendom copper pot still. The spirit is matured for one month in charred barrels made of American Oak. The second expression was released in June 2010 under the name Chatoe Rogue Oregon Single Malt Whiskey. It is made from barley grown on Rogue´s own farm in Tygh Valley. The malt is smoked using Oregon Alder wood chips and the spirit is matured for three months. At the moment 300 cases of Dead Guy Whiskey and 100 cases of Chatoe Rogue are produced monthly. The whiskey can be bought in 30 states in the US and is also exported to Canada, Puerto Rico, Philippines, Japan and Australia.

Canada

DISTILLERY: Glenora Distillery,
Glenville, Nova Scotia
FOUNDED: 1990
OWNER/MANAGER: Lauchie MacLean
www.glenoradistillery.com

Situated in Nova Scotia, Glenora was the first malt whisky distillery in Canada. The first launch of in-house produce came in 2000 but a whisky called Kenloch had been sold before that. This was a 5 year old vatting of some of Glenora's own malt whisky and whisky from Bowmore Distillery on Islay. The first expression, a 10 year old, came in September 2000 and was named Glen Breton. Since then several expressions have been launched, among them single casks and sometimes under the name Glenora. A new expression, Glen Breton Ice (10 years old), the world's first single malt aged in an ice wine barrel, was launched in November 2006. Interest was massive and another release came onto the market in spring of 2007. In 2008 a 15 year old version was available from the distillery only. A 15 year old version of Glen Breton single malt was released under the name Battle of the Glen in June 2010. The release commemorated the distillery's victorious outcome of the ten year-long struggle with Scotch Whisky Association (see below).

Glenora's whisky has not been easy to obtain outside Canada, but exports currently go to countries such as the USA, Poland, Sweden, Switzerland, Spain and Singapore.

Since 2001 Glenora was been locked in a legal fight with Scotch Whisky Association (SWA) over the name of Glen Breton. The opinion of SWA is that the use of the word Glen is misleading and confusing for the customer and will make many believe that they are actually buying a Scotch whisky. The distillery, on the other hand, states that Glen is an established geographical name in this part of Canada. In 2007 the Trademarks Opposition Board in Ottawa ruled in favour of the distillery´s right to continue to sell the whisky under the name Glen Breton. SWA appealed and won in April 2008 when a Federal Court reversed the previous ruling. The next step was Glenora's appeal to Canada´s Federal Court of Appeal in December 2008 which ruled in favour of the distillery by January 2009. SWA decided not to give up but to petition the Supreme Court of Canada to overturn the Court of Appeal's decision. Finally, on 11 June 2009, the Supreme Court dismissed the application for a third appeal filed by SWA and, in November 2009, Glen Breton was entered as a registered mark on the Trademarks Register of Canada.

DISTILLERY: Victoria Spirits, Victoria (Vancouver Island), British Columbia
FOUNDED: 2008 (whisky since 2009)
OWNER/MANAGER: Bryan Murray
www.victoriaspirits.com

This family-run distillery actually has its roots in a winery called Winchester Cellars, founded by Ken Winchester back in 2002. Bryan Murray, the owner of Victoria Spirits, came in as an investor, but soon started to work with Ken on the distilling part of the business. Before Ken left the business in 2008, he took part in introducing Victoria Gin, which currently is the big-selling product with 10,000 bottles a year. The Murray family left the wine part of the business in order to increase the spirits role and the next product on the list was a single malt whisky. The first batch was distilled in late 2009 by Bryan´s son, Peter Hunt, using wash from a local brewery owned by Matt Phillips. The still is a 120 litre German-made copper pot-still fired by wood. The whisky will initially be matured in small casks (octaves) made of new American Oak, but old Bourbon barrels will also be used. Peter Hunt hopes to use Garry Oak (a.k.a. Oregon White Oak) for maturation in the future. This type of oak can be found from southern California up to British Columbia, but is especially abundant on Vancouver island. The first release is expected sometime in 2013 and the working name of the whisky is Craigdarroch.

Peter Hunt in the Victoria Spirits still house

DISTILLERY: Shelter Point Distillery, Vancouver
Island, British Columbia
FOUNDED: 2009
OWNER/MANAGER: Andrew Currie,
Jay Oddleifson, Patrick Evans
www.shelterpointdistillery.com

In September 2010, Shelter Point Distillery, just north of Co-mox on Vancouver Island, became the fourth Canadian distillery producing malt whisky. Andrew Currie, who co-founded Arran Distillery in Scotland 16 years ago, and Jay Oddleifson, a former accountant who was the CFO of Mount Washington Alpine Resort, are behind the project. The buildings were completed in 2009 and in May 2010 all the equipment was in place. That means a one ton mash tun, five washbacks made of stainless steel and one pair of stills (a 5,000 litre wash still and a 4,000 litre spirit still). Both stills and the spirit safe were made by Forsyth´s in Scotland. The yearly capacity is 92,000 litres of pure alcohol. Barley is grown on the estate and is expected to be used in the whisky production. In common with many other new established whisky distilleries, the first products will consist of spirits not requiring maturation, such as gin and vodka.

DISTILLERY: Pemberton Distillery, Pemberton,
British Columbia
FOUNDED: 2009 (whisky since 2010)
OWNER/MANAGER: Tyler Schramm
www.pembertondistillery.ca

This is one of the most recently established distilleries in Canada. Distilling started in July 2009, with vodka from potatoes being their first product. Almost 98% of all the vodkas of the world are made from grain and Tyler came up with the idea to use potatoes while studying brewing and distilling at the renowned Heriot-Watt University in Edinburgh. The organically grown potatoes are sourced locally, and the distillery itself, is a Certified Organic processing facility. Tyler uses a copper pot still from Arnold Holstein and the

first vodka, Schramm Vodka, was launched in August 2009. In June 2010, Tyler started his first trials, distilling a single malt whisky using organic malted barley from the Okanagan Valley. The first release of this whisky will probably not take place for another five years.

AUSTRALIA & NEW ZEALAND

Australia _____

DISTILLERY: Bakery Hill Distillery,
North Balwyn, Victoria
FOUNDED: 1998
OWNER/MANAGER: David Baker
www.bakeryhilldistillery.com.au

In 2008 Bakery Hill completed the installation of a 2,000 litre brewery and now has total control of all the processes from milling the grain to bottling the matured spirit. During 2009 the brewing part of the production was fine-tuned and Baker's evaluation was that the results were stunning. This, according to Baker, led to 2010 becoming a year of consolidation, to allow for focussing on making larger volumes and targeting more markets. The whisky has recently been introduced in France, Germany and Sweden. Apart from distillation, environmental adjustments and engineering were in focus last year. The distillery waste, spent grain and pot ale used to be disposed of, but are now sent to Yarra Valley to be used as stock feed and fertiliser. The next step on the green agenda will be using rainwater.

The still house of Shelter Point distillery

David Baker - Bakery Hill Distillery

The first spirit at Bakery Hill Distillery was produced in 2000 and the first single malt was launched in autumn 2003. Three different versions are available - Classic and Peated (both matured in ex-bourbon casks) and Double Wood (ex-bourbon and French Oak). As Classic and Peated are also available as cask strength bottlings, they can be considered two more varieties. The whisky is double-distilled in a copper pot still. All unpeated malt comes from an Australian maltster, while the malt for the peated version is imported from the UK.

With the Bakery Hill Distillery being situated about 25 km inland in the southern portion of Australia, the climate is very different to that of Scotland. The overall ambient temperatures are much higher while the air mass is much drier. These factors influence the rate of flavour development and whisky character, and David Baker is constantly experimenting with a wide variety of oak to find the optimal path.

DISTILLERY: Lark Distillery, Hobart, Tasmania
FOUNDED: 1992
OWNER/MANAGER: Bill Lark
www.larkdistillery.com.au

One can consider Bill Lark the father of the modern whisky distilling we see today in Australia. In 1992 he was the first person for 153 years to take out a distillation license in Tasmania. Since then he has not just established himself as a producer of malt whiskies of high quality but has also helped several new distilleries to start up. Recently he co-founded the Tasmanian Distillers Group together with the five other whisky distilleries on the island. But that is not all - in June 2009 he relocated to Scotland to help build the Kingsbarns Distillery in Fife!

Bill Lark's original establishment in Kingston was moved to Hobart in 2001. In 2006 a new distillery was constructed on a farm at Mt Pleasant, 15 minutes from Hobart. The farm grows barley for Cascade Brewery and at the moment that is where Lark Distillery gets its malt from. However, the intention is to set up own floor maltings within two years thereby enabling them to produce everything in-house, from barley field to bottle, at one site. Not only that - in 2004 they secured their own peat bog at Brown Marsh and in January 2007 they also purchased the cooperage that makes the barrels. All in all, they are now very much in control of the whole chain. The "old site" down in Hobart by the waterfront is now a showcase for the Lark whisky with a shop, café and whisky bar with over 100 different single malts.

The core product in the whisky range is the Single Cask Malt Whisky at 43% but Bill Lark has also released a Distillers Selection at 46% and a Cask Strength at 58%, both of which are also single cask. The range is completed by a malt whisky liqueur called Slainte and a Pure Malt Spirit at 45%. The latest release made its appearance at Whisky Live in Sydney in August 2010 when a single malt finished in dark rum was presented. The whisky is double-distilled in an 1,800 litre wash still and a 600 litre spirit still and then matured in 100 litre "quarter casks". The current production is 10-12 barrels per month.

Apart from whisky, Lark Distillery also produces Lark Bush, Pepperberry Vodka (triple distilled) and Apple Schnapps.

DISTILLERY: Hellyers Road Distillery, Burnie, Tasmania
FOUNDED: 1999
OWNER/MANAGER: Betta Milk Co-op/ Laurie House
www.hellyersroaddistillery.com.au

Hellyer's Road Distillery is the largest single malt whisky distillery in Australia. The capacity allows for 500 casks per year to be produced but there are also 2,500 200-litre casks in bond. The Tasmanian barley is malted at Cascade Brewery in Hobart and peat from Scotland is used for the peated

expressions. Batches of 6.5 tonnes of grist are loaded into the mash tun and then the wash is fermented for 65 hours. There is only one pair of stills but they compensate for numbers by size. The wash still has a capacity of 60,000 litres which is twice that of the largest wash still in Scotland at Glenkinchie Distillery. The spirit still's capacity is 30,000 litres and the interesting part here is the really slow distillation. The foreshots take around 4-5 hours and the middle cut will last for 24 hours, which is six to seven times longer compared to practice in Scotland. Maturation takes place in ex-bourbon casks but they also use Tasmanian red wine barrels for part of it.

There are three varieties of Hellyers Road Single Malt Whisky in the range: Original, Slightly Peated and Peated. There is also the premium expression Hellyers Road Distillers Choice which is available only to visitors who take the guided tour at the distillery.

The produce has, so far, only been sold in Australia but the vodka exports to the USA started in autumn 2009 and the first batches of whisky reached France in 2010.

DISTILLERY: Tasmania Distillery, Cambridge, Tasmania
FOUNDED: 1996
OWNER/MANAGER: Patrick Maguire
www.tasmaniadistillery.com

Three generations of whisky can trace its origin from Tasmania Distillery. The first was distilled between 1996 and 1998 and, according to the current owner Patrick Maguire, the quality is so poor that he does not want to bottle it. Instead, it has been sold to bakeries to be used in Christmas cakes and similar pastries and just a few barrels remain. The second generation was distilled from November 1999 to July 2001 and is bottled today under the name Sullivan's Cove. The third generation is the whisky distilled from 2003, until now under Patricks and his three partners' ownership, and will not be bottled until it has reached 12 years of age.

The range used to be made up of three different 7 year old whiskies - Sullivan's Cove cask strength (60%) matured in either bourbon casks or port casks and Sullivan's Cove Double Cask (40%) which is a marriage of port and bourbon casks. In May 2010, the distillery launched its first 10 year old versions of both the bourbon and the port matured. Tasmania distillery obtains wash from Cascade brewery located in Hobart, near to the distillery. Cascade is the only brewery in Australia to malt its own barley. The whisky is then double distilled, although there is only one still at the distillery. The model is of a French brandy design with a worm condenser attached. 12,000 litres of wash from Cascade make up one production run and it takes five wash runs and two spirit runs to complete the process. There is generally one production run every two weeks. Patrick has converted from steam heating the still to using electric elements, which in turn, makes it possible for him to run the still a little cooler and slower giving more control of the quality. Annual production amounts to 120 casks of 200 litres each of non chill-filtered whisky, which is matured in American Oak bourbon casks and French Oak port barrels.

Patrick recently bought a disused train tunnel, a few kilometres from the distillery, in which he shortly will stock all whisky and, perhaps, in a few years' time build a new distillery. The tunnel provides a cooler and more even temperature, not to be taken on lightly in this part of the world, where great differences in temperature occur during the year.

Following a number of awards, the rest of the world has now started to take an interest in the whisky, which is available in Scandinavia, Holland, Korea, Singapore, Taiwan, Hong-Kong, China and most recently, France, Belgium and Canada.

DISTILLERY: Great Southern Distilling Company, Albany, Western Australia
FOUNDED: 2004
OWNER/MANAGER: Great Southern Distilling Company Pty Ltd/Cameron Syme
www.distillery.com.au

This is the only whisky distillery in the western part of Australia. It was built in Albany on the south-western tip of Australia in 2004 with whisky production commencing in late 2005. Throughout the initial years production of whisky, brandy, vodka and gin took place in a set of sheds on the outskirts of Albany. A move was made in October 2007 to a new, custom-built distillery with a visitor centre on Princess Royal Harbour.

Production takes place in pot stills (one wash still of 1,900 litres and one spirit still of 580 litres) and a 600 litre copper pot antique gin still has also been installed. For maturation a mix of ex-bourbon, ex-house brandy and ex-sherry barrels are used as well as new and reshaved/charred American Oak and French Oak casks. Great Southern Vodkas and Gin have been available for sale since October 2006.

The first expression of the whisky, called Limeburners, was released in April 2008 with the second appearing a couple of months later. Both releases were single casks and non-chill filtered. Limeburner single malt whisky releases are named M for malt with a unique barrel number. To date M3, M4, M5, M9, M11, M15, M19 and M24 have been released, either at 43% or 63% barrel strength. There are plans for other varieties including a peated version, using peat from local peat bogs. The first peated expression went into barrel in August 2008.

DISTILLERY: Nant Distillery, Bothwell, Tasmania
FOUNDED: 2007
OWNER/MANAGER: Keith Batt
www.nantdistillery.com.au

Nant distillery, in Bothwell in the Central Highlands of Tasmania, started when Queensland businessman, Keith Batt, bought the property in 2004. He embarked on refurbishing the Historic Sandstone Water Mill on the Estate that was built in 1823 and converted it into a whisky distillery. The first distillation took place on 5th April 2008. Keith´s idea is to manage the whole production process on site. Barley has been grown on the estate since 1821 and continues to this day. On the Estate there was also a 180 year old water-driven flour mill which is now

The first release from Nant Distillery, July 2010

used for grinding the barley into grist. Keith plans to start with floor malting on the site in the near future and peat from the original Nant summer highland grazing property, Lake Echo, will be used in the malting process. The distillery is equipped with a 1,800 litre wash still and a 600 litre spirit still and wooden washbacks are used for the fermentation. Keith uses quarter casks of 100 litres, previously used for port, sherry and bourbon, for maturation. The capacity of the distillery is about three hundred 100-litres barrels per year.

In summer of 2010 the first bottlings from the distillery saw the light of day. The release was split into two different styles - the Blood Tub series with five individual bottlings at 43% from five different 20 litre casks that had previously contained port and a Double Wood bottling, with maturation both in French Oak port casks and American Oak sherry.

DISTILLERY: Victoria Valley Distillery, Essendon Fields, Melbourne, Victoria
FOUNDED: 2008
OWNER/MANAGER: David Vitale, Lark Distillery m fl
www.victoriavalley.com.au

This is the very latest distillery to come on stream in Australia. Co-founder, Managing Director and Head Distiller is David Vitale who previously worked with sales and marketing at Lark Distilleries in Tasmania. Bill Lark from the aforementioned distillery has also taken part in the start-up of Victoria Valley. The owner is still looking for a final location for the production but settled for an interim site at Essendon Fields, Melbourne´s original airport. The distillery is actually fitted into an old Qantas maintenance hangar. The stills (an 1,800 litre wash still and a 600 litre spirit still) were bought from Joadja Creek Distillery in Mittagong and contribute to an initial capacity of 20,000 cases of whisky in a year. The target is to increase to 50,000 cases in the future.

David is planning to produce three types of whisky - a single malt, an American-style bourbon and an Australian-style whisky that will provide a clear point of difference. Part of the whisky will mature in Pedro Ximinez sherry butts of which David has already ordered 250. The first products will be ready to launch in October 2011.

DISTILLERY: Old Hobart Distillery Blackmans Bay, Tasmania
FOUNDED: 2007
OWNER/MANAGER: Casey Overeem

This distillery in Tasmania (previously known as Overeem Distillery) came on stream in 2007. By summer 2007 four barrels (100 litres) had been produced and the distillery will continue to produce at least two barrels per month. The omnipresent Bill Lark (see Lark distillery) has also assisted here. The two stills (wash still of 1,800 litres and spirit still of 600 litres) were made by the Hobart still maker Knapp-Lewer. The spirit is matured in casks that have previously contained either port or sherry. Overeem´s plan is to release the first bottlings when they have reached the age of four years, i.e. sometime in 2011.

DISTILLERY: Timboon Railway Shed Distillery, Timboon, Victoria
FOUNDED: 2007
OWNER/MANAGER: Tim Marwood
www.timboondistillery.com

The small town of Timboon (circa 1500 inhabitants) lies 200 kilometres southwest of Melbourne. Here Tim Marwood established his combination of a distillery and a restaurant in 2007 in a renovated railway goods shed, hence the name. Using a pilsner malted barley, Marwood obtains the wash

(1,000 litres at a time) from the local Red Duck microbrewery. The wash is then distilled twice in a 600 litre pot still. It is made by Knapp Lewer in Hobart with a Macallan spirit still as a model. For maturation, resized (20 litres) and retoasted ex-port, tokay and bourbon barrels are used. At the moment, Tim has approximately 1,600 litres of spirit maturing. In June 2010 the first release was made.

The distillery also produces vodka, limoncello and schnapps.The whisky-making tradition dates back to the late 1800s in Timboon, when an illicit still was operated by Tom Delaney, who produced the legendary Mountain Dew.

New Zealand

DISTILLERY: New Zealand Malt Whisky Co, Oamaru, South Island
FOUNDED: 2000
OWNER/MANAGER: Warren Preston
www.nzmaltwhisky.co.nz
www.milfordwhisky.co.nz

It seems that we will have to wait a bit longer for New Zealand`s first proper malt whisky distillery to come on stream. New Zealand Malt Whisky Co was evicted from its premises in Oamaru in February 2010 and one month later the company was placed in receivership with a debt of NZ$3 million.

In 2001, Warren Preston bought the entire stock of single malt and blended whisky from decommissioned Wilsons Willowbank Distillery in Dunedin. The supplies Preston acquired consisted of, among other things, 400 casks of single malt whisky including production dating back to 1987. Before he bought it, the whisky was sold under the name Lammerlaw, but Preston renamed it Milford. There have been 10, 12, 15, 18 and 20 year bottlings. Due to the company entering into receivership, it is now unclear who actually owns the remaining stock of Milford.

Preston's long-term objective was to establish a whisky distillery at a highland property near Queenstown at Nevis Bluff on the Kawaru River. He was granted a 5 year consent in 2007 from the local authorities to build a boutique distillery. In August 2009, however, the site was offered for sale at an auction. Preston had decided it would make more sense to build the distillery adjacent to the existing warehouses in Oamaru with a plan to start distilling in 2009.

ASIA

India

DISTILLERY: McDowell's, Ponda, Goa
FOUNDED: 1988 (malt whisky)
OWNER/MANAGER: UB Group
www.clubmcdowell.com

In 1826 the Scotsman Angus McDowell established himself as an importer of wines, spirits and cigars in Madras (Chennai) and the firm was incorporated in 1898. In the same town another Scotsman, Thomas Leishman, founded United Breweries in 1915. Both companies were bought by Vital Mallya around 1950 and today United Breweries (in which the spirits division consists of United Spirits) is the second largest producer of alcohol in the world after Diageo. Vijay Mallya, the son of Vital, is acting as chairman since 1983.

United Spirits dominates the Indian spirits market of which it has a share of 60%. In the fiscal year ending March 2010, sales of just over 100 million cases of spirit could be reported compared to 90 million the previous year. Since 2009 another brand has made it into the so-called Millionaire's Club to which brands that sell more than 1 million nine-litre cases per year belong. It was Bagpiper Rum and United Spirits now has 20 brands on that list.

The major brands in the group are huge sales-wise. Bagpiper blended whisky is the world's best-selling whisky with more than 16 million cases sold in 2009/2010. McDowell's No 1 is one of the fastest growing whiskies in the world. It sold almost 15 million cases in 2009/2010 compared to 2.5 million 10 years ago. Single malt sales are, of course, negligible compared to these figures. McDowell's Single Malt is made at the distillery in Ponda (Goa) and sells some 20,000 cases each year. It has matured for 3-4 years in ex-bourbon casks. McDowell's launched the world's first diet whisky, McDowell's No.1 Diet Mate, in 2006. It is a blend of whisky and the herb, garcinia, which increases the rate of metabolism. In 2007 United Spirits Limited acquired the Scottish whisky-maker, Whyte & Mackay, (with, inter alia, Whyte & Mackay blend and Dalmore, Jura and Fettercairn distilleries) for £595m.

DISTILLERY: Amrut Distilleries Ltd., Bangalore
FOUNDED: 1948
OWNER/MANAGER: Jagdale Group
www.amrutdistilleries.com
www.amrutwhisky.co.uk

The family-owned distillery, based in Bangalore, south India, started to distil malt whisky in the mid-eighties. More than 6 million litres of sprits (including rum, gin and vodka) is manufactured a year, of which 1 million litres is whisky. Most of the whisky goes to blended brands, but Amrut single malt can be bought outside of India since 2004. It was first introduced in Scotland, can now be found in more than 20 countries and has recently been introduced to the American market. In 2009 total sales on the export market were 5,000 cases, an increase of more than 40% compared to the previous year.

Two Continents and the new Intermediate Sherry Matured from Amrut

The distillery is equipped with two pairs of stills, each with a capacity of 5,000 litres. The barley is sourced from the north of India, malted in Jaipur and Delhi and finally distilled in Bangalore. The small amount of peated malt that is used comes from Inverness. Ex bourbon casks are most commonly used for maturation, but sherry casks and casks made of new oak can also be found in the warehouse. The whisky is bottled without chill-filtering or colouring. The conditions for maturation differ much from the Scottish environment. The temperature in the summer is close to 40° C and it rarely falls below 20° C in winter. Hence the much larger evaporation, between 10-16% per year.

The Amrut family of single malts has grown and has seven official expressions today; unpeated and peated versions bottled at 46%, one cask strength (released in 2006), a peated cask strength (first released in 2008), Amrut Fusion which is based on 25% peated malt from Scotland and 75% unpeated Indian malt and, finally, Amrut Two Continents, where maturing casks have been brought from India to Scotland for their final period of maturation. The most recent addition is a lmited edition called Intermediate Sherry Matured, which means that the new spirit has matured in ex-bourbon or virgin oak, then re-racked to sherry butts and with a third, and final, maturation ex-bourbon casks. This was launched end of September 2010 through La Maison du Whisky in Paris.

Pakistan

DISTILLERY: Murree Brewery Ltd., Rawalpindi
FOUNDED: 1860
OWNER/MANAGER: Bhandara family
www.murreebrewery.com

Murree Brewery in Rawalpindi started as a beer brewery supplying the British Army. The assortment was completed with whisky, gin, rum, vodka and brandy. Three single malts have been available for some time; 3, 8 and 12 years respectively. In 2005 an 18 year old single malt was launched and the following year their oldest expression so far, a 20 year old, reached the market. There are also a number of blended whiskies such as Vat No. 1, Lion and Dew of Himalaya.

Company sources mention a supply of half a million litres of whisky in underground storage. The brewery makes its own malt (using both floor maltings and Saladin box) and produces 2.6 million litres of beer every year and, ap-

proximately, 440,000 litres of whisky. Total annual sales in 2008/2009 amounted to Rs. 2,3 billion ($28 million). Murree Brewery consists of three divisions – the liquor division (responsible for 70% of income and almost 100% of the profit), Tops division (mainly fruit juices) and a glass division (which manufactures glass containers for the company and other customers).

Taiwan

DISTILLERY: Yuan Shan Distillery, Yuanshan,
              Yilan County
FOUNDED: 2005
OWNER/MANAGER: King Car Food Industrial Co.
www.kavalanwhisky.com

The first whisky distillery in Taiwan lies in the north-eastern part of the country, in Yilan County, just one hour from Taipei. The area is flat between two mountain ranges and it was built in record time with construction lasting just eight months. The first distillation took place on 11th March 2006.

The distillery is divided into two units, with the first completed in 2006. It is equipped with a semi-lauter stainless steel mash tun with copper top and eight closed stainless steel washbacks with a 60 hour fermentation time. The malted barley is imported with Baird's of Inverness as the main supplier. There are two pairs of lantern-shaped copper stills with descending lye pipes. The capacity of the wash stills is 12,000 litres and of the spirit stills 7,000 litres. After 10-15 minutes of foreshots, the heart of the spirit run takes 2-3 hours. The cut points differ from what is common in Scotland. To capture the sweetness (important to the Chinese consumers), collecting starts at 78% and stops already at 72%. The extreme cut points are also determined by the climate and the quick maturation. The spirit vapours are cooled using tube condensers but due to the hot climate, subcoolers are also used. The total capacity of this unit is 1.3 million litres per year.

The second unit of the distillery was completed in 2008 and consists of a full lauter Steinecker mash tun, 12 stainless steel washbacks and eight Holstein stills. The stills function, unusually enough, in pairs and two pairs have rectification columns with four plates, while the other two pairs have

Yuan Shan Distillery in Taiwan - home of Kavalan Single Mat

seven plates. This unit, with a 2.6 million litre capacity, is used for spirits other than whisky and for experimentation. The warehouse is five stories high with the first four floors palletised and the top floor more of a traditional dunnage warehouse. The casks are tied together four and four due to the earthquake risk and also the pallets are bound together. The climate in Taiwan is very hot and humid and on the top floors of the warehouse the temperature can reach 42° C. Hence the angel´s share is quite dramatic - no less than 15% is lost every year. The warehouse harbours 30,000 casks and there is a need for more warehousing capacity within the near future. The ideal solution would be to build up in the cooler mountains, but in order to do that, the legislation must be changed, as warehousing must currently be in close proximity to the production plant. The whisky matures mainly in ex bourbon barrels and ex sherry casks with a few other types used for experimentation.

There is also an impressive visitor centre on site. No less than one million visitors come here per annum, which is roughly the same number as all Scottish distilleries' visitor centres together.

The first release of Kavalan (as the whisky from the distillery is called) was in December 2008 and this is now the core expression. In July 2009, a port finish version called Concertmaster appeared and then in August, two different single casks were launched - one ex-bourbon and one ex-Oloroso sherry, both bottled at cask strength. A third single cask, this time from a Fino cask, was released just in time for Chinese New Year in 2010. The recipe of the Classic Kavalan is quite complex and includes six different types of casks - fresh bourbon, fresh sherry, refill bourbon, red wine casks from Spain and two different white wine casks from Portugal. The most important market is primarily mainland China, but it is possible that the whisky will be exported to other destinations in the near future.

Kavalan Concertmaster - a port cask finish

The owning company, King Car Group, with 2,000 employees, was already founded in 1956 and runs businesses in several fields; biotechnology and aquaculture, among others. It is also famous for its canned coffee, Mr. Brown, which is also exported to Europe.

Turkey

DISTILLERY: Tekel (Mey Corporation), Ankara
FOUNDED: 1930 (whisky since 1963)
OWNER/MANAGER: Texas Paficic Group (TPG)
www.mey.com.tr

Both production and sales of tobacco and alcohol in Turkey have been administered by the national company Tekel, which also has a salt division. A change in legislation in 2001 opened a window for privatization and the wine and spirits division was sold to four companies, Nurol, Limak, Özaltin and Tütsab, in 2004 for $292 million. They formed a holding company, Mey Industry & Trade to market and distribute the products but kept the company name Tekel. In 2006 Mey Corporation was sold to the American Texas Pacific Group for $900 million.

There is a large range of beverages, mainly consisting of wine and raki, but vodka, gin, 'cognac' and whisky are also included. The company has produced a whisky named Ankara Turk Viskisi since 1963. It can probably not be called a single malt as it is reported to contain a portion of malted rye and rice mixed with malted barley. The whisky is aged for three years on oak casks.

AFRICA

South Africa

DISTILLERY: James Sedgwick Distillery, Wellington, Western Cape
FOUNDED: 1886 (whisky production 1990)
OWNER/MANAGER: Distell Group Ltd.
www.distell.co.za

Owners Distell Group Ltd. was formed in 2000 by a merger between Stellenbosch Farmers' Winery (founded 1925) and Distillers Corporation (founded 1945,) although the James Sedgwick Distillery was already founded in 1886. The company produces a huge range of wines and spirits. One of the most successful brands was introduced in 1989 - Amarula Cream, today the second best-selling cream liqueur in the world.

The James Sedgwick Distillery has been the home to South African whisky since 1990. The distillery is currently under major expansion in order to enable it to continue meeting the growing demand for whisky in South Africa. After the expansion, the distillery is equipped with one still with two columns for production of grain whisky, two pot stills for malt whisky and one still with six columns designated for neutral spirit (re-distillation of feints etc. from other processes). There are also two mash tuns and 23 washbacks. Grain whisky is distilled for nine months of the year, malt whisky for two (always during the winter months July/August) and one month is devoted to maintenance. The barley for the

malt whisky is imported from UK maltsters.

The distillery's line of blended whiskies is huge: Three Ships Select, Three Ships Premium Select 5 years, Three Ships Bourbon Cask Finish (the first 100% South African blended whisky), Harrier and Knights, which all together amount to circa 7 million bottles a year. In the autumn of 2003 Three Ships 10 year old, South Africa's first single malt whisky, was launched in a limited edition of 6,000 bottles. After that nothing happened but on the 26 October 2010 it was relaunched.

James Sedgwick distillery has the capability of producing both malt and grain whisky and last year produced yet another first for South Africa. A "single grain" whisky was released under the name Bain's Cape Mountain Whisky. It is double matured in the same style of cask and, although it has no age statement, it is matured for a minimum of five years.

Andy Watts, originally hailing from Yorkshire, became the manager of James Sedgwick Distillery in 1991, after having spent time working on Auchentoshan, Glen Garioch and Bowmore distilleries in Scotland.

DISTILLERY: Drayman's Distillery, Silverton, Pretoria
FOUNDED: 2006
OWNER/MANAGER: Moritz Kallmeyer
www.draymans.com

Being a full-time beer brewer since 1997, Moritz Kallmeyer began distilling malt whisky in July 2006. Until now, production has been small (one cask of 225 litres a month), but operations have currently been expanded to two pot stills.

The distillery already sells whisky that is bought from Scotland, blended and solera-matured at Drayman's. He calculates a first release of his own whisky sometime in 2010 of about 4,000 bottles. This version will be unpeated, distilled exclusively from South African dry-land barley malt from the Swartland area. It will be aged in used red wine barrels (Pinotage and Cabernet) of European Oak origin. Kallmeyer has for most of the time, apart from brewing craft beers, also produced Mampoer, a local and for South Africa a very typical brandy. He also has plans for a Polish style vodka distilled from potatoes in order to maintain cash flow in the company.

The biggest obstacle for owners of micro-distilleries is often capital. Creativity and innovation are essential traits to possess, especially when it comes to equipping the distillery.

At Drayman's there is a new wash still (1,500 litres) but the spirit still (800 litres) was cleverly reconstructed from a stainless steel tank in which perfume was imported. Kallmeyer let a local welder rebuild it and then connected it by himself to a column still. He also believes in letting the wash spend a long time in the washback, often up to ten days, to allow the malolactic fermentation to transfer its character to the spirit.

Kallmeyer is also, together with property lawyer, As Botha, involved in a new whisky venture called Hatherley Agri Estate. The estate lies in Mpumalanga province 80 km northeast of Pretoria. The concept consists of a whisky distillery and boutique beer house on a working farm, with the development of a residential component consisting of 575 residential units. A distillery with a capacity of 350,000 litres of alcohol per year (20 mashes per week) is also planned. The project is yet in its infancy, with Kallmeyer and Botha looking for financial investors and the plan is that 2014 will see the start of the construction. When the distillery opens, it will not be the first on the estate, as Paul Kruger already established Hatherley Distillery there in 1883, producing whisky and gin.

Moritz Kallmeyer - owner of Drayman's Distillery

James Sedgwick Distillery

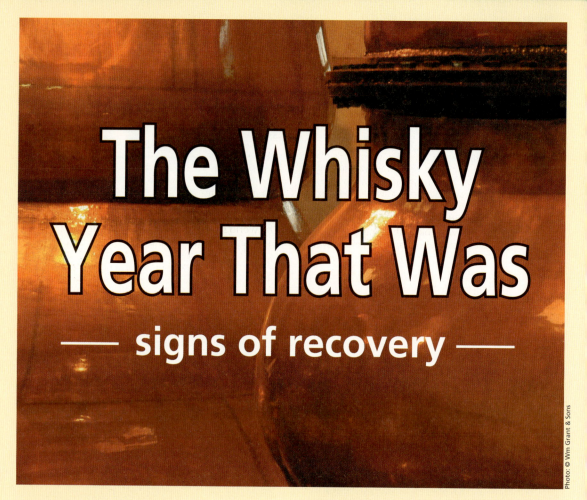

The Whisky Year That Was

—— signs of recovery ——

Sales of Scotch whisky
- slowing down but still increasing!

The Scotch whisky industry continued, albeit with some difficulty, defying the economic downturn that started in 2008. The first three months of 2009 saw the trade de-stocking and weaker confidence among the consumers. Much of the previous decrease was gained during the second quarter, and in the final six months exports rose to make 2009 another record year for Scotch whisky. In 2008 whisky exports broke the £3 billion barrier for the first time and in 2009 it increased by 3% to £3.13 billion. Volumes also increased by 4% to the equivalent of 1.1 billion 70 cl bottles. So does this mean that whisky exports were unaffected by the recession? Not quite, despite values going up by 3%, they increased by 8% in 2008 and by 14% in 2007, so it is obvious that the pace of increase has slowed due to the harsher economic climate. It remains to be seen if the figures will also be increasing in 2010. During the last 30 years, there have only been three years when the value of Scotch whisky export has fallen - 1983, 1998 and 2004.

The picture for 2009, if broken down into malt and blends, is as follows (note that bulk shipments are not included):

BOTTLED MALT - EXPORT
Value: +1% to £502m
Volume: -10.4% to 64.5m bottles

BOTTLED BLENDED SCOTCH - EXPORT
Value: +3% to £2.50bn
Volume: +4.2% to 884m bottles

Not surprisingly, the single malts, which are more expensive, took a tougher beating in 2009 compared to the more affordable blended whiskies. Still, the export value did increase by 1% even though volumes slipped by 10%. Apparently, the producers can squeeze more money out of a bottle of single malt than they could a couple of years ago. If we look at the ratio value/volume, i. e. how much money the exporters get for one bottle, we can see that since 2006 a bottle of single malt has increased in export value by no less than 45% while a bottle of blended Scotch has increased by 12%. Even though fewer bottles are sold, each bottle costs more, so obviously in times of crisis like these, there will still be consumers who are unaffected by the downturn and who can afford the more expensive brands.
The most important market in terms of value is still

the US. During 2009 exports to it increased by 13%, in contrast to the previous year's 11% decrease. The total value is now £419m. Also Mexico showed strong figures with an increase in value by 25% even if that pales in significance when comparing to the previous year's 59% increase.

The most impressive figures for 2009 can be found In Central and South America. Venezuela, for example, increased 73% by value and 77% by volume and is now the sixth largest consumer of Scotch whisky. Brazil is not far behind with an increase in value of 44% in 2009. One should remember that conditions in South America are volatile which Venezuela's decrease by 36% the previous year shows. The absolute majority of Scotch exported to these countries consists of blended whiskies, while single malts make up a very small part. If we look at the whole region, the increase by value was 18%, the best performance of all regions in 2009, and, together with North America, it was the only region that showed growth compared to 2008. In absolute figures though, it is still number four after Europe, Asia and North America.

Asia, the second biggest market for Scotch after Europe, was a disappointment in 2009 with a decrease of 9% in terms of value. If we look at volumes, three of the top six countries decreased: Thailand (-29%), South Korea (-12%) and China (-12%), while the other three increased, Taiwan (+21%), India (+10%) and Singapore (+6%). Singapore is number one of Asian countries with a total import of 14.5 million litres of alcohol but, as we have pointed out before, this figure does not say anything about consumption. The vast majority of the shipments to Singapore are re-exported to China as many of the big producers use Singapore as a hub.

In Africa the figures by value were up 6% to a total of £150m. 72% of this concerns South Africa, which is the eighth largest market for Scotch whisky in terms of value and the fifth in terms of volume. In the Australasian region (read Australia, which stands for 90% of the total) export by value increased by 3% compared to a 32% increase in 2008.

Last, but not least, Europe remains the biggest market for Scotch whisky. With a total value of £1.26bn it equals North America, Asia, Africa and Australasia combined. It was one of two regions (Asia being the other) where sales slipped, albeit only by 1%, in 2009. Bottled single malts were hit most severely as volumes dropped by 25% compared to 2008 and the figures are now down at 2004 levels. It went better for bottled blends, which decreased by only 5%. As always, Europe turns up a heterogeneous region when breaking down the numbers into single countries. First, we have the biggest consumer of Scotch whisky in the world, France, where the export value for the first time surpassed the £400m barrier (+13% to £407m). Total volumes increased by 12% to the equivalent of 179 million bottles. Bottled malts fell by 20% and malts shipped in bulk (+32%) are now bigger than the bottled category.

The second place in Europe has alternated between Spain and the UK during the last decade. UK managed to come second in 2009 despite a volume decrease of 11%. Spain lost even more, almost 15%, due to a falling economy even if total value managed a little better (-5%). The Spanish market is very much about blended whiskies and only 2% of the total Scotch market there is made up of malt whiskies. That can be compared to the global total where the single malt ratio is 10%, in Germany 7% and in countries like Germany and Italy 16% and 20% respectively. Apart from France, very few markets in Europe managed to grow in 2009. Poland and Sweden were two of them. It remains to be seen if the sluggish economy of the Mediterranean countries will continue to keep volumes down also in 2010.

The big players

Diageo
The world's largest drinks company's figures for the fiscal year ending 30th June 2010 hinted that the market is slowly, but steadily, about to turn. Net sales rose by 2% to £9.78bn and operating profit also increased organically by 2% to £2.75bn. When looking at single brands it becomes clear that the second half of the fiscal year (January-June) was a great improvement for sales. Johnnie Walker, for example, decreased its volume by 11% during the full year 2009, while it instead increased by 11% if one follows Diageo's fiscal year. Black Label was responsible for a large share of the increase in, especially, South America and south-east Asia. The company's second largest Scotch blend brand, J&B, on the contrary, decreased by 7%, which to a great deal can be explained by the sluggish market in Spain.

While Asia is a market where Pernod Ricard dominates (when looking at the international companies), the same can be said for Diageo and South America. Especially Johnnie Walker, but also Buchanan Scotch blend, is in the lead as regards the growth in Venezuela, Brazil and Mexico and net sales in the region increased by 15%. If we look at the Diageo global priority brands that are not whisky, Smirnoff, Baileys, José Cuervo and Guinness all saw slipping sales. The only convincing brand was Captain Morgan rum.

When it comes to possible acquisitions it will be interesting to keep an eye on Diageo. Of the three leading companies it is undoubtedly Diageo that possesses the greatest war chest.

Pernod Ricard
For quite some time now, Pernod Ricard has been the second largest drinks company after Diageo. This year, however, Indian United Spirits announced that they had surpassed the French company in terms of volume, i. e. cases sold.

For the full year ending 30 June 2010, Pernod Ricard showed declining sales figures with net sales slipping 2% to €7.08bn. On the other hand, if one excludes the effect of unfavourable currency rates, like-for-like sales actually increased by 2%. Net profits were up by 1% to €951m but again, not counting exchange rates' impact, net sales increased by 7%. As for Diageo, strength was shown during January to June. The financial burden on the company has been great since the acquisition of V&S two years ago and great effort has been made to decrease the debts. Total debt was reduced by €1bn during the year and

sales of further brands have not been ruled out in order to decrease it.

Most of the Top 14 brands (corresponding to 55% of the company's sales) were in the black with Jameson Irish whiskey as the shining star at a 12% increase, while Glenlivet (+7%) and Chivas Regal (+5%) increased at a slower rate. Ballantine´s blended Scotch decreased by 4%. The geographical markets show similarities to the business as a whole, i. e. a rebound in Russia and South Korea, reasonably good figures for the USA and declining sales in Western Europe, especially in Spain and Greece.

United Spirits

United Spirits Limited, part of the Indian UB Group, have their objective set to become the world's largest spirits company in terms of volume. Sales' volumes increased with 13% to 100.2 million cases in 2009 and the company declared that it had overtaken the number two on the list, Pernod Ricard. The next goal is to overtake Diageo, today selling 113 million cases, before March 2011. The company says it is confident to reach that position with more than 100 million Indian consumers entering the legal drinking age in the next five years.

Large volumes are important for the Indian company and there was reason to rejoice when a whisky of their own was established as the number one in the world in 2009. Bagpiper sold 16.2 million cases during 2009 while Johnnie Walker only managed to reach 14.5 million. It should be noted that while the volumes are bigger, in terms of global revenue, Johnnie Walker is still six to seven times bigger than Bagpiper.

Net sales for United Spirits for the fiscal year ending March 2010, were up almost 20% to Rs. 49.6bn. Net profits for the same period increased by no less than 35% to Rs. 4.01bn. During the year, Bagpiper rum became the company's 20th "millionaire brand", i. e. a brand selling over one million cases in a year. The company also announced that they were not shunning overseas acquisitions in the near future. The Far East and Africa were specifically mentioned as interesting areas.

In 2007, United Spirits entered the Scotch whisky market for the first time when Whyte & Mackay was acquired for £595m. Four malt distilleries (Dalmore, Isle of Jura, Fettercairn and Tamnavulin), a bottling plant and stocks of 115 million litres were included in the deal.

Morrison Bowmore

In 2008, Morrison Bowmore (owner of Bowmore, Auchentoshan and Glen Garioch distilleries) saw sales slip by 7% but for 2009 it managed to turn that around to an increase of 6% to £39.3m. Part of the increase is due to the terrific 12% growth of Bowmore single malt. Pre-tax profits also increased by 7% to £3.8m which was not as much as the previous year's 13%. One reason therefore may have been the new agreement with Drambuie Liqueur Company to provide Drambuie with supply chain services covering whisky procurement, blending, bottling, warehousing and logistics. 2009 saw a lot of investments preparing for the different services

Photo: © Edrington Group

Edrington´s CEO, Ian Curle, was pleased with last year´s results

but the actual production of Drambuie did not start until early 2010. It is said that 4 million bottles of the whisky liqueur will be produced per year at the Springburn plant near Glasgow.

Edrington

Last year the Edrington Group showed extraordinary increases in both sales and profit right in the middle of the economic turmoil. That time, figures were boosted by the purhase of Brugal rum. When CEO Ian Curle announced this year´s result (for the year ending March 2010) he still had reasons to be pleased. The group´s turnover was up by 11.5% to £468m and profits before tax soared by 25% to £118.6m. Of the brands, Macallan was the star and managed to gain market shares compared to the other single malts on the Top Five list. It is number three on that list in terms of volume but according to Edrington it has surpassed Glenlivet in terms of value and is now number two. Sales of other key brands like Famous Grouse, Highland Park and Brugal were also satisfying but in spite of these good figures, Ian Curle prefers to be careful in his approach.

"We remain confident about the long term growth prospects for premium authentic spirits brands, however, the board remains cautious in its view of trading prospects in the short to medium term, due to challenging market conditions, especially in Europe." The purchase of Cutty Sark from Berry Brothers was completed in April (read more on page 242).

LVMH

LVMH Moët Hennessy Louis Vuitton SA is the world's leading luxury goods vendor. It provides products ranging from champagne and perfumes to designer handbags and jewellery. The Wines & Spirits business group includes brands such as Moët & Chandon Champagne and Hennessy Cognac with Glenmorangie and Ardbeg as representatives of Scotch whisky.

In spite of the severe economic downturn, LVMH showed good resilience in Europe and continued to grow on the Asian market. For the fiscal year of 2009, total turnover decreased but only with 1% to €17,053m. Wines & Spirits declined by 12% which now makes it only the fourth largest business area with a revenue of €2,740m. In terms of profit, however, it comes in as number two after Fashion with a 2009 profit of €760m, a 28% decrease compared to 2008. The profit for the whole group decreased by 8% to €3,352m.

The decline of cognac and champagne that set in during 2008 continued in 2009. LVMH's sales of champagne have since 2007 decreased by 22%. The corresponding figures for cognac is -10% while whisky has fared better (see Glenmorangie below).

Glenmorangie Company

The owner of Glenmorangie and Ardbeg distilleries is in a phase of transition and it is difficult to compare results from 2008 to those of 2009 without looking at recent changes. Pre-tax profits for the year ending in December 2009 dropped to £12.7m compared to £39.3m in 2008. Then one has to remember that in 2008 there was a large, one-off, gain from the sale of Glen Moray distillery, as well as sales of bulk whisky stocks which augmented financial results. Net sales also declined in 2009 to £73.1m against £112.6m in 2008. One reason for that was the decision by the company to withdraw from the low margin blended whisky market in connection with selling Glen Moray to La Martiniquaise. The only brands retained in the company are Bailie Nicol Jarvie and Martin's.

Glenmorangie recently sold their Broxburn facility, including head office and bottling plant, to Diageo. In 2009 a new site for the bottling plant was chosen at the Alba Business Park in Livingston, West Lothian. The 11-acre site was ready in summer of 2010. Meanwhile it found a place for the new head-quarters at The Cube in the east end of Edinburgh.

Ian Macleod Distillers

One of the largest family-owned companies in the UK spirits industry, Ian Macleod Distillers, act as distiller (Glengoyne distillery), blender and independent bottler. The latest available report for the year ending 30 September 2009 shows an impressive turnover increase by 18% to £26m. Profit after tax was up 90% to £2.2m. The company produces and sells 15 million bottles of spirits in a year, of which 10 million bottles are whisky and the rest are divided between gin, rum and vodka. Glengoyne single malt was responsible for 480,000 bottles of whisky totals.

Fortune Brands

The American company with its headquarter in

Photo: © Ian MacLeod Distillers

Peter Russel (Chairman) and Leonard Russel (Managing Director) can reflect on a good year for IanMacleod Distillers

Deerfield, Illinois is active in three different business areas; Home & Security, Golf and Spirits. The latter is contained within subsidiary Beam Global Spirits & Wine, which has major spirits brands such as Jim Beam, Maker's Mark, Canadian Club, Courvoisier and, in Scotch, Teacher's and Laphroaig. A recent addition to the line-up is Cruzan rum.

The diversity of the company's business activities has made it difficult to maintain a decent growth in recent years. Like last year, and the year before, total sales slipped in 2009 by 12% to $6.69bn. Home & Security and Golf went down (20% and 11% respectively) while Beam Global just decreased by 0.5% to $2.47bn.

The net income for the whole company decreased by 22% to $243m. Beam Global is still the trump card contributing more than 80% of the operating income. Cruzan rum, in particular, was strong with a double-digit growth, while the bourbon segment and Scotch showed smaller increases. One exception was the newly introduced Jim Beam Red Stag, a cherry-infused version of the flagship brand. Courvoisier made out poorest with a double-digit decrease. Like so many of the other big blended Scotch brands, volumes of Teacher's slipped during 2009. It finally ended up with 1.8 million sold cases (down 9%). Even Laphroaig lost during 2009 with 171,000 cases (down 7%). Part of the problem for Laphroaig is, according to the owners, inventory issues and the single malt is sold on allocation. The owners count on starting to increase volumes again from 2010.

Gruppo Campari

After a quiet and uneventful 2008 with a net profit increase by just 1%, the owners of Glen Grant, Italian Davide Campari-Milano, can look back at a considerably better 2009. Sales increased by 7% to €1,008m but organic growth, however, was down by 1%. The reason for increased sales was the acquisition of Wild Turkey in May 2009, which significantly impacted the full year result. Net profits increased by 8% and reached €137m.

The company is divided into three divisions - spirits, wines and soft drinks, where spirits make up 74% of total sales. Apart from Wild Turkey, Ouzo 12 showed good results (+7%) as well as the low-alcohol aperitif Aperol (+40%). On the other side of the scale were Campari (-7%) and Glen Grant (-4%). The Italian market, where Glen Grant is market leader, has been sluggish but in spite of decreasing sales the brand managed to gain market shares.

The big brands

For the last two years, the market for whisky has proven very volatile due to the economic climate. Most of the top brands took a beating in 2009. The winners on the other hand can be found among the less expensive brands, especially in the blended Scotch segment. Clan Campbell and William Lawson´s both grew their sales volumes, but the real winners are a handful of low-priced brands with a strong following, especially in France - William Peel, Label 5 and Sir Edward´s. These whiskies, produced in Scotland but more or less unknown to most of the whisky drinkers of the world, sell between 1 and 3 million cases per year!

Amongst single malts, the top 5 remain the same for the last couple of years with Glenfiddich at the top. However, during 2009 sales dropped to 874,000 cases while the figures improved for number 2, Glenlivet, showing an increase to 612,000 cases. For the past few years Glenlivet has approached Glenfiddich

and its long-term goal is to take over as number one. Macallan is number three, selling well over 500,000 cases a year while number four and five, Glen Grant and Glenmorangie, sell around 300,000 cases per year.

The blended Scotch category also has an obvious number one but Johnnie Walker dominates even more than Glenfiddich. Despite a loss of 11% during 2009, the brand sells almost 15 million cases in a year. This should be compared to the number two, Ballantine´s, with merely 6 million cases. Rankings three to five are held by Jim Beam and Grant´s, selling just below 5 million cases, and Chivas Regal with around 4 million cases. The sales from these five decreased in 2009, some of them even showed double digit losses.

India and China
- the future for Scotch whisky?

The two most densely populated countries in the world have been assumed by many analysts to be the incomparable largest growth markets for Scotch whisky. But what does the market there look like and are there differences between the two in terms of consumer behaviour, distribution network and company cultures?

An advantage to India is that the people are used to drinking whisky since colonial times. It is what we call a brown spirits country, contrary to China, where white, domestically produced spirits have been in demand for a long time. India is, in fact, the country where most whisky is drunk, but only 1% of that is Scotch. The Indian alcohol market is divided into three categories; beer, country liquor (CL) and Indian-made Foreign Liquor (IMFL).

In the IFML whisky category, both the traditional malt and grain whiskies, as well as spirits made from molasses are found. In 2005, IFML surpassed 125 million cases. This had increased to 200 million in

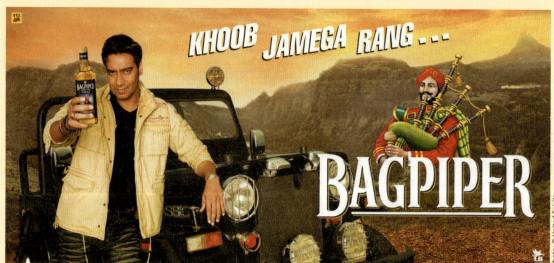

Bagpiper is the biggest brand on the Indian market and also the biggest in the world in terms of volume

2010 with an estimation that it should increase to 310 million in 2015. The whisky part of the IMFL is 100 million cases and, obviously, the whisky market in India is dominated by the big Indian companies such as United Spirits (with a 60% market share), John Distilleries, Radico Khaitan and Allied Distillers & Blenders. They have, between them, the eight largest, out of ten, whisky brands in India. The other two belong to Pernod Ricard, which took over the position built up by Seagrams in the country. Diageo, on the other hand, have never had as strong a position in India and that was the reason for the joint venture with Radico Khaitan in 2006. The biggest advantage for Diageo was that they acquired access to a well-built distribution network, something that is of the utmost importance in a country where each state has its own distribution setup.

The challenge for Pernod Ricard, Diageo, Bacardi, Beam Global and other Scotch producers is now to make the consumers upgrade from the cheaper Indian whisky to Scotch. So far this has been difficult, as import duties have been around 500% and even if they have been lowered by the government in recent years to 150%, each state can veto and decide on its own taxes. Export of Scotch to India has increased by 265% since 2003 to an estimated 1.5 million cases in 2010.

With China probably overtaking the US's position as the world's biggest economy by 2020, it is only natural that the country is looked upon by the producers of Scotch as a future goldmine. More than five billion litres of spirit is consumed every year and only 1% consists of foreign brands. Contrary to India, the habit of drinking whisky is not well established. Rice spirits and wine are definitely the largest categories and the biggest single type of spirit is baijiu, which is distilled from rice or sorghum. There are more than 18,000 producers of baijiu in the country and it is not hard to understand that several of the big Scotch producers have acquired shares in some of the larger producers. After all, most of the big companies producing Scotch are also big on other types of spirit, so for them to be a part of the baijiu market is sound business. At the same time, it is a way to build up a distribution network for their whiskies as has been done in India.

Nevertheless, because of the white spirit traditions, education and information about whisky require a much larger effort in China than in India. An advantage in China is a better retail infrastructure, which contains, among others, a growing network of supermarkets that are allowed to sell alcohol. A further advantage is that, compared to India, there is a low import duty of 15%. One problem in China for foreign producers though, has been the fear of being copied by local producers with whisky-like spirits. However, in summer of 2010, the Chinese government decided to introduce Geographic Indication (GI) of Origin Status to ensure that all whisky labelled as Scotch is also produced in Scotland.

The most popular Scotch whisky brands in China are Chivas Regal and Ballantine's, both owned by Pernod Ricard, and Diageo's Johnnie Walker Black and Red Label. Chivas Regal is the undisputed leader

with sales of 600,000 cases per year which makes China the brand's largest export market. Exports of Scotch to China has increased by 535% since 2003 to an estimated 1.8 million cases in 2010.

Changes in ownership - mergers and acquisitions

Last year we could report on several rumours regarding take-overs and mergers within the industry, but most of them ended up being just that, rumours. Apparently, 2009 was a year of consolidation for most companies, struggling to keep market shares and with little room for grand plans. But economically challenging times often make the best opportunity to grow one's own business through acquisitions.

William Grant & Sons put words into action when it increased its Scotch whisky emporium to include Irish whiskey. The spirit and liqueur part of the C&C Group was acquired in May 2010 at a price of £260m. C&C Group is an Irish company which, apart from spirits, produces cider (Bulmer's) and beer (Tennent's). The brands W Grants takes over are especially Tullamore Dew whiskey, but also Irish Mist and the two liqueurs, Carolans and Frangelico.

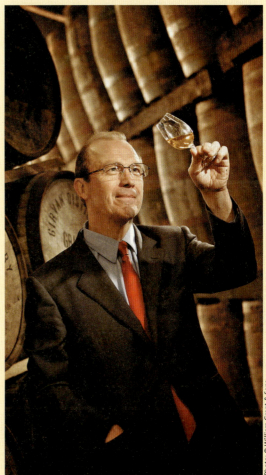

Peter Gordon, chairman of William Grant & Sons, the new owner of Tullamore Dew

The flagship brand is, of course, Tullamore Dew, which with its 600,000 cases, is the second most sold Irish whiskey in the world after Jameson. Tullamore Dew was already established in 1829 and was produced in its own distillery until it closed in 1959. With time, ownership transferred to Irish Distillers (later acquired by Pernod Ricard) and the whiskey has since been produced at Midleton Distillery. In 1994, C&C Group bought the brand from Irish Distillers and recently expanded the range of blended whiskeys with an inclusion of Tullamore Dew 10 year old single malt. Apart from buying the brand, there has also been speculation in W. Grant's having plans to build a new distillery in Ireland for the production.

A classic Scotch blended whisky and a prestigious single malt shifted owner in a deal announced in February 2010. Berry Bros & Rudd sold their Cutty Sark brand to The Edrington Group who, in turn, sold the single malt Glenrothes to BBR, but kept the distillery. Cutty Sark was established as a brand by BBR in 1923 and for many years this blend was the milk cow of the company. The wine business of BBR has grown considerably during the last 20 years, simultaneously with the world of whisky mega brands, requiring companies with massive muscles to make volumes increase. Cutty Sark has, from being the most sold in the seventies, decreased in sales and is today just outside the Top 10 with its 1.5 million cases. A brand such as Glenrothes single malt is completely in line with BBR's desire to go for the high premium brands, and BBR has already contributed to the development of the brand since 1994. Edrington will continue to provide BBR with whisky from Glenrothes distillery.

Belvedere S.A., established in 1991, is a company based in France and is a relative newcomer to the drinks business. It has grown rapidly, having Eastern Europe (especially Poland) and France as its springboard. The flagship brand is the Sobieski vodka, created in the late 1990s and now the 14th biggest vodka brand in the world, selling 3 million cases per year. Recent years' growth has been at the expense of debts, which totalled €580m in late 2009. To avoid bankruptcy, it is now forced to sell off Marie Brizard International, with its fine old history, which was acquired in 2006. Two Scotch whiskies that are comparatively unknown to most whisky drinkers, save the French, were included there. William Peel blended Scotch is the biggest in its category in France and included in the portfolio is also Glen Roger's - with both a blended and a single malt. The growth of William Peel is especially impressive. In difficult times during 2009, sales increased by 11% to 2.35 million cases and it is now the eighth best selling Scotch in the world. Several companies have been interested in acquiring Marie Brizard with ThaiBev (owners of Inver House Distillers) and La Martiniquaise (Label 5, Glen Turner and Glen Moray) as the biggest contesters. In July, only La Martiniquaise remained and negotiations between the two companies commenced. If a deal is struck, it will entail that La Martiniquaise, through both William Peel and Label 5, can take a solid grip on the lucrative French Scotch whisky market.

Photo: © Springbank

Gavin MacLaghlan, the new Distillery Manager for Springbank

Photo: © William Grant & Sons

David Stewart and his successor Brian Kinsman

Annandale may in a few years be the southernmost distillery in Scotland

Changing of the Guards

John MacLellan left Bunnahabhain for another job on Islay after having been there since 1989 (the last 12 years as Distillery Manager). He went to Kilchoman distillery as General Manager to tend to the daily running of that business.

An Ileach who decided to leave the island was Malcom Rennie, Distillery Manager at Kilchoman since the opening and who formerly held the same position at Ardbeg. In July 2010 he moved to the Lowlands to become Distillery Manager of Annandale distillery. The distillery is not functional yet and one of Rennie's first duties will be to specify the equipment requirements together with Forsyth's.

The first locally born person in 60 years became Distillery Manager at Springbank and Glengyle during the summer. Gavin McLaghlan, 36 years old, succeeded Stuart Robertson whom he had been Assistant Manager to for the last four years. Robertson himself moved to Huntly where he will supervise the building of the Huntly distillery - the brainchild of Euan Shand of Duncan Taylor.

Jason Craig, Global Controller for Highland Park and one of the people responsible for the brand's success in recent years, stays within Edrington but obtains new duties as Brand Controller for newly acquired

Cutty Sark. Matthew Turner, previous Marketing Controller of Macallan, replaced Craig at Highland Park.

In December 2009 Brian Kinsman became the sixth Master Blender for Grant's blended whisky since the family firm was founded in 1887. He has been with the company since 1997 and worked alongside his predecessor, David Stewart, for the last eight years. Stewart is Scotland's longest serving Master Blender and one of the most respected persons in the industry. He will remain part of the company, now as Malt Master for Balvenie single malt.

New, revived and planned distilleries

Annandale Distillery

In May 2010 consent was given from Dumfries & Galloway Council for the building of the new Annandale Distillery. The old one was closed in 1921 and in December 2008 the site was bought by Professor David Thomson and his wife, Teresa Church, with the aim to resurrect this, the southernmost distillery in Scotland. The old mash house and warehouses will be restored while a new tun room and still house will be built. As for the equipment (the original has all disappeared), this will be made by Forsyth's in Rothes. In July 2010, Malcolm Rennie, who managed

Kilchoman distillery on Islay, joined the company as Distillery Manager. He will be leading the restoration process and the discussions with Forsyth's regarding the final design. The equipment specification, as it currently looks, will be one semi-lauter mash tun (2.5 tonnes), four wooden washbacks (12,000 litres each), one wash still (12,000 litres), one intermediate still and one spirit still (4,000 litres each). The planned output is 250,000 litres per annum. There is no fixed date when the distillery will be in production, but a decision has been made to primarily produce a peated whisky. Major archaeological, on-site research has been conducted by the Glasgow University Archaeological Research Division (GUARD) the previous year in waiting for planning consent. Through this work it has been established what the distillery may have looked like during the Johnnie Walker era (1895-1919).

Falkirk Distillery

The construction of the first distillery in Falkirk since Rosebank was closed in 1993, came to a halt temporarily in autumn of 2009 after the plans had been approved by the local council in spring of 2009. Objections were raised by Historic Scotland that the distillery would be built too close to the Antonine Wall. The Wall was built in 142 AD to stop Caledonian tribes attacking the Romans and it was given World Heritage Status in 2008. However, in May 2010 Scottish ministers gave the final approval arguing that the distillery would not interfere with the wall but could boost tourism to the area instead. Falkirk Distillery Company, owned by Fiona and Alan Stewart, is behind the £5m project. The facilities will include a visitor centre, restaurant and shops apart from the distillery itself and could create up to 80 jobs. The Stewarts hope to be able to use the name Rosebank for their whisky but the trademark is owned by Diageo who, from time to time, release bottlings under that name from existing stocks. Diageo have stated that the trademark is not for sale even if the Stewarts are hopeful for a change once the stocks of Rosebank have drained

Dingle Distillery

Once there were hundreds of whisky distilleries on Ireland but today only four remain - Bushmills, Midleton, Cooley and the recently restarted Kilbeggan. Perhaps they can soon be five. Planning permission to build a distillery in Dingle, Co Kerry, was applied for in autumn 2008 and in March 2009 it was granted by Kerry County Council. Jerry O'Sullivan, managing director of Southbound Properties who bought the old creamery which will be converted into a distillery, and Porterhouse Brewing Company are behind it all. The project will cost in the region of €2.9m and Jerry O'Sullivan and two other owners, Liam LaHart and Oliver Hughes will put €900,000 of their own money into the project and another €400,000 will be received as a grant. The remaining €800,000 will be raised by private investors. Initially, it was said that the distillery would be up and running in late 2009 while the most recent information states that production will start

some time during 2010. The company will develop a Dingle Cream Liqueur and a Dingle Dew Liqueur to provide income before the whisky has matured. The whiskey will be triple distilled and the first bottlings could be ready by 2013.

Barra Distillery

The classic film, Whisky Galore, based on the equally classic novel by Sir Compton Mackenzie, was filmed on the island of Barra in the Outer Hebrides. It is a story of the SS Politician which was stranded in 1941 and 264,000 bottles of whisky which were among her cargo were lost. The island where the ship went missing was in fact Eriskay, a smaller island to the north of Barra, but that did not deter Peter Brown who had moved to Barra from Edinburgh 12 years ago. He wants to build a distillery there and is convinced that the connection with the film location will be favourable for the business.

In November 2005, the Loch Uisge reservoir on the west of the island was acquired in order to secure water supply for the future distillery. Future casks have been sold to the public since early 2008 and most of the plans regarding building and construction are ready. In July, Peter Brown bought all the shares owned by Andrew Currie (of Arran Distillery fame) who has been part of the project since its inception. The original idea was to start building in autumn of 2009, but the recession has made funding difficult.

Kingsbarns Distillery

Fife will get its third distillery in 2011 if everything goes as planned. The first two are the huge grain spirit complex Cameronbridge and the small farm distillery, Daftmill. Kingsbarns Company of Distillers,

Tamdhu Distillery

Photo: © Edrington Group

HRH The Prince of Wales, together with Christian Porta and Alan Winchester, attending the opening of the new Glenlivet.

Photo: © Chivas Brothers

spearheaded by Greg Ramsay and Doug Clement, are behind the new plans. Greg, who is from Tasmania, met Doug when they were working with establishing the Nant Distillery in Tasmania. Their idea is to build a distillery in the vicinity of St Andrews, an area with thousands of visitors each year but lacking a whisky distillery. Greg and Doug have consulted Bill Lark as advisor. He is the owner of Lark Distillery in Tasmania, godfather of modern whisky-making in Australia, and advisor to several other whisky companies in his native Australia. The idea is to convert a farmstead on the Cambo Estate which has been home to the Erskine family since 1688 and is owned today by Sir Peter Erskine. The distillery will have one pair of stills (to be built in Tasmania) and the capacity will be around 100,000 litres per year. The latest report was that they were anticipating planning permission to be granted during September 2010, after which the work on getting financiers for the remaining £2m required to complete the project would be intensified.

Tamdhu distillery mothballed

The Edrington Group announced their decision to temporarily close Tamdhu Distillery in Speyside in November 2009. It would be put in "care and maintenance" or, as is commonly phrased, mothballed. The reason, according to the owners, was the economic downturn and that they had to "rebalance their distillation capacity". The distillery, founded in 1897, has a capacity of producing 4 million litres of alcohol per year and there is also a maltings operation from which other distilleries within the group have sourced their malted barley. It is obvious that Edrington consider themselves to have excess capacity within the group with Macallan having recently increased its capacity. Furthermore, the maltings were quite old-fashioned and in need of substantial refurbishing and upgrade. Even though the distillery is only mothballed, it is likely that the Tamdhu will not be producing again, at least not under the Edrington regime. The distillery was closed in April 2010 and a total of 30 jobs were affected by the decision.

Investments

One could assume that the current financial climate would not encourage larger, future investments. However, the whisky industry must plan for what will happen five to ten years from now, at least when it comes to production matters. Warehouses and bottling plants can be constructed fairly quickly should there be a need, while the distillation itself must be thoroughly planned if one wishes to have mature whisky to sell.

There were not any announcements of new distilleries or major expansions of current capacities in 2009/2010, but most of what was announced in 2007 and the first half of 2008 has been executed. Examples are new distilleries in Roseisle and Ailsa Bay and capacity expansion at Glenmorangie, Macallan,

245

Glenlivet and Cameronbridge.

Dewar´s expansion of storing and blending capacity at Poniel, South Lanarkshire, which was already announced in 2008 has come well underway. The beginning of 2009 saw two warehouses complete, each holding 72,000 casks. Six months later another four had been built and by December 2010 there will be a total of nine warehouses with a total capacity of 648,000 casks. But it will not stop at that. As Dewar´s has an agreement with Diageo regarding storage, another nine warehouses will be constructed in the near future.

Last year, Diageo took a number of unpopular decisions to close Kilmarnock bottling plant, Carsebridge cooperage and Port Dundas distillery. The total loss of jobs amounted to 900. However, a total of 470 new jobs were to be created due to an £86m expansion of the bottling plant in Fife and a new £9m cooperage in Cambus, both of which will be operational from summer 2011. Port Dundas grain distillery was closed in March 2010 and that production will now move to Cameronbridge instead. Talking about Cameronbridge, sometimes we, the malt whisky drinkers, tend to forget the sheer size of the other side of Scotch whisky production, namely, distilling of grain whisky for the blends. During the last couple of years Diageo have invested a staggering £105m into the Cameronbridge plant. The capacity was increased through a £40m investment

from 65 million litres to 105 million and it is now the biggest distillery in Scotland. The other £65m have been invested in a bio-energy plant at the distillery. The plant will be commissioned in March 2011 and provide 98% of the thermal steam and 80% of electrical power used at the distillery. The reduction of annual CO_2 emissions will be 56,000 tonnes (the equivalent of taking 44,000 family cars off the road).

An example of smaller-scale investments, but still showing the company´s ambition to grow, was the opening of a new bottling line at Inver House Distillers´ Airdrie plant. The cost was £1m and the new facility, which became operational during 2009, has a capacity of 2.4 million bottles per year.

Another company in need of expanded bottling facilities was BenRiach Distillery Company. Instead of building a new plant it bought Chivas Brothers´ existing plant in Newbridge on the outskirts of Edinburgh. The new plant is not just for bottling of the company´s single malts - Glendronach and BenRiach - but also for an expansion in the blended whisky segment. The deal was finalised end of July 2010.

Chivas Brothers was in for an unpleasant surprise when it came to investments, as the roofs of 31 warehouses collapsed under the weight of heavy snow in January 2010. In Mulben, 29 warehouses were affected and in Keith another two. Damages to the inventory were reportedly small but the reconstruction of the warehouses will take time. The company

The third and fourth generations of the owners of Gordon & MacPhail (with David and Michael Urquhart in the middle) who released Mortlach 70 year old - the oldest single malt ever bottled.

will build each new warehouse's outer wall six feet from the existing walls of the damaged warehouse, before tearing down the old.

Whyte & Mackay, the owner of Dalmore distillery, has realised that a high-profile premium brand like Dalmore must be supplemented with an equally high-profile visitor centre. The current area where visitors are welcomed has been small and slightly run-down. Plans are now being made in which the visitor centre and the shop will be refurbished, distillery buildings improved and training provided for tour and distillery staff. It should all be complete within a two-year period at a cost of £1m.

Bottling grapevine
(see pp 254-257 for a detailed listing)

The re-launch of a brand can sometimes entail opportunities for us consumers to try new exciting bottlings, or, at other times, it can just be a matter of introducing new packaging. The most joyous cases occur when the owner decides to put the limelight on a brand or distillery that has been neglected for years and one which the more than average inte- rested whisky buyer never would have contemplated buying. Two such brands stepped out of obscurity this year. The first was *Deanston*, albeit that it already started its journey last year with a new version of the *12 year old*. That was followed up by a *Virgin Oak* in 2010 and the next year both an *Organic Deanston* and an older expression will be released. *Fettercairn* is the other distillery which, in autumn of 2009, presented a range of older whiskies (*24, 30* and *40 year olds*) and in summer of 2010 launched its new core expression *Fior*.

We find established brands at the other end of the scale, competing in the field of "as old bottlings as possible" and, not so rarely, bottles which are works of art themselves. The oldest was, of course, the *70 year old Mortlach* from *Gordon & MacPhail*, the oldest single malt ever bottled. *Highland Park* launched its *50 year old* in a spectacular bottle wrap- ped in an extraordinary creation of silver. *Bowmore* bottled a *40 year old* and for their presentation they chose molten glass. But both distilleries had other aces up their sleeves. *Bowmore* pulled out a *Vintage 1981* and *Highland Park* did the same with *Saint Magnus*, the second in a series of three. Four *Vintages* destined for duty free also came from the Orcadian distillery.

Respectably aged malts were presented by other distilleries; by *Glenfarclas* in the shape of a *40 year old* while *Glenfiddich* released the sixth edition of its *40 year old* and neighbouring *Balvenie* launched its first *40 year old*. *Bunnahabhain* delighted its fans with a *30 year old* as did *Talisker*. The owners of Talisker, Diageo, continued to release single cask expressions from all of their 27 distilleries in the *Manager's Choice* series and in autumn, its annual *Special Releases* were presented. Fans of closed distil- leries went for the 30 year old *Brora* or the 31 year old *Port Ellen*. Others were delighted by bottlings of *Lagavulin* (12 year old cask strength), *Caol Ila* (12 year old, unpeated), *Cragganmore* (21 year old) and *Glenkinchie* (20 year old). But together with "the usual suspects", every year sees a couple of distil- leries that rarely are bottled by the owners. This year the surprises were *Auchroisk 30 year old* and *Glen Spey 21 year old*.

Grandeur 31 year old from GlenDronach and Bunnahabhain 30 year old

Glen Grant's Distillery Manager, Dennis Malcolm, chose the casks for the 170th Anniversary bottling

Our friends from *BenRiach* now have two distilleries to "play" with and it was therefore no surprise that it made quite an effort with no less than 19 new expressions from *Glendronach*: from the young (8 years) *Octarine* to the ´grande dame´ of *Grandeur* (31 years). In between were *four wood finishes*, a *distillery exclusive* and *12 different vintages*. *BenRiach*, of course, got their share of attention with both *wood finishes* and *vintages*, but also some rather unusual items like the triple-distilled *Solstice* and *The Firkin* with 32 years of maturation in such a small (Firkin) cask.

Glenglassaugh re-started its production just two years ago, so the owners had to dig deep into the warehouses to find new whiskies from days gone by. They came up with a *26 year old* but also presented new produce in the shape of *four spirit drinks* (younger than the required 3 years). *Ardbeg* celebrated the 10th anniversary of the Ardbeg Committee with the *Rollercoaster*, a vatting of casks from 10 years and it also launched the 2010 edition of last year's hit, *Supernova*. *Glenmorangie* released *Finealta*, the second in Private Collection, which started last year with Sonnalta. "The sixteen men (and women) of Tain" are also saving up for something spectacular at the beginning of the New Year. Keep your eyes open!

Glengoyne made a huge impression last year with its *40 year old* and followed it up in 2010 with two new *single casks* from *1987* and *1997*, as well as a *13 year old port finish*. *Glenfiddich* expanded its core

range with the *14 year old Rich Oak* which has matured in ex-bourbon casks, but with an additional finish in new European casks. Angus Dundee continue building up the range of *Glencadam* single malts and this year saw the release of a *12 year old port finish*, a *14 year old Oloroso finish* and a *21 year old*. Sister distillery, *Tomintoul*, came up with a *12 year old port finish* as well.

Laphroaig launched two new expressions - a *master edition* of the *Cairdeas* and a *20 year old double cask* matured, exclusive for duty free in France. *Kilchoman* followed the path that it started last year with its first release and followed up with *three new bottlings* and a launch on the American market. If we stay in the young whiskies section, we can report of the oldest producing whiskey distillery, namely *Kilbeggan* in Ireland and their first release, the *three year old Kilbeggan Distillery Reserve*.

Kilkerran from Glengyle distillery has now reached four years of age with the *Kilkerran Work in Progress II*. The owners of Glengyle are also the owners of *Springbank* and they started early in 2010 with *Springbank Claret Wood*, *Springbank 12 year old cask strength* and a new edition of the *18 year old*. Later in the year they continued with new versions of *Springbank CV*, *Longrow CV* and *Hazelburn CV*. *Jura* distillery celebrated its 200th anniversary with a *21 year old* which had matured in a sherry cask from 1963 the year when the distillery, which was already founded in 1810, was resurrected. Another distillery which found itself in a celebratory mood was *Glen*

Gerry Tosh, Global Brand Manager for Highland Park, is obviously proud of the new 50 year old

Photo: © Edrington Group

Grant who marked its 170th anniversary with a vatting of casks from 1976 to 1999, all selected by Distillery Manager, Dennis Malcolm.

Tomatin started to release a number of exciting bottlings two years ago and continued in 2010, with its first *peated* expression, a *4 year old* destined for the Japanese market, among others. The manager of *Ben Nevis* distillery explored the warehouse and came up with a *25 year old* which was launched in February. It sold out instantly and a new release was made during the summer. *Arran* distillery is slowly, but steadily, building its future core range. It was time for the *14 year old* this year, but it also released a young, peated expression called *Machrie Moor* and *Rowan Tree*, the second edition of Icons of Arran. *Auchentoshan* followed up the success of its re-launch two years ago with two *vintages - 1977* and *1998*, with the last one having matured in a Fino sherry cask and from *Benromach* came the third edition of *Peatsmoke* and batch two and three of *Origins*.

Finally, we had reserved lots of space for the traditional line-up of 15-20 new *Buichladdichs*, but the distillery has kept a relaxed pace this time. "Only" seven new bottlings saw the light of day with the second and third release of heavily peated *Octomore, Black Art 2, PC Multi Vintage* and a *40 year old* among them.

One of two new vintages from Auchentoshan this year

Independent Bottlers

The independent bottlers play an important role in the whisky business. With their innovative bottlings, they increase diversity. Single malts from distilleries where the owners' themselves decide not to bottle also get a chance through the independents. The following are a selection of the major companies. All tasting notes have been prepared by Ian Wisniewski.

Gordon & MacPhail................www.gordonandmacphail.com
Established in 1895 the company which is owned by the Urquhart family still occupies the same premises in Elgin. Apart from being an independent bottler, there is also a legendary store in Elgin and, since 1993, an own distillery, Benromach. There is a wide variety of bottlings, for example *Connoisseurs Choice, Private Collection, MacPhail's Collection* and *Pride of the Regions*. Many of the bottlings have been diluted to 40%, 43% or 46%, but the series *Cask Strength* obviously, as the name implies, contains bottlings straight from the cask. Another range called *Rare Old* consists of unusually old single malts which quite often come from closed distilleries as well. The Gordon & MacPhail warehouses in Elgin contain probably the largest collection of matured malt whisky in the world which was a prerequisite for the 2010 launch of the world's oldest single malt ever bottled - a 70 year old *Mortlach*. There are also large volumes of *Macallan* dating all the way to 1940 enabling the release of a special range of whisky from this distillery called *Speymalt*. Several blended whiskies, e. g. *Ben Alder, Glen Calder* and *Avonside* are also found in the company's range.

Connoisseur's Choice, Caol Ila 1996

Nose: Apples, garden in full bloom, rich honey, vanilla, background hint of earthy peatyness and subtle oak.
Palate: Creme caramel sweetness with subtle, underlying oak dryness, apples, honey, vanilla, background waft of smoke and toastyness.
Finish: Creamy creme caramel, honey, wafting smoke and embers, dried fruit and oak.

Linkwood 15 year old

Nose: Dark chocolate, cappuccino, dried fruits and toastyness, with more chocolate and toffee following.
Palate: Lightly creamy dark chocolate, a wave of dried fruits, creme brulee, cappuccino and underlying dryness, remains poised and balanced.
Finish: Rich, dark chocolate and creme caramel, hint of prunes and raisins, and lingering subtle dry oak.

Berry Bros. & Rudd..www.bbr.com
Britain's oldest wine and spirit merchant, founded in 1698 has been selling their own world famous blend, Cutty Sark. since 1923. Berry Brothers had been offering their customers private bottlings of malt whisky for years, but it was not until 2002 that they launched *Berry's Own Selection* of single malt whiskies. Under the supervision of Spirits Manager, Doug McIvor, some 30 expressions are on offer every year. Bottling is usually at 46% but expressions bottled at cask strength are also available. The super premium blended malt, *Blue Hanger* is also included in the range. So far, four different releases have been made, each different from the other. While the 3rd edition was a 30 year old, the fourth edition contains whiskies from 16 to 34 years of age and the distilleries involved are Glen Elgin, Glenlivet and Mortlach. 2010 turned out to be an exciting year for BBR. First it sold Cutty Sark blended Scotch to Edrington and obtained *The Glenrothes* single malt in exchange. A strategic partnership with American Anchor Brewers & Distillers, best known for Old Potrero single rye in a whisky context, was announced in summer of 2010. Anchor Brewers & Distillers will assist BBR in selling part of their range in the USA.

Berry's Speyside Reserve

Nose: Honey, cider, underlying oak and digestive biscuits, with orange marmalade emerging, then increasingly fruity with vanilla overtones.
Palate: Silky texture, honey, then a wave of chocolate, apples, dryness lies beneath fruit sweetness, then creamy cappuccino.
Finish: Digestive biscuits, dryness builds, garnished with apples.

Blue Hanger 4th release

Nose: Toastyness extending with oak, chocolate, vanilla, and fruit cake with a lemon garnish.
Palate: Rich dried fruit, dark chocolate, creme caramel, espresso, hint of background toastyness and dry oak, with lemon and apricots emerging.
Finish: Rich fruit leads, with dark chocolate, cappuccino and dryness emerging.

Signatory Vintage Scotch Whisky
Founded in 1998 by Andrew and Brian Symington, Signatory lists at least 50 single malts at any one occasion. The most widely distributed range is *Cask Strength Collection* which sometimes contains spectacular bottlings from distilleries which have long since disappeared. Another range is *The Unchill Filtered Collection* bottled at 46%. Andrew Symington bought *Edradour Distillery* from Pernod Ricard in 2002.

Ian Macleod Distillers ....www.ianmacleod.com
The company was founded in 1933 and is one of the largest independent family-owned companies within the spirits industry. Gin, rum, vodka and liqueurs are found within the range, apart from whisky and they also own *Glengoyne Distillery*. In total 15 million bottles of spirit are sold per year. Single malt ranges like *The Chieftain's* and *Dun Bheagan* are single casks either bottled at cask strength or (more often) at reduced strength, always natural colour and unchill-filtered. There are two *As We Get It* expressions - Highland and Islay, both 8 year olds. Bottled at 40% are the five *MacLeod's Regional Single Malts* (one for every region and Campbeltown is not included). The blended *Six Isles Single Malt* contains whisky from all the whisky-producing islands and is bottled at 43%. A recent development of this is the limited Pomerol finish. Finally, *Smokehead*, a heavily peated single malt from

Islay, was introduced in 2006. There is also a *Smokehead Extra Black 18 years old*.

The Six Isles

Nose: Hint of toastyness, then vanilla, dark chocolate, a hint of fruitcake emerges, with toffee, oak and lemon hints.
Palate: Elegant vanilla and chocolate emerge on a luscious wave, lively lemons and oranges, hint of toffee, background dry oak, toastyness.
Finish: Hint of sweet fruitiness, then dryness opens up accompanied by malty-ness and mellow vanilla.

Smokehead

Nose: Earthy, heather moors, woodyness, apples, chargrilled, barbecue smokey-ness.
Palate: Creamy vanilla accompanied by dried fruit, smoke arrives mid-way, hints of spice, dryness and oak, providing a rich, balanced palate.
Finish: Creamy vanilla with background earthy, toasty notes, and wafting back-ground smoke.

Douglas Laing & Co .... www.douglaslaing.com

Established in 1948 by Douglas Laing, it is currently run by his two sons, Fred and Stewart. One of their most talked about ranges is *The Old Malt Cask* which contains rare and old bottllngs. More than 100 different expressions can be found regularly in this range where bottlings are diluted to 50%. Some malts are released in an even more exclusive range - *The Old and Rare Selection*, offered at cask strength. A third range is called *Provenance*, often aged around 10-12 years and almost always diluted to 46%. What started as a one-off with a blend of Macallan and Laphroaig single malts, has now turned into a small range of its own called *Double Barrel*, where only two malts are vatted together and bott-led at 46%. In May 2009, the company launched *Big Peat*, a vatting of selected Islay malts (among them Ardbeg, Caol Ila, Bowmore and Port Ellen) and also bottled at 46%. Some-times some very old and rare single grains are released in the *Clan Denny* range. Douglas Laing & Co also has a range of blended whiskies in which *John Player Special*, *The King of Scots* and *The McGibbon Golf Range* are the biggest sellers.

Double Barrel Highland Park & Bowmore

Nose: Apples, digestive biscuits, vanilla, dark chocolate, lemon zest, hint of earthyness, background waft of smoke and sea breeze.
Palate: Light creamyness with smoke, luscious creme caramel and lemon emerge, orange marmalade, subtle dryness ac-centuates the details.
Finish: Light dryness with waft of subtle smoke, spice and oak.

Big Peat

Nose: Chargrilled notes, embers, distinct but controlled, vanilla and honey, oak, sea breeze garnished with lemon.
Palate: Creamy vanilla and choco-late unfold in waves, with smo- and toasty notes, hints of dried fru-honey, balanced by oak.
Finish: Smoke continues to waft, balanced by growing sweetness and dryness.

Duncan Taylor .... www.duncantaylor.com

Duncan Taylor & Co was founded in Glasgow in 1938 and in 2001, Euan Shand bought the company and operations were moved to Huntly. The company bottles around 200 expres-sions per year. The range includes *Rarest of the Rare* (single cask, cask strength whiskies of great age from demolished distilleries), *Rare Auld* (single cask, cask strength malts and grains with the vast majority aged over 30 years), *Peerless* (a unique collection of single malts over 40 years old), *NC2* (mainly single casks, 12-17 years, non chill-filtered at 46%), *Battlehill* (younger malts at 43%) and *Lonach* (vattings of two casks from same distillery of the same age to bring them up to a natural strength of over 40%). *Auld Reekie* is a 10 year old vatted malt from Islay, which is similar to *Big Smoke*, although the latter is younger, more peated and available in two strengths, 40% and 60%.
The latest addition to the range involves the concept of re-racking the whisky from larger casks (hogsheads or barrels) to the smaller quarter casks (ca 125 litres) or octaves (ca 60 litres). This will speed up the maturation due to the higher whisky to wood ratio, i. e. the whisky is more in contact with the oak. The whisky is allowed to be in the smaller casks for a minimum of 3 months before it is bottled. Duncan Taylor also offers sales of a whole Octave or Quarter Cask.

Black Bull 12 year old

Nose: Digestive biscuits, dried fruit, then tof-fee, a hint of creme caramel and espresso.
Palate: Rich fruityness with underlying dry oak hints, toastyness, honey, digestive biscuits, vanilla, chocolate, with a garnish of lemon zest.
Finish: Fruity sweet-dry balance, toffee, chocolate, with lingering dried fruit and honey.

Octave Glen Grant 1987

Nose: Toastyness, rich, dark chocolate notes, honey, vanilla then spice, oak and dried fruit, focussed and integrated.
Palate: Creamy dark chocolate with underlying dryness, then vanilla, prunes, raisins, a wave of luscious ripe fruit sweetness and cappuccino.
Finish: Lightly toasty notes with some dark chocolate, prunes, oak and lingering dryness.

Blackadder International .... www.blackadder.se

Blackadder is owned by Robin Tucek, together with John Lamond. Apart from the Blackadder and *Blackadder Raw Cask*, there are also a number of other ranges - *Aberdeen Distillers*, *Clydesdale Original* and *Caledonian Connections*. All bottlings are single cask and in the case of Raw Casks, they are also completely unfiltered. Most of the bottlings are diluted to 43-45% but there are also cask strength expres-sions on offer. Around 100 different bottlings are launched each year.

Wm Cadenhead & Co .... www.wmcadenhead.com

This company was established in 1842 and is owned by J & A Mitchell (who also owns Springbank) since 1972. The single malts from Cadenheads are neither chill filtered nor co-loured. When it comes to whisky, they work essentially with three different ranges; *Authentic Collection* (cask strength), *Original Collection* (diluted to 46%) and *Chairman's Stock* (older and rarer whiskies). *Duthie´s*, a new range of single malts reduced to 46%, was launched in 2009. A chain of ten whisky shops working under the name Cadenhead´s can be found in the UK, Denmark, The Netherlands, Germany, Poland, Italy and Switzerland.

Speciality Drinks............................. www.specialitydrinks.com

Sukhinder Singh, known by most for his two very well-stocked shops in London, The Whisky Exchange, is behind this company. Since 2005 he is also a bottler of malt whiskies operating under the brand name *The Single Malts of Scotland*. He has around 50 bottlings on offer at any time, either as single bottles or as batches bottled at cask strength or at 46%. In 2009 a new range of Islay malts under the name *Port Askaig* was introduced, starting with a cask strength, a 17 year old and a 25 year old. *Elements of Islay*, a series in which all Islay distilleries are, or will be, represented was introduced around the same time. The list of the product range is cleverly constructed with periodical tables in mind (see www.elements-of-islay.com) in which each distillery has a two-letter acronym followed by a batch number. New release 2010 was Pe2 (Port Ellen) which will be followed by Bn1 (Bunnahabhain) and Kh1 (Kilchoman).

Elements of Islay Lg1

Nose: Waft of toastyness, bonfire and sea breeze, rich oak notes, then honey, vanilla and lemon zest freshness.
Palate: Wafting smoke grows, followed by a wave of sweet vanilla creamyness, luscious lemon and underlying dry oak, continuing lemon freshness.
Finish: Sweet-dry balance, background smoke and lemon zest continues with lingering dryness.

Port Askaig 25 year old

Nose: Honey, dried fruit, apple, hint of lemon peel, with underlying oak, toastyness, creme caramel and gingerbread.
Palate: Initial rich-dry balance, then creamy vanilla and rich fruit sweetness, with hints of dark chocolate, lemon zest and apricots.
Finish: Dryness emerges with underlying digestive biscuits, leading to light spice and oak.

Murray McDavid .... www.murray-mcdavid.com

Established in 1995 by Mark Reynier, Gordon Wright and Simon Coughlin. Murray McDavid makes three to four releases a year, averaging 25 expressions per time. The range is highly selective and all casks are chosen by Jim McEwan who has more than 40 years experience in the whisky industry. Unlike most independent bottlers, the bottlings are vattings of four or five casks (same age) at 46% without chill filtration or tinting. The range can be divided into three categories: – the *Murray McDavid* range, the *Mission* range (unusual aged stock) and, finally, the *Celtic Heartlands* range - exceptionally old or unique casks from the sixties and seventies.

Master of Malt .... www.masterofmalt.com

One of the biggest whisky retailers in the UK, Master of Malt, also have ranges of its own bottled single malts. One range is called *Secret Bottlings* and are bottled at 40%. No distillery names appear on the label. Instead, the region is highlighted (40 year old Speyside, 12 year old Lowland etc.). The bottlings are very competitively priced, not least the older ones. A 50 year old Speyside is only £249.95. Master of Malt also bottles single casks from various distilleries. Some of the latest are a 19 year old Tomatin and a 26 year old Bowmore. The people behind Master of Malt have also come up with the brilliant idea to sell single malts (and other spirits) in 30 ml bottles. They call it *Drinks by the Dram* and it gives the customer an opportunity to sample a whisky before they buy it. At the moment there are more than 300 different drams to choose from.

Compass Box Whisky Co ....www.compassboxwhisky.com

The company was started by John Glaser with a past in the wine trade and, later, in Diageo working with premium malts. Most of the people within the whisky industry acknowledge the fact that the cask has the greatest influence on the flavour of the final whisky, but none more so than John Glaser. His philosophy is strongly influenced by meticulous selection of oak for the casks, clearly inspired by his time in the wine business. But he also has a lust for experimenting and innovation to test the limits, which was clearly shown when *Spice Tree* was launched in 2005. For an additional maturation, Glaser filled malt whisky in casks prepared with extra staves of toasted French oak suspended within the cask. Scotch Malt Whisky Association deemed this non-traditional and threatened with court action unless the production was halted. Glaser had to give up but returned in 2009 with *Spice Tree II* with the difference that the controversial casks had been equipped with new French Oak heads to achieve the same effect. The company today divides its ranges into a *Signature Range* and a *Limited Range*. *Spice Tree*, *The Peat Monster* (a combination of peated islay whiskies and Highland malts), *Oak Cross* (where Glaser uses casks of American oak but fitted with heads of French oak) and *Asyla* (a blended whisky matured in first-fill ex-bourbon American oak) are included in the former. The Limited range consists of *Hedonism* and *Hedonism Maximus* (vatted grain whiskies), *Lady Luck* (a vatted malt made up of old Caol Ila and Imperial), *Flaming Heart* (a vatted malt with a second maturation in new French oak) and *Canto Cask* (a series of single cask bottlings).

Flaming Heart '10

Nose: Peaches, apricots, underlying layer of digestive biscuits, oak, and a hint of orange marmalade.
Palate: Initially integrated, then waves of luscious peaches, apricots, citrus, vanilla creamyness, digestive biscuits and underlying hint of dryness.
Finish: Maltyness and dryness lead, with a hint of oak and orange marmalade emerging.

Creative Whisky Company .... www.creativewhisky.com

David Stirk, who has worked in the business with, among others, several independent bottlers the last 15 years, is behind this company that started in 2005. He is also author of The Distilleries of Campbeltown and of features in most editions of Malt Whisky Yearbook. The range, exclusively of single casks, is divided into three parts: *Exclusive Malts* are bottled at cask strength and vary in age between 8 and 40 years. Around 20 bottlings are made annually. *Exclusive Range* are somewhat younger whiskies, between 8 and 16 years and is, according to Stirk himself, for "easy-drinkers". Finally, *Exclusive Casks* are single casks, which have obtained a finish of three months in another cask, e. g. madeira, sherry, port or made of another type of oak.

Dewar Rattray .... www.adrattray.com

This company was founded by Andrew Dewar and William Rattray in 1868. In 2004 the company was revived by Tim Morrison, previously of Morrison Bowmore Distillers and fourth generation descendent of Andrew Dewar, with a view to bottling single cask malts from different regions in Scotland. All whiskies are bottled at cask strength, without colouring or chill filtration. To give customers a choice, a new range of single malts bottled at 46% was recently introduced. A 12 year old single malt named *Stronachie* is also found in their portfolio. It is named after a distillery that closed in the 1930s. Tim Morrison bought one of the

few remaining bottles of Stronachie and found a Highland distillery that could reproduce its character. The distillery in question was shrouded in secrecy until 2010, even if some whisky fans had made a correct guess, when it was revealed as *Benrinnes* in Speyside. Each Stronachie bottling is a batch of 6-10 casks from Benrinnes. The 12 year old Stronachie was joined in 2010 by another expression - an 18 year old.

Stronachie 12 year old

Nose: Summer in a meadow, rich fruit, honey and oak, with background toasty notes.
Palate: Balanced, revealing details as it opens up with creme caramel, apples, pears, honey, oak, maltyness and background toastyness.
Finish: Dryness builds and leads, with ripe fruit and honey emerging.

Cask Collection, Bowmore 1990

Nose: Oak and rich fruit, nutmeg, hint of toastyness, embers, followed by a waft of dried fruit and lemon zest.
Palate: Vanilla and rich fruit extend with digestive biscuits, rich honey, a wave of creamyness and gentle smoke.
Finish: Waft of smoke with a rich-dry balance, apricots and lemon freshness.

Adelphi Distillery .... www.adelphidistillery.com

The Adelphi Distillery, one of the largest whisky distilleries in Scotland at the time, ceased production in 1902. The name was revived in 1992 by the great-grandson of the last owner, Jamie Walker, who established the company as an independent bottler of single cask single malts. He then sold the company in 2004 to Keith Falconer and Donald Houston, who recruited Alex Bruce from the wine trade to act as Marketing Director. Their whiskies are always bottled at cask strength, uncoloured and non chill-filtered. Furthermore, a decision was made to work only with ex-sherry or ex-bourbon casks, meaning that wood finishes from any other type of casks are out of the question. Adelphi bottles around 50 casks a year. Unusual for an independent, Adelphi has an on-line shop on their website. The company affords its customers the opportunity to join the Adelphi's Dancey Man Whisky Club which has special offerings for its members, discounts and first choice of the latest releases. Rumour also has it that Adelphi is looking to build a distillery of its own in the near future.

Liddesdale 18 years

Nose: Integrated oak toastyness, honey, rich dried fruit with raisins and apricots, hint of espresso and gingerbread.
Palate: Lightly creamy, toffee, raisins, orange marmalade, with creme brulee emerging on a wave of richness, underpinned by dry oak.
Finish: Rich and rounded, but composed and balanced, ending on raisins, oak and chocolate.

Fascadale 10 years

Nose: Oak, honey and mellow spices, with a waft of background toastyness, then apples, creme caramel and lemon.
Palate: Mellow vanilla grows richer with chocolate overtones, hint of honey, lemon, dried fruit and subtle oak dryness, builds with confidence.
Finish: Fruity, sweet-dry balance with a hint of lingering oak.

Wemyss Malts .... www.wemyssmalts.com

This family-owned company, a relatively newcomer to the whisky world, was founded in 2005. The family owns another three companies in the field of wine and gin. Based in Edinburgh, Wemyss Malts takes advantage of Charles MacLean's experienced nose when choosing their casks. There are two ranges; one of which consists of single casks bottled at 46% or 55%. The distillery name is not used on the label, instead, the names are chosen to reflect what the whisky tastes like, for instance, *Admiral of the Sea, Chocolate Heaven, Dried Fruit Basket* and *Barbecue Sauce*. All whiskies are unchill-filtered and without colouring. The other range is made up of blended malts of which there are three at the moment - *Spice King, Peat Chimney* and *Smooth Gentleman*. They are bottled at 40% and are available in two age expressions, 5 and 8 year olds.

Glenkeir Treasures .... www.whiskyshop.com

The Whisky Shop, the biggest whisky retail chain in the UK, is soon to open their 16th shop in Guildford in Surrey. The company was founded by the owner, Ian Bankier, in 1992 when it opened its first shop in Edinburgh. Apart from having an extensive range of malt (and other) whiskies, they also select and bottle their own range of single malts called Glenkeir Treasures. Once a cask has been chosen it is re-racked into smaller oak casks which are then put out for display in each store. The whisky is bottled to order and the customer can also try the whisky in the shop before buying. Glenkeir Treasures come in three bottle sizes - 10, 20 and 50 cl and is bottled at 40%. The current range consists of Aberlour 12, Ben Nevis 15, Deanston 12, Ledaig 9, Linkwood 12 and Macallan 18 year old.

Malts of Scotland .... www.malts-of-scotland.com

This is one of the more recently established independent bottlers. The German, Thomas Ewers, bought casks from Scottish distilleries and decided in the spring of 2009 to start releasing them as single casks bottled at cask strength and with no colouring or chill filtration. At the moment he has released circa 50 bottlings from a Port Charlotte distilled in 2001 to a Bunnahabhain from 1967. He also has two new expressions called Glen First Class (a Glenfarclas) and Glen Peat Class (a vatting of Ardbeg, Laphroaig and Bowmore), both bottled at 50%. According to Ewers, there are several hundreds of casks from more than 60 distilleries maturing in the warehouse.

Mackillop's Choice .... www.mackillopschoice.com

Mackillop's Choice, founded in 1996, is an independent bottler owned by Angus Dundee Distillers (owner of Tomintoul and Glencadam distilleries). The brand is named after Lorne McKillop who selects the casks. The whole range is single casks with no colouring or chill filtration. Some of the bottlings are at cask strength, while others are diluted to 40 or 43%.

Scott's Selection .... www.speysidedistillers.co.uk

Speyside Distillers in Glasgow are the owners of Speyside distillery but also has a wide range of whisky brands in their domains. One of these is Scott's Selection, a range of single cask malt whiskies, previously selected by the Master Blender Robert Scott, who now is retired. Emphasis is placed on whisky distilled in 70's and 80's and some unusual distilleries such as North Port, Linlithgow and Convalmore are represented. Perhaps the most interesting bottling is a single grain, North of Scotland 1973. This was the grain distillery that the founder of Speyside distillery, George Christie, had built in 1958 and has since closed down in 1980. All the whisky in the Scott's Selection range are bottled without colouring or chill-filtration and at cask strength. There is an additional range of single malts in the company, Private Cellar, but these are all diluted to 43%. In addition to single malt Speyside Distillers produces a range of blended whiskies, such as Glen Ross and Scotchguard.

New bottlings

It is virtually impossible to list all new bottlings during a year,
there are simply too many and sometimes it is difficult to find information on them.
In this list we have selected 500 that were released from late 2009 until autumn 2010.
All bottlings (except for certain official ones) are listed with year of distillation, age,
finish or special maturation (if applicable), alcohol strength and bottler.
Read more about the major independent bottlers on pages 250-253.

Aberfeldy

	19		OB
1994	15	57,3%	DR
	14	46,0%	CAD
1983	26	50,0%	DL

Aberlour

a'bunadh batch 30		59,6%	OB
1996	14	46,0%	DR
1993	17	55,2%	DT
1995	14	46,0%	DT
1992	16	46,0%	SD

Ardbeg

Supernova 2010		60,1%	OB
Rollercoaster		57,3%	OB
1994	15	53,0%	IM
1999	12	43,0%	IM
1994	15	56,0%	CAD
1998	11	57,9%	AD
1991	18	50,0%	DL

Ardmore

1992	17	46,0%	IM

Arran

	14	46,0%	OB
1999	Rowan Tree	46,0%	OB
	Port	50,0%	OB
	Sauternes	50,0%	OB
	Amarone	50,0%	OB
	Amontillado	54,6%	OB
	Machrie Moor		OB
1997		55,0%	BA

Auchentoshan

1977		49,0%	OB
1998		54,6%	OB
2000	9	46,1%	DT
1992	16	56,6%	SD

Auchroisk

1999	Man. Choice	61,0%	OB
1990	20	58,1%	OB
	20	46,0%	CAD
1999	10	46,0%	DT
1975	34	47,7%	DL

Aultmore

1997	12 Oloroso	43,0%	IM
1974	35	49,6%	AD

Balblair

1978		46,0%	OB
2000		43,0%	OB
1991	US market	43,0%	OB
1981	19	46,0%	DR
1990	20	53,0%	CAD
1990	20	48,0%	AD

Balmenach

1984	25	51,8%	SIG
1993		43,0%	GM
2000	9	46,0%	DT

Balvenie

	40		OB
	17 Peat.Cask	43,0%	OB
	14 Carr. Cask	43,0%	OB

Banff

1975	34	44,1%	DR
1971	38	53,4%	DL

Ben Nevis

	25	56,0%	OB
1996	13	58,2%	DR
1999	10	43,0%	DT
1990	19	56,4%	DT
1998	11	46,0%	DT

Benriach

Solstice 12yo triple		50,0%	OB
Horizons 15yo		50%	OB
The Firkin Cask 32yo			OB
	16 Claret	46,0%	OB
	17 Burgundy	46,0%	OB
	17 Rioja	46,0%	OB
10 different Vintages			OB
1996	13 Pomerol	46,0%	IM
1995	14 Rum	46,0%	IM
1996	13 Sauternes	43,0%	IM

Benrinnes

1996	Man. Choice	59,7%	OB
1994		45,0%	BA

Benromach

Peatsmoke 3rd ed.		46,0%	OB
Origins batch 2		50,0%	OB
Origins batch 3		50,0%	OB

Bladnoch

1990	20	52,2%	CAD

Blair Athol

1995	Man. Choice	54,7%	OB
	Dist. Exclusive	55,8%	OB

Bowmore

	40	44,8%	OB
1981		49,6%	OB
1989	20	50,1%	DR
1996	13	46,0%	DR
1997	13	56,4%	CAD
	17	46,0%	CAD
2001	8	59,9%	AD
2000	10	54,7%	AD
2002	8	40,0%	DT
1998	12	46,0%	DT
1982	27	50,2%	DT
2002	Ch. Latour	46,0%	MM
2000		46,0%	MM
1999	Ch. d'Yquem	46,0%	MM
1996	Ch. Petrus	46,0%	MM
1987		58,7%	BA
1987	22 Sherry	56,1%	DL

Braeval

1989	20	59,3%	SD
1996		57,3%	BA

OB = Official bottling from the owner, AD = Adelphi Distillery, BA = Blackadder, BB = Berry Brothers, CAD = Cadenhead, DL = Douglas Laing, DR = Dewar Rattray, DT = Duncan Taylor, GM = Gordon & MacPhail, IM = Ian MacLeod, MM = Murray McDavid, SIG = Signatory, SD = Speciality Drinks

Brora

Year	Age	ABV	Bottler
	30	54,3%	OB
1981	28	57,4%	DL

Bruichladdich

Year	Age/Name	ABV	Bottler
Organic MV		46,0%	OB
PC Multi Vintage		46,0%	OB
Octomore Orpheus		61,0%	OB
Octomore/3_152		59,0%	OB
1977			OB
	40		OB
Black Art 2 1989			OB
1991	19	56,9%	CAD
1990	19	51,8%	AD
1991		50,2%	BA

Bunnahabhain

Year	Age/Name	ABV	Bottler
	30	45,4%	OB
	18 PX sherry	51,4%	OB
Cruach-Mhòna		50,0%	OB
1974	35	44,3%	DR
1991	18	53,7%	DR
1985	24	48,0%	IM
1997	12 Peated	46,0%	IM
1997	11	58,6%	AD
2000	9	59,2%	AD
1968	41	41,2%	AD
1975	35	47,3%	AD
1997	12 Peated	55,7%	SIG
1997	12	46,0%	DT
1979	29	46,0%	SD
1997	Ch. d'Yquem	46,0%	MM
2005	Rioja, peated	46,0%	MM
1997	Ch. Lafite	46,0%	MM
1997	Moine	54,0%	BA
1978	30	50,0%	DL

Caol Ila

Year	Age/Name	ABV	Bottler
	25	43,0%	OB
1997	Man. Choice	58,0%	OB
	12 Unpeated	57,6%	OB
1980	30	58,8%	DR
1999	10 Pomerol	46,0%	IM
1997	13	43,0%	IM
1999	11 S. Giovese	46,0%	IM
1996	13 Sauternes	43,0%	IM
1999	10 Oloroso	43,0%	IM
1984	25	55,2%	CAD
1982	27	57,6%	AD
1979	30	53,3%	BB
1984	25	50,9%	SIG
1979	30	55,6%	BB
1984	25	53,8%	DT
1981	29	55,2%	DT
1996	Ch. d'Yquem	46,0%	MM
2003		61,4%	BA
1984	26	50,0%	DL
1979	30	50,0%	DL

Caperdonich

Year	Age	ABV	Bottler
1972	37	53,4%	DT
1968	41	52,6%	DT
1998	12	57,0%	SD

Clynelish

Year	Age/Name	ABV	Bottler
1997	Man. Choice	58,8%	OB
1997	12	59,4%	DR
1993	16	56,8%	CAD
1993	16	56,4%	AD
1982	28	46,0%	BB
1997	Ch. Lafite	46,0%	MM
1995	Ch. Lafite	46,0%	MM
1990		57,1%	BA
1992	17	46,0%	SIG

Cragganmore

Year	Age/Name	ABV	Bottler
1997	Man. Choice	59,7%	OB
1989	21	56,0%	OB
1997	12	46,0%	DR
1985	24	50,7%	SIG
1992	17	46,0%	SIG
1989	20	50,0%	DL

Craigellachie

Year	Age	ABV	Bottler
1999	10	57,1%	DT

Dailuaine

Year	Age/Name	ABV	Bottler
1997	Man. Choice	58,6%	OB
1998	11 S. Giovese	43,0%	IM
1989	20	56,5%	CAD
1994		43,0%	GM
1982	27	46,0%	SD

Dallas Dhu

Year	Age	ABV	Bottler
1981	29	53,0%	DT
1981		55,8%	BA

Dalmore

Year	Age/Name	ABV	Bottler
1951	58 Selene	44,0%	OB
Mackenzie 1992		46,0%	OB
1999	11	59,1%	DR
1996	14 S. Giovese	43,0%	IM
1995	14 Rum	46,0%	IM
1997	12 Oloroso	43,0%	IM
1990	19	59,0%	SIG
1990	20 Sherry	50,0%	DL

Dalwhinnie

Year	Age	ABV	Bottler
1992	Man. Choice	51,0%	OB

Deanston

Year	Age/Name	ABV	Bottler
Virgin Oak		43,0%	OB
1994	15	50,0%	DL

Dufftown

Year	Age	ABV	Bottler
1997	Man. Choice	59,5%	OB

| 1984 | 25 | 57,5% | SIG |
| 1997 | Zinfandel | 46,0% | MM |

Edradour

Year	Age/Name	ABV	Bottler
2000	10 Sherry	59,1%	OB
Ballechin #5 Marsala		46,0%	OB
1999	10	46,0%	SIG

Fettercairn

Year	Age	ABV	Bottler
Fior		42,0%	OB
	24	44,4%	OB
	30	43,3%	OB
	40	40,0%	OB

Glenallachie

Year	Age	ABV	Bottler
1973	36	48,1%	AD
1995	14	59,7%	SD

Glenburgie

Year	Age	ABV	Bottler
1998	11	43,0%	IM
1990	18	62,2%	SD
1989		46,0%	MM

Glencadam

Year	Age/Name	ABV	Bottler
	12 Port	46,0%	OB
	14 Oloroso	46,0%	OB
	21	46,0%	OB
1990	19	56,3%	DR
1989	20	55,7%	SIG
1977	32	54,9%	DL

Glendronach

Year	Age/Name	ABV	Bottler
Octarine 8yo		46,0%	OB
Grandeur 31yo		45,8%	OB
1996	Dist. exclusive	59,7%	OB
	14 Virgin oak	46,0%	OB
	14 Sauternes	46,0%	OB
	15 Moscatel	46,0%	OB
	20 Port	46,0%	OB
12 different Vintages			OB
1994	15	61,8%	SD

Glendullan

Year	Age/Name	ABV	Bottler
1995	Man. Choice	59,2%	OB
1993	Ch. de Haux	46,0%	MM

Glen Elgin

Year	Age	ABV	Bottler
	18	46,0%	CAD

Glenfarclas

Year	Age	ABV	Bottler
	40	46,0%	OB
Family Casks, at least 12 vintages			OB

Glenfiddich

Year	Age/Name	ABV	Bottler
	14 Rich Oak	40,0%	OB
1978 Vintage Reserve		50,7%	OB

	40 6th edition	45,8%	OB
	30	43,0%	OB
	Snow Phoenix 15yo	47,6%	OB

Glen Garioch
	12	48,0%	OB
1990	20	56,0%	DR
1991	18	50,3%	CAD
1990	19	53,8%	AD

Glenglassaugh
| | 26 | 46,0% | OB |
| 1984 | 25 | 50,0% | DL |

Glengoyne
1987	single cask		OB
1997	single cask		OB
	13 Port	46,0%	OB
1996	14	55,9%	CAD

Glen Grant
	170th Anniversary	46,0%	OB
1985	24	55,8%	DR
1985	25	55,0%	AD
1969	40	44,3%	SIG
1969	40	51,6%	DT
1972	37	51,8%	DT
1974	35	48,8%	DT
1987	22	57,9%	DT
1976	32	50,0%	DL

Glengyle
| Kilkerran Work in Pr. | 46.0% | OB |

Glen Keith
1992	17	59,7%	DR
1995	15 S. Giovese	46,0%	IM
1996	13	54,2%	CAD
1989	20	46,0%	SD

Glenkinchie
1992	Man. Choice	58,1%	OB
	Dist. Exclusive	59,1%	OB
1990	20	55,1%	OB

Glenlivet
Founder's Reserve		55,6%	OB
1978	31	53,9%	AD
1995	14	46,0%	SIG
1987	22	56,1%	DT
1970	40	49,9%	DT
1989	19	46,0%	SD
1997		61,4%	BA

Glenlochy
| 1980 | 29 | 52,8% | SIG |

Glenlossie
| 1999 | Man. Choice | 59,3% | OB |
| 1993 | 16 | 55,8% | CAD |

Glen Mhor
1982	27 Sherry	56,8%	CAD
1982	27	55,0%	SIG
1982		55,8%	BA
1982	27	50,0%	DL

Glenmorangie
| Finealta | | 46,0% | OB |

Glen Moray
1996	13 Sauternes	43,0%	IM
1982	17 Rum	57,0%	CAD
1975	35	50,3%	DT
1988	21	57,1%	DT
1971	38	48,7%	DT
1983	26	54,6%	DT
1973	36	53,1%	DT

Glen Ord
| 1997 | Man. Choice | 59,2% | OB |

Glenrothes
1990	19	49,9%	DR
1997	13	48,0%	IM
1997	12	43,0%	IM
1994	15	53,8%	CAD
1969	40	45,8%	DT
1968	41	43,0%	DT
1989	19	46,0%	SD
1998	Ch. d'Yquem	46,0%	MM
1989		54,2%	BA
1988		52,5%	BA

Glen Scotia
1992	17	59,4%	DR
1977	33	57,0%	DR
1977	32	56,0%	IM
1992	18	52,1%	CAD
1991	18	57,6%	DT

Glenspey
1996	Man. Choice	52,0%	OB
1988	21	50,4%	OB
1995	15	56,1%	CAD

Glenugie
| 1980 | 30 | 50,0% | IM |
| 1977 | 32 | 58,6% | SIG |

Hazelburn
| Hazelburn CV | | 46,0% | OB |
| Hazelburn Sauternes | | | OB |

Highland Park
	50			OB
Saint Magnus 12yo		52,6%	OB
1970	Orcad. vintage	48,0%	OB
1973		50,6%	OB
1990		40,0%	OB
1994		40,0%	OB
1998		40,0%	OB
1998	11	46,0%	DR
1990	19	56,7%	SIG
1991	18	46,0%	SIG
1995	Ch. Lafite	46,0%	MM
1988		46,0%	MM
1997		53,8%	BA
1996		55,1%	BA
1983	26	50,0%	DL

Imperial
1982	27	58,3%	SIG
1998	11	46,0%	DT
1997	13	46,0%	DT

Inchgower
| 1993 | Man. Choice | 61,9% | OB |

Inchmurrin
| 1996 | | 60,7% | BA |

Jura
1993	Oloroso	54,0%	OB
1995	Bourbon	56,5%	OB
1999	Peated	55,0%	OB
200th Anniver. 21yo			OB
Prophecy		46,0%	OB
1997	12	43,0%	IM
1999	10 St Etienne	55,0%	IM
1996	13	43,0%	IM

Kilchoman
Second release		46,0%	OB
Third release		46,0%	OB
Fourth release		46,0%	OB

Knockando
| 1996 | Man. Choice | 58,6% | OB |
| 1994 | | 60,6% | BA |

Lagavulin
1993	Man. Choice	54,7%	OB
	Dist. Exclusive	51,5%	OB
1998	12	56,5%	OB

Laphroaig
Cairdeas Master Ed.		57,3%	OB
	20 Double C.	46,6%	OB
1998	11	61,6%	DR
1997	13	58,0%	DR
2001	9	46,0%	SIG

Year	Age/Type	ABV	Bottler
1990	19	53,6%	SIG
1990	19	54,2%	SIG
1997	12	54,9%	DT
1997	13	46,0%	DT
1999	Ch. Margaux	46,0%	MM
1999	Ch. Lafite	46,0%	MM
1998	Ch. Petrus	46,0%	MM
1997	Ch. Latour	46,0%	MM
1998	Ch. Petrus	46,0%	MM
1998		57,4%	BA
1989	20	50,0%	DL

Ledaig
Year	Age/Type	ABV	Bottler
1997	12	46,0%	IM
	13	46,0%	CAD
2005		62,7%	BB
2004		46,0%	MM

Linkwood
Year	Age/Type	ABV	Bottler
1997	12	43,0%	IM
1989	20	55,4%	CAD
1984	25	56,4%	AD
1989	20	53,4%	SD

Littlemill
Year	Age/Type	ABV	Bottler
1991	19	58,1%	CAD

Lochside
Year	Age/Type	ABV	Bottler
1981	18	50,0%	DL

Longmorn
Year	Age/Type	ABV	Bottler
1990	20	52,8%	DR
	19	46,0%	CAD
1992	17	53,6%	AD
1990	20	50,5%	AD
1992	17		SD
1990	19	54,5%	SD
1989	19	46,0%	SD
1999		62,0%	BA

Macallan
Year	Age/Type	ABV	Bottler
Oscuro		46,5%	OB
Fine Oak Master Ed.		42,8%	OB
1991	19	58,9%	DR
1989	20	52,1%	CAD
1995	14	57,0%	AD
1996	13	58,8%	AD
1988	21	53,9%	SIG
1991	18	55,3%	DT
1996	13	46,0%	DT
1995	Ch. d'Yquem	46,0%	MM
1995	Ch. Petrus	46,0%	MM
1997	Ch. Latour	46,0%	MM
1992		46,0%	MM
1997		53,2%	BA
1977	32 Pinot Noir	49,4%	DL
1985	24	50,0%	DL
1990	19 Red Wine	50,0%	DL

Macduff
Year	Age/Type	ABV	Bottler
1984	25	52,2%	BB

Mannochmore
Year	Age/Type	ABV	Bottler
1998	Man. Choice	59,1%	OB
1982	27 Claret	58,4%	CAD

Miltonduff
Year	Age/Type	ABV	Bottler
1991	18	51,3%	OB
1987	23	46,0%	IM

Mortlach
Year	Age/Type	ABV	Bottler
1938	70	46,1%	GM
1990	19	58,6%	DR
1998	12	43,0%	IM
1995	14	43,0%	IM
1990	19	57,5%	SIG
1991	18	46,0%	SIG
1994	Fresh Oak	46,0%	MM
1997	Ch. d'Yquem	46,0%	MM
1989	21	50,0%	DL
1992	17	56,1%	DL

Mosstowie
Year	Age/Type	ABV	Bottler
1979	31	50,4%	SIG

Oban
Year	Age/Type	ABV	Bottler
	Dist. Exclusive	55,0%	OB

Octomore
Year	Age/Type	ABV	Bottler
Octomore Orpheus		61,0%	OB
Octomore/3_152		59,0%	OB

Port Charlotte
Year	Age/Type	ABV	Bottler
PC Multi Vintage		46,0%	OB

Port Ellen
Year	Age/Type	ABV	Bottler
	31	54,6%	OB
1982	28	50,0%	IM
1983	27	55,7%	SIG
1982	27	58,6%	SIG
1983	26	54,6%	DT
1979	30	52,6%	DL
1983	27	46,0%	DL
1983	26	50,0%	DL

Pulteney
Year	Age/Type	ABV	Bottler
WK499 Isabella Fort.		52,0%	OB
1982	27	53,5%	DR
1974		43,0%	GM
1995		60,5%	GM

Rosebank
Year	Age/Type	ABV	Bottler
1990	20 Fr Oak fin.	46,0%	IM
1991	19		SD
1990	19	50,0%	DL

Royal Lochnagar
Year	Age/Type	ABV	Bottler
1994	Man. Choice	59,3%	OB
1986	23	54,5%	DT

Speyside
Year	Age/Type	ABV	Bottler
1993	17	61,2%	SD
1991	18 Pomerol	54,9%	DL

Springbank
Year	Age/Type	ABV	Bottler
	12 cask str.	54,6%	OB
	12 Claret	54,4%	OB
	18	46,0%	OB
	CV	46,0%	OB
2001	8 Cognac	58,5%	CAD
1992	17	54,3%	AD
1998	12	51,5%	AD
2000	Ch. d'Yquem	46,0%	MM

Strathmill
Year	Age/Type	ABV	Bottler
1996	Man. Choice	60,1%	OB
1991	18	46,0%	DR

Talisker
Year	Age/Type	ABV	Bottler
1994	Man. Choice	58,6%	OB
1980	30	57,3%	OB

Tamdhu
Year	Age/Type	ABV	Bottler
1994	16	46,0%	IM
1987		49,5%	BA
1989	20	55,6%	DL

Tamnavulin
Year	Age/Type	ABV	Bottler
1992	16	54,1%	SD

Tobermory
Year	Age/Type	ABV	Bottler
1994	Ch. Haut Brion	46,0%	MM

Tomatin
Year	Age/Type	ABV	Bottler
1997	12	57,1%	OB
1999	10	57,1%	OB
1990	18	54,0%	OB
	21	52,0%	OB
1999	Tempranillo		OB
	4 Peated		OB
1988	21	55,2%	DR
1994	16	53,6%	CAD

Tomintoul
Year	Age/Type	ABV	Bottler
	12 Port		OB
1967		45,9%	BA

Tormore
Year	Age/Type	ABV	Bottler
1988	21	64,8%	SD

Tullibardine
Year	Age/Type	ABV	Bottler
Aged Oak		40,0%	OB

OB = Official bottling from the owner, AD = Adelphi Distillery, BA = Blackadder, BB = Berry Brothers, CAD = Cadenhead, DL = Douglas Laing, DR = Dewar Rattray, DT = Duncan Taylor, GM = Gordon & MacPhail, IM = Ian MacLeod, MM = Murray McDavid, SIG = Signatory, SD = Speciality Drinks

Whisky Shops

AUSTRIA

Potstill
Strozzigasse 37
1080 Wien
Phone: +43 (0)676 965 89 36
www.potstill.org
Austria's premier whisky shop with over 1100 kinds of which c 900 are malts, including some real rarities. Arranges tastings and seminars and ships to several European countries. On-line ordering.

BELGIUM

Whiskycorner
Kraaistraat 16
3530 Houthalen
Phone: +32 (0)89 386233
www.whiskycorner.be
A very large selection of single malts, no less than 1100 different! Also other whiskies, calvados and grappas. The site is in both French and English. Mail ordering, but not on-line. Shipping worldwide.

Jurgen´s Whiskyhuis
Gaverland 70
9620 Zottegem
Phone: +32 (0)9 336 51 06
www.whiskyhuis.be
An absolutely huge assortment of more than 2,000 different single malts with 700 in stock and the rest delivered within the week. Also 40 different grain whiskies and 120 bourbons. Online mail order with shipments worldwide.

Huis Crombé
Engelse Wandeling 11
8500 Kortrijk
Phone: +32 (0)56 21 19 87
www.crombewines.com
A wine retailer with a heritage dating back to 1894 and now covers all kinds of spirits. The whisky range is very nice where a large assortment of Scotch is supplemented with whiskies from Japan, the USA and Ireland to mention a few. Regular tastings in the shop.

CANADA

Kensington Wine Market
1257 Kensington Road NW
Calgary
Alberta T2N 3P8
Phone: +1 403 283 8000
www.kensingtonwinemarket.com
With 400 different bottlings this is the largest single malt assortment in Canada. Also 2,500 different wines. Regular tastings in the shop.

DENMARK

Juul´s Vin & Spiritus
Værnedamsvej 15
1819 Frederiksberg
Phone: +45 33 31 13 29
www.juuls.dk
A very large range of wines, fortified wines and spirits. Around 500 single malts. Also a good selection of drinking glasses. On-line ordering. Shipping outside Denmark (except for Scandinavian countries).

Cadenhead´s WhiskyShop Denmark
Vestergade 21
5000 Odense C
Phone: +45 66 139 505
www.cadenheads.dk
Whisky specialist with a very good range, not least from Cadenhead's. Nice range of champagne, cognac and rum. Arranges whisky and beer tastings. On-line ordering with worldwide shipping.

Whiskydirect.dk
Braunstein
Carlsensvej 5
4600 Køge
Phone: +45 7020 4468
www.whiskydirect.dk
This on-line retailer is owned by newly established Braunstein Distillery. Aside from own produce one can find an assortment of 200 different whiskies, including own single cask bottlings from Scottish distilleries.

Kokkens Vinhus
Hovedvejen 102
2600 Glostrup
Phone: +45 44 97 02 30
www.kokkensvinhus.dk
A shop with a complete assortment of wine, spirit, coffee, tea and delicatessen. They started selling whisky five years ago and now stock around 500 different kinds, mostly single malts. They are specialists in independent bottlings. On-line ordering for shipments within Denmark.

ENGLAND

The Whisky Exchange (2 shops)
Unit 7, Space Business Park
Abbey Road, Park Royal
London NW10 7SU
Phone: +44 (0)208 838 9388

The Whisky Exchange
Vinopolis, 1 Bank End
London SE1 9BU
Phone: +44 (0)207 403 8688
www.thewhiskyexchange.com
This is a great whisky shop established in 1999 and owned by Sukhinder Singh. Started off as a mail order business which was run from a showroom in Hanwell, but since some years back there is also an excellent shop at Vinopolis in downtown London. The assortment is huge with well over 1000 single malts to choose from. Some rarities which can hardly be found anywhere else are offered much thanks to Singh's great interest for antique whisky. There are also other types of whisky and cognac, calvados, rum etc. On-line ordering and ships all over the world.

The Whisky Shop
(See also Scotland, The Whisky Shop)
Unit 1.09 MetroCentre
Red Mall
Gateshead NE11 9YG
Phone: +44 (0)191 460 3777

11 Coppergate Walk
York YO1 9NT
Phone: +44 (0)1904 640300

510 Brompton Walk
Lakeside Shopping Centre
West Thurrock, Essex RM20 2ZL
Phone: +44 (0)1708 866255

7 Turl Street
Oxford OX1 3DQ
Phone: +44 (0)1865 202279

3 Swan Lane
Norwich NR2 1HZ
Phone: +44 (0)1603 618284

7 Queens Head Passage
Paternoster
London EC4M 7DY
Phone: +44 (0)207 329 5117

25 Chapel Street
Guildford GU1 3UL
Phone: +44 (0)1483 450900
www.whiskyshop.com
The first shop opened in 1992 in Edinburgh and this is now the United Kingdom's largest specialist retailer of whiskies with 16 outlets. A large product range with over 700 kinds, including 400 malt whiskies and 140 miniature bottles, as well as accessories and books. The own range 'Glenkeir Treasures' is a special assortment of selected malt whiskies. On-line ordering and shipping all over the world except to the USA.

Royal Mile Whiskies
3 Bloomsbury Street
London WC1B 3QE
Phone: +44 (0)20 7436 4763
www.royalmilewhiskies.com
The London branch of Royal Mile Whiskies. See also Scotland, Royal Mile Whiskies.

Berry Bros. & Rudd
3 St James´ Street
London SW1A 1EG
Phone: +44 (0)870 900 4300
www.bbr.com/whisky

A legendary shop that has been situated in the same place since 1698. One of the world's most reputable wine shops but with an exclusive selection of malt whiskies. There are also shops in Dublin and Hong Kong specialising primarily in fine wines.

The Wright Wine and Whisky Company
The Old Smithy, Raikes Road, Skipton
North Yorkshire BD23 1NP
Phone: +44 (0)1756 700886
www.wineandwhisky.co.uk
A very good selection of over 750 different whiskies to choose from. There is also a nice range of armagnac, rum, calvado etc. 900 different wines are likely to impress the visitor.

Master of Malt
2 Leylands Manor
Tubwell Lane
Crowborough
East Sussex TN6 3RH
Phone: +44 (0)1892 888 376
www.masterofmalt.com
Independent bottler and online retailer since 1985. A very impressive range of more than 1,000 Scotch whiskies of which 800 are single malts. In addition to whisky from other continents there is a wide selection of rum, cognac, Armagnac and tequila. The website is redesigned and contains a wealth of information on the distilleries. They have also recently launched "Drinks by the Dram" where you can order 3cl samples of almost 400 different whiskies to try before you buy a full bottle.

Whiskys.co.uk
The Square, Stamford Bridge
York YO4 11AG
Phone: +44 (0)1759 371356
www.whiskys.co.uk
Good assortment with more than 600 different whiskies. Also a nice range of armagnac, rum, calvados etc. On-line ordering, ships outside of the UK. The owners also have another website, www.whiskymerchants.co.uk with a huge amount of information on just about every whisky distillery in the world and very up to date.

The Wee Dram
5 Portland Square, Bakewell
Derbyshire DE45 1HA
Phone: +44 (0)1629 812235
www.weedram.co.uk
Large range of Scotch single malts (c 450) with whiskies from other parts of the world and a good range of whisky books. Run 'The Wee Drammers Whisky Club' with tastings and seminars. On-line ordering.

Mainly Wine and Whisky
3-4 The Courtyard, Bawtry
Doncaster DN10 6JG
Phone: +44 (0)1302 714 700
www.whisky-malts-shop.com
A good range with c 400 different whiskies of which 300 are single malts. Arranges tastings and seminars. On-line ordering with shipping also outside the UK. Was known as Mainly Malts before they joined with a local wine shop.

Chester Whisky & Liqueur
59 Bridge Street Row
Chester
Cheshire CH1 1NW
Phone: +44 (0)1244 347806
www.chesterwhisky.com
A shop that specialises in single malt Scotch and American, Irish, Japanese and Welsh whisky. There is also a good range of calvados, armagnac and rum and the shop has its own house blend, Chester Cross Blended Scotch Whisky, as well as three casks for tasting and bottling in the store.

Nickolls & Perks
37 Lower High Street, Stourbridge
West Midlands DY8 1TA
Phone: +44 (0)1384 394518
www.nickollsandperks.co.uk
Mostly known as wine merchants but also has a good range of whiskies with c 300 different kinds including 200 single malts. On-line ordering with shipping also outside of UK

Gauntleys of Nottingham
4 High Street
Exchange Arcade
Nottingham NG1 2ET
Phone: +44 (0)115 9110555
www.gauntley-wine.co.uk
A fine wine merchant established in 1880. The range of wines are among the best in the UK. All kinds of spirits, not least whisky, are taking up more and more space and several rare malts can be found. The monthly whisky newsletter by Chris Goodrum makes good reading and there is also a mail order service available.

The Wine Shop
22 Russell Street, Leek
Staffordshire ST13 5JF
Phone: +44 (0)1538 382408
www.wineandwhisky.com
In addition to wine there is a good range of c 300 whiskies and also calvados, cognacs, rums etc. They also stock a range of their own single malt bottlings under the name of 'The Queen of the Moorlands'. Mailorders by telephone or email for UK delivery.

The Lincoln Whisky Shop
87 Bailgate
Lincoln LN1 3AR
Phone: +44 (0)1522 537834
www.lincolnwhiskyshop.co.uk
Mainly specialising in whisky with more than 400 different whiskies but also 500 spirits and liqueurs and some 100 wines. Mailorder only within UK.

Milroys of Soho
3 Greek Street
London W1D 4NX
Phone: +44 (0)20 7437 2385
www.milroys.co.uk
A classic whisky shop in Soho now owned by the retail wine merchant Jeroboams Group. A very good range with over 700 malts and a wide selection of whiskies from around the world. Tastings are arranged in the tasting cellar in the shop. On-line ordering for shipping within the UK.

Arkwrights
114 The Dormers
Highworth
Wiltshire SN6 7PE
Phone: +44 (0)1793 765071
www.whiskyandwines.com
A good range of whiskies (over 700 in stock) as well as wine and other spirits. Regular tastings in the shop. On-line ordering with shipping all over the world except USA and Canada.

Cadenhead's Whisky Shop
26 Chiltern Street
London W1U 7QF
Phone: +44 (0)20 7935 6999
www.whiskytastingroom.com
Used to be in Covent Garden but moved and was expanded with a tasting room. One in a chain of shops owned by independent bottlers Cadenhead. Sells Cadenhead's product range and c 200 other whiskies. Regular tastings and on-line ordering.

The Vintage House
42 Old Compton Street
London W1D 4LR
Phone: +44 (0)20 7437 5112
www.sohowhisky.com
A huge range of 1400 kinds of malt whisky, many of them rare or unusual. Supplementing this is also a selection of fine wines. On-line ordering with shipping only within the UK.

Whisky On-line
Units 1-3 Concorde House, Charnley Road, Blackpool, Lancashire FY1 4PE
Phone: +44 (0)1253 620376
www.whisky-online.com
A good selection of whisky and also cognac, rum, port etc. On-line ordering with shipping all over the world.

Constantine Stores
30 Fore Street
Constantine, Falmouth
Cornwall TR11 5AB
Phone: +44 (0)1326 340226
www.drinkfinder.co.uk
A full-range wine and spirits dealer with a good selection of whiskies from the whole world (around 800 different, of which 600 are single malts). Worldwide shipping except for USA and Canada.

FRANCE

La Maison du Whisky (2 shops)
20 rue d'Anjou
75008 Paris
Phone: +33 (0)1 42 65 03 16

(2 shops outside France)

47 rue Jean Chatel
97400 Saint-Denis, La Réunion
Phone: +33 (0)2 62 21 31 19

The Pier at Robertson Quay
80 Mohamed Sultan Road, #01-10
Singapore 239013
Phone: +65 6733 0059
www.whisky.fr
France's largest whisky specialist with over 1200 whiskies in stock. Also a number of own-bottled single malts. Three shops and on-line ordering. Ships to some 20 countries.

GERMANY

Celtic Whisk(e)y & Versand
Otto Steudel
Bulmannstrasse 26
90459 Nürnberg
Phone: +49 (0)911 450974-30
www.whiskymania.de/celtic
A very impressive single malt range with well over 1000 different single malts and a good selection from other parts of the world. On-line ordering with shipping also outside Germany.

SCOMA - Scotch Malt Whisky GmbH
Am Bullhamm 17
26441 Jever
Phone: +49 (0)4461 912237
www.scoma.de
Very large range of c 750 Scottish malts and many from other countries. Holds regular seminars and tastings. The excellent, monthly whisky newsletter SCOMA News is produced and can be downloaded as a pdf-file from the website. On-line ordering.

The Whisky Store
Am Grundwassersee 4
82402 Seeshaupt
Phone: +49 (0)8801-23 17
www.thewhiskystore.com
A very large range comprising c 700 kinds of whisky of which 550 are malts. Also sells whisky liqueurs, books and accessories. The website is a veritable goldmine of information about the whisky business and especially so when it comes to photographs of distilleries. There are 7500 photos of 168 distilleries. On-line ordering.

Cadenhead's Whisky Market
Luxemburger Strasse 257
50939 Köln
Phone: +49 (0)221-2831834
www.cadenheads.de
This first Cadenhead shop outside of the UK was established in 2001. Good range of malt whiskies (c 350 different kinds) with emphasis on Cadenhead's own bottlings. Other products include wine, cognac and rum etc. Arranges recurring tastings and also has an on-line shop.

Cadenhead's Whisky Market
Mainzer Strasse 20
10247 Berlin-Friedrichshain
Phone: +49 (0)30-30831444
www.cadenhead-berlin.de
Good product range with c 350 different kinds of malt with emphasis on Cadenhead's own bottlings as well as wine, cognac and rum etc. Arranges recurrent tastings.

Malts and More
Hosegstieg 11
22880 Wedel
Phone: +49 (0)40-23620770
www.maltsandmore.de
Very large assortment with over 800 different single malts from Scotland as well as whiskies from many other countries. Also a nice selection of cognac, rum etc. Orders can be placed on-line or through Email and telephone.

Reifferscheid
Mainzer Strasse 186
53179 Bonn / Mehlem
Phone: +49 (0)228 9 53 80 70
www.whisky-bonn.de
A well-stocked shop which has been listed as one of the best in Germany several times. Aside from a large range of whiskies (among them a good selection from Duncan Taylor), wine, spirit, cigars and a delicatessen can be found. Holds regular tastings.

Whiskywizard.de
Christian Jaudt
Schulstrasse 57
66540 Neunkirchen
Phone: +49 (0)6858-699507
www.whiskywizard.de
Large assortment of single malt (over 500) and other spirits. Only orders on-line, shipping also outside Germany.

Whisky-Doris
Germanenstrasse 38
14612 Falkensee
Phone: +49 (0)3322-219784
www.whisky-doris.de
Large range of over 300 whiskies and also sells own special bottlings. Orders via email. Shipping also outside Germany.

Finlays Whisky Shop
Limesstrasse 9 A
61381 Friedrichsdorf
Phone: +49 61 75 79 79 58
www.finlayswhiskyshop.de
Whisky specialists with a large range of over 700 single malts. Finlays also work as the importer to Germany of Douglas laing, James MacArthur and Wilson & Morgan. There is an impressive listing of 700 bottlings of Port Ellen on the website (The Port Ellen Archive). Shop in Friedrichsdorf as well as on-line orders.

Weinquelle Lühmann
Lübeckerstrasse 145
22087 Hamburg
Phone: +49 (0)40-25 63 91
www.weinquelle.com
An impressive selection of both wines and spirits with over 1000 different whiskies of which 850 are malt whiskies. Also an impressive range of rums. General information about whisky on the site, part of which is in English. On-line ordering with shipping also possible outside Germany.

Liquids
Heerstrasse 335
50169 Kerpen-Brüggen
Phone: +49 (0)2237-975491
www.liquids-and-more.de
A good range (over 200 single malts) and a fine assortment of whiskies from other countries. Also books and accessories. On-line ordering.

The Whisky-Corner
Reichertsfeld 2
92278 Illschwang
Phone: +49 (0)9666-951213
www.whisky-corner.de
A small shop but large on mail order. A very large assortment of over 1600 whiskies. Also sells blended and American whiskies. The website is very informative with features on, among others, whisky-making, tasting and independent bottlers. On-line ordering.

World Wide Spirits
Hauptstrasse 12
84576 Teising
Phone: +49 (0)8633 50 87 93
www.worldwidespirits.de
A nice range of c 500 whiskies with some rarities from the twenties. Also large selection (c 1000) of other spirits.

Banneke
Kreuzeskirchstr. 37
45127 Essen
Phone: +49 (0)201 247710
www.banneke.de
Very impressive assortment of 4500 different kinds of spirit and wine. Good range of malt whiskies (c 400) and rum (c 200). On-line ordering and will deliver outside of Germany.

WhiskyKoch
Weinbergstrasse 2
64285 Darmstadt
Phone: +49 (0152) 29 51 75 72
www.whiskykoch.de
The English chef, Christopher Pepper, and his wife Marion own this combination of a whisky shop and restaurant. The shop has a nice selection of single malts as well as other Scottish products and the restaurant has specialised in whisky dinners and tastings.

Whisk(e)y Shop Tara
Rindermarkt 16
80331 München
Phone: +49 (0)89-26 51 18
www.whiskyversand.de
Whisky specialists with a very broad range of, for example, 800 different single malts. On-line ordering.

Mara Malt-Rarities
Roland Puhl & Co. GbR
Cahenslystr. 14
65549 Limburg
Phone: +49 (0)6431-41176
Phone: +49 (0)6432-508690
www.maltwhisky-mara.com
Probably the main experts on rare whisky offering over 1000 kinds. Also arranges tastings. Mail orders by fax or phone. Shipping also outside Germany.

Single Malt Collection
(Glen Fahrn Germany GmbH)
Hauptstraße 38
79801 Hohentengen a. H.
Phone: +49 (0)77 42 -857 222
www.singlemaltcollection.com
A very large range of single malts (c 600). Newsletter. On-line ordering. Shipping also outside Germany.

Kierzek
Weitlingstrasse 17
10317 Berlin
Phone: +49 (0)30 525 11 08
www.kierzek-berlin.de
Over 400 different whiskies in stock (of which 250 are single malts). In the product range 50 kinds of rum and 450 wines from all over the world are found among other products. Mail order is available within Germany.

Whisky & Cigars
Sophienstrasse 8-9
10178 Berlin-Mitte
Phone: +49 (0)30 2820376
www.whisky-cigars.de
Over 1000 kinds of whisky and a large
selection of cigars from all over the
world. Tastings are arranged.

House of Whisky
Ackerbeeke 6
31683 Obernkirchen
Phone: +49 (0)5724-399420
www.houseofwhisky.de
Aside from over 1,200 different malts
also sells a large range of other spirits
(including over 100 kinds of rum).
On-line ordering with shipping also
outside Germany.

Whiskyscheune
Alte Bornstrasse 4
61250 Usingen
Phone: +49 (0)6081-582642
www.whiskyscheune.de
Large selection with c 500 Scottish
malts in addition to whiskies from
other countries. Also mail order.

Whiskyworld
Ziegelfeld 6
94481 Grafenau / Haus i. Wald
Phone: +49 (0)8555-406 320
www.whiskyworld.de
A very good assortment of more than
1,000 malt whiskies. Also has a good
range of wines, other spirits, cigars and
books. Also on-line ordering.

Wine, Spirits & Cigars
(Whiskypack Spirituosenhandel)
Schnakenberg 15-19
31608 Marklohe/Lemke
Phone: +49 (0)5021-888150
www.nurvomfeinsten.de
Has a nice selection of cigars in
addition to whisky, wines and spirits.
On-line ordering.

World Wide Whisky (2 shops)
Eisenacher Strasse 64
10823 Berlin-Schöneberg
Phone: +49 (0)30-7845010

Hauptstrasse 58
10823 Berlin-Schöneberg
www.world-wide-whisky.de
Large range of 1,500 different whiskies.
Arranges tastings and seminars. Has a
large number of rarities. Orders can be
made via email.

HUNGARY

Whisky Net / Whisky Shop
Kovács Làszlò Street 21
2000 Szentendre

(shop)
Veres Pálné utca 8.
1053 Budapest
Phone: +36 1 267-1588
www.whiskynet.hu, www.whiskyshop.hu
A whisky trader established in 2007. In
the shop in downtown Budapest one
finds the largest selction of whisky in
Hungary. Agents for Douglas Laing, Cadenhead, Bruichladdich and Glenfarclas
among others. Also mailorder.

IRELAND

Celtic Whiskey Shop
27-28 Dawson Street
Dublin 2
Phone: +353 (0)1 675 9744
www.celticwhiskeyshop.com
More than 70 kinds of Irish whiskeys
but also a good selection of Scotch,
wines and other spirits. On-line ordering with shipping all over the world.

ITALY

Cadenhead's Whisky Bar
Via Poliziano, 3
20154 Milano
Phone: +39 (0)2 336 055 92
www.cadenhead.it
This is the tenth and newest addition
in the Cadenhead´s chain of shops.
Concentrating mostly on the Caden-
head´s range but they also stock
whiskies from other producers.

THE NETHERLANDS

Whiskyslijterij De Koning
Hinthamereinde 41
5211 PM 's Hertogenbosch
Phone: +31 (0)73-6143547
www.whiskykoning.nl
An enormous assortment with more
than 1400 kinds of whisky including
c 800 single malts. Also whisky-related
items like decanters, books etc.
Arranges recurring tastings. The site is
in Dutch and English. On-line ordering.
Shipping all over the world.

Whisky- en Wijnhandel Verhaar
Planetenbaan 2a
3721 LA Bilthoven
Phone: +31 (0)30-228 44 18
www.whiskyshop.nl
A wide selection of wines and spirits
with 1300 whiskies of which 1000 come
from Scotland. Email orders.

Wijnhandel van Zuylen
Loosduinse Hoofdplein 201
2553 CP Loosduinen (Den Haag)
Phone: +31 (0)70-397 1400
www.whiskyvanzuylen.nl
Excellent range of whiskies (c 1100)
and wines. Email orders with shipping
to some ten European countries.

Wijnwinkel-Slijterij
Ton Overmars
Hoofddorpplein 11
1059 CV Amsterdam
Phone: +31 (0)20-615 71 42
www.tonovermars.nl
A very large assortment of wines,
spirits and beer which includes more
than 400 single malts. Arranges
recurring tastings. Orders via email.

Van Wees - Whiskyworld.nl
Leusderweg 260
3817 KH Amersfoort
Phone: +31 (0)33-461 53 19
www.whiskyworld.nl
A very large range of 1000 whiskies
including over 500 single malts. On-line
ordering.

NEW ZEALAND

Whisky Galore
797 Colombo Street
Christchurch 8013
Phone: +64 (3) 377 6824
www.whiskygalore.co.nz
The best whisky shop in New Zealand
with 550 different whiskies, approximately 350 which are single malts. The
owner Michael Fraser Milne, has also
founded The Whisky Guild which has,
as one of its aims, to produce exclusive
single cask bottlings for members.
There is also online mail-order shipping
within New Zealand.

POLAND

George Ballantine´s
Krucza str 47 A, Warsaw
Phone: +48 22 625 48 32

Pulawska str 22, Warsaw
Phone: +48 22 542 86 22
www.sklep-ballantines.pl
These two shops have the biggest
assortment in Poland with more than
360 different single malts. Apart from
whisky there is a full range of spirits
and wines from all over the world.
Recurrent tastings are arranged and
mail-orders are dispatched.

PORTUGAL

Whisky & Co
Rua Visconde de Seabra 12-A
1700-370 Lisboa
Phone: +351 217 933 314
www.whiskyco.com
Established in 2001 this is the foremost
whisky shop in Portugal with more
than 800 different whiskies and also a
Whisky Museum with more than 10.000
bottles on display.

RUSSIA

Whisky World Shop
9, Tverskoy Boulevard
123104 Moscow
Phone: +7 495 787 9150
www.whiskyworld.ru
Opened in 2003 in the centre of
Moscow. The assortment is huge with
more than 1,000 different single malts,
mainly from independent bottlers. It
also stocks a selection of rare and old
whiskies and a blended Scotch under
their own label, Glen Clyde. The range
is supplemented with a nice range of
cognac, armagnac, calvados, grappa
and wines. Tastings are also arranged.

SCOTLAND

Gordon & MacPhail
58 - 60 South Street, Elgin
Moray IV30 1JY
Phone: +44 (0)1343 545110
www.gordonandmacphail.com
This legendary shop opened already in
1895 in Elgin. The owners are perhaps
the most well-known among independent bottlers. The shop stocks more
than 800 bottlings of whisky and more

than 600 wines and there is also a delicatessen counter with high-quality products. Tastings are arranged in the shop and there are shipping services within the UK and overseas. The shop attracts visitors from all over the world.

Royal Mile Whiskies (2 shops)
379 High Street, The Royal Mile
Edinburgh EH1 1PW
Phone: +44 (0)131 2253383

3 Bloomsbury Street
London WC1B 3QE
Phone: +44 (0)20 7436 4763
www.royalmilewhiskies.com
Royal Mile Whiskies is one of the most well-known whisky retailers in the UK. It was established in Edinburgh in 1991. There is also a shop in London since 2002 and a cigar shop close to the Edinburgh shop. The whisky range is outstanding with many difficult to find elsewhere. They have a comprehensive site regarding information on regions, distilleries, production, tasting etc. Royal Mile Whiskies also arranges 'Whisky Fringe' in Edinburgh, a two-day whisky festival which takes place annually in mid August. On-line ordering with worldwide shipping.

The Whisky Shop
(See also England, The Whisky Shop)
Unit L2-02
Buchanan Galleries
220 Buchanan Street
Glasgow G1 2GF
Phone: +44 (0)141 331 0022

17 Bridge Street
Inverness IV1 1HD
Phone: +44 (0)1463 710525

11 Main Street
Callander FK17 8DU
Phone: +44 (0)1877 331936

93 High Street
Fort William PH33 6DG
Phone: +44 (0)1397 706164

Shop Unit 1
Station Road
Oban PA34 4NU
Phone: +44 (0)1631 564409

Unit 14
Gretna Gateway Outlet Village
Gretna DG16 5GG
Phone: +44 (0)1461338004

Unit RU58B, Ocean Terminal
Edinburgh EH6 6JJ
Phone: +44 (0)131 554 8211

Unit 23
Princes Mall
Edinburgh EH1 1BQ
Phone: +44 (0)131 558 7563

www.whiskyshop.com
The first shop opened in 1992 in Edinburgh and this is now the United Kingdom's largest specialist retailer of whiskies with 16 outlets. A large product range with over 700 kinds, including 400 malt whiskies and 140 miniature bottles, as well as accessories and books. The own range 'Glenkeir Treasures' is a special assortment of selected malt whiskies. On-line ordering and shipping all over the world except to the USA.

Loch Fyne Whiskies
Inveraray
Argyll PA32 8UD
Phone: +44 (0)1499 302 219
www.lfw.co.uk
A legendary shop with an equally legendary owner, Richard Joynson. Joynson is known as a person with a high degree of integrity who does not mince his words on whisky matters. The range of malt whiskies is large and they have their own house blend, the prize-awarded Loch Fyne, as well as their 'The Loch Fyne Whisky Liqueur'. There is also a range of house malts called 'The Inverarity'. Loch Fyne Whiskies also publish the highly readable 'Scotch Whisky Review' which previously was produced by Joynson but now has authorities such as Charles MacLean and Dave Broom on the staff. Also on-line ordering with worldwide shipping.

Single Malts Direct
36 Gordon Street
Huntly
Aberdeenshire AB54 8EQ
Phone: +44 (0) 845 606 6145
www.singlemaltsdirect.com
Duncan Taylor, one of Scotland's largest independent bottlers, also has a shop in Huntly. In the assortment is of course the whole Duncan Taylor range but also a selection of their own single malt bottlings called Whiskies of Scotland. Add bottlings from other producers and you end up with a good range of almost 700 different expressions. Also has an on-line shop with shipping worldwide. The website has information on the production of whisky and a very comprehensive glossary of whisky terms.

Parker's Whisky
27 Low Street, Banff AB45 1AU
Phone: +44 (0)1261 812353
www.parkerswhisky.co.uk
Dedicated malt whisky specialist with a very nice range of more than 500 malt whiskies. On-line ordering with worldwide shipping.

The Whisky Shop Dufftown
1 Fife Street, Dufftown, Keith
Moray AB55 4AL
Phone: +44 (0)1340 821097
www.whiskyshopdufftown.co.uk
Whisky specialist in Dufftown in the heart of Speyside, wellknown to many of the Speyside festival visitors. More than 500 single malts as well as other whiskies. Arranges tastings as well as special events during the Festivals. On-line ordering with worldwide shipping.

The Scotch Whisky Experience
354 Castlehill, Royal Mile
Edinburgh
Phone: +44 (0)131 220 0441
www.whisky-heritage.co.uk
The Scotch Whisky Heritage Centre is a must for whisky devotees visiting Edinburgh. An interactive visitor centre dedicated to the history of Scotch whisky. This five-star visitor attraction has an excellent whisky shop with almost 300 different whiskies in stock.

The shop is open to the general public and not only to those who have taken the whisky tour. Do not miss the award-winning Amber Restaurant where whisky is being used in the cooking.

Cadenhead's Campbeltown Whisky shop (Eaglesome)
7 Bolgam Street
Campbeltown
Argyll PA28 6HZ
Phone: +44 (0)1586 551710
www.wmcadenhead.com
One in a chain of shops owned by independent bottlers Cadenhead. Sells Cadenhead's products and other whiskies with a good range of, for example, Springbank. On-line ordering.

Cadenhead's Whisky Shop
172 Canongate, Royal Mile
Edinburgh EH8 8BN
Phone: +44 (0)131 556 5864
www.wmcadenhead.com
The oldest shop in the chain owned by Cadenhead. Sells Cadenhead's product range and a good selection of other whiskies and spirits. Arranges recurrent tastings. On-line ordering.

Robbie's Drams
3 Sandgate, Ayr
South Ayrshire KA7 1BG
Phone: +44 (0)1292 262 135
www.robbiesdrams.com
A whisky specialist with over 600 whiskies available in store and over 900 available from their on-line shop, including a large range of Irish, Japanese and American Bourbons. Specialists in single cask bottlings, closed distillery bottlings, rare malts, limited edition whisky and a nice range of their own bottlings. Worldwide shipping.

Luvian's Bottle Shop (2 shops)
93 Bonnygate, Cupar
Fife KY15 4LG
Phone: +44 (0)1334 654 820

66 Market Street, St Andrews
Fife KY16 9NU
Phone: +44 (0)1334 477752
www.luvians.com
Wine and whisky merchant with a very nice selection of more than 600 malt whiskies.

The Maltman
(S. R. & E. Barron (Dyce) Ltd.)
119 Victoria Street, Dyce
Aberdeen AB21 7BJ
Phone: +44 (0)1224 722208
www.maltman.co.uk
A good range with over 350 malts in stock, including a 'Collector's Corner' with some very rare malts. There is a mail order service, but not on-line. Only shipping within the UK.

Robert Graham Ltd (3 shops)
194 Rose Street
Edinburgh EH2 4AZ
Phone: +44 (0)131 226 1874

Finlay House
10-14 West Nile Street
Glasgow G1 2PP
Phone: +44 (0)141 248 7283

Robert Graham's Treasurer 1874

254 Canongate
Royal Mile
Edinburgh EH8 8AA
Phone: +44 (0)131 556 2791
www.whisky-cigars.co.uk
Established in 1874 this company
specialises in Scotch whisky and cigars.
They have a nice assortment of malt
whiskies and their range of cigars is
impressive. On-line ordering with shipping all over the world

Whisky Castle
Main Street
Tomintoul
Aberdeenshire AB37 9EX
Phone: +44 (0)1807 580 213
www.whiskycastle.co.uk
Whisky specialist situated in the heart
of malt whisky country. With over 500
single malts, the specialisation is in
independent bottlings. There is also a
mail order shipping worldwide with
the exception of USA.

John Scott & Miller
15-19 Bridge Street, Kirkwall
Orkney KW15 1HR
Phone: +44 (0)1856 873146
www.jsmorkney.co.uk
A very large range of whisky from all
over the world and a special selection
from Orkneys' two distilleries. There
is also a range of Havana, Dominican
Republic and Dutch cigars.

Scotch Malt Whisky Society
www.smws.com
A society with more than 20 000 members worldwide. They are specialised
in own bottlings of single casks and
release between 150 and 200 bottlings
a year. Orders on-line for members
only. Shipping only within UK.

SWITZERLAND

P. Ullrich AG
Schneidergasse 27
4051 Basel
Phone: +41 (0)61 338 90 91
Another two shops in Basel:
Laufenstrasse 16
Unt. Rebgasse 18
www.ullrich.ch
A very large range of wines, spirits,
beers, accessories and books. Over 800
kinds of whisky with almost 600 single
malt. On-line ordering. Recently, they
also founded a whisky club with
egular tastings (www.whiskysinn.ch).

Eddie's Whiskies
Dorfgasse 27
8810 Horgen
Phone: +41 (0)43 244 63 00
www.eddies.ch
A whisky specialist with more than
700 different whiskies in stock with
emphasis on single malts (more than
500 different). Also arranges tastings.

World of Whisky
Via dim Lej 6
7500 St. Moritz
Phone: +41 (0)81 852 33 77
www.world-of-whisky.ch
A legendary shop situated in the Hotel
Waldhaus Am See which has an also

legendary whisky bar, the Devil's Place.
It was created by Claudio Bernasconi,
owner of the hotel and a whisky aficio-
nado. With over 2,500 whiskies, the
bar appears in the Guinness Book of
Records. The shop, run by Christian
Lauper, stocks almost 1,000 different
whiskies and has a good range of
other spirits such as rum, cognac and
armagnac. There is also a World of
Whisky Malt Club and mail order.

Glen Fahrn (5 shops)
Glen Fahrn N°1 "the origin"
Fahrnstrasse 39
9402 Mörschwil
Phone: +41 (0)71 860 09 87

Glen Fahrn N°2 "the pearl"
Oberdorfstrasse 5
8001 Zürich
Phone: +41 (0)44 520 09 87

Glen Fahrn N°3 "the museum"
Paradeplatz 3
8001 Zürich
Phone: +41 (0)43 343 09 87

Glen Fahrn N°4 "the store"
Glen Fahrn Germany GmbH
Hauptstrasse 38
79801 Hohentengen a.H.
Germany
Phone: +49 (0)7742 857 222

Glen Fahrn N°5 "the hotel"
Bernstrasse 7
3280 Murten
Phone: +41 (0)26 678 81 91
www.glenfahrn.com
A wide range of spirits, fortified wines
and champagnes. A large selection of
whisky, with over 600 from Scotland.
On-line ordering. Ships within
Switzerland and to adjacent countries.

Monnier
Büetigenstrasse 30
2557 Studen
Phone: +41 (0)32 373 43 53
www.whiskytime.ch
A large range of whisky including
600 single malts. Also grappas and
champagnes. On-line ordering.
Shipping mainly within Switzerland.

Scot & Scotch
Wohllebgasse 7
8001 Zürich
Phone: +41 44 211 90 60
www.scotandscotch.ch
A whisky specialist with a great
selection including c 560 single malts.
Mail orders, but no on-line ordering.

Angels Share Shop
Unterdorfstrasse 15
5036 Oberentfelden
Phone: +41 (0)62 724 83 74
www.angelsshare.ch
A combined restaurant and whisky
shop. More than 400 different kinds
of whisky as well as a good range
of cigars. Scores extra points for
short information and photos of all
distilleries. On-line ordering.

Cadenhead's Whisky & More
Mittlere Gasse 15
5400 Baden
Phone: +41 (0)56 222 04 44
www.cadenheads.ch
A new member of the chain of Caden-

head's stores with a nice range of
whiskies, especially Cadenhead's. Also
rum, cognac and other spirits.

USA

Binny's Beverage Depot
5100 W. Dempster (Head Office)
Skokie, IL 60077
Phone:
Internet orders, 847-581-3186
Whisky Hotline, 888-817-5898 (toll free)
www.binnys.com
A chain of no less than 24 stores in
the Chicago area, covering everything
within wine and spirits. Some of the
stores also have a gourmet grocery,
cheese shop and, for cigar lovers, a
walk-in humidor. The whisk(e)y range
is impressive with 700 single malts, 120
bourbons, 40 Irish whiskeys and more.
Among other products almost 200
kinds of tequila should be mentioned.
Online mail order service.

Traverso's
2097 Stagecoach Road,
Santa Rosa, CA 95404
Phone: +1 707 542-2530
www.traversos.com
Traverso's Gourmet Foods was established by Charles Traverso in 1922 and
today specialises in food, wine and
liquors. They have a very nice range of
malt whiskies with regular tastings in
the shop.

The Whisky Shop
360 Sutter Street
San Francisco, CA 94108
Phone: +1 415-989-1030
www.whiskyshopusa.com
Whisky specialist with 600 different
whiskies of which over 400 are single
malts. Mail order with delivery to most
states.

The Wine Specialist
2115 M St. NW
Washington, DC 20037
Phone: +1 202 833 0707
www.winespecialist.com
Wines but also complete when it comes
to spirits with over 300 different single
malts. Another exciting part of the
range is 100 different kinds of sake and
soju. Mail order within the USA.

Park Avenue Liquor Shop
292 Madison Avenue
New York, NY 10017
Phone: +1 212 685 2442
www.parkaveliquor.com
Legendary whisky shop already established in 1934. A very large assortment
of wine and spirits with 400 different
expressions of single malt.

McScrooge's Wines and Spirits
307 N. Peters Rd
Knoxville, TN 37922
Phone: +1 865 691 6463
www.mcscrooges.com
Extensive assortment of wines, spirits
and beer. More than 350 different
single malts from over 80 distilleries.

Statistics

Photo: © Chivas Bros

The following pages cover statistics and forecasts on production, sales, exports, consumption and capacity. The pages have been made possible thanks to kind cooperation from three sources - Euromonitor International, The Scotch Whisky Industry Review and Scotch Whisky Association.

Euromonitor International
is the world's leading provider of global business intelligence and strategic market analysis. They have more than 30 years experience of publishing market reports, business reference books, bespoke consulting projects, and integrated online databases: GMID and Passport. Euromonitor International is headquartered in London with offices in Chicago, Singapore, Shanghai, Dubai, Vilnius, Cape Town and Santiago.
More information on **www.euromonitor.com**

The Scotch Whisky Industry Review 2010
is written and compiled by Alan S Gray, Sutherlands Edinburgh. It is now in its 33rd consecutive year and provides a wealth of unique business critical information on the Scotch Whisky Industry. Copies can be obtained from Sutherlands Edinburgh, 61 Dublin Street, Edinburgh EH3 6NL. Details also on the website **www.scotchwhiskyindustryreview.com**

Scotch Whisky Association (SWA)
is the trade association for the Scotch Whisky industry. Its members account for more than 95% of production and sales of Scotch Whisky. Their main objective is to promote, protect and represent the interests of the whisky industry in Scotland and around the world. They also produce a plethora of statistical material covering production and sales of Scotch whisky. More information can be found on **www.scotch-whisky.org.uk**

EUROMONITOR INTERNATIONAL
making sense of global markets

Whisk(e)y forecast (volume & value) by region and sector 2009-2014

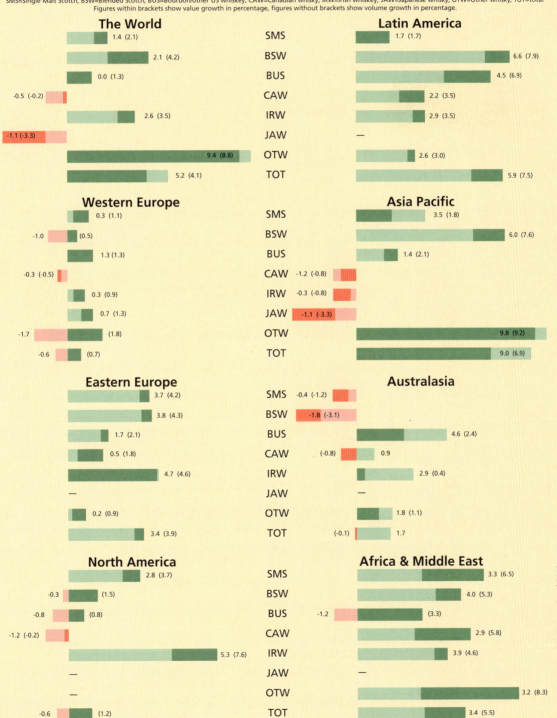

= positive volume growth   = positive value growth   = negative volume growth   = negative value growth

NB! The figures show CAGR% (Compound Annual Growth Rate) i. e. year-over-year growth rate.

SMS=Single Malt Scotch, BSW=Blended Scotch, BUS=Bourbon/other US whiskey, CAW=Canadian whisky, IRW=Irish whiskey, JAW=Japanese whisky, OTW=Other whisky, TOT=total
Figures within brackets show value growth in percentage, figures without brackets show volume growth in percentage.

The World

SMS	1.4 (2.1)
BSW	2.1 (4.2)
BUS	0.0 (1.3)
CAW	-0.5 (-0.2)
IRW	2.6 (3.5)
JAW	-1.1 (-3.3)
OTW	9.4 (8.8)
TOT	5.2 (4.1)

Latin America

Sector	
SMS	1.7 (1.7)
BSW	6.6 (7.9)
BUS	4.5 (6.9)
CAW	2.2 (3.5)
IRW	2.9 (3.5)
JAW	—
OTW	2.6 (3.0)
TOT	5.9 (7.5)

Western Europe

Sector	
SMS	0.3 (1.1)
BSW	-1.0 (0.5)
BUS	1.3 (1.3)
CAW	-0.3 (-0.5)
IRW	0.3 (0.9)
JAW	0.7 (1.3)
OTW	-1.7 (1.8)
TOT	-0.6 (0.7)

Asia Pacific

Sector	
SMS	3.5 (1.8)
BSW	6.0 (7.6)
BUS	1.4 (2.1)
CAW	-1.2 (-0.8)
IRW	-0.3 (-0.8)
JAW	-1.1 (-3.3)
OTW	9.8 (9.2)
TOT	9.0 (6.9)

Eastern Europe

SMS	3.7 (4.2)
BSW	3.8 (4.3)
BUS	1.7 (2.1)
CAW	0.5 (1.8)
IRW	4.7 (4.6)
JAW	—
OTW	0.2 (0.9)
TOT	3.4 (3.9)

Australasia

Sector	
SMS	-0.4 (-1.2)
BSW	-1.8 (-3.1)
BUS	4.6 (2.4)
CAW	-0.8 (0.9)
IRW	2.9 (0.4)
JAW	—
OTW	1.8 (1.1)
TOT	-0.1 (1.7)

North America

SMS	2.8 (3.7)
BSW	-0.3 (1.5)
BUS	-0.8 (0.8)
CAW	-1.2 (-0.2)
IRW	5.3 (7.6)
JAW	—
OTW	—
TOT	-0.6 (1.2)

Africa & Middle East

Sector	
SMS	3.3 (6.5)
BSW	4.0 (5.3)
BUS	-1.2 (3.3)
CAW	2.9 (5.8)
IRW	3.9 (4.6)
JAW	—
OTW	3.2 (8.3)
TOT	3.4 (5.5)

Top 5 Scotch Whisky Single Malt brands UK market share %

Glenfiddich	2009	14,1
	2008	13,2
	2007	13,1
Glenmorangie	2009	13,1
	2008	13,8
	2007	15,2
The Glenlivet	2009	10,0
	2008	9,8
	2007	9,1
Glen Moray	2009	6,1
	2008	5,7
	2007	5,4
Laphroaig	2009	5,5
	2008	5,4
	2007	5,6

Top 5 Scotch Whisky Single Malt brands export market share %

Glenfiddich	2009	14,4
	2008	14,8
	2007	15,2
The Glenlivet	2009	10,4
	2008	10,3
	2007	9,8
The Macallan	2009	9,9
	2008	8,3
	2007	8,2
Glen Grant	2009	6,5
	2008	6,9
	2007	7,3
Cardhu	2009	5,7
	2008	6,1
	2007	6,4

Top 5 Scotch Whisky Single Malt brands world market share %

Glenfiddich	2009	14,4
	2008	14,6
	2007	14,9
The Glenlivet	2009	10,4
	2008	10,2
	2007	9,7
The Macallan	2009	9,1
	2008	8,8
	2007	8,7
Glen Grant	2009	5,7
	2008	5,9
	2007	6,2
Glenmorangie	2009	4,9
	2008	5,4
	2007	5,3

Source: Euromonitor International 2010
The figures exclude grey and black
market and duty free / travel retail.
2009 shares are provisional.

Top 5 Scotch Whisky Blended brands UK market share %

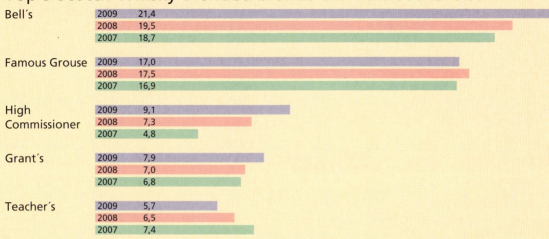

Bell's	2009	21,4
	2008	19,5
	2007	18,7
Famous Grouse	2009	17,0
	2008	17,5
	2007	16,9
High Commissioner	2009	9,1
	2008	7,3
	2007	4,8
Grant's	2009	7,9
	2008	7,0
	2007	6,8
Teacher's	2009	5,7
	2008	6,5
	2007	7,4

Top 5 Scotch Whisky Blended brands export market share %

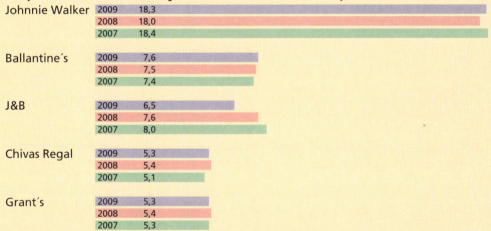

Johnnie Walker	2009	18,3
	2008	18,0
	2007	18,4
Ballantine's	2009	7,6
	2008	7,5
	2007	7,4
J&B	2009	6,5
	2008	7,6
	2007	8,0
Chivas Regal	2009	5,3
	2008	5,4
	2007	5,1
Grant's	2009	5,3
	2008	5,4
	2007	5,3

Top 5 Scotch Whisky Blended brands world market share %

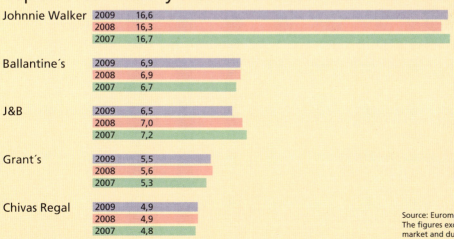

Johnnie Walker	2009	16,6
	2008	16,3
	2007	16,7
Ballantine's	2009	6,9
	2008	6,9
	2007	6,7
J&B	2009	6,5
	2008	7,0
	2007	7,2
Grant's	2009	5,5
	2008	5,6
	2007	5,3
Chivas Regal	2009	4,9
	2008	4,9
	2007	4,8

Source: Euromonitor International 2010
The figures exclude grey and black
market and duty free / travel retail.
2009 shares are provisional.

World Consumption of Scotch Whisky

■ = 2007 ■ = 2008 ■ = 2009

Staples show major markets. Units in million litres of pure alcohol.
Total world consumption*; 339,8 (2009), 331,4 (2008), 347,0 (2007)

Please note that these figures show the actual amount of Scotch consumed in a particular market, excluding grey and black market and duty free / travel retail. Export figures may differ from consumption figures, especially for those countries that are used as hubs for re-exports to other markets.

Based on export figures - Australia, Germany and Singapore would have entered the table on this page. A large share of the whisky exported to Singapore is re-exported to China and the same goes for Germany where imported whisky to some extent is forwarded to Eastern Europe.

France 47 48 50 | USA 32 32 32 | Spain 30 29 26 | UK 28 28 28 | Thailand 13 13 13 | Venezuela 11 10 11 | Brazil 10 10 9 | South Korea 9 8 8 | China 7 8 7 | Greece 8 8 7 | South Africa 6 6 6

Source: Euromonitor International 2010 and for* Scotch Whisky Industry Review 2010

Exports of Scotch Whisky

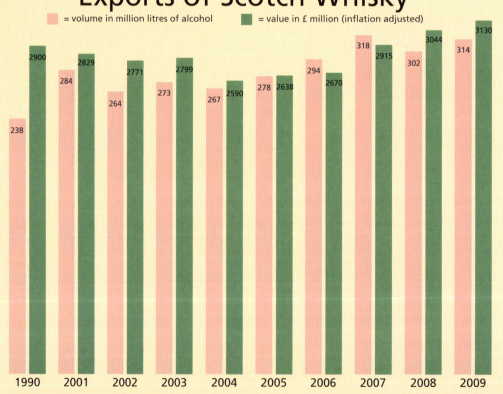

■ = volume in million litres of alcohol ■ = value in £ million (inflation adjusted)

1990: 238 / 2900
2001: 284 / 2829
2002: 264 / 2771
2003: 273 / 2799
2004: 267 / 2590
2005: 278 / 2638
2006: 294 / 2670
2007: 318 / 2915
2008: 302 / 3044
2009: 314 / 3130

Source: Scotch Whisky Association and Office for National Statistics

Distillery Capacity
Litres of pure alcohol, Scottish, active distilleries only

Glenlivet	10 500 000	Ben Nevis	1 800 000	Glen Garioch	1 000 000
Glenfiddich	10 000 000	Blair Athol	1 800 000	Tobermory	1 000 000
Roseisle	10 000 000	Glenlossie	1 800 000	Arran	750 000
Macallan	8 750 000	Auchentoshan	1 750 000	Glengyle	750 000
Ailsa Bay	6 000 000	Glen Elgin	1 700 000	Glen Scotia	750 000
Glenmorangie	6 000 000	Bruichladdich	1 500 000	Springbank	750 000
Glen Grant	5 900 000	Knockdhu	1 500 000	Oban	670 000
Caol Ila	5 800 000	Pulteney	1 500 000	Speyside	600 000
Dufftown	5 800 000	Scapa	1 500 000	Benromach	500 000
Balvenie	5 600 000	Glendronach	1 400 000	Royal Lochnagar	450 000
Glenrothes	5 600 000	Glenspey	1 390 000	Glenturret	340 000
Miltonduff	5 500 000	Balblair	1 330 000	Bladnoch	250 000
Ardmore	5 200 000	Glencadam	1 300 000	Kilchoman	110 000
Tomatin	5 000 000	Knockando	1 300 000	Edradour	90 000
Kininvie	4 800 000	Ardbeg	1 150 000	Daftmill	65 000
Glentauchers	4 500 000	Glenglassaugh	1 100 000	Abhainn Dearg	20 000
Teaninich	4 400 000	Glengoyne	1 100 000		
Clynelish	4 200 000				
Glenburgie	4 200 000				

Summary of Malt Distillery Capacity by Category

Category	Litres of alcohol	% of Industry	Average capacity
Speyside (44)	172 290 000	59,8	3 916 000
Islands (7)	10 570 000	3,7	1 510 000
Rest of the Highlands (30)	74 220 000	25,8	2 474 000
Islay (8)	18 160 000	6,3	2 270 000
Lowlands (5)	10 415 000	3,6	2 083 000
Campbeltown (3)	2 250 000	0,8	750 000
Total (97)	**287 905 000**	**100**	**2 968 000**

(Tormore 4 100 000; Allt-a-Bhainne 4 000 000; Braeval 4 000 000; Glen Ord 4 000 000; Loch Lomond 4 000 000; Tamnavulin 4 000 000; Royal Brackla 3 900 000; Auchroisk 3 800 000; Aberlour 3 700 000; Dalmore 3 700 000; Craigellachie 3 600 000; Mortlach 3 600 000; Aberfeldy 3 500 000; Linkwood 3 500 000; Longmorn 3 500 000; Mannochmore 3 450 000; Glendullan 3 400 000; Macduff 3 340 000; Dailuaine 3 300 000; Tomintoul 3 300 000; Cardhu 3 200 000; Aultmore 3 000 000; Deanston 3 000 000; Glenfarclas 3 000 000; Glenallachie 3 000 000; Laphroaig 2 900 000; Benriach 2 800 000; Inchgower 2 800 000; Tullibardine 2 700 000; Talisker 2 600 000; Benrinnes 2 500 000; Bunnahabhain 2 500 000; Highland Park 2 500 000; Strathisla 2 400 000; Glenkinchie 2 350 000; Fettercairn 2 300 000; Strathmill 2 300 000; Glen Moray 2 200 000; Jura 2 200 000; Lagavulin 2 200 000; Balmenach 2 000 000; Bowmore 2 000 000; Cragganmore 2 000 000; Dalwhinnie 2 000 000; Speyburn 2 000 000)

Summary of Malt Distillery Capacity by Owner

Owner (number of distilleries)	Litres of alcohol	% of Industry
Diageo (28)	87 310 000	30,3
Pernod Ricard (12)	50 900 000	17,7
William Grant (4)	26 400 000	9,2
Bacardi (John Dewar & Sons) (5)	17 340 000	6,0
Edrington Group (4)	17 190 000	6,0
Whyte and Mackay (4)	12 200 000	4,2
Pacific Spirits (Inver House) (5)	8 330 000	2,9
Beam Global (2)	8 100 000	2,8
Moët Hennessy (Glenmorangie) (2)	7 150 000	2,5
C L Financial (Burn Stewart) (3)	6 500 000	2,3
Campari (Glen Grant) (1)	5 900 000	2,0
Tomatin Distillery Co (1)	5 000 000	1,7
Suntory (Morrison Bowmore) (3)	4 750 000	1,6
Loch Lomond Distillers (2)	4 750 000	1,6
Angus Dundee (2)	4 600 000	1,6
Benriach Distillery Co (2)	4 200 000	1,5
J & G Grant (Glenfarclas) (1)	3 000 000	1,0
Tullibardine Distillery Ltd (1)	2 700 000	0,9
La Martiniquaise (Glen Moray) (1)	2 200 000	0,8
Nikka (Ben Nevis Distillery) (1)	1 800 000	0,6
Bruichladdich Distillery Co (1)	1 500 000	0,5
J & A Mitchell (2)	1 500 000	0,5
Ian Macleod Distillers (Glengoyne) (1)	1 100 000	less than 0,5
Scaent Group (Glenglassaugh) (1)	1 100 000	- " -
Isle of Arran Distillers (1)	750 000	- " -
Speyside Distillers Co (1)	600 000	- " -
Gordon & MacPhail (Benromach) (1)	500 000	- " -
Co-ordinated Developm. (Bladnoch) (1)	250 000	- " -
Kilchoman Distillery Co (1)	110 000	- " -
Signatory Vintage (Edradour) (1)	90 000	- " -
Francis Cuthbert (Daftmill) (1)	65 000	- " -
Mark Thayburn (Abhainn Dearg) (1)	20 000	- " -

Do you want to find out more in detail where the different distilleries are situated? We suggest that you pay a visit to www.maltmaps.com designed by Johannes de Jong. There you will find not only Scottish distilleries but all the other distilleries presented in Malt Whisky Yearbook. For Scottish distilleries there is also a nice, interactive map made by Johannes van den Heuvel at www.maltmadness.com/whisky/map/Scotland/ The latest addition to whisky maps on the internet is the excellent version by Steffen Bräuner found at bit.ly/cgpHsX

ORKNEY ISLANDS

Wick

NORTH HIGHLANDS

Isle of Lewis
129

SKYE
73

Barra
1

Kyle of Lockalsh

Inverness

SPEYSIDE

Aberdeen

Loch Ness

CENTRAL HIGHLANDS

Fort William

EAST HIGHLANDS

Pitlochry

Dundee

WEST HIGHLANDS

Loch Tay

Oban

MULL

Perth

St. Andrews

Loch Lomond

Stirling

JURA

Glasgow

Edinburgh

ISLAY

ARRAN

Campbeltown

Ayr

THE LOWLANDS

Dumfries

Stranraer

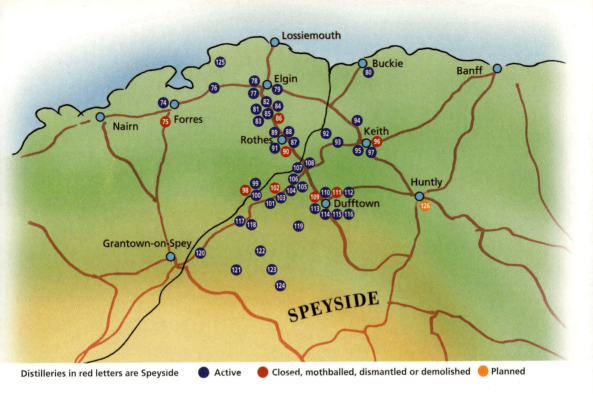

Distilleries in red letters are Speyside   ● Active   ● Closed, mothballed, dismantled or demolished   ◖ Planned

Index

Bold figures refer to the main entry in the distillery directory.

Index

Bold figures refer to the main entry in the distillery directory.

Index

Bold figures refer to the main entry in the distillery directory.